A WORLD OF RELATIONSHIPS:
ITINERARIES, DREAMS, AND EVENTS IN
THE AUSTRALIAN WESTERN DESERT

A World of Relationships is an ethnographical account of the cultural use and social potential of dreams among Aboriginal groups of the Australian Western Desert. The outcome of fieldwork conducted in the area in the 1980s and 1990s, it was originally published in French as *Les jardins du nomade: Cosmologie, territoire et personne dans le désert occidental australien.*

In her study, Sylvie Poirier explores the contemporary Aboriginal system of knowledge and law through an analysis of the relationships between the ancestral order, the 'sentient' land, and human agencies. At the ethnographical and analytical levels, particular attention is given to a range of local narratives and stories, and to the cultural construction of individual experiences. Poirier also investigates the cultural system of dreams and dreaming, and the process of their socialization, analysing their ideological, semantic, pragmatic, and experiential dimensions. Through the synthesis of a complex and diverse range of theoretical and empirical materials, *A World of Relationships* offers new insights into Australian Aboriginal sociality, historicity, and dynamics of cultural change and ritual innovation.

(Anthropological Horizons)

SYLVIE POIRIER is a professor in the Department of Anthropology at Université Laval.

ANTHROPOLOGICAL HORIZONS

Editor: Michael Lambek, University of Toronto

This series, begun in 1991, focuses on theoretically informed ethnographic works addressing issues of mind and body, knowledge and power, equality and inequality, the individual and the collective. Interdisciplinary in its perspective, the series makes a unique contribution in several other academic disciplines: women's studies, history, philosophy, psychology, political science, and sociology. For a list of the books published in this series see page 305

A World of Relationships

Itineraries, Dreams, and Events in the Australian Western Desert

Sylvie Poirier

UNIVERSITY OF TORONTO PRESS
Toronto Buffalo London

© University of Toronto Press Incorporated 2005
Toronto Buffalo London
Printed in Canada

ISBN 0-8020-3544-2 (cloth)
ISBN 0-8020-8414-1 (paper)

Printed on acid-free paper

Library and Archives Canada Cataloguing in Publication

Poirier, Sylvie, 1953–
    A world of relationships : itineraries, dreams and events in the Australian
Western Desert / Sylvie Poirier.

    Includes bibliographical references and index.
    ISBN 0-8020-3544-2 (bound).   ISBN 0-8020-8414-1 (pbk.)

    1. Dreamtime (Australian aboriginal mythology) – Australia – Western
Desert (W.A.)   2. Dreams – Australia – Western Desert (W.A.)
3. Aboriginal Australians – Australia – Western Desert (W.A.) – Social
life and customs.   4. Ethnology – Australia – Western Desert (W.A.)
5. Western Desert (W.A.) – Social life and customs.   I. Title.

    GN667.W5P65 2005   305.89′91509415   C2004-905144-X

This book has been published with the help of a grant from the Canadian
Federation for the Humanities and Social Sciences through the Aid to Scholarly Publications Programme, using funds provided by the Social Sciences
and Humanities Research Council of Canada.

University of Toronto Press acknowledges the financial assistance to its
publishing program of the Canada Council for the Arts and the Ontario
Arts Council.

University of Toronto Press acknowledges the financial support for its
publishing activities of the Government of Canada through the Book
Publishing Industry Development Program (BPIDP).

In memory of
Muntja Nungurrayi and
Sunfly Tjampitjin

Contents

Acknowledgments

I first wish to express my gratitude and deepest respect for the families of the Aboriginal communities of Balgo Hills (Wirrimanu) and Yagga Yagga, who welcomed me to their camp hearths and shared with me their stories and knowledge, their joys, their pain, their concerns – in short, their daily lives. I sincerely hope that this book will show how much I honour their teachings and the values that they hold dear, and in some measure acknowledge the friendship and confidence they showed me. I especially want to thank Muntja Nungurrayi, Bye Bye Napangarti, Mindi Napanangka, Balba Napangarti, Nancy Napanangka, Freeda Napanangka, Njammi Napangarti, Patricia Lee Napangarti, Ivi Napangarti, Doreen Nampitjin, Dora Nungurrayi, Elsie Nungurrayi, Margaret Napurrula, Dora Napaltjarri, Butja Butja Napangarti, Sunfly Tjampitjin, Moskito Tjapangarti, Donkeyman Tjupurrula, Larry Loddi Tjupurrula, Jimmy Flatnose Tjampitjin, Thomas Galova Tjapangarti, Mark Moora Tjapangarti, John Lee Tjakamarra, Kenny Gibson, Bumblebee Tjapanangka, Mick Tjakamarra, and all their children and grandchildren.

Among these people, many elders (men and women both) passed away during the 1990s. It is to these elders and their kin that I dedicate this book. Since Aboriginal Law forbids the use of the names of the deceased for an indeterminate period after their deaths, many of the names listed above will not appear elsewhere in this book. Where I recount the experiences and the stories told to me, the tellers will be designated only by their subsections.

I first arrived at Balgo in August 1980 and stayed until January 1982. I owe a great debt to Warwick Nieass, an Australian free-lance artist who was my partner at the time and who first introduced me to Balgo and its people. Curiously enough, my first contact with Balgo was as a lone traveller rather than as an academic. While there, I worked as the cook for the non-Aboriginal staff of the Catholic mission, who numbered about twenty at the time. I wish to thank the mission's superintendent at the time, Father Ray Hevern. Despite our many differences of opinion, Father Hevern eventually did not interfere in my interaction with the Aborigines. He was a little worried and uncertain at first about the possible repercussions of it; at the time it was not considered proper for White employees to mingle with the Aborigines outside the workplace. In 1982, when I returned to Quebec City, my birthplace, I decided to further my anthropological studies at Université Laval and thereby express my experience in an academic language.

I returned to Balgo with my spouse and two-year-old son in March 1987, and stayed a year, mostly in Yagga Yagga, an outstation situated 100 kilometres south of Balgo. During this time I was able to share the daily lives of Aboriginal families and to devote myself entirely to my research. This second stay would not have been as productive and agreeable without the presence and active participation of my former spouse, Alain Sachel Tjampitjin, an anthropologist who worked many years for First Nations in Quebec. I am grateful to my son Mathieu Tjangala, notwithstanding his habit of running off with my notebook, both for his talents as a tracker (despite his youth), and for his endurance. He was able to make Yagga Yagga and Balgo his home, and I hope that he will be able to benefit from what he learned there. All three of us owe a great debt to Chris Carey, who was then the Balgo accountant. When the rainy season came and we (and the Aboriginal families) were forced to leave our camp at Yagga Yagga, Chris helped us to find a house in the community. I also thank my other son, Toma. Though he has never visited the Australian desert, he has shown a daily interest in the progress of this book. I returned to Balgo and Yagga Yagga for two short visits, from August to October of 1994, and from June to August of 1998.

Financial support for this research, and for the fieldwork since 1987, was provided by the Social Sciences and Humanities Research Council of Canada. The Australian Institute of Aboriginal and Torres Strait Islander Studies (AIATSIS) (Canberra) also provided financial support for the 1987–8 and 1994 fieldwork. Included in the institute's support was the use of a four-wheel-drive vehicle, which is necessary in a place like Balgo. I thank them sincerely. This book has been published with the help of a grant from the Canadian Federation for the Humanities and Social Sciences, through the Aid to Scholarly Publications Programme, using funds provided by the Social Sciences and Humanities Research Council of Canada.

I am grateful to the journal *Man*, which allowed extensive citations of extracts from my article 'Nomadic Rituals: Networks of Ritual Exchange between Women of the Australian Western Desert' (*Man* 27 [1992]: 757–76). I also used material taken from two other articles that appeared in the journal *Anthropologie et sociétés*: 'Cosmologie, personne et expression artistique dans le désert occidental australien' (16 [1992]: 41–58); and 'La mise en œuvre sociale du rêve. Un exemple australien' (18 [1994] : 105–19).

For fruitful exchanges, for professional and personal support, or for comments on earlier versions of the manuscript, sincere thanks go to Eric Schwimmer, Ellen Corin, Yvan Breton, Fred Myers (who wrote the preface to the French version of the book), Nicolas Peterson, the late Daniel de Coppet and the members of his research team (Erasme, CNRS), Warwick Dix, Kyngsley Palmer, Maggy Brady, Stephen Wild, Robert Tonkinson, Barbara Glowczewski, and Yvan Simonis. I also thank the late Father Anthony Peile, missionary and ethnologist at Balgo for almost twenty years, who agreed to compare information during my first two stays at Balgo, and who helped me translate numerous local terms. My father and mother supported me constantly, in more ways than I can state here. Their assistance was priceless, and I will always be grateful to them. I thank Martha Radice, Sylvie Fortier, and Kirsten Oravec for their precious help in translating and revising the manuscript, and Andrée Héroux for the maps.

I owe my deepest respect to the late Professors Ronald M. Berndt and Catherine H. Berndt, who were the first anthropologists to visit Balgo, and whose work has been a constant source of inspiration to me.

This book is a much revised version of one originally published in French entitled *Les jardins du nomade. Cosmologie, personne et territoire dans le désert occidental australien* (1996: Lit: Münster). It was imperative that I translate my work into English so as to make it available to those who are most concerned: my Aboriginal friends and their families.

A WORLD OF RELATIONSHIPS:
ITINERARIES, DREAMS, AND EVENTS IN
THE AUSTRALIAN WESTERN DESERT

Introduction

This book explores dialectical aspects of Australian Aboriginal social and cosmological realities that have been brought to light by recent ethnographic work.[1] With a focus on some Western Desert groups, I discuss the facets of their world where intransigence gives way to negotiation, constraint yields to strategy, repetition allows innovation, rigidity bends to openness and flexibility, formal rules flex under the performative, structures are moulded by the event, and univocality gives voice to plurivocality. This ethnographic study focuses on the manifold and dynamic relations among the ancestral order, the land, and human and non-human agencies, and underlines the local sense of historicity and identity. By investigating the different modes of experience as they are recognized and lived locally, including dreams and dreaming, I attempt to understand a contemporary Aboriginal system of knowledge and law, and Aboriginals' specific way of being-in-the-world and of relating to it.

This book is the outcome of three years spent in the Aboriginal community of Balgo Hills, now known as Wirrimanu, and its neighbouring communities, located on the northern edge of the Gibson Desert in Western Australia. The Gibson Desert, with the Great Victoria Desert and the Great Sandy Desert, form the immense Western Desert. The Balgo Hills Catholic Mission was first established in 1939 and became the Wirrimanu Aboriginal Corporation in the mid-1980s. In the region of Wirrimanu, there are three other Aboriginal communities: Mulan, Billiluna (Kururrungku), and Yagga Yagga. These four communities now total about one thousand people. The main language groups of the area, which constitute more or less bounded territorial, cultural, and linguistic entities, are the Kukatja and the Walmatjari. The ancestral lands of the Kukatja stretch from the north of Lake Mackay to the Stansmore Range, while traditional Walmatjari country spreads all the way to the Canning Stock Route and includes Lake Gregory. Other groups are also represented in the area: the Ngarti, the Wangkatjunga, the Mandiltjarra, the Tjaru, the Pintupi, and some Warlpiri (see maps 1 and 2, at the front of the book). While these groups differ in their respective territorial affiliations, they none the less share a whole series of cosmological, social, cultural, and historical elements. As R. Berndt (1959) proposed originally, we could envisage the Western Desert groups as extensive, complex, flexible, and dynamic networks of social, territorial, and ritual connections and responsibilities. In the context of settlement life, these identities have endured and, at the same time, been transformed, while new group identities have emerged. The first chapter of this book presents my own narrative of the history of the relationships between Aborigines and non-Aborigines in the Balgo area.

Classical and positivistic anthropological views and paradigms have tended to emphasize the 'prescriptive' nature of Aboriginal Australian socialities, 'where all is execution and repetition' (Sahlins 1985: xii), portraying these as rigid and closed structures, a view that denies and conceals their potential for transformation and reinterpretation. With the advent of new paradigms in the discipline as a whole (Ortner 1984), the empirical and theoretical emphasis in Australian Aboriginal studies has shifted to 'human agency, individual choice, event and action' (Myers 1986b: 139). This shift has allowed a deeper understanding of the active and creative engagement of Aborigines in the world through their own ontological and epistemological principles; it has also paved the way for insightful studies on the nature and extent of Aboriginal forms of resistance to wider Australian (and Western) society, and the relationships and dialogues they have engaged in with that society.[2]

In their present-day, ever-changing expression, Australian Aboriginal socialities are characterized by a continuously negotiated and somewhat paradoxical dynamic between 'the forms of permanence' (to use Stanner's expression, meaning the existing mythological and ritual expressions), and their structural transformations. In the Western Desert, this dynamic of change is barely noticeable, because the Aborigines themselves have a very conservative discourse in relation to their ancestral Law and order. They portray themselves as being simply the executors of such Law: 'This is Law from our fathers and grandfathers, and we follow that Law.' Because of this prevalent attitude that emphasizes the unchanging and rigid character of the Law, the peoples of the Western Desert are 'known throughout Australia for their conservatism and the strength of their adherence to the Law' (Myers 1986a: 297).[3] This dominant standpoint effectively conceals from outside observers all possible mechanisms through which mytho-ritual elements can be modified and transformed, both through reinterpretation and through innovation. However, another reality is revealed when one analyses the dimensions of openness and flexibility inherent in the Law.

Among the main themes of this book are the qualities of 'openness' and 'flexibility' inherent in the Aboriginal system of law and cosmological order – usually known as the Dreaming, or *Tjukurrpa* in most Western Desert languages. By 'openness' I mean the capacity to introduce new forms, new variants of existing themes, and to suggest new readings of older structures. While these accretions remain true to the founding principles of the Law, they show the potential for transformation, reinterpretation, and reformulation of the structures of permanence. The dimension of 'flexibility'[4] refers to the pragmatics of individual choices; in other words, it shows that the dictates of ancestral Law can be negotiated on the basis of one's own knowledge and understanding of the Law and its mythological and ritual expressions. The Law is far from being closed to novel interpretations. Western Desert Aborigines constantly re-evaluate the different elements of the existing cosmological order, depending on circumstance. Paramount in such a process is the polysemous and contextual value of signs. In other words, within the imperatives of the Law, creativity, negotiation, and different levels of interpretation are primordial for the reproduction of the world of the ancestors.

The dimensions of openness and flexibility are the avenues through which I examine the structural transformations of the mytho-ritual elements of the Law and try to understand the meanings that Aborigines confer upon events and local, regional, or supraregional historicity. This investigation also examines how social actors participate, creatively and strategically, in the process of re-evaluating and rereading the existing mytho-ritual elements (and their territorial inscriptions), in addition to the social and cultural avenues available for such an endeavour. Any given social group must draw on the cognitive and innovative potential of its members if it wishes to ensure the continuity of its identity, as well as the social regeneration of the world of the ancestors. This is even more pertinent in contexts of major social and cultural transformation created by the colonial and neocolonial setting.[5]

Sahlins wrote that the transformation of a culture is also a mode of its reproduction (1985: 138). In a more recent essay, he states that 'the very way societies change has its own authenticity' (1993: 2). Whenever the historicity of a group does not appear in an explicit manner to an outside observer, it is often because such a historicity is grounded upon markers and constructed upon signifiers belonging to a radically different cultural order and elaborated on modalities of interpretation that are imperceptible to a modern Western gaze. Hence, it is important for the ethnographer to investigate the local sense of history in any given society (Rosaldo 1980). Furthermore, the dialectic and dialogic relationships between individual experiences and collective expressions (Bruner 1986), between structure and event, and between creative action and cultural change are what we may call an 'endogenous historicity' (Comaroff and Comaroff 1992). An ethnographic inquiry into the processes that ground such historicity and into meaningful local practices and local historical imagination offers different ways of investigating the varying forms and expressions of Aboriginal accommodation and resistance to the wider Australian society. In the Western Desert, such an 'endogenous historicity' can only be understood by considering the value of ancestrality and its encompassing, immanent, and coeval nature, and by considering the paramount role of spatial, rather than temporal, referents. In the Wirrimanu area, as elsewhere in Aboriginal Australia, the sense of events and the sense of place are intimately linked.[6] Chapters 2 and 3 of this book explore these qualities of 'openness' and 'flexibility' in relation to cosmological, territorial, and social configurations.

The ethnography of the dynamic and manifold relations among cultural expressions, individual experiences, events, the ancestral realm, and – eventually – cultural changes requires identifying the underlying thread that could guide the ethnographer in her exploration. In the Wirrimanu area, dreams and dreaming, and the process of their socialization, have proved extremely relevant in this endeavour because they are granted a particular status, value, and role at the ideological, pragmatic, and experiential levels. As an integral part of human actions in the world, dreams and dreaming represent a mode of experiencing and knowing the world and one form of engagement with one's surroundings; they are a way to 'open out' to the world as a whole. The dream realm is a privileged space-time of encounter and communication with the ancestors and deceased relatives. The dream realm offers a cognitive and narrative potential; it is an opportunity for individual or collective reflection, interpretation, and objectification of events and experiences, as part of a (re)evaluation of the state of relationships among the human, the ancestral, and the non-human constituents of the world, including the land as a sentient actor. The aim, then, is to understand the role granted to dreams and dreaming in the processes by which Aborigines interpret and give meaning to events in the world around them. On a broader and more universal level, are dreams not a major source of a people's imaginary – the last frontier to the 'colonization' of the mind – and a source of transformation of that imaginary?

When studying a cultural system of dreams, we cannot limit our analysis to 'dreams as objects' (or products of the mind). We must investigate the ontological and epistemological principles as well as the semantic and pragmatic dimensions of dreams and dreaming in a given world. Only then can we hope to develop a basis for an anthropology of dreams.[7] At the methodological and analytical levels, I find it relevant to consider five aspects in the process of dream socialization. While each element does not necessarily apply to every dream narrative and experience, as a group they nevertheless offer a wider view that locates the role of dreams in local understanding, discourses, and practices. The five aspects are as follows: (1) Local dream theories and what they can reveal about the local notion of the person and about local ontology and epistemology. (2) Dream narratives as a process of translating, structuring, and communicating a dream experience – a process in which the embodied social, cultural, and symbolic components, as well as the contextual and personal variables, come into play from the moment a dream is remembered until it is communicated.[8] (3) The modes of dream sharing: that is, where, when, why, how, and with whom one shares dreams. Herdt (1987) has identified public, private, and secret spheres of dream sharing in one Melanesian society. In many respects, this classification also applies to the Western Desert context. It should be added that in some societies dream sharing can also be considered as 'narrative events' (Bauman 1986); this is by no means an unimportant point, considering the social and political ramifications of dreams in addition to their entertainment and aesthetic value. (4) Local modes of dream interpretations and local dream typologies, both of which are a rich source of information as long as

their true value is not undermined in favour of grids of dream interpretation based upon the anthropologist's own culture.[9] (5) The revelatory, mediatory, and often creative and innovative role ascribed to
dreams in a number of societies throughout the world, including Australian Aboriginal societies. This dimension of the dream experience
reveals that a dream and its narrative, in whole or in part, are often
received as the spoken word of the ancestors, which is then subjected
to collective scrutiny and approbation (or refusal) as to its relevance.
Afterwards, it may eventually be integrated into existing cultural
forms and expressions and can contribute to cultural transformation of
different kinds and scopes.

The potential of revelation and innovation granted to dreams in a
number of non-Western (and non-modernist) societies, as well as the
relation between dreams and myths, are subjects commonly discussed
in the anthropological literature.[10] For the ethnographer, this moment
in the process of dream socialization is no doubt relevant in the understanding of cultural change because it establishes a relation between
changes, the imaginary, the flow of events (dreams being part of the
event here), and the creative participation of cultural agents. However,
one cannot reach a clear understanding of such a dynamic relationship
without inquiring into the other aspects and elements inherent in the
local systems of dreams.

To varying degrees, and in a sporadic manner, a number of ethnographic writings on Australian Aboriginal peoples have stressed the
importance of dreams in 'Aboriginal experience and cultural creation'
(Maddock 1976: 169). According to R. Berndt, all aspects of Aboriginal
life and thought are expressed through the medium of dreams (1951:
71). The realm of dreams as the place of revelation of new mytho-ritual
elements (or of elements that had been concealed from human consciousness) by the ancestors is not a novel idea in the ethnographic
literature on Australian Aborigines.[11] This book contributes many elements of analysis to the existing literature. In it, I present an analysis of
the different aspects of the socialization of dreams. I examine the relationship between dreams, the flow of events, and local historicity, and
expose the role that dreams play in local cultural politics. I wish to
emphasize what I call the 'relational' role of dreams in Aboriginal Australia and to highlight the fact that, in many respects, the activity of
dreaming (i.e., dreaming as a human action in the world, and as a
social process) is more valued than the actual dream content, than
dreams as mere objects. In any given society, one cannot make assump-

tions as to the place and status granted to dreams in relation to other modes of experience or states of being. It is therefore necessary to identify and evaluate the modes of experience and the contexts of actions that are culturally meaningful. The different realms of action and modes of experience, as well as the cultural system of dreams and dreaming in the Wirrimanu area, are the topics of chapters 4 and 5, while chapter 6 analyses ritual innovation through the medium of dreams.

It is only recently that anthropology has started to take seriously and at face value local ontological and epistemological principles and stances, and to examine and investigate how and to what extent these principles ground and inform others' objectivity,[12] as well as other ways of being, knowing, and relating to the 'natural' world. Concomitant with these considerations are a number of critically and historically informed studies that deconstruct the two analytic categories that have been the cornerstones of anthropology (and modernist epistemology) since the eighteenth century: 'nature' and 'culture.' These studies question the absolute dichotomy between nature and culture, as well as the presumed universality of such a dualism, which was and is propounded by the modernist and mechanistic views of the world.[13] In modernist thought, what we call 'nature' is reduced to an object at the service of humankind, something that can be quantified, mechanized, and dehumanized, 'in a way that made us think that knowledge of nature was independent of our relations with it' (Ellen 1996: 13). In his argument for re-establishing the necessary unity between nature and mind, Bateson presented modernist epistemology as an 'anti-aesthetic' (1980: 240). Because 'the disjuncture between nature and society ... is the key foundation of modernist epistemology,' Descola and Pálsson, among others, argue about the insufficiency of simply deconstructing the dualist paradigm (1996: 12). They add that 'Going beyond dualism opens up an entirely different intellectual landscape, one in which states and substances are replaced by processes and relations; the main question is not any more how to objectify closed systems, but how to account for the very diversity of the processes of objectification' (ibid.). Considering that modernity itself is one 'nature-culture' among many others (Latour 1993), and one that strongly advocates an absolute dichotomy between nature and culture, animality and humanity, matter (body) and mind, instinct and reason, and so on, then worlds that do not advocate such a dualistic mode are viewed as non-modern.[14] In today's context, non-modern societies, such as that of the Australian Aborigines, continue to challenge and to resist the hegemony of the modernist and dualistic mode of thought and way of being-in-the-world.

A number of recent studies propose novel avenues along which to investigate the socialities of hunter-gatherers, their relationships with a sentient landscape, and the manifold interactions between human and non-human agencies. Based on her work among the Nayaka of south India, Bird-David (1999) introduces the concept of a 'relational epistemology' where the notions of the person and sentient agents are not limited to humans only and where 'maintaining relationships with ... other local beings is critical to maintaining ... personhood' (Bird-David 1999: S73). She contrasts the guiding principle of modernist epistemology, 'I think therefore I am,' with one that emphasizes the relational nature of knowing and being: 'I relate therefore I am,' and 'I know as I relate' (ibid.: S78). We could argue, however, with Viveiros de Castro (1999: S79), that Bird-David's emphasis on epistemology rather than ontology echoes a modernist concern with 'knowing' rather than 'being.' It is at this point that Ingold's work represents an important contribution to the new understanding of non-modernist realities.

Drawing from a series of 'thick descriptions' and ethnographic work carried out among contemporary hunter-gatherer societies, Ingold presents what he calls an 'ontology of dwelling,' in which 'apprehending the world is not a matter of construction but of engagement, not of building but of dwelling, not of making a view *of* the world but of taking up a view *in* it' (1996: 121) (emphasis in original). However, Ingold's purpose is not to contrast hunting (and nomadic) traditions with Western ones, but rather to show the limits inherent in the modernist dualistic mode of thought and action. He considers that the universal human condition is 'that of a being immersed from the start, like other creatures, in an active, practical, and perceptual engagement with constituents of the dwelt-in world' (ibid.: 120–1).[15] Like Descola and Pálsson, he seeks to go beyond the limits inherent in an extreme constructivist perspective, 'which subsumes the environment under the symbolism of tradition and culture,' and where 'the environment has no active role at all' (Descola and Pálsson 1996: 11). From an Aboriginal perspective, the view of the land (and its constituents) as a passive agent is untenable.

In Australian Aboriginal studies, Povinelli (1993a, 1995) emphasizes that in order to understand the Aboriginal notions of human actions and labour on the land, it is necessary to consider the reality of the 'sentient landscape,' or, more accurately, the named places. These places are perceived and experienced as sentient and intentional and endowed with consciousness. I would also add that the constituents of the world, whatever forms they may take – animal, vegetable, mineral, celestial, and so on – are not passive entities upon which humans project their mental representations; rather they engage as active agents in intimate and reciprocal relations with humans. The ontological boundaries between the different states of being, as well as between the forms of being in the physical world, are permeable and flexible. Permeability and flexibility of forms are the basis for all metamorphoses and transformations experienced in the Aboriginal world, both in the mundane and in the ancestral realms, on the basis of their co-presence.

Ontologies are not only thought, they are lived out.[16] While each society's ontological principles may be very different, each opens onto varieties of 'true' experiences. The process of objectification by which ethnographers develop a certain understanding of other ontologies and epistemologies requires that one take 'seriously' what others say about their social worlds and their experiences (Overing 1985). Still, the ethnographer must remain aware that she is not necessarily experiencing and perceiving the world in the way the cultural Other is perceiving it (Geertz 1983: 55–9). This inherent danger is even more marked when we are dealing not so much with different world-views but with different ways of apprehending the world (Ingold 1996: 121). Accordingly, acquaintance with the ontologies and epistemologies of other cultures requires a certain degree of humility on the part of the ethnographer. The intersubjective mode of objectification that emerges from these encounters can therefore be an explicitly creative one (Hastrup 1995; see also Poirier 2004).

In order to arrive at an understanding of the Kukatja world, or at least certain aspects of it, I listened 'seriously' to their stories and various narrative forms. The narrative dimension includes the narrated events (and experiences) as well as the narrative events (Bauman 1986). I found that stories – not only those about the mythical landscape that have a particular value, but also stories of everyday life and dream stories – provided a meaningful avenue to investigate the local structuration of experience, the production and transmission of knowledge, and the interpretation and objectification of events. In worlds of oral tradition such as those of the Australian Aborigines, stories and storytelling play a paramount role in everyday life. Stories of many kinds were told to me as we sat around the camps at Wirrimanu (Balgo), Yagga Yagga, or Mulan. Stories were told, too, as we drove about the countryside, during trips out into the bush or while on our way to neighbouring or far-away communities, or even as we walked for hours at a time across the desert land while hunting and gathering.[17] One elderly man, now deceased, told me that my work was 'to write down their stories.' This book is my story about their stories.

This constant travelling and moving about leads me to another major element of contemporary Aboriginal reality: nomadism. This aspect of their sociality should never be downplayed, because it is also their specific way of apprehending the world. Classical studies on hunter-gatherers have focused primarily on the geopolitical and socio-economic aspects and impacts of a nomadic way of life. While considering these aspects, I also look into what we may rightly call a nomadic mind and way of being-in-the-world (as opposed to the highly valued sedentary way of the Western world). The Aborigines' nomadic way of life has gone through major transformations since their first contact with Whites. Their motivations for travelling about – to and fro between the communities, for instance – are no doubt different from what they were in traditional times.[18] However, in the Wirrimanu area, as in other parts of Aboriginal Australia, not only do the nomadic ways retain importance, they permeate the very ways in which Aborigines relate to their lives in the more settled communities. Their contemporary redefinition of nomadism is one of the multiple expressions of their accommodation and resistance to the Australian government's decades-long efforts to foist a sedentary way of life upon them.

Embodied in the Aboriginal peoples' identity, knowledge, and ethos, their nomadism is tied to a strong sense of territoriality. This territoriality is most vibrantly expressed by the reality of the places along mythical itineraries that were formed and named by the ancestral beings. These places and itineraries are the basis of the formation and transformation of the complex and dynamic networks of social belonging and ritual responsibilities. The mythical landscape in which the Aborigines live is infused with ancestral essence and presence. The French title of this book, *Les jardins du nomade*, refers to the continuous cultivation of the mythical landscape by passing generations, influenced by the flow of experiences and events in the region.

In the book, I also pay particular attention to the local concept of person, which I find to be a key concept in understanding the ways of being, knowing, and relating to the world.[19] Generally speaking, in the Western Desert, people, places, and ancestors are tightly linked together; the social, territorial, and cosmological components of the world are indissociable from one's sense of self. Each person is a node within a complex and dynamic network of agencies, social (including territorial and ritual) relationships, and responsibilities. What I call the 'personal configuration of belonging' (see chapter 3) stresses the composite character of one's identity and the 'dividual' dimension of the person.[20] By 'dividual' I mean that networks of social relationships are intrinsic to the Aborigines' sense of self and composite identities, rather than extrinsic (as in an 'individualistic' notion of person). In other words, these relationships are an integral part of an Aborigine's *raison d'être* and way of being-in-the-world; they are embodied. Another characteristic of a 'dividual' mode rather than an individual one is that, in the former, subjectivity and agency are embodied, as T. Turner explains about the Kayapo, 'in discrete bodily processes and modes of activity rather than ... attributes of a disembodied and integral Cartesian ego' (1995: 166). In other words, in a dividual mode, an action is always an interaction, a subjectivity (or agency) is always conceived as intersubjectivity (or interagency) between the different constituents of the world. What I call the 'bodily-self' stresses the sense of unity between body and mind, as well as the embodied character of all knowledge and identity. It also stresses the way the holistic being – as an active and moving agent or subject – is constantly engaged in interactions with the surrounding environment, and is permeable to its essences and humours. We will also see how local notions of person and of bodiliness[21] are interwoven into local theories of dreams and dreaming.

Stanner was the first researcher to pinpoint the existence of a dynamic relation among cultural change, human creative action, and the imaginary in Aboriginal Australia. He stressed the strength and the richness of the Aborigines' imaginary and mythopoetic thought. He wrote that not only have the Aborigines the power to create forms that endure, they also have 'the power to adapt the work of their imaginative mind to the unfolding of history' (1966: 80). Stanner argued that there exists a strong adherence to traditions and to the Ancestral Law, but that the traditions themselves are a constant source of inspiration (ibid.: 85).

These inspirations and improvisations are, in turn, 'part of the process by which mythopoetic thought nurtures and is nurtured' (ibid.). Stanner's work recognized a historical imagination and consciousness at work on the collective level. I take that recognition farther and examine the elements of analysis and understanding of this historical imagination and consciousness and its intimate links with ancestrality, the land, and dream experiences and narratives.

In this book, I discuss the different elements of the structural, moral, social, and symbolic codes, along with their dialectic and dialogic interrelations with variables of a more contingent and experiential nature. The Aboriginal system of Law, the mythical itineraries and their dimension of 'openness' (chapter 2), the social morphology and the flexibility inherent in it (chapter 3), the local modes of experiencing and knowing the world, with an emphasis on dreams and dreaming (chapters 4 and 5), and the intensity of the ritual sphere (chapter 6) are explored in relation to sociocultural logic and its dynamic unfolding.

Chapter 1

A Place like Balgo: A Story of Accommodation, Resistance, and Misunderstandings

This chapter presents a brief social history of the Wirrimanu Aboriginal Corporation from its establishment as the Balgo Hills Catholic Mission in the late 1930s, through the 1990s. It is also a narrative about the nature and extent of the relationships between Aborigines and non-Aborigines in the area. Considering the number of different social groups that have, over the decades, contributed to shaping the place through their experiences, their projects, desires, and disillusionments, and their sufferings, it is evident that the history of a place like Balgo cannot be reduced to a single narrative. In other words, the multivocality and multilocality of this place can hardly be contained by a single voice.[1] My narrative of the major events and reconstruction of the social groups at Balgo over time is constructed from one given point of view, and is obviously incomplete. Therefore, it could be contested by both the Aborigines and the non-Aborigines, namely the missionaries, the church and government staff who have worked and lived there for years, and anthropologists, each of whom have different narratives to share about the historical unfolding of the community and its present-day dynamics.

I present here only a glimpse, the tip of the iceberg, of a complex, inchoate, and dialectic interplay between two worlds. Even though they have coexisted together in Balgo for more than five decades, the Aboriginal and non-Aboriginal worlds still remain incompatible in many ways. The unequal relations of power that underlie this coexistence prevent the emergence and expression of tangible dialogical and reciprocal relationships. This chapter discusses the shift from a colonial to a so-called postcolonial context, during which the national policy of assimilation changed to one of self-determination. It recounts local

expressions of accommodation and resistance, of continuity and discontinuity.[2] I also discuss the significant and less significant events and
actors, at the local, regional, and national levels, that have contributed
to shaping local Aboriginal historicity, projects, experiences, and identities. In the course of this narrative, some fundamental differences
between the Aboriginal and the non-Aboriginal sense of place will
emerge: in terms of their respective involvement with place, with
regard to cultural practices and imaginary towards place, and with
respect to the different forms that these take over time.[3]

The *Kartiya*:[4] First Encounters

In the second half of the nineteenth century, prospectors and pastoralists settled in the Halls Creek area, which became an important gold-
producing centre at the turn of the century. Around 1910, gold miners
established themselves at Tanami and the Granites. Of all these newcomers, only a few attempted to go farther south into the desert, and
those few did not stay long. The Halls Creek gold rush was short-lived,
as was the one at the Tanami and the Granites. The mining industry
would have to wait until the 1970s and the 1980s, and the arrival of
modern technology, in order to establish itself on a large scale in the
area.

The pastoralists, though, found a suitable area for their activities in
the eastern Kimberley District. Coming mostly from Queensland in the
1880s, they established themselves with their herds along the Victoria,
Ord, and Stirling Rivers. For these settlers, the desert areas were totally
devoid of attraction, and they regarded them as 'waste land.'

The explorers, however, were driven by different goals from the pastoralists and miners. From the 1850s onwards, expeditions followed
each other into the Gibson Desert in order to expand the frontier of
colonization. In 1855, Gregory travelled down Sturt Creek all the way
to a large lake, since then known as Lake Gregory. In 1872, Warburton
succeeded in crossing the desert westward from Alice Springs to the
Indian Ocean. He travelled not far north of the present-day Aboriginal
community of Yagga Yagga. These expeditions and those that followed
were severely handicapped by the harshness and the size of the territory through which they attempted to travel.

In 1896, David Carnegie, a young explorer, accompanied by a few
men, horses, and a caravan of camels, travelled north and crossed the
Gibson Desert, from Coolgardie to Halls Creek. During his return jour-

ney, he travelled near the Stansmore Range, which he named. His passage did not go unnoticed by local Aborigines. In sheer desperation for water south of the Stansmore Range, Carnegie captured a local Aborigine whom he forced, chained, to lead his party to water. Among the local Aborigines, this was the first instance of their being chained and forced to walk long distances, though certainly not the last.

From the gold mining town of Coolgardie on the southern edge of the Western Desert, Carnegie had hoped, by penetrating farther north into the desert, to find either gold, a suitable region for grazing, or a route to drive cattle from the Kimberley to southern towns for butchering. His hopes were not fulfilled and he wrote, 'What heart breaking country, monotonous, lifeless, without interest, without excitement, save when the stern necessity of finding water forced us to seek the natives in their primitive camps ' (1898: 292). The writings of Carnegie express more a desire to be the first to cross the desert from south to north than an interest in the local inhabitants, whom he considered, as did the majority of his contemporaries, to be still existing at the dawn of humanity.

In 1906–7, A.W. Canning, like Carnegie, succeeded in crossing the Gibson Desert, but this time along its western edge. Unlike Carnegie, though, Canning was more inclined to establish friendly relationships with the local Aborigines, and that is presumably why they agreed to show him the location of water sources along what was to become the Canning Stock Route (250 km to the west of the Stansmore Range). By 1910, the stock route was fully functional. It was used to drive cattle from Halls Creek, through the Billiluna Station and around Lake Gregory, which is mostly Walmatjari country, on through to Lake Disappointment, in Mardu country, and then all the way to Wiluna. A series of wells were dug along this 1200-kilometre desert trail. A number of Aboriginal men, mostly from the Kimberley area, would accompany the stockmen on these months-long and surely quite epic expeditions. The stock route and the wells were abandoned in the early 1950s with the development of roads on the periphery of the desert.

An elderly Walmatjari woman, now deceased, told me that when she was still a child and living south of Lake Gregory, her family would hide behind the hills to look at these impressive convoys as they slowly travelled through their country. As a child, she was afraid not only of the White men, of whom she had certainly not seen many, but also of the Aborigines who accompanied them and whom she did not know. She was also quite intrigued by the camels. On a few occasions, her family did join the newcomers in their camps when the strangers seemed to be well intentioned, and sometimes received food and provisions from them. These first fleeting encounters lasted only the time of a meal or overnight, and they were opportunities for the adults to exchange news with the Aboriginal men from the Kimberley region.

These expeditions would not have been possible without the use of camels. They had been brought to Australia in the second half of the nineteenth century from Afghanistan, along with a few knowledgable camel drivers, precisely for the purpose of exploring the desert areas and ensuring the flow of supplies to settlers in remote areas. In some of these regions, camels were used until the 1950s. With the construction of the railway and the advent of roads and motorized transport, the camels were then simply left to fend for themselves. They proliferated in great numbers in the Gibson Desert, almost unbeknownst to Euro-Australians. Today, in the areas south of Balgo and Yagga Yagga, it is not uncommon to come across a small herd of camels. As my Aboriginal friends and I would drive around hunting and gathering, we would stop to watch them from a distance. My friends would comment on the various members of the group – the males, the females, the youngsters, and the elders – but under no circumstances would they go near them. Their sentiments about camels are mixed. There is both respect and fear, but also resentment because they pollute the water holes. The Aborigines definitively refuse to kill them, and consider their meat to be 'rubbish.'

The Aboriginal groups whose territories lay at the periphery of the Western Desert were the first to come in contact with the *Kartiya*. In the first half of the twentieth century, mission stations and settlements were established to receive them as they left the desert, but not, of course, without creating tension and discontent (Meggitt 1962a; Myers 1986a; Tonkinson 1974). In the 1940s, at the peak of the federal policy of Aboriginal settlement (implemented to better control the nomads), there were still nomadic families in the heart of the desert. In the 1950s and 1960s, police patrols still combed the desert in search of these families (Peterson 1986; Nathan and Japanangka 1983). By the 1960s, the authorities thought that they had finally achieved the depopulation of the Western Desert, and in many respects they had. However, as late as 1984 a family was found in the Gibson Desert between Yagga Yagga and Kiwirrkura. They have since joined their relatives at Balgo and Kiwirrkura (Myers 1988a).

During the 1930s, the Aboriginal families living around Lake Gregory and to the south, between the Stansmore Range and Lake Mackay, including Lake Hazlett and Lake White, maintained a nomadic lifestyle as hunters and gatherers. They were aware, though, of the presence of newcomers on the edges of their countries. Not only had they heard about (and some had seen) the stock convoys along the Canning Stock Route, but we can be sure that news about the *Kartiya* had circulated for quite some time. Messengers from neighbouring groups already in contact with the newcomers and local people who had been travelling to distant places for ceremonial, exchange, or other purposes, had brought the news. In no way do I wish to imply here that the desert people were 'isolated.' They had always been involved in economic and ritual exchanges with neighbouring groups, some from quite far away, with different linguistic and cultural traditions. In local historicity, accommodation but also resistance to these differences had always been a dynamic and ongoing process. The *Kartiya* were radically different in that they showed no interest in exchange or reciprocal relationships.

From the turn of the century until the 1940s, the Walmatjari and Kukatja families living around Paruku (Lake Gregory) and Mungkayi (Stansmore Range) suffered at the hands of a few of the newcomers, who were in search of gold or of pasture for their animals. The stories surrounding these first fleeting contacts vary from one extreme to the other, from the sharing of food and overnight camps to manslaughter. In the confrontations that occurred, both *Kartiya* and Aborigines lost their lives.

With their characteristic sense of humour, the elders at Balgo, male and female, would take pleasure in recalling anecdotes inspired by these first contacts. These covered a wide range of reactions: The stupor felt by one man at his first sight of a *Kartiya*, who he thought was a *wanya* (malevolent spirit); as he prepared to throw his spear, he saw the stranger's beard and concluded that it must be a man. The amazement at the first camel sighted, which someone had mistaken for one of the ubiquitous termite mounds in the area. The savouring of the first sweet tea, a drink that has since become part of their daily lives. The first *bullucki* (the Aboriginal word for bullock) killed, which was then cooked in the classic earth oven. They laughed when they recalled the huge hole they had to dig, and the amount of wood they had to gather for the occasion. To be on the safe side, they gave the first piece of meat to the dogs. In years to come, cattle were to take an increasingly important place in the lives of those who were to become identified as 'the Balgo mob.'

In 1939, three Pallottine missionaries, a Catholic order of German origin, left Halls Creek in the eastern Kimberley region of Western Australia and undertook a 250-kilometre journey south, down to the northern edge of the Gibson Desert, a region at that time largely unknown to the Euro-Australians. This expedition followed an unsuccessful first attempt by the Pallottines to establish a mission settlement at Rockhole Station, next to Halls Creek, which they had acquired in 1934. These men were Bishop Raible, Father Ernest Worms (also an ethnologist), and Father Alphonse Bleischwitz. A few years prior to this move, Father Worms had explored the Lake Gregory area in search of a suitable place to establish the new mission station. It took many months to gather all the material necessary for the trip: carts full of provisions, as well as mules and sheep (a thousand had been bought along with the Rockhole Station). Accompanying them were a few Aboriginal men from the Kimberley region. These men would be useful for surveying the new area and tracking down the Aboriginal families living around Lake Gregory and in the desert to the south. Father Alphonse Bleischwitz became the superintendent of the Balgo Hills Catholic Mission[5] for the following two decades.

The 'Old Mission' Days

Some of the families who had experienced painful events at the hands of passing explorers or settlers welcomed the arrival of Father Alphonse Bleischwitz and his friends to the area. They saw in them a guarantee of security in the face of the ever-increasing number of strangers. The majority of the local families, however, remained reluctant to join the mission settlement, at least initially. The Aborigines who had accompanied Father Alphonse from Halls Creek travelled over the countryside around Lake Gregory, trying to contact the local families and convince them to join the new settlement. Over the following years, more and more families walked in from the desert, partly out of curiosity but also to visit their close kin or when in need of water or rations.

Father Alphonse, as the Aborigines called him, tried at first to establish the mission station at Tjaluan (Point Alphonse) on the Balwina reserve, some forty kilometres to the south of the actual site. Bores were put down and water was struck at seventy feet. But the lack of wind to drive the bore windmill made the site unsuitable for permanent settlement. A year later, the mission moved to Darbi, a better watering place situated within the boundaries of Billiluna Station, which was then privately owned. The war was raging in Europe, and for different reasons this made the lives and work of the missionaries of German origin difficult. They stayed only a few months at Darbi before they moved to the Balgo Hills, where they finally established their mission in the mid-1940s. In 1965, they abandoned that location, which has since been called the 'old mission' or the 'old Balgo,' and moved to the present site, some twenty kilometres to the north-east.

During the 1940s and 1950s, local Aboriginal families gradually walked in to the old mission from the desert. In 1953, there were about 100 Aborigines living at Balgo Hills; in 1958, according to official sources, there were 130 people (R. Berndt 1959: 85), but this number fluctuated considerably. The people were mostly Kukatja and Walmatjari and came from the Stansmore Range and the Lake Gregory areas, respectively. There were also some Wangkatjunga, Mandiltjarra, Ngarti, and Pintupi[6] (see map 2). For the Kukatja and their neighbours, the gradual move from their ancestral lands to the mission settlement was done willingly as they became aware of the changing context. The Kukatja and Walmatjari established at Balgo could and would return on foot to their territories, sometimes for extended periods, knowing that they could go back to the mission settlement when necessary. The children who were raised in the 1940s and the 1950s recall the times when they lived with their kin on their homelands, mostly to the south of Balgo, and the occasional return to the mission settlement when needed.

At the old mission, bores were put down, buildings of mud brick and blackwood timber were erected, and in 1947 an airstrip was opened. During the 1950s, the mission grew bigger, and a few brothers, nuns, and lay missionaries joined Father Alphonse. By 1953, a mud-brick school and dormitory had been built. It became compulsory for the children to stay there most of the time, which displeased some parents. The fear of being forcibly separated from their children while on the mission grounds was one of the reasons why families occasionally preferred to leave the mission for their countries.

On the periphery of the *Kartiya* area of the mission were the Aboriginal camps, where makeshift shelters were constructed of branches, canvas, and sheets of galvanized iron. The Aboriginal men participated in the construction of the mission's main buildings, but without sharing the enthusiasm of Father Alphonse. The women, who had traditionally prepared unleavened bread made from local seeds, were shown how to prepare and bake bread in the White man's fashion. Both sexes were responsible for herding the sheep, moving them from pasture to pasture, and protecting them from the wild dogs or dingoes. While all the men and women learned these new skills, they only practised them on an irregular basis because they would often leave the mission settlement for days or weeks at a time, either to engage in ritual activities or to resume their nomadic life as hunters and gatherers. This caused great discontent to the missionaries.

In areas like the Kimberley, the history of the relationship between Aborigines and *Kartiya* can be traced back to what the latter considered a major offence: the spearing and theft of cattle. The theft of livestock, the cattle from the neighbouring Billiluna Station and the mission sheep, was a frequent occurrence, which entailed quite severe penalties. Obviously, the Aborigines understood the unlawfulness of such practices, but the easy availability and the size of the game seem to have outweighed any fear of the sanctions they might suffer if caught. These offenders were indeed severely punished by Father Alphonse and the Halls Creek police. During the 1940s and early 1950s, a number of Balgo men experienced the humiliation of being chained and forced to walk from Balgo all the way to the Halls Creek jail, and even as far as Wyndham. During the 250-kilometre march, they were kept under close scrutiny by the mounted police. With intense bitterness, some of these men recounted to me these difficult events that have now become an integral part of local collective memories. And yet, this element in the collective memory, of having known the weight of chains – a punishment experienced not only by men in the Balgo area but by Aborigines all through the Kimberley and all the way to the West Coast around Broome and Derby (Ryder 1935) – has been creatively channelled and re-expressed as an important travelling cult, the *Tjulurru*. It originated in the first half of the century on the West Coast and was eventually transmitted to the Balgo mob in the mid-1970s (see chapter 6).

As concerns the theft of livestock at Balgo, the Aborigines do not represent themselves as victims and certainly never as thieves. A number of stories tell how some Aboriginal hunters succeeded in escaping *Kartiya* reprisals either by hiding in the bush for a while or by some other glorified feat of skill. The negative collective memory of humiliation finds its positive expression in narratives of great feats. It is said that a Kukatja man (in other versions, and depending on the narrator, it could be a Walmatjari or a Ngarti), living at the time in the Halls

Creek area, had just killed a *bullucki*. He butchered it, cutting it into large pieces that he then strung over a piece of wood carried over his shoulder, as he would have done for any other large game. As he was getting ready to walk back to his camp, a *Kartiya* mounted on a horse saw him and started galloping after him. But the man ran so fast, despite the heavy weight he was carrying, that the horseman never succeeded in catching him. Another story in the same vein tells about a *maparn* (medicine man) in the Halls Creek area who had just killed a *bullucki*. He was also chased by a horseman, who started to shoot at him. Not only did the Aboriginal man succeed in avoiding the shots, but he intercepted a few of these with his shield and deflected them back, killing the rider. These two stories were told to me on various occasions and by different narrators, and always with a great sense of pride. They summarize decades of difficult relations in the eastern Kimberley resulting from the theft of livestock.

In contrast, such feats of skill are typically absent from stories about the spearing and theft of cattle by Balgo people. A number of stories from Balgo tell how a relative, usually a father or an uncle, after having killed a sheep from the mission herd, had to hide and live a few weeks in the bush in order to avoid Father Alphonse's reprisals. This difference from the previous narratives can be explained by the fact that, unlike in the Kimberley area, the focus of the relationships between Aborigines and Euro-Australians in Balgo did not primarily revolve around livestock. In the stories from both regions, the Aborigines, men and women alike, far from representing themselves as dispossessed victims, reaffirm their own identity as hunters and warriors and as the first dwellers in the land. Furthermore, these actions, considered as theft by the *Kartiya* and thus punishable, were for the Aborigines a response of active resistance towards the theft of their land by the newcomers. From the Aboriginal perspective, these 'thefts' may have represented a form of reciprocity, but they were in a form that the *Kartiya* did not easily accept or understand.

From the first contacts onward, both in the Kimberley and at Balgo, the 'cowboy' became an important figure at all levels of social and cultural reality. The cattle industry in the Kimberley employed much of the Aboriginal workforce (both men and women), at least up until the late 1960s. Even though in Balgo the situation was different, Father Alphonse, Father McGuire (the superintendent in the 1960s), and, after them, Father Hevern saw this profession as the only possible future for young Aboriginal men. At the same time, they needed a skilled workforce to care for the increasing livestock of the mission station. These same young men who had seen their fathers, uncles, or grandfathers chained and jailed for the theft of a cow or a sheep quickly learned the stockman's trade. In the early 1960s, a dispute between the manager of the Billiluna Station (which had been supplying the mission with meat since its opening) and Father McGuire prompted the latter to buy some 600 head of cattle, enlarging his own herd. He also greatly expanded the herd of horses. The mission station thus joined the cattle and horse industries while still selling wool from its sheep. Through this expansion Father McGuire had ensured not only the financial survival of the mission but also the meat supply for a growing Aboriginal population. Besides their evangelical and pastoral duties, Father Alphonse, Father McGuire, and Father Hevern were keen administrators and business-men.

One of the points that I wish to stress is how strongly and symboli-cally the 'cowboy' figure has been appropriated by the people of Balgo. From their first sightings of the Canning Stock Route convoys to their subsequent experiences over the years, either around Balgo or in the stations farther north where a number of them worked on a casual basis during the 1950s and 1960s, the people of Balgo became familiar with the cowboy image. Even though the number and influence of cowboys declined during the 1980s and the 1990s in the Balgo area, today there are still love songs sung by the women about Aboriginal cowboys. These characters are also present in the song lines of the women's rituals such as *Tjarada* (see chapter 6). Furthermore, through a process of creative appropriation, the cowboy has locally acquired mythical status. He has become a cultural hero, part of the contempo-rary cosmology (see chapter 4). The Aborigines have appropriated one of the dominant characters of the colonial period, one that also person-ifies their own skilful participation in the *Kartiya* world.

Today, only a few ruins remain at the old mission's location. When I used to drive by it during an afternoon outing with Aboriginal friends heading off on hunting or gathering trips, they would often ask me to stop there. As we walked around, they would point to the remains of the communal dining hall, the dormitory, the bell tower, and the bread oven, and would recall life during the old mission days. Some talked of the day when they walked into the mission for the first time, who the other members of their party were, and the direction from which they came. A woman showed me the location of the camp where her father died. Most people would then recall all those who had died, or the few who had chosen to walk back to their countries to die there. One old man smiled when he told me about the times he used to sneak to the dormitory's window to court the young woman who was to become his second wife. Another man, now deceased, remembered the numerous trips he had made to Halls Creek along with one of the brothers or a lay missionary and a string of donkeys to get basic goods such as flour, tea, and sugar. The women spoke of kneading bread dough at dawn and about the smell of the bread oven, while others remembered how they had to protect the sheep from the dingoes.

However, the general feelings about the time at the old mission are mixed. The elders, those who had been young adults when they first walked to the mission settlement from their desert homelands, out of curiosity or to meet their close kin, felt deeply sorry for the country they had abandoned. They felt, they said, 'worry for the country' they had left behind, as if they had abandoned a relative. One woman told me how her father-in-law, already an elderly man when he had come to the mission settlement, sang himself to death so that his spirit would go back to his country around the Lake Hazlett area. The elders remembered, too, a time when they were separated from a number of their relatives in the 1940s and 1950s because they had chosen to walk to other distant settlements established on the outskirts of the desert. Those of Walmatjari descent, for example, missed their relatives who had gone to Christmas Creek, while those of Pintupi descent worried about their relatives who had walked to Papunya. Most people in Balgo had to wait until the 1960s and the 1970s and access to motorized vehicles before they could resume contact with these kin.

During the old mission period, from the 1940s to 1965, they deplored the separation from their children, who were required to stay in the dormitory, and also the hard work they were forced to do by the head missionary. Despite these memories of sorrow and bitterness, the adults and the elders had an immense respect for Father Alphonse, even though they still resisted conversion to Catholicism. In many ways, Father Alphonse's control over them was far from absolute. As I mentioned above, the people could, and would, leave the mission grounds for weeks or months at a time to resume their nomadic life. They still maintained a fair degree of autonomy. It seems as if both parties had been able to arrive at a *modus vivendi*, perhaps because of their relative isolation from the settlers or from the larger Euro-Australian centres.

While they shared their memories, stories, and anecdotes about the first encounters and life at the old mission, my Aboriginal friends never presented themselves as victims or survivors, but rather, and with a characteristic sense of humour, as a strong and proud desert people who had followed a new path and whose ancestral Law stood on equal terms with the *Kartiya* law. While both individuals and local groups maintained their specific ancestral connections and ritual responsibilities, a new identity had emerged and took shape under the conditions of settlement life, that of the Balgo mob.

'Our Law is strong:' The Balgo Mob and the Church

In the early 1960s, two main factors compelled the church to find a new location for the mission. First, the old mission was located on part of the Billiluna Station, and this prevented it from obtaining assistance from the Education Department at a time when the mission sought to expand its teaching facilities. Second, the old mission site was on low-lying ground and was frequently cut off during the wet season. The church needed to find a place offering better terrain and security of tenure. This was achieved when the church obtained a 3,000-acre freehold site within the Balwina Aboriginal Reserve, some twenty kilometres to the north-east of the old location. They moved to the present site in 1965.

Officially, the mission kept the name of the Balgo Hills Catholic Mission. From an Aboriginal perspective, however, and on the basis of the local toponymy, the new site's name is Wirrimanu. This refers to a small local depression formed in the ground by *Luurn* (the Kingfisher), an ancestral being, while on his way south to the Kukatja country (see chapter 2). R.M. Berndt (1970: 245) identified the new location as Ngarili, which is a site on the ancestral track of the *Wati Kutjarra*, Two Initiated Men, along their route to the Walmatjari country. The present settlement is actually located between these two sites, with Wirrimanu to the south-east and Ngarili to the south-west. From an Aboriginal perspective, these ancestral imprints and presences add to the multivocality and multilocality of the place. In the mid-1980s, following the transfer of power from the church to the government, the Aborigines opted for Wirrimanu as the name of the new corporation. This choice may be explained by the presence of a majority of Kukatja people within the Balgo mob.

Clearly, the missionaries had high expectations when they moved to the new location. A few hundred tons of steel were shipped from Perth to Wyndham and then carted 750 kilometres or so to Balgo to build the settlement. All through the 1960s, Father McGuire, who was then the superintendent, kept expanding the herds of cattle and horses to ensure the financial independence of the mission. A total of seventeen bores were put down around the Balwina Reserve to supply water for the livestock. Business flourished. A White manager and a few Aboriginal families, mostly of Tjaru and Ngarti descent, were established at the Balgo Homestead, also known as Ngulyipi, 100 kilometres to the east. The sheep population declined gradually from 1,200 head in the early sixties. When it became apparent that the cost of keeping the sheep exceeded the profit from the wool, the superintendent decided to use them solely for food. By the end of the 1960s, none were left. According to the Aborigines, a great number fell prey to dingo attacks.

The Aborigines had to participate in the construction of the new Balgo mission. Some remember those first years after moving to the new location as if they had been sentenced to hard labour. One man, now deceased, recalled with resentment his days at the quarry, some forty kilometres away, having to break the stone, load it, and then cart it back to the mission settlement. This stone was used to build the school, the church, its bell tower, and the monastery. Mud bricks were also made locally and used for the most part to build small shelters for the Aborigines. The women continued in the tasks that they had been introduced to at the old mission, such as kitchen or laundry work. In fact, it was only by doing the various mission tasks, as maids, stockmen, or kitchen helpers, or by doing minor maintenance work, that the Aborigines could have access to the communal dining hall run by the church. This, though, was mostly funded by the Native Welfare Department, which became the Department of Aboriginal Affairs in the early 1970s. Two dormitories, one for girls and one for boys, were also built. The children were kept under close supervision by a few brothers, nuns, and lay missionaries who had arrived in Balgo to give a hand in the task of 'civilizing the primitives.'[7] The autonomy that the Balgo mob had maintained at the old mission was soon replaced by a high level of economic dependency. The opportunities to visit their country or to resume a nomadic life, even for just a short while, gradually diminished, for various reasons. The main reason was that they felt they were abandoning their children, who were not allowed to join them. It must be emphasized, however, that under the mission regime, the Aborigines in Balgo were not subjected to the kind of abuses and ill-treatment that those living and working on cattle stations farther north experienced.[8]

The Balgo mob grew steadily during the 1960s. A few new families trickled in from the desert, while others left settlements or stations farther north to join their close kin in Balgo. In the early 1970s, the mission settlement experienced a sudden population increase. From 130 people in 1958, the population rose to more than 600 in the mid-1970s, though with fluctuations. This increase corresponded to an important and very well-documented episode in Euro-Australian–Aboriginal relations. In 1967, a national referendum, passed by a 93 per cent majority, gave the federal government the right to legislate all matters affecting Aboriginal people, and resulted in the granting of Australian citizenship to the Aborigines. The station owners and managers, who up until then had been exploiting the Aboriginal workforce by paying them in kind with rations of food, clothes, and tobacco, were now legally obliged to give them wage parity with their Euro-Australian counterparts. Most refused to comply, and so their Aboriginal workers were laid off. Because of this, the Aboriginal groups who had been living on the station grounds since the first contacts, typically on their own ancestral lands, were forced to move away and to find another place to live. A few families who had been living on cattle stations to the north, such as Sturt Creek and Gordon Downs, but also as far as the Turkey Creek area, came to Balgo. Most of these newcomers to the mission identified themselves as Ngarti, Tjaru, or Warlpiri, with territorial links and ancestral connections to the east and north-east of Balgo. The majority of them, however, were related to the Kukatja mob on either their father's or their mother's side.

The mission staff, still at the time only about a dozen in number, managed this population increase relatively easily because the Balgo Homestead was functioning well and the mission was also receiving funding from the Department of Aboriginal Affairs. Some problems developed, though, primarily because of tensions and conflicts between the different Aboriginal groups. These conflicts faded with the establishment of two settlements, Billiluna (now known as Kururrungku), some eighty kilometres to the north-west, and Lake Gregory (Mulan), some sixty kilometres to the west of Balgo. Both of these places had been part of the Billiluna cattle station, with Mulan always having served as an outpost to the station owner and his stockmen. The Western Australia government acquired the Billiluna Station on behalf of the Aborigines following the establishment of an Aboriginal Lands Trust in 1972. Most of the Walmatjari and Wangkatjunga families who had been living at Balgo moved to these communities. They took over the responsibility of the cattle with the help of a White manager employed by the local Aboriginal Council. The two communities now have a population of about 150 people each. By the end of the 1970s, the Aboriginal population at Balgo was down to about 500 people. This number was reduced again during the 1980s and the 1990s with the establishment of outstations in the area (see below).

In the late 1960s, Aboriginal movements and claims for greater social justice and recognition gained increasing impetus in different parts of Australia. The federal Labour government elected in 1972 promoted a policy of Aboriginal self-determination and implemented a series of measures at the national level to this end. Although these did not have the effect of a magic wand that would instantly erase all previous (and outrageous) colonial injustices, they most certainly opened the way to significant changes. They gave a voice to Aboriginals at the national level. One of the policy's most significant outcomes, at least for the Aboriginal groups living in the Northern Territory, was the implementation of the Aboriginal Land Rights Act (Northern Territory) 1976. Since then, the act, 'a legal discourse on Aboriginality' (Povinelli 1993a: 53), has been at the core of the multifaceted relations and negotiations between the Aborigines and the *Kartiya* in the Northern Territory. On the downside, only Balgo people of Warlpiri and Ngarti origins, whose countries lie east of the Western Australia/Northern Territory border, have been directly involved in land claims and have acquired the status of 'traditional owners.' The Catholic church in Balgo resisted this ideological turn towards Aboriginal self-determination during the 1970s. As the freeholder of the 3,000 acres of the Balgo site, and because of all the efforts and monies the mission had invested over the years, it saw itself as the sole master of the settlement grounds and of the Aboriginal population. The church at that time had complete control over the economic and decision-making aspects of the settlement, leaving no space for the Aborigines' involvement in community affairs and business. During this time the relations between the church and the government became strained. The church refused to hand over to the Aborigines the full amount of whatever state or federal monies they were entitled to, such as unemployment benefits, child benefits, or old age pensions. It kept a substantial percentage of these funds to finance the operation of the mission settlement. The superintendent considered the Aborigines too inexperienced in dealing with cash and feared also that they might simply stop their 'work' at the mission if they did not feel compelled to

do it. The families who left for Billiluna and Mulan were no longer subjected to this treatment and gained access to their own government
benefits.

Finally, in the mid-1970s, the dormitories and communal dining hall
at the mission were closed, and the youth were allowed, at last, to
resume camp life, which meant a greater involvement in the daily
dynamics and activities of the camps, including rituals. In 1982, after
intense pressure from the state and federal governments, the mission
superintendent finally agreed to comply with their demands to hand
over to the Aborigines whatever governmental allowances or unemployment benefits they were allowed. These benefits were referred to
by the Aborigines as 'sit down money' (welfare and unemployment
benefits), 'kids' money' (family allowances), and 'pension money' for
the old people. This was the first time that the Aborigines had participated directly in the cash economy since they had moved into the mission settlement. This contributed, in some ways, to the lessening of the
mission's control over the lives of the Aborigines.

In 1980, following the national movement towards internal decoloni-
zation and a greater implementation of Aboriginal self-determination,
a local Aboriginal Council was elected in Balgo. However, because the
mission kept control over the politics and land of the mission settlement, the local council had little, if any, authority and decision-making
power with regard to the running of Balgo. The council member turnover, then as now, was very high. In the late 1970s, the community
adviser, a representative of the government, arrived on the scene. His
role was supposedly to advise the local council and share with the mission superintendent the administrative and political responsibilities of
Balgo until the complete transfer of power from the mission to the government in 1984. I will return to this topic in the next section.

In some respects, the Aborigines in Balgo had decided to leave the
Kartiya to tend to business, as they had always done. In the meantime
they employed their newly acquired though still very limited autonomy to follow their own agenda, focusing on the production and transmission of their Law and on the generation of social and symbolic
capital. In Balgo, as in most of Aboriginal Australia (Bell and Ditton
1980), two laws coexist for the Aborigines, who recognize a clear distinction between the '*Kartiya* law' (or 'whitefella' law) and their own
Law, the Ancestral Law, also known in most Western Desert languages
as the *Tjukurrpa* (or Dreaming).

In the 1970s, different factors promoted the growth and renewal of

ritual activity in Balgo. The closing of the dormitories and the reunifi-
cation of families led the adults and the elders, both male and female,
to reintroduce the young people to the Ancestral Law and to their ritual responsibilities. Although the transmission of ritual and mythical
knowledge and the performance of ceremonies had continued while at
the mission – out in the bush away from the missionaries' gaze – and in
spite of the missionaries' vigorous denigration of these – there had
been some disruption of ritual activity due to the migration of the various groups on the fringe of the desert and the breakdown of traditional
networks. Furthermore, the Aborigines' newly gained autonomy, in
part derived from welfare benefits and government allowances, along
with a greater mobility due to the availability of motorized vehicles,
prompted the Aborigines to travel more and more to neighbouring settlements both to visit relatives and for ritual purposes.

Beginning in the 1970s, a ritual renewal of some importance occurred
throughout the Kimberley region (Akerman 1979; Kolig 1981) and in
desert-affiliated communities such as Balgo, Lagrange, Jigalong, Yuendumu, Papunya, and Kintore, with gatherings involving up to several
hundred Aborigines (see chapter 6). Traditional networks of ritual
exchanges were revitalized, and new ones were created.[9] After decades
of relative isolation, the Balgo mob had the chance to renew contacts
with their relatives who had joined other settlements on the fringe of
the desert. They started travelling, for example, to Christmas Creek,
Lagrange, and even as far as Jigalong in the west, to Turkey Creek and
Lajamanu in the north and north-east, and to Yuendumu, Papunya, and
Kintore to the south-east. These journeys, which might last from a few
days to a few weeks and which are still very frequent today, had many
purposes: to visit relatives or to participate in initiation ceremonies,
mourning rituals, or ritual exchanges. In this sense, the Aborigines
never ceased to be nomads. They kept a travelling lifestyle and a socia-
bility that they express today with modern means. Trucks, cars, and
four-wheel-drive vehicles have acquired a particular status, not only in
Balgo but throughout Aboriginal Australia. They have become a prized
item, the main symbol of today's nomadism, and one that has been
appropriated in a particularly Aboriginal fashion.

While the church continued to exercise its hegemony with regard to
the administration of the mission settlement all through the 1970s and
until the early 1980s, the same could not be said on the religious level.
The majority of the Balgo mob, after more or less thirty years of living
on the mission settlement, still refused to convert to Catholicism and,

with a few exceptions, strongly resisted conversion.[10] Changes such as the closing of the dormitories, along with access to 'sit down money' and other government allowances, prompted the Aborigines to invest their energies and their time in 'real hard work': the initiation of the young men and ritual exchanges. In brief, 'real hard work' is the strengthening of the Law, in terms of both the production and the reproduction of ancestral territorial and ritual connections and responsibilities. This occurred to the great despair of the church and government observers, who would have much preferred to see the Aborigines involved in the kinds of 'work' more in tune with Western ideology and value systems. From an Aboriginal perspective, however, it was far more rewarding and meaningful to participate in an initiation ceremony than it was to water the lawn in front of the missionary's house.

Resistance to Christian ideology and cosmology,[11] though, was accompanied by an equivalent respect towards the church and its representatives. As long as the two laws were kept separate, the Aborigines were confident that coexistence was possible. While they lived in the dormitories, the youth had followed the discipline imposed upon them by the nuns and the brothers and endured a discourse that strongly denigrated the values and the lifestyle of their parents and grandparents. After the closing of the dormitories, it seemed as if the result of that discourse had been to strengthen the youths' commitment to their own ancestral Law. Those who chose to maintain religious ties with the church did not do so at the expense of their attachment to the Law but tried instead to find an intermediate position. Over the years, the strategy of the three mission superintendents had always been one of absolute condemnation of Aboriginal ways and Law. When it became evident that such strategies did not bear the expected results, the church decided to adopt a different attitude.[12] The relationship between the church and the Aborigines changed in the early 1980s.

At this point, I should explain my presence and activities in Balgo. In May 1980 I had arrived in Alice Springs, determined to work and live with Aborigines. An opportunity arose for me to work at the Central Land Council. My partner at the time, Warwick Nieass, a free-lance artist, took a job as cook for the mission staff at Balgo. As my principal goal at the time was to live in an Aboriginal community, I decided at once to join him and to assist him in his job. Because we were not married, he had to negotiate with Father Hevern to let me join him. I arrived in Balgo in August 1980. A few months later Warwick became an art teacher (and manager) at Balgo, so I took over the cook's job until January 1982, when the church closed the dining hall for lack of money. While the job was time consuming, I still had opportunities to be with the Aborigines, to visit their camps at night, to invite them to our house, and, whenever possible, to go into the bush with them (as mission staff, I had access to a vehicle). At first, Father Hevern expressed his disapproval. He was not used to such friendly relationships between the mission staff and the Aborigines and saw us as 'political troublemakers.' He explained to us a few implicit rules: no Aborigines were allowed in the *Kartiya* houses, and contact between both groups should be restricted to the workplace only. We did not heed his warnings, however, and began to be viewed with much suspicion by the other *Kartiya*. There were about twenty of them at the time: the Catholic mission staff and the schoolteachers from the State Department of Education. Over the months, however, our relationship with Father Hevern improved significantly (and not only because he liked our cooking). He came to realize, as he was to tell me later, that the kind of relationships we had established with some of the families and the fact that we made our vehicle available for bush trips almost daily had a more than beneficial effect. It gave the Aborigines the opportunity to leave the community and engage in hunting and gathering activities farther afield. At the same time, it provided an outlet for several teenagers who were regarded as troublemakers.

In the 1980s, the church was being confronted with an increase in the level of ritual activities and the strengthening of traditional Law, at both the local and regional levels. With the implementation of national policies for Aboriginal self-determination, the church realized that it would soon have to withdraw from its administrative responsibilities and opted for a radical change in its discourse, practices, and strategies. In this new endeavour, Father Hevern was greatly helped by Sister Alice Dempsey, who arrived in Balgo in 1980 and who promoted greater recognition of and tolerance towards Aboriginal ways, a discourse surely more in tune with the times. For example, the men were asked in 1981 to paint a series of banners inspired by their traditional designs for the jubilee of Father Peile, one of the missionaries.[13] These banners were used afterwards to decorate the inside of the church building. For the same occasion, the men were asked to perform ritual sequences, dressed in their ceremonial regalia, in front of the Whites and representatives of the Catholic diocese. This was the first time such a request had been put to them, and the Aborigines took the matter very seriously, with evident pride and dignity, while concealing to the

Kartiya gaze any elements of sacred-secret significance. Furthermore, the St John's Adult Education Centre, which had been operating on a rather small scale throughout the seventies, expanded its activities. Sister Alice, as the Aborigines called her, worked on the translation into Kukatja of some passages from the Bible and of religious hymns, and Bible reading classes were organized for the adults, together with a number of training programs for young people. In the translation endeavour, Sister Alice was assisted by Father Peile, who knew the Kukatja language, and by a few young Aboriginal men and women who had been studying at the Nulungu Aboriginal College in Broome.

The new politics of conversion, which displayed more openness and tolerance, quickly bore fruit. In 1981, I observed the mass baptism of nearly forty adults and elders of Balgo, both men and women. These were people who were born in the bush, who had lived the first part of their lives outside the confines of the mission, and who had, up until then, refused to convert to Catholicism. I have retained one very vivid image from that ceremony. As the neophytes and the priests were getting ready to enter the church building, an elder, Arthur Tjapanangka, a very widely respected Law man and one of those who still refused to be baptized, sat silently on the ground at the foot of the altar for a long while. He left the church as the others were entering and was not seen for several weeks; according to his relatives, he had 'gone bush.' This mass baptism came from a collective decision and had thus a strategic and political tone to it. One thing, however, was clear to the Aborigines: their baptism did not mean a lessening or a contradiction of their involvement in the Law and responsibilities towards it.

A few days after the mass baptism, all the Aborigines in the community welcomed a ritual convoy from Jigalong that they had been impatiently expecting for the last two weeks. This convoy of trucks and cars, carrying about 200 men, women, and children, had taken many days to travel from Jigalong through Broome, Christmas Creek, Halls Creek, and finally Balgo. They had come for the initiation ceremonies. The convoy was bringing back two young novices from Balgo who had been sent by plane to Jigalong a few weeks earlier for the first steps of their initiation. Two ceremonial camps, one for the men and one for the women, were erected to the west, at the outskirts of the settlement and out of sight of the *Kartiya*. The two weeks that followed were filled with intense ritual activities under the umbrella of the ancestral Law. One evening, as the sounds of beating boomerangs and of ritual songs echoed in the mission settlement, an elderly nun, who had been in

Balgo for nearly twenty years, complained to me with obvious resentment how, in spite of all the missionaries' efforts, the Aborigines were 'quick to go back to their savage ways.' Six years later (in 1987), this same woman would drive around the Aboriginal camps on Sunday mornings to prompt the Aborigines to go to mass.

The nature and extent of the religious and political relationship – both being intrinsically intertwined in Aboriginal ideology, sociality, and experience – between the church law and their own Law that was worked out over the years by the Aborigines in Balgo is a complex and delicate issue that will not be dealt with here in any great detail. Suffice it to say that in 1987, when I came back to Balgo, the extent to which the two Laws could and should be mixed still remained a puzzling matter for most Aborigines. The following example shows the complexity of such theological cohabitation. In 1987, the Catholic diocese organized a religious meeting in Broome to which a number of communities from the Kimberley area were invited. A group of about fifteen people from Balgo accompanied the church people. Among them, a young man, involved then with the church, travelled to Broome in an old car he had just bought and which, as it turned out afterwards, was in rather poor repair. Accompanying him were his pregnant wife, their children, his mother and father, and his classificatory mother, the first spouse of his father. On their way back, in the vicinity of Halls Creek, they had an accident in which the young man's classificatory mother (a Walmatjari elder from Mulan) was killed. The news of the accident and of the death reached Balgo only the following day. At once, crying and wailing started echoing in the top and bottom camps. It went on all night. Early the next morning, their faces and chests painted with kaolin as a sign of mourning, and the men armed with their boomerangs, the men and the women from the top camp walked towards the bottom camp where they were awaited. There, the close kin of the deceased and those of the young man formed two lines and confronted each other with boomerangs and insults. This animated expression of grief lasted for a few moments, after which everyone sat down and gathered to cry and wail, sharing their sorrows. The female close kin of the deceased injured themselves by hitting their heads with stones or any other convenient hard objects, while a few of the male relatives had speared their thighs the previous night in the intimacy of their camp or in the bush. These moments were the preludes to the 'sorry business' (mourning ceremonies) and to a ritual of conflict resolution that was to be held a few days later.

From the *Kartiya* point of view, one of the causes of the accident was the car's poor state of repair. In addition, the police accused the young man of drunken driving and of driving without a licence. On the other hand, Aboriginal causality and objectivity required that the explanation for this sad event had somehow to be found elsewhere. In the days following the accident, as the atmosphere overflowed with grief, discussions, speculations, and interpretations were offered as to the causal chain of events that might account for the death. Nungurrayi, a very respected Law woman, perceived in this unfortunate event the confirmation of their own mistake in bringing their own Law into the church. A few people seemed to agree with her, though no one else expressed it in such an explicit manner. This is what she said: 'Nobody can stop us thinking. We can think long way. For long time we kept the Law in the camp, for us. Before we never used to mix up. Now we been mixing. We been bring some Law in the church. This is no good.'

Two days after the accident, the young man was released from the Halls Creek prison, awaiting his trial according to *Kartiya* law. The young man was held responsible for the death of his classificatory mother and, in order to alleviate the grief of the deceased's relatives, he had to be punished according to Aboriginal Law. A ritual of conflict resolution had to take place. Everyone in Mulan, not only the relatives of the deceased, was strongly affected by the death. Considering the intensity of their grief, the family of the young man feared the worst. On the fourth day after the accident, a few hundred people from Balgo and Mulan gathered at the bottom camp for the ritual of conflict resolution. While the young man stood in the middle, his brothers – and also the sons of the deceased – real and classificatory, formed a half-circle around him. Over the next few moments, they threw spears and boomerangs at him. He protected himself with a shield, which he handled awkwardly. During the attack, his cross-cousins were allowed to protect him, which a couple of them did. His mother and one of her sisters ran by his side and succeeded in intercepting a few blows. The intention was certainly not to kill him, but the whole performance was necessary in order to give a lesson to the offender and soothe the pain and grief of the deceased relatives. The young man received a head injury, and it was the two sisters of the deceased who afterwards cleaned it and comforted him. The conflict was over, and the mourning ceremonies were held two days later in Mulan. The whole of Balgo and Mulan participated alongside relatives of the deceased who had come from Billiluna and Christmas Creek. A few weeks later, the young man had to face the *Kartiya* law and was sentenced to a few months in jail. Over the decades, a fair number of Balgo men have gone to the prisons of Halls Creek, Broome, or Perth, for periods of varying length. Such stays in jail have become an integral part of their relationships with *Kartiya* law. Moreover, and by analogy, in pidgin English they now call 'jail' the seclusion camp where, during the initiation ceremonies, the novices are isolated while being introduced to Ancestral Law.

In 1984, power was transferred from the church to the government. While the church withdrew from administrative responsibilities, it continued in its pastoral role. The Balgo Hills Catholic Mission became the Balgo Hills Aboriginal Community, and then a few years later, the Wirrimanu Aboriginal Corporation. Having lived under the mission-aries' authoritarian rule and the church's paternalistic supervisor for several decades, the Balgo mob were inexperienced in dealing with their new responsibilities in community affairs and anticipated this transfer of power with some anxiety. In the negotiations that then took place between the government and the mission, it was agreed that the church would resume responsibility for the school, which had been under the State Department of Education since the mid-1970s, and also retain its responsibility for the Adult Education Centre. The church therefore ensured its continuing presence and influence in the community of Wirrimanu.

Wirrimanu: Neocolonial and Postcolonial Encounters

The socio-spatial arrangement of the settlement reveals the social distance between the *Kartiya* and the Aborigines. The settlement is divided into three distinctive areas, the *Kartiya* area and two Aboriginal camps, the 'top camp' and the 'bottom camp.' The *Kartiya* area forms a half-circle around a large oval where local or regional sports events are held and where Aboriginal soccer teams meet on a regular basis. Starting from the western end of the horseshoe formed by the main buildings are the store, the Adult Education Centre, the community office (during the mission period, a large stone building that was later replaced by a small, and now derelict, prefabricated house), the monastery, the church, the art centre (formerly mission staff dining hall), the convent, the school complex (which includes the teachers' residences), and a number of houses for visitors and for the regular church and government staff. Some of these buildings, and particu-larly the private houses, are protected with fences to keep out Aboriginal youths, who are often tempted to break into the *Kartiya* houses. Indeed, a number of buildings have been totally destroyed by these youths over the years. The fences stand as a symbol of the nature of the relationship between the *Kartiya* and the Aborigines.

A few hundred metres to the east is the 'top camp.' The Kukatja, Ngarti, and Tjaru peoples mostly live here, and have territorial affiliations to the east and south-east of Wirrimanu. To the west of the *Kartiya* area is the 'bottom camp,' where mostly the Walmatjari, Wangkatjunga, and Mandiltjarra peoples live; their countries lie to the west and south-west.[14] Some Pintupi, whose countries are to the south, live here as well. As a general rule, the Aborigines circulate freely between both camps. Sometimes, someone might be confined to one or other of the camps for a limited period after the death of a close relative or after a conflict. Most families in Wirrimanu are now related in some way or other, and residence in one or the other of the camps is characterized by great mobility and flexibility. Some people might live a few years or a few months in the top camp and then move to the bottom camp for an indeterminate period, or vice versa. Within the camps, there is also a fair amount of shifting around, and very rarely would one family occupy a house for many months in a row without at some point moving to another location. All these movements, which constitute yet another expression of contemporary nomadism, are based on different factors. Prominent among these is the state of the relationships among kin. A quarrel or a disagreement, for example, might prompt some people to move somewhere else for a while. Alternatively, a family that goes to visit relatives in another settlement for a few weeks or a few months might, on its return, have to find another location. Or a move would become necessary after a death, since custom requires that the house or camp of a recently deceased relative be abandoned for a few months to alleviate the grief of the living relatives.

In the early 1980s, there were still very few modern houses in either of the camps. Small mud-brick shelters and a number of makeshift camps made with canvas, branches, and sheets of galvanized iron were most common. Over the years, through government funding, houses were built in the bottom and the top camps to replace many of the makeshift shelters. The houses are inhabited in a specific way that reflects Aboriginal sociality. They are usually devoid of furniture – though some are now equipped with a television – with swags (bedrolls) and personal effects lying on the floors in the different rooms. The main living and gathering areas are the verandas and yards.

Although some houses are equipped with electric stoves (when they are not out of order), people still prefer to cook outside on the fire, with each house or location having its own firepit. Whenever game is brought to the settlement, it is cooked in the earth oven. The camp-fire has maintained the same importance it always had in Aboriginal sociality, and fetching wood is still a daily concern and activity. In the early morning, fires are rekindled at the family camps.

During mission times, the majority of the Aborigines had to assume minor tasks around the community, such as laundry or kitchen work for the women, garbage removal and lawn watering (in front the *Kartiya* houses) for the men. Since then, things have not changed much. The few jobs available for Aboriginal men and women, usually under the Community Development Employment Project (CDEP) scheme, either are at the store, the clinic (as health worker), the school (as a teacher's aide), or the Adult Education Centre. Aborigines are always under the close supervision, authority, and paternalism of the *Kartiya*. The jobs are worked irregularly by the Aborigines, are subject to high turnover, and are done at a rhythm that is seldom the one expected by the *Kartiya*. On pay-days, a majority desert the workplace to play cards, grouped on the ground throughout the community. Clearly, the Aborigines in Wirrimanu refuse to comply with the White values of 'work' and 'working,' and this contributes to widen the social distance between the two groups.[15] As a general rule (with the exception of a few of the church people), the relations between the White staff and the Aborigines are reduced to their strictest minimum, that is, the workplace during working hours. Following the transfer of power in 1984, the 1980s and the 1990s were marked by an overt competition between the two hegemonic bodies, the church and the government, both claiming that they were acting on behalf and for the good of the Aborigines. This rivalry found another expression during the 1980s in the struggle for control over the 3,000 freehold acres that the Catholic church had acquired in the late 1950s. In many ways, the control of the land meant also the control of the local population. The negotiations, which peaked in the late 1980s, were finally concluded in the early 1990s when most of the settlement land came under the Aboriginal Lands Trust (Western Australia), while the church retained its freehold over those sites where its own buildings stood. The local Aboriginal Council was largely excluded from the negotiations between the two hegemonic bodies, in complete contradiction to the national policy regarding Aboriginal self-determination.

Following the transfer of power to the government, there was a huge increase in the number of White staff in Wirrimanu, from about twenty to as many as fifty during the 1980s. (Ironically, the Aboriginal population decreased markedly following the establishment of outstations in the 1980s.) The sudden increase of Whites in the community began to trouble the Aborigines. During mission times, the *Kartiya* population in Balgo was kept to the absolute minimum, scarcely over twenty people. This included the church staff, a few teachers from the State Department of Education, and the health and maintenance staff. As a result of the expansion of activities at the St John's Adult Education Centre and at the school, the church staff grew steadily over this decade, as did government staff. During my second stay at Wirrimanu in 1987–8, there were more than fifty *Kartiya* in the community, employed by the church or the government. There were also official visitors almost daily. Staff from the Department of Aboriginal Affairs, which was restructured at the end of the 1980s as the Aboriginal and Torres Strait Islanders Commission (ATSIC), became very numerous. Besides the community adviser and the office staff, there were a number of 'project officers' in charge of different training programs that ran parallel with church training programs. The Aborigines now had to deal with two competing hegemonic bodies and were continually being requested to participate in a range of activities, mostly designed and organized by the *Kartiya*. 'Meetings' with *Kartiya* were held daily. In the camps, there was much talk about the fact that there were 'too many meetings,' and people expressed their discontent with an arrangement that left them little time for their own responsibilities. This whole situation had a definite neocolonial air to it, the most noticeable sign of which was the daily siren that echoed from the office all through the settlement at precisely 8:00 a.m., apparently calling the Aborigines to 'work.' The siren was a holdover from mission times, and to my great astonishment it was still in use in 1987. The practice was finally abandoned in 1988.

This state of affairs was clearly at odds with the federal discourse on Aboriginal self-determination and self-management. Furthermore, the situation made it difficult for the local council and the Aborigines to promote their own concerns, since they were still inexperienced in dealing with *Kartiya* institutions and decision-making structures. In many ways, the council and the community became hostages to the quarrel and competition between the two hegemonic bodies. The local council membership, which had gained some confidence and decision-making power during the 1980s, started withdrawing from its responsibilities. Membership turnover became frequent, and it became more and more difficult to find someone to act as chair, a position that had never been easy to fill. The government preferred and sought to recruit young adults rather than elders in the hope that the former would be more able to deal with 'modern' matters and, probably, easier to control. On the other hand, the kind of decision-making power that is assigned to the council members stands in contradiction with Aboriginal politics and decisional processes, in which it was and still is very rare for someone to impose his or her point of view upon others. Furthermore, these young adults, usually only in their thirties, had not yet acquired the necessary knowledge and ritual maturity within the Law that would enable them to exercise some influence on collective matters. In the 1980s, to alleviate the strain and discomfort of the local council members, a Council of Elders was formed to assist them, but was dissolved towards the end of the decade. Conflicts between Aboriginal groups and families, and among the young leaders, and the stresses put on the council members by their relatives also contributed to the high turnover and the eventual non-participation in the council.[16] All the chairs whom I have known over the years lived through their one-year mandate with uneasiness, sometimes even with great anxiety, torn between the often very different interests of the government and their own people.

The increased White population and the high turnover of White staff, the apparent conflict between the church and the government, the administrative problems of the community, the fact that the council wielded little real power, and the endless requests imposed upon the Aborigines contributed to their increasing discontent and anxiety. This was compounded by a significant increase in alcohol consumption on community land during the 1980s. When the Aborigines had been controlled by the mission, the missionaries had succeeded in keeping alcohol-related problems at bay (though on their return journeys from Halls Creek or Rabbit Flat Roadhouse, while still outside the community grounds, people would usually drink whatever they had brought back). No one now had sufficient authority or charisma to forbid the consumption of alcohol on community land, despite Wirrimanu's status as a 'dry community.' The Ancestral Law had no real mechanism to deal with such issues. An increase in the availability of motorized vehicles led to more frequent trips to Halls Creek or Rabbit Flat Roadhouse, the closest places at which to buy liquor. Outbreaks of violence in the camps became an almost daily matter. Over the 1980s this increasing collective despair was aggravated by the deaths of young men from the community in car crashes, or during fights in northern towns.

By 1988, the social climate had become very tense, and the situation culminated in a local crisis during which some young Aboriginal men physically threatened some *Kartiya*. Matters reached a point where, fearing for their security, most of the *Kartiya* asked to leave the community temporarily. At that time the government decided to transfer the community office to Kununurra, a township several hundred kilometres to the north, where it is situated to this day. The church and government staff were reduced to a minimum for a short period, and even the Health Department had difficulty finding nurses for the clinic during the crisis.

When I returned for a short visit in 1994, the White staff had grown back to what it had been in the late 1980s even though the Aboriginal population had declined, with a greater number of Aborigines now living at the outstations. A small police station, only occasionally visited by the Halls Creek police, had been built. Because the community office was still in Kununurra, the involvement and the responsibility of the local council in the administration and decisional affairs of the community had been considerably reduced. The government still refused to return the office to the community, citing staff security requirements and the need for a more 'controlled' management. The local council turnover was higher than ever, and one could easily sense among the Aborigines a clear indifference to, if not complete disillusionment with and withdrawal from, the community's official decisional process. These feelings could be interpreted as a form of resistance and opposition both to the White system of administration and to an institution that had been imposed upon them, an institution that they refused to appropriate for themselves. This lack of interest in the affairs of the community council is also the outcome of a particular context in which the Aborigines had lost the little power they had been given in the 1980s.

In 1998, when I last visited the area, the government seemed bereft of innovative ideas on how to solve the 'Balgo problem,' but the same could not be said of the church staff. During the 1990s, the church expanded its pastoral and educational activities, and its staff of the parish, the school, and the Adult Education Centre greatly outnumbered the government's staff. Strengthened by its long experience in dealing with the Balgo mob, and having gained the confidence of the

Aborigines over the years, the church seemed far better organized and efficient than the government. More and more elements of local Aboriginal 'culture' have been introduced into the school and into church activities. Even though some Aborigines still actively oppose the presence of the church, the majority welcome it and participate in the Catholic religious activities with varying degrees of interest, while at the same time maintaining a distinction between these practices and those of their own Law.

Reconnecting with 'Country'

In the decades after the migration to the mission, very few people had returned to the vast desert areas between the Canning Stock Route, the Stansmore Range, and Lake Mackay where they had originally come from. The adults and the elders who had been born in the bush had never ceased, however, to recall the places where they were born and grew up, and where their parents and grandparents had died. They had continued to perform the rituals associated with those places. Access to these territories improved in the 1980s due to (1) the out-station movement, and (2) increased mining exploration in the areas south of Wirrimanu. Two events foreshadowed a return to the bush by many Aborigines.

In 1979, Father Hevern, then the superintendent at Balgo, went on a bush trip with a group of Aboriginal men. They travelled farther than they had for twenty years, around the Stansmore Range and east towards Lappi Lappi. This two-week trip, funded by the Aboriginal Arts Board, left a strong impression on the men and the missionary. Father Hevern told me afterwards that he had been quite surprised by the metamorphosis of his fellow travellers, which occurred as soon as they left the mission grounds. Suddenly, he was no longer the 'boss.' They were at home here, and they were the bosses. Even though he had known these men for years, it was the first time he saw them at their true value, on their own ground, and he was highly impressed by their bush skills and their knowledge of the countryside. For the Aboriginal men, after an absence of twenty years or more, this brief return to their distant ancestral lands meant a great deal. All along the way, they sang songs about the country, performed ritual sequences, and renewed their acquaintance with the land and with their ancestors. They found a skeleton, which apparently was the remains of one man's father, who had decided to die in his country during the early years of the old Balgo mission. His bones were treated as tradition demanded. On their return journey, they encountered the footprints of a 'bush man,' an Aborigine unknown to them.

During my first stay at the mission in 1981, rumours were circulating about some people who had refused to join the mission settlement and who were still living in the desert, and the tracks seen during the trip with Father Hevern were talked about. In October of that year, two of these 'bush men' were seen in the vicinity of the settlement by a young couple while they were fetching wood. Upon hearing the news, the camp residents reacted immediately and organized a plan of action. Fearing that these men might try to kidnap some women, the women and children gathered at the mission oval, in the centre of the *Kartiya* area. The men armed themselves with spears, shields, and boomerangs and formed a long line at the southern edge of the community to guard the community during the night. The 'bush men' were not seen, but in the morning footprints bore witness to their passage. The rumours had proved true, although the identity and the intentions of these 'bush men' remained unknown. Talking about the event then, I sensed mixed feelings of fear and excitement. In 1987, during my second stay, I learned that these 'bush men' belonged to a family that was found in the Gibson Desert in 1984 (Myers 1988a). They were feared in 1981 because the people knew neither their intentions nor their affiliations. Today, they regularly visit their relatives in Wirrimanu. These two events might seem innocuous, but they nevertheless brought some hope to the Aborigines for a return to their respective ancestral lands.

Other events at both the national and international levels were to be important for the Balgo mob in helping them realize their dream of returning to their countries. Among these events, geological exploration activities in the Gibson Desert contributed to easier access to the distant ancestral lands, in spite of what such activities represented in terms of exploitation of Aboriginal lands by exterior multinational interests. After unsuccessful drilling attempts in the 1960s and early 1970s at Tjawa Tjawa (Point Moody) and Walkarli (White Hills), oil exploration teams continued to explore in the areas south of Wirrimanu, mostly in Walmatjari and Kukatja countries. Over the years, the tentacles of multinational imperialism have scarred the desert landscape with a multitude of grid 'cut lines.' The Aborigines started using these tracks, despite their foreign aesthetic, because they were suitable for motor vehicles and allowed the locals to go farther into the desert for hunting and gathering activities, and to reconnect with various sites. Following the passage of the Heritage Protection Act, prior to any activity the mining companies were required to obtain an Aboriginal cartography of the area they intended to explore. This was to make them aware of and to protect sites of Aboriginal significance. During the 1980s, anthropologists and men from Balgo (later, women) mapped some of the areas south of Balgo. These mapping and survey trips became more and more frequent. Some Kukatja and Pintupi men and women travelled with Scott Cane (1984) on several occasions to perform archaeological surveys and outstation projects. The Rainmaker, a Walmatjari man, travelled to Kutal (see map 2) with his relatives in 1986 and performed the rainmaking ritual for the first time in years.

The oil exploration teams have continued prospecting in the area. During my last visit in 1998, a team was attempting to drill for oil and gas near Walkarli (White Hills), but they knew that their chances of drilling were rather unlikely because of the hardness of the ground. The Aborigines are highly suspicious of what they consider to be the desanctification of the underground, the sacred dwelling place of the ancestral beings, including the Rainbow Snake, *Warnayarra*. An elder told me that he felt that the ancestral beings, particularly the Rainbow Snake, would 'look after the country' and protect the people's interests on the land better than 'Canberra,' which they know to be the centre of *Kartiya* power. They were also aware that the land-rights issues had hardly begun in the area.[17]

The Aborigines' renewed access to their ancestral lands arrived just in time, when the elders who had walked over the territory in their youth were still alive to introduce the younger generation to their countries. The young adults, in their thirties and younger, who knew the country only from stories and through rituals and sand drawings performed at the mission settlement, finally had the opportunity to explore and experience on the ground with the elders all the sites of significance they had heard about so often. They finally discovered their land, the campsites of their forebears, the places where significant events had occurred, the water points, and all the myriad hunting and gathering resources of the land.

Another important factor in reconnecting with their ancestral lands for the Balgo mob was the outstation movement. Begun in the 1970s by Aboriginal groups in Arnhem Land, Northern Territory (Coombs and al. 1982), and supported from its inception by government subsidies, the outstation movement quickly gained impetus all through the Northern Territory, the northern regions of Western Australia, and

South Australia. Aborigines in Arnhem Land decided to reoccupy their ancestral lands on a more permanent basis, spurred by the threat that the mining companies represented to them. There were nearly 600 outstations by the end of the 1980s, with populations that varied between 5 and 150 people (Cane and Stanley 1985; AGPS 1987). The outstation movement, as a major social movement, resolved the tensions and conflicts building up in the more densely populated settlements. This dispersion was beneficial to a people whose sociality had been best developed at the band level, a generation or two before, with intrinsic and complex ties to ancestral lands. At the outstations, the Aborigines not only could renew their ties with their lands but also could live in a social and cultural environment that was more in tune with their needs, values, and desires. Some of these outstations have since acquired administrative and political autonomy from the main settlements.

The population of Wirrimanu dropped from nearly 500 in the early 1980s to half of that by the end of the decade following the establishment of the outstations. Ringer Soak, an outstation 150 kilometres to the north-east of Wirrimanu, attracted a few Ngarti-Warlpiri families. Other families joined their relatives at Nyirripi, an outstation near Yuendumu in Warlpiri country. Some Pintupi families moved to Kiwirrkura, on the southern edge of the Gibson Desert. These outstations have since become well-established communities with their own local councils. These examples of diffusion of the population over a large territory reflect the different territorial connections of the Balgo mob and the persistence of their ties to their ancestral lands. For the Balgo community, Yagga Yagga became the most important outstation because of its location near Mungkayi (the Stansmore Range), a cluster of sites of significance to the Kukatja.

In the late 1970s, a few Kukatja families had planned to establish an outstation near Mungkayi. In 1984, a water bore installed and used by an oil company some 100 kilometres south of Balgo was vacated. The families concerned took advantage of this situation to ask the government for the funds necessary to develop the basic infrastructures of an outstation, and so Yagga Yagga was founded (see chapter 2 for further information on Yagga Yagga). When I returned to the area with my family in 1987–8, we decided immediately to establish our camp at Yagga Yagga. Several factors prompted our decision to join the Yagga Yagga mob, even though at the time the outstation had no electricity, houses, or facilities (only four tin sheds and a water bore). The main reason we chose Yagga Yagga, however, was the fact that the families there were those which had adopted me in the early 1980s during my first stay.

There were about thirty people living there at the time, though on an irregular basis. Trips back and forth to Balgo for food supplies, for medical care, or to get money were quite frequent. Sometimes the outstation would be deserted for a few weeks when ritual responsibilities and activities prompted the Yagga Yagga mob to travel to neighbouring communities. As well, because the track flooded during the wet season, at that time we all moved back to Balgo for a few months. Such mobility is often perceived negatively by government bodies and officials, who expect the outstation to be occupied on a permanent basis. From an Aboriginal point of view, however, the outstation is an expression of their renewed nomadism.

The results of the Yagga Yagga experiment proved satisfactory to the government. Following repeated demands from the Yagga Yagga and Kiwirrkura outstations, funds were released in 1988 to built a bush track south to Kiwirrkura from Yagga Yagga. The track became functional, at least by Aboriginal standards, a few years later. This track meant a great deal to these desert people, mostly Kukatja and Pintupi. Previously, travellers wanting to get to Kiwirrkura from Yagga Yagga had to take the 1000-kilometre road from Wirrimanu, through the Granites, Papunya, and Kintore (see map 1). Now, with this direct track between the two outstations, there is only about 200 kilometres to travel. Equally important, the new track has allowed access to the remote parts of the desert and the ancestral places that the Pintupi and the Kukatja had been longing to reconnect with for many decades. Though they might just stay at a place overnight, or just walk around an area for a short while before driving away, they have left their tracks as a sign of their presence, and their noise and voices will be heard by the ancestors as a sign that they still care for the country. Three more outstations were established along that bush track in the early 1990s, Walkarli, Lamanpanta, and Piparr (see map 2). Each has a bore and four tin houses. Even though they are seldom occupied, they represent the contemporary expression of Aboriginal nomadism and presence in the land, and the Aborigines' care for the country.[18]

Yagga Yagga became an incorporated community in the early 1990s, and acquired administrative and political autonomy from Wirrimanu. The population of Yagga Yagga grew steadily through the 1990s, to nearly 200 in 1998, though with fluctuations. The community infrastructure now includes a few large houses, a small store, an office, a garage, and a small school. White staff were still minimal in 1998. The Yagga Yagga mob have established their own identity, distinct from the Balgo one. They are recognized at the regional level also, when they visit more distant communities or participate in ritual meetings. There is also a Yagga Yagga music band, and a football team. Tensions have increased over the years between the Balgo and the Yagga Yagga mobs because of competition for the various funding programs available from different government sources. There, as elsewhere in Aboriginal Australia, the contemporary politics of identity and place between Aboriginal groups are interwoven and entangled in complex and ever-changing ways. As we will see in chapter 2, the Yagga Yagga mob went through a process of mythological creative innovation in order to ground and validate their new identity.

For the Kukatja and other Western Desert groups, the outstation movement is their response to earlier colonial practices. It is also a contemporary expression of the persistence of their relationships to their ancestral lands, social orders, and identities. The acrylic painting movement is another form of contemporary accommodation and expression. The acrylic painting movement started in the 1970s at the Pintupi settlement of Papunya (Bardon 1979; Myers 1992, 2002). It has since spread rapidly to other settlements of Western Desert affiliation such as Yuendumu (Anderson and Dussart 1988), Lajamanu (Glow-czewski, ed., 1991), Balgo, and Yagga Yagga (Poirier 1992a; Watson 1996). Accustomed to painting on their bodies, on the ground, or on ritual objects using ochre, kaolin, and charcoal mixed with animal fat, they have creatively adopted the newly introduced medium of acrylic paint on canvas. Their main sources of inspiration are traditional designs and iconography. These designs are representations and mani-festations of their relationships to places, depictions of ancestral and human actions, and expressions of their engagement with the land. Traditionally, these designs were performed and exhibited solely in rit-ual contexts, and they were reproduced anew when needed. Through negotiation, agreement about what is allowed to be painted has been reached among Aboriginal groups, in order to preserve the sacred-secret character of the designs (Kimber 1995) in the face of the perma-nent character of acrylic paint and in response to the commercial mar-keting of the pieces.

An exhibition of the Balgo paintings at the Art Gallery of Western Australia in Perth in 1986 was highly successful. This stimulated other people in Balgo and Yagga Yagga to start painting, each person having his or her own creative style. Since then, a number of national and international exhibitions of their work have been held. Until 1987, the Adult Education Centre at Wirrimanu had assumed the responsibility for and management of the acrylic paintings. An autonomous art centre was established, the Warlayirti Artists Corporation, under the supervision of a White manager. Like the outstation movement, the opportunity to paint in acrylic arrived at the time when the generation of elders who grew up before mission times were still living and could use the medium to transmit the knowledge and the stories of the country to the younger generations. These works of art also constituted a dialogue with the world at large, a way to express and assert a specifically Western Desert aesthetic, and the Aborigines' own way of being-in-the-world. Besides its aesthetic dimension, each painting is also a political act, in that it reasserts the artist's identity and connection to the country depicted. Not unimportantly, the paintings are a source of money, which is at once shared and reinvested in social relations, rather than representing a personal gain for the artists themselves.[19]

As I stated at the beginning of the chapter, this narrative is only an imperfect glimpse of Balgo. It is impossible to recount all the explicit and implicit compromises, reinterpretations, and negotiations that have occurred over the decades and contributed to shaping the relations between the Aborigines and the *Kartiya* in the Balgo (Wirrimanu) area. One thing is clear, however: the expectations, desires, values, discourses, and practices of both groups are largely incompatible and incomprehensible to each other. The church and the government promote an ideology of 'progress' and 'development' – the magic concepts of Western hegemony – while the Aborigines rarely respond as expected by the *Kartiya*. These expectations and the paternalism of the majority of the White staff in Wirrimanu (who are often oblivious to Aboriginal ways, values, and practices) adds to the social distance between both groups. It seems as if the Balgo of White imagination and desire has no room for the Aborigines as they are but only as the *Kartiya* expect them to be.

The resistance of the Aborigines to *Kartiya* ideology and expectations is expressed in different ways. Most often the resistance is seen by the White staff as the incapacity of Aborigines to come to terms with modernity. Everyday life in the camps is more often than not understood as 'laziness,' 'drunkenness,' and 'filthiness.' One of the main sources of discomfort in the relations between the Aborigines and the *Kartiya*, at least in my understanding, is the complete absence of reciprocity. If the Aborigines now expect to some extent that the government and the church will 'look after them,' there is no way, no space or opportunity, for them to reciprocate and 'look after the *Kartiya*.' The value of reciprocity is at the core of Aboriginal sociality and sense of self and shared identity, and it finds no means of expression in the (neo)colonial setting of Balgo. The *Kartiya* are so busy 'working for' and 'helping' the Aborigines, no doubt with the best of intentions, that they have not had the time to pause and ask themselves how the Aborigines could, in turn, maybe 'help us' (rather than just help themselves). This absence of reciprocity on the part of the *Kartiya* could be one reason for the Aboriginal resistance to Whites' expectations and for their suspicion or lack of interest in any project presented to them by the *Kartiya*. Such absence of reciprocal relations is an expression of the unequal relations of power at Wirrimanu. However, with the exception of a few young leaders, the Aborigines rarely express themselves in terms of inequality.[20] In the Balgo area, the persistence and transformation of Aboriginal social orders, identities, and cultural consciousness within the contemporary context are expressed by the outstation and the acrylic movements, the transmission and transformation of social and ritual networks on a regional scale, and renewed nomadism. The final outcome of some of these projects, the changes manifest in the context of the coexistence of the two laws, are still unknown. For instance, in 1980–2, during my first stay, the Aborigines used the English term 'business' (by analogy to *Kartiya* values) to refer to all matters pertaining to the Ancestral Law, especially ritual activities. This word highlighted the sociopolitical character of these activities. By 1987, another expression had been introduced, this one taken from the neocolonial vocabulary: 'culture.' At Balgo, as in other parts of the postcolonial world, the word 'culture' was on everyone's lips (Sahlins 1993). The Aborigines no longer used the term 'business meetings' but spoke rather of 'cultural meetings.' Aboriginal Culture and Law meetings started to be held regularly by regional Aboriginal organizations in the late 1980s and even more frequently in the 1990s, with the *Kartiya* being allowed to participate on a larger scale. However, the Aborigines distinguish between these 'cultural meetings' organized by regional bodies, and their own 'cultural' (ritual) activities and responsibilities.

The narrative presented in this chapter is incomplete in that I intentionally excluded a group of actors who are intrinsic to Aboriginal historicity, experience, sociality, and sense of place. I am talking here of the ancestral beings – their continuing presence and actions in the world. The *Kartiya* see the ancestors simply as beliefs and refuse to consider Aboriginal assertions as truth; however, the ancestral realm is inherent in the Aboriginal way of being in, knowing, and relating to the present-day world and to places such as Balgo and Yagga Yagga. Obstacles to intercultural relations between the Aborigines and the *Kartiya* are not only ideological but also ontological and epistemological.

Chapter 2

Ancestrality, Sentient Places, and Social Spaces

Two realities or key embodied symbols, *Tjukurrpa* and the mythical itineraries, are necessary to understand the sociality, cultural expressions, individual experiences, and composite identity of the Kukatja and neighbouring groups. These realities enable us to grasp the ways in which Western Desert Aborigines might possibly understand, structure, express, and negotiate their multifaceted social relationships with each other, the land, and the cosmos. The first of these realities is *Tjukurrpa*, the term most widely used by the Western Desert language groups and generally translated as 'Dreaming.' *Tjukurrpa* is a cosmology, an ancestral order, and a mytho-ritual structure. As a generative force, *Tjukurrpa* breathes life into the universe by giving it form and vital substance. Knowledge of the world emanates from *Tjukurrpa* and at the same time is grounded in it. *Tjukurrpa* and its multiple expressions are embodied in the land and are intrinsic to an Aborigine's sense of self and experience of the world.

The second key symbol flows from the first and highlights the paramount importance of social and territorial spaces as networks of named and sentient places. These are the 'mythical itineraries' or 'ancestral tracks,' which are spatio-physical narratives of the ancestors' journeys, actions, and performances across the land. These itineraries meander over the land, forming criss-crossing networks that define the social spaces of territorial and ritual knowledge, belonging, and responsibilities. These ancestral tracks and the networks they form represent 'forms of permanence' (Stanner), while they are also subject to transformation and reinterpretation over the course of time. Western formal constructs such as the social, natural, and cosmological codes are, in the Kukatja world, interwoven into a seamless whole where there are no ontological dichotomies between these dimensions.

Tjukurrpa: A Multidimensional Complex

The term *Tjukurrpa* is used by all the language groups represented in the Wirrimanu area: the Kukatja, the Walmatjari, the Wangkatjunga, the Ngarti, the Mandiltjarra, the Pintupi, and the Warlpiri. While all Australian Aboriginal groups recognize the existence of this primary principle, its designation varies from region to region. Before inquiring into the different meanings and expressions associated with *Tjukurrpa*, it is appropriate to raise the problem posed by the translation of that key term. Spencer and Gillen (1927) offered the expression 'Dream Time' as a translation for the term *Alcheringa,* which is used by the Arrernte (Aranda) groups of the Central Desert and which designates the same thing as *Tjukurrpa.* The fact that the Arrernte also used the term *altjira* to designate the dream experience surely motivated their choice, since the suffix *-inga* means 'belonging to.' Furthermore, with the expression 'Dream Time,' Spencer and Gillen meant to underline the notion of eternity that comes to a Western (and Judeo-Christian) mind whenever the Aborigines talk about the ancestral past.[1] Later, in an effort to delineate that pivotal reality and to make readers aware that our arid and abstract language could hardly offer an adequate translation, Stanner, in a first comprehensive essay on the topic (1953, see Stanner 1979), popularized the 'Dreaming' expression, which he in fact borrowed from Aboriginal English. Today, the second translation is the one most widely used in ethnographic writings, if not in popular usage. The 'Dream Time' expression has gradually become obsolete because it neglects *Tjukurrpa*'s spatial dimension as well as its capacity to combine both times and spaces. The 'Dreaming' expression not only evokes an action, it also implies the dynamic and immanent character of *Tjukurrpa.* Nevertheless, any translation is always to the detriment of the original term, which expresses an all-encompassing concept. In many respects both of these translations are restrictive to the point of being misnomers.[2]

Though incomplete in relation to the meaning of the Aboriginal term, both translations, 'Dreaming' and 'Dream Time,' no doubt facilitate communication between Aborigines and non-Aborigines. However, this does not mean that there is a shared understanding of the concept of ancestrality, which is central to the term *Tjukurrpa*. The misunderstanding is exacerbated when we consider that Aboriginal and Western theories about dream experiences are in many respects very different (see chapters 4 and 5). The translations, which may express a Western imagination in search of the exotic, reflect a simplistic view of a cosmic order and symbolic system whose sources are not found solely in the realm of dreams. The unfortunate consequence of the choice of such terms is that they fail to capture the complexity and the specificity of the Aboriginal concept of ancestrality and of the underlying ontological and epistemological principles that underpin their world-view and their way of being-in-the-world. On the other hand, these translations do attest to an intimate relationship in local expressions and experiences between the ancestral and dream realms. This relationship is reinforced by the fact that such groups as the Arrernte and the Warlpiri (Glowczewski 1991; Dussart 2000) use the same term to designate both the ancestral order and the dream experience. While it is clear that, in Aboriginal thought, dreams and the Dreaming are closely related modes of experience and realms of action, they none the less represent two structurally distinct levels of reality. They are not confused in Aboriginal thought, except in their shared epistemology. Unlike the Arrernte or the Warlpiri, the Western Desert groups such as the Kukatja, Walmatjari, and Pintupi, have a specific word for the dream experience: *kapukurri*. Therefore, I have chosen to use the term *Tjukurrpa* to distinguish that cosmic order and mythopoesis from the mundane dream realm (*kapukurri*). This is to avoid any confusion about their respective meanings and to respect the encompassing dimensions brought to the Kukatja world and experiences by *Tjukurrpa*.

Stanner wrote that the Dreaming (*Tjukurrpa*) encompassed 'a complex of meanings' and that it is 'many things in one' (1979: 23–4). It represents a multidimensional complex, a primary principle through which the universe was created and that permeates and animates everything there is and still actualizes and manifests itself today. As an all-encompassing reality, *Tjukurrpa* defines – or at least offers a moral code with which to evaluate and negotiate – the social rules and cultural practices and the levels of discourse and experience of everyday life. Stanner presented the Dreaming as a cosmogony, 'a study about creation,' and as a cosmology, a theory of 'how the universe became a moral system' (ibid.: 28), but also as 'a poetic key to Reality' (ibid.: 29). Following his work, Munn and Myers, among others, have further contributed to our understanding of *Tjukurrpa* as an ontology, a hierarchically superior value, and a cosmic order. Both of these authors, however, find it difficult to reconcile the ancestral past and the ongoing present, or the coexistence of the realms of the ancestral and the human. This difficulty stems partly from their emphasis on the transcendental dimension of *Tjukurrpa*, to the detriment of its coeval nature and consubstantiality with the human realm. Munn, for example, wrote that none of the persons and events of *Tjukurrpa*, as the ancestral period, overlap in time with the living (1986a: 24). To muddy the waters, she writes elsewhere, 'the ancestral past is continuously coming out of the ground and being re-embodied as a living entity, as well as continually returning to the ground in death' (1973: 199). While the first of these statements emphasizes an absolute division between the two realms, the second stresses their coexistence and interrelation. We find the same ambiguity in Myers, when he writes that the Dreaming transcends the immediate and the present (1986a: 69). At the same time, he offers potent ethnographic examples of intimate relationships between human and ancestral actors and between humans and named places as the embodiment of ancestral actions and as intrinsic to one's sense of self. Munn's and Myers's insightful and classic contributions to Aboriginal ethnography and to *Tjukurrpa* have now been taken a step farther, looking 'closer to the ground' (Dubinskas and Traweek 1984) in terms of local theories of human and non-human actions, and 'closer to the skin' in terms of local notions of person and bodiliness.[3] The 'ground' and the 'skin' (or the body) are used here as metaphors for an embodied ancestrality that unfolds and reveals itself through its multifaceted interactions with the human realm.

In other words, one of the ways by which we can approach Aboriginal experiences and achieve a better understanding of Kukatja sociality and way of being-in-the-world is to look seriously into the immanent dimension of *Tjukurrpa*. It is first an active and dynamic principle that permeates all that there is – be it rock, wind, plant, human, or animal. It is a realm of actions and a mode of experiences that are coeval and consubstantial with the mundane world and interact with it. In the Kukatja ideology and value system, that which is 'from *Tjukurrpa*' is hierarchically superior; but it is also essentially immanent, in contrast, for example, with Judeo-Christian cosmology in which the Creator is transcendent.[4] Partly because of this immanent and embodied character, the communication, reciprocity, and intimacy between the ancestors and humans must be taken seriously – as 'true' (*mularrpa*) – if we are ever to understand the local structuration of experience as an ongoing engagement (and exchange) within a world permeated with ancestral powers and presence.

Tjukurrpa as Law

While the expression *Tjukurrpa* is still the one most widely and frequently used by the Aborigines in the Wirrimanu area, it is sometimes replaced by one of the following English terms: 'Dreaming,' 'Law,' or 'Business.' Each of these terms attests to an aspect of *Tjukurrpa*. As previously discussed, the expression 'Dreaming' conveys the mythopoetic quality of *Tjukurrpa*. The term 'Law' is also widespread over the continent and is used by the Aborigines to confirm the validity of their own system of power and Law, as opposed to the one they have been subjected to since colonization, which they call *Kartiya* law (White man's law). They will say, '*Tjukurrpa* is Law,' and add firmly and convincingly, 'We follow the Law.' The Aborigines are very aware that in today's Australia they have to follow 'two laws,' which in many respects remain incompatible, at least in their respective epistemological and ontological principles. The term 'Law' when used to designate *Tjukurrpa* presents its multiple and wide-ranging contexts of implementation: the ritual sphere, the networks of alliances and exchanges, territorial and social spaces, the classificatory and taboo systems, the preparation and sharing of food, and so on. Those who are said to be 'Law men' or 'Law women,' usually the elders, are those who are knowledgable in all the areas pertaining to *Tjukurrpa* and who have, by participation in ritual activities, 'cultivated' through their lifetime an intimacy with the ancestral realm. A third facet of *Tjukurrpa* is designated as 'Business' and specifically refers to ritual matters, mostly those of a sacred-secret nature. It also stresses the political and economic dimension of *Tjukurrpa*, in terms of the local processes of the production and generation of social, territorial, and cosmological resources. The Aborigines recognize two separate and complementary domains of business: 'men's business' (or men's Law) and 'women's business' (or women's Law), which refer to their respective spheres of responsibility in ritual and daily matters (see chapter 6; Poirier 2001).

Tjukurrpa is no exception to the rule that any law conveys a character of inflexibility, even of intransigence, while at the same time being open to interpretation and thus negotiable. In the Wirrimanu area, any transgression of the Ancestral Law that is recognized as such is usually severely punished. Not long ago the offender could have been speared to death. However, though *Tjukurrpa* first appears to be essentially the place of convention, inflexibility, and permanence, it is much more. Negotiation is possible because of the contextual interpretation of the

. mode of enforcement of the Law. While *Tjukurrpa* attests to the social regeneration of the realm of the ancestors and of the established rules, it is human beings who articulate the modalities of that reproduction in time and space, according to their needs and contexts. It is in that way that the principles of transformation recorded in *Tjukurrpa* express a dialectic and a dialogic between the forms of permanence and their transformations. It is a system that shows a fair degree of rigidity and intransigence while being flexible and open to contingencies and to novel interpretations.

Aborigines and Time

For the Kukatja and neighbouring groups, there is no abstract concept of Time, in contrast to the Western frame of mind in which Time and History are key embodied symbols. The Kukatja are not concerned with the question of 'eternity' or of the beginning of time. This does not mean, however, that they do not have forms of time and a sense of temporality (not to be confused here with chronology) as a principle of transformation. The Aborigines are concerned not with the representation of time, as such, but rather with principles of transformation that are intrinsically linked to *Tjukurrpa*, itself embodied in the land and in people. The Kukatja sense of historicity is intrinsically linked to and cannot be dissociated from the ancestral order. Ancestrality is accountable not only for the past but also for the present and the future. The important fact about *Tjukurrpa* is not so much that it has always been – a fact that cannot be downplayed – but that it is, here and now. The Aborigines are confident that *Tjukurrpa* is 'everywhen,' to borrow again from Stanner.

As the primary essence, *Tjukurrpa* has always existed – has always been – and this ever-existence led to the notion of eternity that was favoured by the first ethnographers. But this so-called timelessness is not the equivalent of a transcendent and ahistorical order. Not only has *Tjukurrpa* always existed, but it continues to permeate and animate all matter, to actualize itself and be actualized in the ongoing present, in a world where networks of social relationships and exchanges involve not just humans but also named places and the ancestors, both acting as sentient agents. From an Aboriginal perspective, reality unfolds and reveals itself through the multiple interactions and relations among the different constituents of the world, be they human, non-human, or ancestral. There lies, I would say, a part of the Aboriginal sense of temporality. The Aboriginal approach to time, I would add, is relational and process-oriented rather than linear and genealogical, and it cannot be dissociated from place, meaning the landmarks where the event occurs.

Swain has argued that, rather than 'prejudicing the issue with the word "time" (either linear or cyclical), it is best to state that Aborigines operate from an understanding of *rhythmed events*' (1993: 19) (emphasis in original). Considering that, from an aboriginal perspective, events occur in place rather than in time, Swain proposes the concept of a 'spatial ontology' (or an 'ontology of place'). The concept is relevant as long as we don't go as far as he does in denying Aboriginal recognition of phenomena such as 'time' and 'the body' (Rose 2000). With this denial, Swain overlooked, first, the fact that 'patterned action and rhythmic events might be indicative of forms of time' (Rose 2000: 288), and second, the relational and embodied character of being-in-place and of moving through places. Such motion of the bodily-self through the landscape implies a sense of temporality. Kukatja representations of time, as principles of transformation and relatedness, are grounded in places, in bodies, events, and 'predictably patterned rhythms' (such as the seasons, celestial activity, and kinship).

As far as 'social' time is concerned, Stanner had observed how the Aboriginal interest 'lies in the cycles rather than in the continuum, and each cycle is in essence a principle for dealing with social inter-relatedness' (1979: 34). This applies to kinship and the subsection system (see chapter 3). It must be stressed here that in the Western Desert, genealogical memory seldom goes back more than three generations from Ego. Beyond this point, persons and events become identified with *Tjukurrpa* and merge with this ancestral order. Such identification with *Tjukurrpa* does not deny their having ever existed or happened but rather recognizes their potential for transformation (or metamorphosis). That which is transformed continues to be, whether it is visible or invisible, and whatever its form. Bell, among others, has stressed how 'the shallowness of genealogical memory is not a form of cultural amnesia but rather a way of focusing on the basis of all relationships – that is the *Jukurrpa* and the land' (1993: 90).

From an Aboriginal perspective, any past event or experience can be woven into a qualitative temporal frame rather than a quantitative one, as the following examples show: 'during the last rainy season,' 'when the goannas come out of the ground,' 'during the X ceremony,' 'following the trip to the Y site,' 'when I was a child,' 'before the mission time,' or 'a long time ago in the bush when my grandfather was a young man.' As we will see (chapter 5), dreams, as events and experiences, also occur in place and time (at a particular time of day or night, and at a particular moment in the dreamer's life trajectory). The reference points to mark past events are never in terms of the number of years or decades.[5] The Aboriginal organization of time, as Merlan has demonstrated, is not governed by an abstract chronology (1998: 66) but is grounded in local Aboriginal historicity and narratives of events and in the spatial landmark where the event actually occurred.

It can also happen that a certain event, for some contextual reasons, captures local attention and imagination and is eventually interpreted in such a way as to become part of local mythical narratives. Once woven into local *Tjukurrpa* narratives or mytho-ritual structure, the event in question becomes estranged from any temporal reference point, irrespective of whether it happened in the past year or half a century ago (see chapter 6 for some examples). Whenever an event or a deceased person is identified with *Tjukurrpa*, it is thus transformed into an expression of ancestrality, in its facet as a regenerative force. The Kukatja show no interest in history as a continuum. Their sense of historicity rather is one of a reality that unfolds and reveals itself in places and through a dynamic and intricate interplay among events and actions from *Tjukurrpa*, the human and non-human realms. The following statement of Swain's is appropriate here: 'The world is not made, but worlds take shape' (1993: 32). Such shaping – or, we could say, unfolding – implies a movement, a transformation, and thus a form of space-time.

From my point of view, one of the most potent examples of Aborigines' lack of interest in time (at least as we know and embody it in the West) is their infinite patience. They are confident that something will happen anyway, irrespective of what it is, which forms it adopts, or how long it takes. During initiation periods, for example, I often saw people 'waiting' for days and days for the arrival of the other participants from neighbouring settlements. The elders would sit under the bough sheds erected at the ceremonial ground, while others would go about their daily business around the settlement or out in the bush. Never, in such situations, have I heard comments or seen signs of impatience or resentment, although rumours would circulate as to the reasons for the late arrival of the other participants. In a similar manner, whenever the car broke down because of a flat tire or mechanical problems, far from being concerned or in a hurry to repair it, the friends with whom I was travelling took it as an opportunity to invest themselves in the immediate place where the event occurred. Some wandered about looking for animal tracks or edible plants, while others sat around or gathered firewood. In other words, they established camp. It was as if the breakdown was an occasion to engage themselves with the place, an opportunity to feel the place and the moment and see what would happen in that space, that time, that moment. Eventually, however, the car was fixed. The narratives of the event that were told afterwards to relatives focused not so much on the breakdown but on whatever was sensed and experienced at that place, at that moment, and before continuing on their journey. These attitudes towards time and the flow of events, as embodied practices, are expressions of a 'poetics of dwelling' (Ingold 1996).

The Ancestors

Ancestral beings are pivotal expressions and manifestations of *Tjukurr-pa*. For the Kukatja, the universe became as it is through the creative actions and performances of these powerful beings. As they travelled the land, they created and named the landscape as one sees it and experiences it today. During the course of their travels, they sowed the reproductive essences known as *kuruwarri* (spirit-children), generally around water points. Each form of existence, human and non-human, is an incarnation and an expression of *Tjukurrpa* as primary essence. The ancestral beings are therefore the ancestors not only of humans but also of the animals, plants, and natural elements. All forms are therefore consubstantial. The ancestors are said also to have handed down to the Aborigines the bodies of knowledge and practices that they, in turn, transmit today. There are numerous ancestors, and it would be impossible to name all those who have left their imprints and essence in the lands south of Wirrimanu. Some of the most important are *Luurn* (Kingfisher), the *Wati Kutjarra* (Two Initiated Men), the *Kanaputa* (Digging Sticks Women), *Marlu* (Kangaroo), *Karnti* (Yam), and *Warnayarra*, one of the many names for the Rainbow Snake. The ancestors, whether male or female, are often said to have unusually prominent sexual organs and pubic hair. In the Western Desert, as elsewhere in Aboriginal Australia, their sexual identity is self-evident, except for the Rainbow Snake, who is ambiguous, being 'neither exclusively male nor female' (Rose 1992: 224).

At the conclusion of their epic adventures, some of these ancestral beings are said to have returned underground, whence they are often said to have originated. While some have risen to the heavens to be transformed into constellations and unflaggingly continue their travels, others have infused the water points and become the inexhaustible sources of the spirit-children (*kuruwarri*), while others have metamorphosed into permanent features of the landscape. Whatever the case, they have never ceased to exist. On the basis of their embodiment within the landscape and their ongoing presence, the ancestors are not only everywhere but also 'everywhen.' Although they are very rarely seen, the ancestral beings are able to make their presence known by a variety of means and to manifest themselves in a range of different forms. For example, they can send messages through the wind, or assume the form of clouds, or slap someone on the shoulder. A person may also just 'feel' their presence. Such manifestations will be given meaning and interpreted contextually, in accordance with recent events (accident, pregnancy, or death) and with the site where they occurred. The ancestors also can be encountered in dreams, the privileged medium of communication between them and humans, through which they may reveal new knowledge. These ancestral beings are endowed with magical powers and engage in intimate and reciprocal relationships with humans.

The ancestral beings are nomads *par excellence*. In the course of their being-in-the-world, in the course of walking, hunting, foraging, dancing, singing, fighting, dreaming, breathing, sweating, copulating, or urinating, they have imprinted and shaped the landscape and infused it with the reproductive essences. In this sense, Povinelli, talking about the Belyuen of Northern Australia, is right in saying that, from an Aboriginal perspective, 'all matter is the congealed labor of ancestral action' (1993a: 137).[6] The ancestors travelled not only over the land but also underground and in the heavens. As they did so, they named the places that represent today the social spaces of belonging and ritual responsibilities. The actions, footprints, body parts, corporeal fluids,[7] and belongings (spears, boomerangs, digging sticks, sacred boards, and so on) of the ancestors underwent a process of metamorphosis. These are now embodied in the landscape (Munn 1970). They *are* the landscape. The land and the named places are the embodiment of ancestral actions and events, of metamorphosed and 'dividual' bodies. By 'dividual' I mean that body parts or corporeal fluids still carry the essence, and thus subjectivity and agency, of the ancestors even once separated from the body itself. Slight hollows in the ground are the footprints of *Karlaya* (Emu); a hill, the tail of *Marlu* (Kangarou); a tree, the spear of one of the *Wati Kutjarra* (Two Initiated Men); a rock hole was formed as they urinated; white pebbles are the fat of *Warnayarra* (Rainbow Snake); a water soak, the place where the *Kanaputa* (Digging Sticks Women) have gone underground to travel to the south-east. From the Kukatja perspective, these topographical, plant and mineral features still embody the essences and the spirits of the ancestors and also those of deceased relatives, whose spirits (*kurrunpa*) have merged with the ancestral order. One can say that in many respects the features of the landscape are gendered, identified with either male or female principles and expressions. Imbued with ancestral essence and presence, the landscape and named places are thus sentient entities. These mythical beings have become the land, and that is how the Kukatja and their neighbours not only express but experience their manifold relationships with their country.

Places, Itineraries, and Networks

Through their actions and deeds over the land and underground, the nomadic ancestors shaped and named places, be it a hill, a water soak, a rock hole, an outcrop, and so on. These specific places are known as *ngurra*, the dwelling places of the ancestors. *Ngurra* are socialized spaces created by the *Tjukurrpa* beings, and each human person identifies with a series of these *ngurra*. A set of *ngurra*, spread over a more or less extended stretch of land and identified with one or more of the ancestral beings, represents one's 'country' (*ngurrara*, 'one's own country'). This network of ancestral connections constitutes an Aborigine's identity and sense of self.

   The term *ngurra* also refers to the human camps the Kukatja set up for the night or for a longer period in the settlements or on the land while visiting relatives in neighbouring communities or during a visit to town. After a day's hunt or while travelling to distant places, people set up a camp; that is, they clear a space, sometimes erect a windbreak, and gather around the fire. The space is now one's home. The *ngurra*, the camp, is a dwelling place but only a temporary one. As 'home,' the camp also involves social relationships. For example, to live as husband and wife, and thus to share a camp, is referred to as *ngurrangkarriwa* (Valiquette 1993: 155). Thus, the single word *ngurra* includes two concepts of social space. As one's country, *ngurra* refers to one's relationship with the land and to the ancestors; as one's camp, it refers to a set of relationships with close relatives. In both cases, *ngurra* appears as a place of dwelling, belonging, and relating. As Myers has pointed out, *ngurra* is not only the human creation of 'camp' but also the *Tjukurrpa* creation of 'country' (1986a: 55). We could add that both leave traces on the ground and inscribe the landscape, whether in an enduring or a more temporary manner.

It was by travelling over the countryside with the Aborigines or sitting around the camps that I gradually became acquainted with the 'stories' (*wangka*, in their public form; *turlku*, when they are sung, usually in ritual contexts) that recreate the journeys of the *Tjukurrpa* beings. In this way I came to realize that the various *ngurra* shaped and named by the ancestors form mythical itineraries. Through hearing the stories, I also came to realize that these 'ancestral tracks' or 'mythical itineraries'[8] extend over tens, hundreds, even thousands of kilometres, in many different directions, and that usually the more extensive ones possess a greater social, political, and ritual importance. Each mythical itinerary re-creates the events and actions from one or a group of *Tjukurrpa* beings. For example, the *Marlu* (Kangaroo Man) *Tjukurrpa*, which comprises dozens of sites, meanders on a north-south axis, starting from the East Kimberley area, across the Gibson Desert, all the way to Pintupi country; while the *Wati Kutjarra* (Two Initiated Men) track goes on an east-west axis, from Warlpiri country to Walmatjari country and probably beyond. The stories portraying the travels of the ancestors also tell how and where in the course of their journeys other *Tjukurrpa* beings were encountered. It is told, for example, how at one site two groups of ancestors decided to perform a ritual together before parting; or how at another site, a lone ancestral traveller tried to seduce a group of *Tjukurrpa* women. At the local and regional levels, these meeting places 'from *Tjukurrpa*' usually represent nodal points, sites of greater significance. In desert areas, more often than not, these nodal points are the main water points. As narrated and experienced by the Aborigines, the whole desert landscape thus presents itself and unfolds into a rich and enduring drama of ancestral events and performances. These itineraries define, in turn, the complex and dynamic networks of social relationships, of territorial and ritual responsibilities, of exchanges and alliances (see chapter 3).

Seldom, however, would my Aboriginal friends narrate these itineraries in full. They would limit themselves by telling me the stories that relate to their respective 'country,' as a series of named sites. That is to say, these ancestral tracks are divided into segments, each of which delineates a country as a more or less bounded territorial space that comes under the responsibility of a local group (see chapter 3). As the *Tjukurrpa* stories form a sequence, it is apparent that a segment seldom, if ever, stands alone; it derives some of its meaning from its relation to other segments on the same or neighbouring itineraries. This also applies to a 'country,' which is necessarily connected to its neighbouring countries, and so on down the sequence. I find the metaphor of the rhizome, as expounded by Deleuze and Guattari (1987), most appropriate here. Unlike the root system of a tree, but rather like a rhizome,[9] all the segments are equal and self-generating while being connected in one way or another.[10]

From the Kukatja perspective, the whole desert, as well as areas far beyond, is thus criss-crossed with ancestral tracks that not only link the surface of the earth, the underground, and the heavens, but also tightly bind together humans, ancestors, and named places within complex and dynamic networks of social relationships and responsibilities. The stories (*wangka*; or *turlku* as song) recounting the unfolding of these itineraries throughout the land, the manner in which they connect and intersect and disappear underground to (re)emerge farther on, offer some clues as to their underlying rhizomatic logic and their dimension of 'openness' – that is, their potential for transformation and reinterpretation.

The Politics of Sacred Knowledge

In Kukatja epistemology, to know a country is to have a first-hand experience of it. When one has travelled through a country, has seen it, sensed it, and left her or his footprints in it, when one has foraged or hunted in the area, then one can be said to know a country. In addition, linked to this physical aspect of knowing the country, is knowledge of a sacred character. Each country, as a series of named sites, corresponds to bodies of ritual knowledge and practices derived from *Tjukurrpa*. This sacred knowledge comes in the form of stories and mythical narratives but also as ritual songs, designs, dances, and objects. These elements form a mytho-ritual corpus that can be more or less elaborate depending on the social, political, and spiritual relevance of the site and country thus celebrated. These elements also correspond to the Law of a country, as bequeathed by the *Tjukurrpa* beings. These bodies of knowledge, in their public and secret forms and flowing from all of the *Tjukurrpa* itineraries of a given region, attest to the breadth and wealth of Aboriginal cosmology. Furthermore, ritual activities are highly valued modes of knowledge and experience.

In Aboriginal sociality and experience, the concept of knowledge is land-based. Rose has aptly summarized the politics of sacred knowledge in the following manner: 'Within country, access to knowledge (subject to the 'usual' circumscriptions of age, gender and intelligence) is a right. Beyond the parameters of what can legitimately be defined as one's country, access to knowledge is a privilege' (1994: 3). The criteria of exclusion from/inclusion within sacred knowledge are relative rather than absolute and are contextually re-evaluated and negotiated according to events and individual abilities, requests, and acquaintances with such knowledge. (Local criteria with regard to rights and responsibilities towards country and associated ritual knowledge will be dealt with in more detail in chapter 3.)

From childhood onwards, each individual is gradually introduced to the Law of his or her country. This familiarization comes first through listening to the *Tjukurrpa* stories, in their public form, either at the camps or when the children travel in the bush with their relatives, but also during public ritual performances. The acquisition of knowledge of the various countries to which an individual may claim rights is a lifelong process. There exist formal and less formal means to acquire that knowledge, as well as different degrees of secrecy associated with mythical and ritual knowledge. The question of one's interest and maturity is relevant in this learning process, even more so today than in earlier times. In the Wirrimanu area, the initiation rites in which young boys are circumcised still carry a great deal of importance and significance. These rites are held every year and, intermittently over a few months, draw on the time and energy of many groups over a vast area. A second level of initiation, still for boys, follows a few years later. Kukatja women do not hold initiatory rites *per se* but act as guardians of specific mytho-ritual corpuses that make their participation in the boys' initiation essential (see chapter 6). Therefore, only sustained interest and participation in women's rituals and in public ones enable young women to become gradually acquainted with and 'initiated' into the secrets of the Law to which they are entitled. In the Wirrimanu area, men and women, in so far as they distinguish between men's Law and women's Law, share the ritual responsibilities for the production and the reproduction of the sociocosmic environment, in distinct but nevertheless complementary ways.[11] When ritual apprenticeship ends – if it ever ends – the elders of both genders, as guardians of the Law, have not only mastered the mythical knowledge and ritual practices but have also evolved intimate relationships with the *Tjukurr-pa* realm.

Each mytho-ritual corpus comprises secret knowledge that is then said to be *tarruku*. Imbued with important and magical powers, this knowledge is disclosed only to those entitled to it through successive initiations; its communication also requires that one has acquired the necessary maturity and skills to deal with such powers. Everything that is *tarruku* – sites, moments, songs, designs, or objects – is governed by a set of rules that are accessible only to knowledgable men and women – Law men or Law women – and that only they can manipulate and, potentially, negotiate. The young and the uninitiated must refrain from what is forbidden; the Law is uncompromising in this regard.

The following story of an event that occurred a few decades ago, before the settlement at the mission, is revealing. It was initiation time, and all the men had gathered at their ceremonial grounds. A young male child, attracted by the distant singing and the beating of boomerangs, came closer and hid behind some bushes. He was caught and was condemned to die. His grandfather pleaded on his behalf, and it was decided instead that the child should be 'sung': by having a sacred board held over his throat while powerful songs were sung, the boy was rendered mute. Thus, he could not divulge the forbidden things that he had seen and heard. Today, Tjupurrula, the young child, has become an accomplished Law man and a respected *maparn* (medicine man) in the Wirrimanu area. Though still mute, he communicates with his surroundings and tells stories by means of sign language, probably the first language that children learn, even today.

By participating in rituals and acquiring knowledge, one has one's composite identity, in terms of ancestral connections and rights to country, collectively recognized. While the ethnographic literature has documented, region by region, the social and political components of ritual life in relation to rights to country, age groups, or gender, very little attention has been given to the experiential and emotive dimensions of rituals. Ritual practices and performances are an objectification and enactment of ancestral actions and deeds, and manifestations of their enduring power. They are also acts of communication with the mythic beings. From an Aboriginal perspective, singing, painting, and dancing are acts of communication with, and participation in, an ancestral realm that is immanent and coeval. When the Kukatja represent a particular country in painting, singing, or dancing, they unequivocally demonstrate their connections and rights to the particular country thus objectified: it is a political act. It is also an aesthetic and communicative act. In painting, singing, or dancing the country, the Kukatja directly address the sensibility of the place-person, as the embodiment and dwelling place of the deceased and the ancestors. These practices enhance the individual's empathy for his or her country. Empowerment is also a recurrent theme in local discourses on ritual activities. One of the manifold purposes of rituals is, as one Kukatja man put it, 'to make people and country stronger (*marrka*).' Such empowerment can be understood on the basis of the permeability of the bodily-self to ancestral powers and on the basis of one's intimate relationships with sentient places that are regarded as kin.

Kuruwarri and Sentient Places

Another pivotal expression of *Tjukurrpa*, one that is sometimes used as a synonym, is that which is called *kuruwarri*. *Kuruwarri* signifies the primary essence and substance, the vital and 'generative force' (Watson 1996) from *Tjukurrpa*. For the Kukatja, the term *kuruwarri* carries two interrelated meanings. First, it refers to the spirit-children; second, to ritual designs. Both are manifestations of ancestral powers and presence, and it is through the agency of the *kuruwarri* that human beings express their privileged relationship with their *ngurra*, as country.

As the original essence, the *Tjukurrpa* represents an ongoing presence that is continuously being re-embodied and actualized. This is made evident in the reproductive cycles and local theories of conception. As mentioned already, the ancestral beings, in the course of their travels, have sown the reproductive essences, the *kuruwarri*, or spirit-children. As a non-human agent, the spirit-child might undergo a series of metamorphoses prior to entering the mother's body. Before entering, it can momentarily take the form of an animal, a plant, an object, or a natural element (cloud, rain, or wind), sometimes taking a malicious pleasure in teasing future relatives. It is for this reason that spirit-children are often presented as tricksters. After coming into contact with the future mother through ingestion or other means, or by manifesting itself in a dream, it transforms into a human foetus (see chapter 4). The site where the event takes place – that is, where the mother realizes she is pregnant, usually after the first morning sickness – becomes the conception site of the child to be. A person is thus the incarnation of the ancestor associated with such a site. Throughout life, a person maintains a privileged and intimate relationship with the conception site. Such intimacy is evident in the way men and women sometimes refer to themselves in the first person ('I') by using the name of the ancestor of whom they are the embodiment.

Metamorphosis is key to understanding the permeability and consubstantiality of forms, or the passage from one state of being to another. The entire landscape came into being through the initial metamorphosis of ancestral actions, body parts, and objects. Humans in turn come into being following the metamorphosis of the spirit-child from *Tjukurrpa*. Like the wind, at once physical and spiritual, that is transformed into breath upon penetrating the human body (Peile 1985),[12] the spirit-child is transformed upon entering the mother's body. At death, one's spirit (*kurrunpa*) is reunited with the ancestral realm, merging and being identified with the ancestral essence of the place of conception. In the process of conception, as in death, the dream acts as mediator between the ancestral and the human realms (see chapter 4). Owing to the principle of consubstantiality involving ancestral, human, and non-human agencies and dimensions, and that of the permeability of forms, such metamorphosis conveys its own cultural objectivity.

Kuruwarri, as an ancestral power and a generative force, also refers to sacred designs painted on bodies and objects, usually in ritual contexts.[13] *Kuruwarri* designs can also be drawn on the sand. They are an essential part of the Law of a country. Whatever the medium used, some of these designs may be concealed from younger, uninitiated, or unauthorized people. More than a mere objectification of the ancestor and the country thus represented, these designs are a manifestation of the ancestors' power, which is in turn communicated to humans when they come in contact with these designs. For example, after a ritual performance, women sometimes delay washing the designs on their breasts in order to let the *kuruwarri* forces penetrate their whole being, thus making them (and their spirit) stronger (*marrka*). This practice testifies to the permeability of the bodily-self. Even if they seem more noticeable in ritual contexts, *kuruwarri* signs are present throughout the landscape, unnoticed until the moment is ripe for their revelation. For instance, the 'natural' designs found on some rocks may be identified as *kuruwarri* from the moment an interpretation is made of the messages bequeathed by some *Tjukurrpa* beings, or as an index (in Peirce's sense) of their passage at that very place.

Named places embody the spirits of the deceased and of the ancestors. As one's country, they are not only a template (or a culturalized, political space) patterning the workings of kinship and ritual networks, they are themselves a fundamental constituent of these networks. The Kukatja refer to the named places with which they are affiliated as *walytja*, 'kin.' While the whole landscape is sentient, some places are considered a 'person' in a literal rather than metaphorical sense; such places are endowed with consciousness and intentionality. The identity and the becoming of the place-person and the human-person are closely intertwined. Accordingly, the Kukatja experience their relationship to their country in a way that is intimate, reciprocal, and communicative. For example, the spirit of the deceased father of a Walmatjari/Wangkatjunga rainmaker now lives in Kutal, one of the many abodes and expressions of *Warnayarra*, the Rainbow Snake. The deceased father and the Snake are both referred to either as Kutal or as the 'old man.' Through the merging of identities, Kutal is at the same time the site, the ancestor, and the deceased relative.

Like their human kin, named places have feelings. Their shared identity is also a shared sensibility. The emotions existing between human kin, such as compassion, anger, shame, or longing, that Myers has so vividly portrayed as the Pintupi's expressions of shared identity with others (Myers 1979, 1986a, 1988b) also apply to some sites, especially the dwelling places of deceased relatives and ancestors. These sites feel a longing for the human persons with whom they are affiliated. In turn, the Aborigines 'feel sorry' for their country (*ngurra*), often saying pityingly, '*yawi*' ('poor fellow' or 'poor bugger'). The spirit(s) of the place-person may send messages to their human kin, most often through dreams, if the affiliated human-persons are far away or have failed to look after the place properly. When Aborigines long for a place that they are unable to visit or when they feel that a site feels lonely because it has not been visited for a long time, they will address the place in song. The song is sung to soothe their pain, communicate feelings to the place, and express contrition for having been negligent and absent.

Places have simultaneously a political, aesthetic, emotive, and mnemonic value. Whenever my Aboriginal friends travelled through a country, by walking or driving, or whenever they engaged in foraging or hunting activities, it was not unusual for them to sing the country, either addressing the ancestor dwelling in the place or singing some verses related to the plants gathered or the animal hunted.

Mythical Itineraries as Spatial Stories

'What the map cuts up, the story cuts across.'

(de Certeau 1984: 129)

It is important at this point to introduce some of the major ancestral tracks of the Wirrimanu area and of the regions to the south, to provide background to some segments of the complex networks that compose the *Tjukurrpa* stories in the Kukatja, Ngarti, and Walmatjari countries. At the same time, we present some of the mythic characters and actions that are part of local reality and understanding of the world. These spatial stories are at the core of local relationships and experiences with the landscape, and of local imagination and improvisation. My main purpose here is to give a general idea of the extent, richness, and multiplicity (and to some extent, multivocality) of these ancestral travels.[14] I have limited myself here to the public versions of such stories, concealing some of their sacred-secret dimensions and putting particular emphasis on the four major tracks in the area that are said to be 'strong Laws.' Since any one mythical track can include a hundred or more named places, the *Tjukurrpa* stories presented are only summarized here. They nevertheless illustrate what Myers suggests when he describes the territory as 'a continuous entity' (1986a: 60).

Very seldom can someone narrate the whole of an ancestral itinerary because of the various criteria limiting access to knowledge (for example, age, gender, or territorial affiliations). Similarly, neither is one person ever entitled to reveal all the different versions of the story in relation to a site or to a series of sites. For the ethnographer, this information is accumulated very gradually and by a variety of means. The best ways to learn are by travelling extensively through the country itself with some of its custodians, by participating in rituals, and by listening to the elders in the camps. The recording of songs (*turlku*) is also a valuable asset and is another way in which men and women may choose to transmit their knowledge of their country. My own partial understanding of such rich, multivocal, and spatially complex stories comes mostly from my close friendship with some middle-aged and elderly couples in Wirrimanu, Yagga Yagga, and Mulan. Had I travelled over the countryside only with men or only with women, or sought information from only one of these groups, my understanding of some stories would have been different. Some sites, often the most prominent ones, have specific female and male versions attached to them, related to a women's Law and a men's Law. These different versions enhance the multivocal and multilocal quality of the stories and the places, and can become the grounds for negotiation or create tensions between either gender or local groups. The elders – both men and women – play upon this ambiguity when communicating the stories to uninitiated youths or ethnographers. This ambiguity confirms what I said earlier about *Tjukurrpa* as an open system, as a body of knowledge and stories open to interpretation, whose meaning is not fixed once and for all but might change with events or as one acquires knowledge.

Wati Kutjarra

The *Wati Kutjarra*, the Two Initiated Men, is one of the region's most important *Tjukurrpa*. The couple theme is quite frequent in the desert regions' structure of myths and other types of narratives (Myers 1986a; Róheim 1945). In the Wirrimanu area, the Two Initiated Men were perceived as unmarried young men endowed with magical powers, and some people presented them as *maparn* (medicine men). They were at times referred to as the Two *Yalpuru* (initiation mates). They belong to the tjapaltjarri subsection (see chapter 3). The *Wati Kutjarra* itinerary, or at least the segment presented here, passes through the territories of the Warlpiri, the Ngarti, the Kukatja, and the Walmatjari, and even beyond. This mythical duo is indeed ubiquitous across the whole Western Desert area, where they travelled widely, and the stories and songs recounting their epics are innumerable.[15] The people in the Wirrimanu area, with a close affinity to the Pintupi or the Mandiltjarra from the southern parts of the Gibson Desert, presented the *Wati Kutjarra* as Two Goanna Men, one black and the other white. However, for the Kukatja, the Ngarti, the Walmatjari, and the Wangkatjunga, the Two Men were often likened to the wind whose form they took when endangered. An elderly woman even called them the Two *Warlpang* (Wind Men). For the groups in the Wirrimanu area, a corpus of songs, designs (*kuruwarri*), and ritual sequences relating to the *Wati Kutjarra* are presented as men's Law, while other examples are under the custody of the women (see chapter 6).

The track of the *Wati Kutjarra* follows an east-west axis. The two heroes arrived from the east, from Warlpiri country, where they seem to have started their journey (Meggitt 1966a: 141). The narrative then recounts their passage through the Mungkayi region (Stansmore Range), which is in Kukatja country. Farther to the north, at Parlku Parlku and Yirli Yirli, on Ngarti land, they each killed and cooked a kangaroo. At Yagga Yagga, they hunted a snake that they had been chasing for a while. Yagga Yagga means 'silence-silence,' or 'quiet-quiet,' which is why the Two Men were whispering to each other so as not to scare their prey away. Near the Yagga Yagga community, a rocky hillock bearing many holes testifies to their unsuccessful digging in search of the snake. At Kunakurlu, a billabong, they killed a kangaroo. At Kungkala, a small rock hole nearby, the *Wati Kutjarra* lit a fire, and it is the friction of their firesticks in the rock that made the rock hole (Watson 1996: 121).

The *Wati Kutjarra* then moved on to a place named Ngantalarra, twenty kilometres to the east of Yagga Yagga. In Ngantalarra, they performed for the first time one of the initiation rituals important to the groups of that region.[16] Nearby, two small, circular billabongs, Ngali Kutjarra, indicate where they set up their *ngurra*, their respective camps. A men's Law and a women's Law are associated with the site of Ngantalarra. They represent each group's shared responsibility in the making of young boys into men (*wati*). South of Ngantalarra, the site of Nakarra Nakarra is also important.[17] There are eight hills at Nakarra Nakarra, said to be the metamorphosed bodies of a group of young ancestral women lying down with their breasts upright. The *Wati Kutjarra* came close to the group and tried to seduce the women but failed; the women fled to the west.

One night at Nampurrungu, near Ngantalarra and Ngali Kutjarra, being threatened by a group of *wanya* (evil spirits, sorcerers, or strangers with harmful intentions), the Two Men were awakened by the nighthawk (*kurnkuta-kuta*), who ordered them to follow him. He told them to place embers in their spear-throwers to serve as torches. He guided them and steered them away from danger. During their journey, they shaped a river bed, dry for most of the year, that runs by Yagga Yagga. That same night, they rested at Tjirrtjiwarri. In the morning, they created wind (or, in some versions, became a small tornado, a willy-willy) along the way to erase their tracks and keep the *wanya* from following them. The following night, they slept in a cave at Walawarra. That night, *Marlu*, Kangaroo Man, passed close by but did not notice that the *Wati Kutjarra* were sleeping inside the cave. In the morning, the Two Men recognized his tracks but decided to go on and ignored the other traveller. This non-meeting of the *Wati Kutjarra* and *Marlu* means that, for the moment at least, there is no junction between the two itineraries. However, such a place conceals an undeniable potential for 'openness' (see below).

The women's songs refer to a number of places where the *Wati Kut-*

jarra performed specific actions. At Wangkatji, they took the guts out of a goanna they had just killed; at Karntawarra, they painted themselves with yellow ochre (*karntawarra*) and white kaolin (*nguntju nguntju*); at Parla Parla, they found and ate some wild figs (*witjirrki*); at Marrapinti, another initiation place, they wore the ceremonial headband made of spun hair and pierced their nasal septum to insert a nose-peg (*marrapinti*); at Pirriwa, they ate bush honey; at Mungkyarra, they undid their hair-bun (*pukurti*).

Continuing their travels to the south-east in Kukatja/Wangkatjunga country, they reached a place called Yunpu, the country of cannibals (*yunpu* or *kunatarkaratja*). Noticing human bones scattered over the territory (seen as rocks today), the *Wati Kutjarra* resolved to brave the cannibals of that region. The two men transformed themselves into a tornado (*ngumi-ngumi*) in order to deceive the cannibals and fight them better. Outsmarted, the cannibals went underground and surfaced farther to the west, in the region stretching between Jigalong and Port Hedland. But that is along another itinerary, and thus is another story.

On the site of and around the old Balgo mission, the *Wati Kutjarra* hunted various animals. A small rock hole in the area formed where they urinated. The landscape in Walmatjari country presents several characteristics attributed to their passage and to their different *ngurra*. In Ngarili, close to Wirrimanu, their journey is marked by two small rocks overlooking a cliff. Nearby, another rock is their mother. In Ngarili, the Two Men once again transformed themselves into wind. They then travelled to Mulan, where two identical hills attest their passage. The story then chronicles their actions farther north, in the Christmas Creek region. Returning south, worn out by their travels, the Two Men decided to end their journey and go underground, at a place named Mulawakal, near the Canning Stock Route. For the majority of the Kukatja, Ngarti, and Walmatjari, the *Wati Kutjarra*'s *Tjukurrpa* ends at Mulawakal. However, the narrators belonging to countries farther to the west continue that mythical itinerary up to the West Coast, where apparently the Two Men found mates. One elderly woman even went so far as to say that two rocks on the seashore, in the vicinity of Lagrange, were left there by the *Wati Kutjarra* when they set out on a journey to the Indian subcontinent.

Marlu

As important and wide-ranging as the mythical track of the *Wati Kutjarra* is that of *Marlu*, the tjapanangka subsection's Kangaroo Man.

Whereas the *Wati Kutjarra* crossed the Western Desert from east to west, *Marlu* crossed it from north to south. According to the versions heard in Wirrimanu, *Marlu*'s travels started far to the north, in Tjaru country. In the region of Halls Creek, *Marlu* was chased by a group of hunters led by a man named *Murtikarlka*, of the tjapangarti subsection.[18] The hunters succeeded in coming close enough to hit *Marlu* with boomerangs. Their attempts to hold him by the tail were unsuccessful because their hands kept slipping. About thirty kilometres south of Halls Creek, a hill embodies him resting. The hunters continued to chase him, but *Marlu* always escaped. Near Rubby Plains, a hundred kilometres south of Halls Creek, *Marlu* set up his *ngurra* close to a rock hole and fell asleep. The hunters caught up with him and tried again to seize him, but *Marlu*'s body was too slippery. The hunt went on for a long time, but *Marlu* kept escaping his adversaries.

He turned back towards Halls Creek, and the men chasing him continued to throw boomerangs at him, but all missed. At Mungkurr, to the east of Halls Creek, a series of termite mounds are the metamorphosed bodies of some of the hunters who fell asleep there. He continued north until he arrived in Kuruntji country, around Wyndham and Turkey Creek. In that region, various landscape forms testify to his passage. Close to Wyndham, a hill represents *Marlu* sleeping. *Murtikarlka*'s band of hunters were still chasing him through that region when they met another group who were also hunting *Marlu*. That group was headed by *Marrakurru*, of the tjangala subsection.[19] *Murtikarlka* told *Marrakurru*'s group that he intended to chase *Marlu* right to the end. And he did, all the way south to Pintupi country, but never succeeded in catching him. His name, *Murtikarlka*, refers to someone who is, as one woman put it, 'run down to the knees (*murti*),' whose lower legs have been worn down from running. As for *Marrakurru* and his companions, the *Marwuntu*, they hunted *Marlu* for a while and then decided to join *Luurn*, the Kingfisher Man, another ancestral traveller (see below).

Murtikarlka chased *Marlu* to the north, maybe even up into the coastal regions, since one man's narrative tells of a large stretch of salty water. Then followed the long trip to the south, through the expanse of the Gibson Desert. The story lists a succession of sites shaped and named by *Marlu*, through Walmatjari, Ngarti, and Kukatja country: where he slept, where he hunted, where he urinated, or where he met with *Kaarnka*, the Crow Woman. At Tjalyirr, in the vicinity of Paruku (Lake Gregory), in Walmatjari country, *Marlu*, in need of a rest, made himself a bough shed out of leaves (*tjalyirr*). At Karntawarra, located in the Stansmore Range, in Kukatja country, *Marlu* met a group of blind people. Not only did the mythical hero cure them of their blindness, he also taught them how to cut trees to make boomerangs, spear-throwers, shields, and digging sticks. The Law with which he entrusted the people then is still performed today by the custodians of the area. *Marlu* continued his journey to the south, towards the country of the Pintupi, and there he instructed them with a Law that is considered, as one man put it, 'the same but different.' Still chasing him, *Murtikarlka* was having his own adventures. In the vicinity of Kiwirrkura, a hill named Walawala testifies to *Marlu*'s passage. According to some Pintupi men living in Wirrimanu, *Marlu* continued his journey into Pitjantjatjarra country. The itinerary is thus spread out over a large expanse. Like the *Wati Kutjarra*'s itinerary, *Marlu*'s journey has imprinted the territories of several Western Desert groups and beyond: the Tjaru and the Kuruntji (as well as other groups of the East Kimberley), the Walmatjari, the Ngarti, the Kukatja, the Pintupi, and finally the Pitjantjatjarra.

Luurn

Another *Tjukurrpa* that has left its imprints and ancestral power in the vicinity of Wirrimanu and also covers a considerable geographical distance is *Luurn*, the Kingfisher, and the novices who accompany him, the *Marwuntu* of the tjangala and tjampitjin subsections. That *Tjukurrpa* is of prime importance to the groups of the region, since it represents one expression of a major initiation cycle, *Tingarri*, a Law bequeathed to them by *Luurn* and other ancestral beings. In some ritual contexts, *Tingarri* becomes a synonym of *Tjukurrpa*. The *Tingarri* stories and itineraries recreate the travels of the initiated men as they accompany the young novices,[20] coordinate the initiation trials, and instruct them in the secrets of the Law. The stories tell also of their often tumultuous encounters with other *Tingarri* groups or with strangers seeking to steal their sacred objects (*tarruku*).[21]

Luurn guided the *Marwuntu* in their initiatory travel to the southeast, towards the Lake Mackay area. From the accounts heard in Wirrimanu, they left from the East Kimberley[22] and journeyed south, leaving many traces of their passage along their way. A few kilometres west of Ringer Soak, at a place called Ngurruring, the *Marwuntu* painted themselves with red ochre and left some behind; the place is to this day an important deposit of red ochre. They passed near Wirrimanu. Wirrimanu means 'the passage newly shaped by *Luurn* to guide the *Marwuntu*.'[23] A large cliff is the windbreak they made for the night.

Nearby, a subtle hollow in the ground is *Luurn*'s footprint, clearly directed towards the south-east. In the middle of the hollow, a series of black, round pebbles were left there by *Luurn*. According to one woman, these are *Luurn*'s eggs. While this observation suggests a certain ambiguity as to *Luurn*'s sexual identity, it could also simply be this woman's way of interpreting and expressing how *Luurn* left the reproductive forces and essences (*kuruwarri*) in the area. At Namalu, a rock hole in the vicinity of Wirrimanu, *Luurn* yelled to the *Marwuntu*, prompting them to take their spears and to follow him to the south-east. One can see today two groups of trees, *kilykilypa* (rough-leafed bloodwood, which has knots that are identified with the female breast) and *mangkapuru* (snappy-gum), which are the metamorphosed bodies of the *Marwuntu* as they were getting ready to follow *Luurn*. To the east, two hills that can be seen from Wirrimanu are again the metamorphosed bodies of two groups of *Marwuntu*, the tjangala/tjampitjin and the tjapangarti/tjapanangka.

At Lintapurru, in the Mungkayi area, in Kukatja country, the *Marwuntu* met another *Tingarri* man, *Tjilkamarta* (Echidna), who was coming from the west. After nightfall, *Tjilkamarta* stole the *Marwuntu*'s sacred objects (*tarruku*) and even went so far as to tease the *Marwuntu* by slapping them on the shoulders as they were sleeping. Awakened, they asked themselves, 'Who is hitting us?,' until they saw him. Annoyed, some *Marwuntu* decided to chase *Tjilkamarta* to the north, while the others stayed behind awaiting their return. The story goes on to mention the various places visited by *Tjilkamarta* and his pursuers. For a long time, he successfully outsmarted his adversaries, lighting fires along the way to keep them at a distance. But finally, the *Marwuntu* overtook him, riddled him with spears, and recovered their *tarruku*. This event occurred at Munturn, a rock hole. While they were wondering what to do with their wounded adversary, Echidna diverted their attention by showing them smoke in the distance, the sign of another *Tingarri* group. *Tjilkamarta* chose that moment to go inside the rock hole and disappear underground.

South of Mungkayi, still in Kukatja country, the *Marwuntu* cut across the *Kanaputa*'s (Digging Sticks Women) road. Still guided by *Luurn*, they reached Tjikarri, in the Lake Mackay area, a very important ritual site. Tjikarri is an underground spring in the rocks that can only be reached through a very narrow aperture; whoever went there needed to be skinny. The place is forbidden to women. To fetch water, the men used to bring with them a *luwantja* (wooden dish). Old man *Luurn* – in the narrative, his name becomes *Warlayirti* – lived in Tjikarri with his dog, *Maturrpilangu*. The dog hunted kangaroo and other game but never shared his kill with his master. Outraged by his conduct, the *Marwuntu* chased *Maturrpilangu* with the intention of killing him. They travelled through the air mounted on their long spears (*kurlarta*). To evade them, the dog managed to slip into the small rock aperture, but the *Marwuntu* captured him nevertheless and killed him by blows to the nape of the neck. According to some informants, *Luurn's Tjukurrpa* continues beyond Tjikarri towards Ayers Rock, where his travels ended. In the vicinity of Tjikarri, at Murungpa, the story tells of a young novice who was going through the last phases of his initiation. One night, he was sleeping by himself near the men's camp. A lone traveller, *Marrakurru* of the tjangala subsection and the leader of the *Marwuntu*, was coming from the east, exhausted from much travelling and hunting. He decided to establish his camp for the night at Murungpa. It was dark and *Marrakurru* did not see the young boy lying down. Inadvertently, he stepped on his abdomen, and the young boy's intestines came out.

Kanaputa

The *Kanaputa* are known as Women of high degree (in reference to Elkin's expression, 1977), filled with magical powers, who refuse men's advances. They do not hesitate to kill those who do not follow the Law and to maim the penises of those who show too much arrogance. Starting in the Lake Mackay region, the *Kanaputa* itinerary is a major *Tingarri* cycle for most of the groups living today in Wirrimanu. It recalls the travels of the Digging Sticks (*kana*) Women, who were then keepers of the sacred objects (*tarruku*) that men have since stolen from them. It is said that these ancestral women began their journey at Wilkin (or Wilkinkarra), one of the many names for Lake Mackay, also known as Maruwa. Lake Mackay and the surrounding countryside are loaded with meaning from *Tjukurrpa*. Many stories, and thus many Laws, seem to converge there, or are said to have started there. Events that occurred at Lake Mackay in the *Tjukurrpa* are highly relevant for many groups, including the Kukatja, Ngarti, Warlpiri, and Pintupi. It is a place of shared identity and shared responsibility.

In the Lake Mackay area, the *Tingarri* men and the novices had established their *ngurra* on the top of a hill, out of sight, in preparation for initiation ceremonies. The *Kanaputa*, at the time young, nubile women, had their camp nearby. They were under the supervision of a few elderly men who kept them in ignorance of the novices' presence. One day, one of the old men brought them a kangaroo killed by one of the novices. As they were eating, the *Kanaputa* found in the meat a small piece of *kularta* (spear) and realized then that they had been deceived about the novices. They decided to make their presence known to the novices by preparing some bread from a variety of local seeds (*lukurarra, mugnilpa*, etc.), which they then sent to the novices. The novices came down the hill to have sexual intercourse with the *Kanaputa*, their promised wives. Outraged by their behaviour, the *Tingarri* men, in their anger, lit a huge bush fire that killed all the novices. The *Kanaputa* were also targeted but managed to escape the fire by diving into a nearby lake and then travelling underground, fleeing from the elders. They felt both sorrow for having lost their (future) husbands and rancour against the elders. Before escaping, however, they stole the magical objects (*tarruku*) and thus the power of the *Tingarri* men. From there, as the story goes, the *Kanaputa* kept on travelling, singing and dancing along the way, while a few elders pursued them, trying either to recover the *tarruku* or to seduce them. Most were killed by the *Kanaputa*. From the Lake Mackay area, the *Kanaputa* separated into two groups.

The first group headed towards Lappi Lappi and Mirmindilli, to the north-east. In today's context, this group and their actions over the land are mainly associated with the Warlpiri. I present here only some segments of a complex and dense story (and Law).

At Kunaputa, the *Kanaputa* came across a man of the tjangala subsection, a *Tjunta* (Bush Onion) Man. When the *Kanaputa* came along, he was spinning hair (threads of spun hair are important ceremonial objects). Out of jealousy, the women started to annoy him by throwing his wool everywhere. He swore at them angrily. The women chased him and killed him with their sticks. A black stone is now his metamorphosed body. Then they went to Kulurr, where an old man of the tjakamarra subsection lived. That old man would hunt and keep all the meat for himself. Today, his meat can still be seen, metamorphosed into stones. Not far away, a woman had just given birth to a girl. The old man wanted to have sexual intercourse with the mother. But she was of the nangala subsection, thus in a mother-in-law (*yumari*) relation to the man (by far the most forbidden relation in Aboriginal Australia). The mother threw her baby into the air. The *Kanaputa* caught her and threw her up again. When she came down again, she had breasts and had grown into a woman.[24] The mother and the *Kanaputa* decided to kill the old man. After injuring him with their *kana*, they dragged him into a cave, where he died. Later on, they came across the Crow (*Kaarnka*) Man, of the tjapanangka subsection. He engaged in lovemaking with two *Kanaputa* of the napaltjarri subsection, his potential 'mothers-in-law' (*yumari*) and therefore forbidden. The *Kanaputa* killed Crow Man. However, the two women had bled to death after the man had penetrated them with his overlong penis. Two hills are the metamorphosed bodies of these two napaltjarri. The *Kanaputa* mourned them for a long time. Then, at Yirrillmanu, they went underground.

The second *Kanaputa* group also left from Wilkin (Lake Mackay) but sang and danced their way towards the north-west, into the Mungkayi area and beyond, in Kukatja, Ngarti, and Wangkatjunga countries. As they walked, they poked the ground with their *kana*, infusing it with their ancestral power. At different places, they also met with men who tried to seduce or deceive them, but the *Kanaputa* managed to kill them or to flee by going underground. Tjawa Tjawa (Point Moody) and Walkarli (White Hills) are two important sites in this *Kanaputa* story. Here are some of the events that occurred in the area. At one site, they dug for *tjalapa* (great desert skink), and where they dug there is water now. A small rock hole was created as they urinated. Somewhere else, they gathered *warturnuma* (the flying form of white ants) and danced as they cleaned them in their wooden dish. Near Tjawa Tjawa, the *Kanaputa* were chased by the Lizard Man, whose sexual overtures they refused. Lizard Man slithered underground and tried to penetrate some of them, but the *Kanaputa* mutilated his emerging penis with their *kana*. His penis is still there today in the form of a stone. At Walkarli (White Hills), they sang and danced. They finally were deceived by a man who stole the *tarruku* from them. They went underground at Tjawa Tjawa (Point Moody) and travelled back to Lake Mackay whence they first came and where they continue to live to this day. According to other versions, the *Kanaputa* changed into a Rainbow Snake. As *Tingarri*, the *Kanaputa* songs (in their secret forms) and rituals are today solely under men's custody.

For the various groups now living in Wirrimanu, Yagga Yagga, and Mulan, the *Wati Kutjarra*, *Marlu*, *Luurn*, and *Kanaputa Tjukurrpa*, as foundations of impressive mythic and ritual corpuses or expressions of the *Tingarri* (as initiation ceremonies), represent major Laws. Though different segments among them come under the guardianship of different local groups, taken as a whole they nevertheless represent a 'shared responsibility.' As regards social and ritual relationships and partnerships, they offer the basis of a shared identity (Myers 1986a) to the extent that every person is able to claim an affiliation to one or more of these *Tjukurrpa*. This shared identity represents an important sociological fact, since it facilitates the cohabitation and ritual cooperation of several families and groups whose territorial claims and ancestral connections are otherwise located outside the immediate Wirrimanu region. While reducing but not eliminating the tensions that could arise, this shared identity enables the ritual participation of everyone and assures everyone an identity that links them to Wirrimanu, even if their ancestral essence stems from another *ngurra*.

However, the region's networks of *Tjukurrpa* stories and ancestral travels and performances are not limited to these four major tracks. The wealth, complexity, and multivocality of such networks testify to the almost inexhaustible character of *Tjukurrpa* stories, as they infuse places with meanings and link one country to the other. Below are a few additional examples.

Kutal (Helena Springs) refers to a place, to an expression of the Rainbow Snake, and to the dwelling place of the present-day rainmaker's ancestors. It is at the site of Kutal that the ancestors of the same man performed the first rainmaking ritual for the groups of the area. Located about 140 kilometres south-west of Yagga Yagga, it comes under the guardianship of people who define themselves primarily as Walmatjari. Kutal consists of a spring and associated outcrops with a claypan. The main rock formation is the metamorphosed body of Kutal, lying down, his head pointing to the west, while other rocks in the vicinity are some of his ceremonial regalia. The waterhole is his navel. Some cavities in one of the rocks are his ears, with which he can hear people coming. Kutal, the mythical hero, travelled from there through the Christmas Creek region and to the West Coast, where he met other rainmakers before returning home. Here again, the story comprises a myriad of named places visited by Kutal. During the 1980s, the rainmaker and some of his relatives made a few visits to Kutal to perform the rainmaking ritual.

Another *Tjukurrpa* is *Warnayarra*, the Rainbow Snake. *Warnayarra* was resting in the Mungkayi region when he heard the sound of a group of people coming from the east, singing and dancing. Intrigued, he travelled underground and emerged at Yunpurtu (site of an underground spring). Listening again, he located the sounds and continued his journey, all the while creating a riverbed. He arrived at Lappi Lappi, a permanent rock hole, where the people were assembled for initiation ceremonies. At the sight of the snake, a young man tried to frighten him by swirling his hair belt and using his shield (*kurtitji*) to protect himself. Two rock formations nearby are the metamorphosed young man and his shield. After spraying all the people with his saliva (or morning dew, according to other versions), *Warnayarra* surrounded the men, women, and children and swallowed them.[25] Nearby, at Tjangkangka, feeling nauseated and dry, he tried to vomit, but at first could only disgorge facial and body hair; he succeeded in regurgitating only some of the people. At Tirlti, as he continued slithering, white pebbles split his belly and he lost his fat, which was transformed into stones. There, he finally vomited the rest of the people he had swallowed. Travelling on with difficulty, he reached Rapi (Lake White), where he went underground and still lives to this day.

Among *Tjukurrpa* itineraries that are the basis of the ancestral connections for a number of people now living in the Wirrimanu area are the stories of *Tjilkamarta* (Echidna), previously mentioned and part of the *Tingarri*, and *Karnti* (the Yam Man). He came from Warlpiri country and, in the vicinity of Mungkayi, was entangled in vines, which made him fall to the ground. As he fell, he dropped all the *karnti* that he was carrying on his head, leaving the region rich in yams. There is also *Karlaya* (Emu), who was chased by the Two Dingos. That itinerary extends over a particularly long distance. Starting their chase south of Mungkayi, the Two Dingos pursued Emu across the Tanami and some Warlpiri country, all the way north to Katherine. Doubling back, Emu travelled down along Sturt Creek, still hunted by his pursuers, until they finally ended their journey at Lake Gregory (Paruku). Finally, the itinerary of the ancestral women *Nangala Kutjarra* (Two Nangalas) and their associated ritual, *Tjipari*, will be dealt with in the last chapter.

Throughout these narratives, the itineraries cross and intertwine; some are narratively, socially, and ritually linked to a given area before they separate again. This brief sketch of much more complex and detailed stories was principally intended to illustrate how the landscape expresses ancestral performances and events and how contemporary Aborigines are sensitive to that reality when they move through the land. The itineraries constitute a basis for experiencing and knowing the land, provide explanations and interpretations for its forms and moods, and represent a source of imagination and improvisation (with regard, for example, to unusual events). From childhood, most people become familiar with these mythic characters and all their different expressions, although each individual develops an affinity to only a few. More extensive knowledge of these ancestral characters and events is acquired gradually, according to one's own ancestral connections and interest in ritual matters. For the Aborigines, the *Tjukurrpa* and all the stories that emanate from the land are 'true' (*mularrpa*). Whenever a narrator, male or female, ended an episode of a story that related to his or her own country, the narrator invariably stated 'This one true story.' This statement not only confirmed the truth-value of the events from *Tjukurrpa*, but also reasserted the narrator's own connection to the site(s) narrated or sung.

Considering the low population density of the Western Desert during the time of traditional nomadism, the wealth and depth of mythical narratives and events reveal the scope of the Aborigines' first-hand knowledge of the territory and show the importance of the links that unite humans, places, and ancestors.

Grounds for Transformation and Negotiation

The distinction that M. de Certeau establishes between the map and the itinerary, as two poles of experience, is most relevant here for introducing an intrinsic quality of these itineraries: that is, their 'openness' and potential for transformation. According to de Certeau (1984: 119), the main ontological difference between the map and the itinerary is that the former is descriptive, 'a plane projection totalizing observations,' whereas the latter is performative, 'a discursive series of operations.' The map describes a space; the itinerary narrates movements in space. Maps present a fixed character, whereas itineraries are open-ended, forever unfolding. This difference could be another way of expressing what the Aborigines call the two Laws, the *Kartiya* and their own. *Tjukurrpa* stories are not only multivocal, that is comprising different versions and levels of interpretation and symbolic (and metaphoric) subtlety, but their manifestations upon the landscape are also open to reinterpretation and negotiation and to further revelation from the ancestors. This process of reinterpretation is actuated, however, only when social, political, or historic imperatives require it, and it is always a very serious 'business.'

The mythical tracks, inasmuch as they delineate networks of territorial and ritual responsibilities, represent the ideological structures of permanence. In the Western Desert, more so than in better-watered areas, there is an intrinsic structural quality to these itineraries, their 'openness,' the possibility that new meanings or new segments relating to ancestral journeys might be revealed. An itinerary with its various segments is never 'set,' neither at its end points nor at any of its named sites. According to circumstances, events, contingencies, or revelation from the ancestors (or deceased relatives), it is possible to transform or reinterpret the course of an itinerary or some of its segments. There is a tension and a dialectic between these ideological structures of permanence and their potential for transformation. Humans are not mere spectators who roam over the countryside, narrating and singing the great deeds of ancestral heroes; nor are they 'confronted with a *fait accompli*, a fixed topographical structure, within which [they] must operate' (Munn 1970: 147). These ancestral journeys and the political and ritual networks they delineate are partly the expressions of a local historicity and consciousness that have been inscribed in named places. In other words, the Aborigines are active agents in the construction, reproduction, and reinterpretation of these mythical tracks. It is at this level that individual and collective knowledge and achievement and active and perceptual engagement come into play with constituents of the mythical landscape. Considering, on the one hand, the political and ritual dimensions of these ancestral tracks and, on the other hand, the intransigence of the Law as regards secret ritual matters, it goes without saying that such transformations or rereadings of the inscription and significance of the mythical tracks cannot be effected without careful thought. None the less, each case of such a transformation or reinterpretation must be consistent with and respect the structural, social, and semantic logic of the existing forms.

This 'openness' and potential for transformation is present not only in the way *Tjukurrpa* stories are inscribed within the land but also in the narrative forms themselves. I will introduce here what I call the metaphors of 'openness,' or grounds for transformation. Let us consider, as a first example, the ability of *Tjukurrpa* ancestors to travel not only across the surface of the land but also underground or even through the air. Consequently, all the segments of a given itinerary are not necessarily recorded on the land, since the ancestral travellers may have left the earth's surface to continue their journeys through the air or under the ground. A typical story tells how the ancestral beings either landed on or (re)emerged from another place. Thus, the segment that has not left visual traces on the land represents a potential area where it will be possible, eventually and if necessary, to (re)discover the presence and the imprints of the ancestor in question.

The story and the complete itinerary cycle would seem, however, to come to an end when it is said that in a given site the ancestors have entered the underworld 'forever.' This is particularly apparent in rhetorical forms such as 'From there, they've disappeared now,' or, 'Finish now, they've gone inside.' Such representations are 'true' (*mularrpa*), inasmuch as the storytellers limit themselves to narrating the segments of the itinerary encompassed by their country or area of responsibility. When their story comes to a close in that locality, nothing proves that the ancestor's journey has indeed ended there, for in other versions of the same itinerary, the ancestor emerges (or lands) in another site located in a neighbouring country that falls under another group's jurisdiction. There, the ancestral being might be known under a different name, like *Luurn*, for example, who becomes known farther south as *Warlayirti*.

Whether or not they evoke closure depends on the narrator's area of responsibility. Such episodes where the ancestral beings have gone underground or flown away always offer a greater potential of openness and grounds for reinterpretation. Should the need arise, it then becomes possible to lengthen the itinerary or to change its course by adding new segments, by having the hero reappear or land in another site, in another country. As reported to Myers by the Pintupi, the following example illustrates this potential for transformation and the possibility for the ancestors to continue their journey beyond familiar territories, unknown to the people until it is revealed to them. It also demonstrates how the places where the ancestral beings are said to have gone 'under the ground' contain a greater potential of openness:

> Until 1975 I had been told that one of the main Pintupi Dreaming tracks ended at a place called Pinari near Lake Mackay. However, after Pintupi from my community visited their long-separated relatives at Balgo, they returned to tell me that 'we thought that story ended, went into the ground at Pinari. But we found that it goes underground all the way to Balgo.' Apparently, this revelation was discovered in a vision by a man from Balgo. (Myers 1986a: 53)

Map 1
NORTH OF WESTERN AUSTRALIA

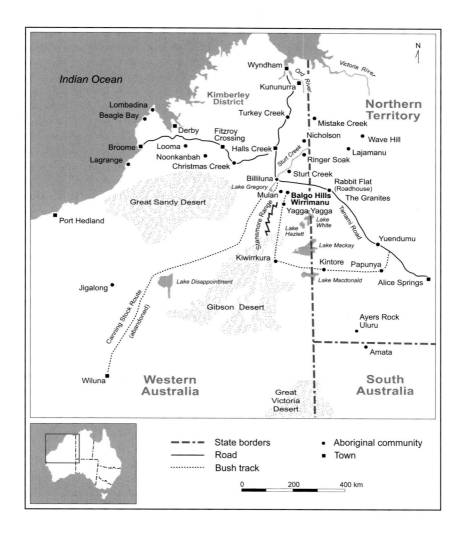

Indian Ocean

N

Wyndham

Victoria River

Ord River

Kununurra

Kimberley District

Northern Territory

Lombadina
Beagle Bay

Turkey Creek

Mistake Creek

Derby

Fitzroy Crossing

Nicholson

Wave Hill

Broome

Looma

Halls Creek

Sturt Creek

Lajamanu

Lagrange

Noonkanbah

Ringer Soak

Christmas Creek

Sturt Creek

Billiluna

Rabbit Flat
(Roadhouse)

Lake Gregory

The Granites

Mulan

Balgo Hills
Wirrimanu

Great Sandy Desert

Yagga Yagga

Port Hedland

Stansmore Range

Lake Hazlett

Lake White

Tanami Road

Lake Mackay

Yuendumu

Kiwirrkura

Kintore

Papunya

Jigalong

Lake Disappointment

Lake Macdonald

Alice Springs

Canning Stock Route
(abandoned)

Gibson Desert

Ayers Rock
Uluru

Amata

Wiluna

Western
Australia

Great
Victoria
Desert

South
Australia

- - - State borders
——— Road
········· Bush track

• Aboriginal community
■ Town

0   200   400 km

Map 2
LANGUAGE GROUPS

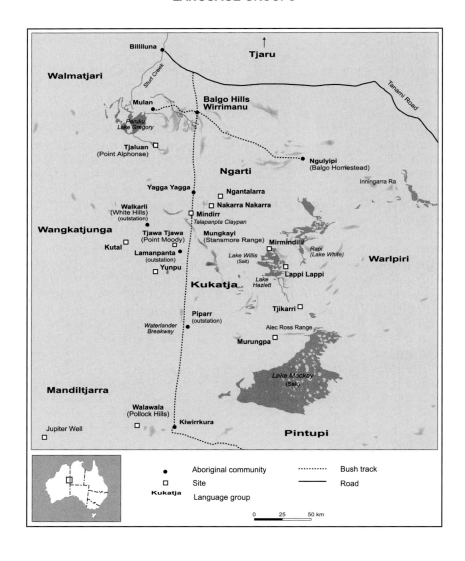

Billiluna

Tjaru

Walmatjari

Sturt Creek

Mulan

Balgo Hills
Wirrimanu

Paruku
Lake Gregory

Tanami Road

Tjaluan
(Point Alphonse)

Ngulyipi
(Balgo Homestead)

Ngarti

Inningarra Ra

Yagga Yagga

Ngantalarra

Nakarra Nakarra

Walkarli
(White Hills)
(outstation)

Mindirr

Talapanpta Claypan

Wangkatjunga

Tjawa Tjawa
(Point Moody)

Mungkayi
(Stansmore Range)

Mirmindilli

Rapi
(Lake White)

Kutal

Warlpiri

Lamanpanta
(outstation)

Lake Willis
(Salt)

Yunpu

Lappi Lappi

Kukatja

Lake
Hazlett

Piparr
(outstation)

Tjikarri

Waterlander
Breakway

Alec Ross Range

Murungpa

Lake Mackay
(Salt)

Mandiltjarra

Walawala
(Pollock Hills)

Jupiter Well

Kiwirrkura

Pintupi

• Aboriginal community

⬚ Site

Kukatja Language group

············ Bush track

——— Road

0   25   50 km

Ochre and charcoal on canvas by Arthur Tjapanangka, Balgo 1980. This painting was made just before the introduction of acrylic painting in the area.

In the vicinity of Balgo, Nungurrayi and Napurrula are grinding seeds. (Photo W. Nieass, 1981)

South of Balgo, Nungurrayi digs for wild yams (*karnti*). With the help of digging sticks, wooden dishes, or curved metal plates, women and men dig in the desert soil for plant foods or small game such as lizards and snakes. (Photo: W. Nieass, 1981)

At the women's ceremonial ground on the outskirts of Balgo, Napangarti is preparing for the *Walawalarra* ritual. She is untangling a thread of spun human hair. Next to her is a ceremonial pole and the stone used to grind the ochre for the body paintings. (Photo by the author, 1981)

At Yagga Yagga, the men have come back from a kangaroo hunt. The game is first cleaned and its hair burned on the flames. It will then be cooked in a hearth oven: a hole is dug next to the fire and lined with hot coals to receive the game, which is then covered with coals and hot sand. (Photo: C. Samson, 1987)

Acrylic painting on a wooden dish by Bye Bye Napangarti, 1987. It depicts an episode of the *Kanaputa* story when, between the sites of Walkarli and Tjawa Tjawa, they are pursued by the Lizard Man and strongly reject his sexual advances.

Families from Balgo en route to Christmas Creek to participate in an initiation ceremony. Motorized vehicles have become indispensable for the constant moving around for hunting and gathering activities, to participate in rituals and ceremonies in neighbouring communities, to visit relatives, or to travel to and fro between the outstations and the main community. (Photo by the author, 1987)

At Yagga Yagga, Tjapangarti is giving the final touch to a boomerang he has just made. (Photo by the author, 1994)

A small sample of a day's hunt. During the season, a party of four to five women can catch up to ten lizards of different kinds in a few hours. (Photo by the author, 1994)

At Yagga Yagga, Tjangala is making a boomerang while Tjupurrula drinks his tea. Boomerangs are no longer used for hunting; they are used during ceremonies to accompany the singing (by beating two boomerangs together) and for trade purposes. (Photo by the author, 1988)

Another ground for transformation stems from an expression often used by people when recounting *Tjukurrpa* itineraries. When relating the travels of the ancestral beings, they often penetrate the stories with the wordings *Wulu Yarra* or *Wulu Watjarninpa*, which mean 'all the way, keep going.' The storytellers here are referring to the continued travels of the nomadic ancestors, who go on tirelessly and relentlessly throughout the land. This is in seeming contradiction to narrators who offer finality: 'finish now that story,' 'they've gone now.' This narrative strategy discloses another facet of the same reality. Indeed, the *Tjukurrpa* beings long to continue their existence, and at times they make their presence known by revealing in dreams to men and women new episodes of their journeys. Once inserted into the mythical landscape network, following a process of collective negotiation and elaboration (see chapter 6), these new episodes transform nomadic spaces and the existing ritual corpus.

Such innovative and creative reinterpretations of the ancestral manifestations in the land are linked to a wide variety of historical circumstances and geopolitical necessities. The need for economic or ritual exchanges or new alliances between groups that may be geographically more or less distant may be a reason for such reinterpretations. In the context of traditional nomadism, these rereadings could stem from a move into other countries due to ecological pressures, such as a prolonged drought or a famine. Therefore, in order to strengthen a ritual or economic exchange or an alliance or to justify a right of residence, the groups concerned have to reinterpret the narrative framework and the mythical inscription of the land. In fact, this happened in some cases when Aborigines had to settle in the missions and communities peripheral to the desert, far from their ancestral territories. Their reinterpretations were legitimate since they were based on the existing *Tjukurrpa* forms and associated Laws.

During the time of traditional nomadism, and from a standpoint of a comprehensive strategy, such practices as changing the course of mythological itineraries, adding new segments, or having them reappear farther on, were not only possible but often proved necessary for the groups concerned. In the Wirrimanu area, adults and elders speak of their respective country as plentiful lands with abundant animals and edible plants, where the water never runs dry. Although quite positive, these perceptions and discourses nevertheless do not erase the well-known fact that the Western Desert is a rather harsh environment. Resources are not scant, but they are irregular (Cane 1984). In traditional times, water supply was one of the major problems, at least during the dry season that lasts usually from May to November. This explains why sites of great mythological significance are, more often than not, the water points.

In light of the irregular distribution of resources in time and space in the Western Desert, groups were occasionally forced to move beyond known territories towards more welcoming regions, sometimes for extended periods. Usually, most of these other regions were already claimed by other groups on the basis of their respective *Tjukurrpa*. The newcomers therefore had to justify their right of cohabitation. That right was often founded on pre-existing mythical forms and ancestral tracks shared by both groups. When such shared or neighbouring segments did not exist, the right of cohabitation and ritual cooperation had to be justified by other means. New segments and ritual sequences were then added, either by continuing an already-existing itinerary or by linking two stories that had been distinct until then. When previously abandoned countries were inhabited again, and when the knowledge relating to the region's *Tjukurrpa* had been lost or become obsolete, the people had to 'recreate' the mythological segment(s) in order to justify their (re)occupation of a country, not only to themselves but to other groups and to the ancestors. This is what R. Berndt meant when he wrote, 'there was considerable local descent group territorial fluctuation or, to put it another way, a tendency for mythic sites to remain "fallow" over a period of time, to be "taken up" and "used" only when specific claims were made' (1976: 142). These claims, he adds, rest on 'mythic resources' – that is, knowledge of local *Tjukurrpa* segments.

The openness of *Tjukurrpa* itineraries and networks allows for spatial and temporal transformations and reinterpretations. The creative and political processes underlying such transformations – in other words, the politics of ritual innovation and ancestral revelation – will be discussed in more detail in the last chapter. Grounds for creative innovation, *Tjukurrpa* stories and various segments are also grounds for discord and negotiation.

The Example of Yagga Yagga

During my second stay in the Wirrimanu area, in 1987–8, I witnessed the process of transformation of a *Tjukurrpa* segment. The new segment started to be 'revealed' in the mid-1980s, not long after the establishment of an outstation at Yagga Yagga (see chapter 1), which is a site on the *Wati Kutjarra* itinerary. The new segment was intended to validate, according to the principles of the Law, a right of residence for the few families who first went to live there. I present here some background information as well as the initial steps that gave rise to the process of innovation.

Initially, the few families concerned (predominantly Kukatja) wanted to establish an outstation closer to their country, which is situated in the Mungkayi area (Stansmore Range). Yagga Yagga was chosen as the site for the outstation because an oil company had installed a water bore there. This was sufficient to prompt the leader of the group, Tjapangarti, to apply to the federal government for funding for an outstation. Yagga Yagga was the first outstation to be established south of Wirrimanu, 100 kilometres away, and closer to their ancestral lands. The reoccupation of the area was significant not only for the families concerned but also for all the people who shared ancestral connections to the site and to surrounding countries, whether they now resided in Christmas Creek, Ringer Soak, or Mulan. The outstation allowed the Aborigines to reconnect with the surrounding countryside and with ancestral essences. From Yagga Yagga, they were in a better position to look after their country.

Even though only a handful of people established themselves at Yagga Yagga at first, the presence of this outstation meant a great deal to all those who claimed ancestral connections to the significant places nearby: Ngantalarra, Nakarra Nakarra, Walkarli, and the Mungkayi area. It was as if Yagga Yagga and the surrounding countryside had come back to life again, after being abandoned for nearly thirty years. The *kuruwarri*, the vital and ancestral essences that had given these places form and animation, were reactivated by the human presence. In the process of this reactivation, Yagga Yagga also became the site of conception for a few children, the first of these being twin girls, one of whom was named Yagga Yagga.

However, the presence of the founding Kukatja families at Yagga Yagga was strongly contested from the start because the site is in Ngarti country. The claim of these Kukatja families had to be mythically grounded. None of the initial Kukatja inhabitants of Yagga Yagga could claim a close ancestral connection to the site itself, apart from the fact that it represented a site on the *Wati Kutjarra* itinerary to which they claimed an affiliation. Therefore, validating their residence at Yagga Yagga on the basis of the *Tjukurrpa* became imperative. Their right of residence was contested by some Ngarti living in Wirrimanu and Ringer Soak. Meetings were held between the Ngarti and the Kukatja established at Yagga Yagga; heated negotiations ensued. At first, Tjapangarti, the middle-aged leader who had negotiated with the oil company and the government for an outstation at Yagga Yagga, claimed he was of Ngarti origin, since his conception site was at Emily Spring, north-east of Yagga Yagga, in Ngarti country. This aspect of his claim, while not contested, was nevertheless insufficient in the eyes of the Ngarti. At the time, all concerned agreed that the man's skills in dealing with *Kartiya* matters were outstanding, but people were also aware that his knowledge of the Law and his interest in ritual matters were rather weak. The Ngarti wanted the claim for a right of residence at Yagga Yagga to come from a ritual leader.

Thus, the process of the (re)discovery of a *Tjukurrpa* segment in the Yagga Yagga region started shortly after the creation of the outstation. The main protagonist was a very respected and prominent Law man, Tjampitjin, brother-in-law to the 'modern' leader. Tjampitjin's country lay to the south-east, between Mungkayi and Lake Mackay, around the Alec Ross Range. His second wife was a Kukatja woman from Mungkayi. They had lived in Balgo since the 1950s and were among the founding families of Yagga Yagga. Tjampitjin 'discovered' a segment of the *Wati Kutjarra* (Two Initiated Men) itinerary that was revealed to him by some of his deceased relatives in a series of dreams. The segment links Yagga Yagga to Mungkayi and Lake Mackay and is an underground episode featuring the *Wati Kutjarra* and the snake they were pursuing. The initial story recounts that the *Wati Kutjarra* lost sight of the snake at Yagga Yagga when he slithered underground. What was revealed to Tjampitjin was that the snake continued his underground journey all the way to Lake Mackay and that the Two Initiated Men followed him before returning to Yagga Yagga. Thus, this new segment even enhanced Yagga Yagga's ritual and spiritual value, while also establishing a right to the site for the inhabitants of the outstation. As a result, the Ngarti were satisfied and the conflict was over.

Tjampitjin received the knowledge from *Tjukurrpa* through a series of dreams. He discussed and shared what he had learned with the other elders before making it partially or totally public. Aside from the new narrative thread, the revelation included a few songs and ritual sequences. In such a process of revelation, the dreamer and the dream-experience act as intermediaries between the ancestral and the human realms. From the perspective of the Aborigines, dreams represent a privileged space-time to encounter and communicate with the ancestral beings and the deceased relatives. It is through dreams that the ancestors reveal to humans knowledge derived from *Tjukurrpa*, knowledge that had always existed in a potential state but that had remained unknown until then. Such a process requires that Tjampitjin and the other elders to whom he turned for help have the skill and the status to translate the contents of the dreams and to propose a new story and songs. Such an innovative and creative process is 'hard work,' as Tjampitjin's wife told me one day. He had acquired, through his travels and extensive participation in rituals, a profound knowledge of and esoteric learning about *Tjukurrpa* and the Laws of a vast region. In the process of reinterpreting the existing forms to validate a territorial affiliation, he thus made a strategic use of his skills as a Law man and the knowledge of the land acquired throughout his lifetime.

Tjampitjin died in the mid-1990s. The new segment was not identified with him (as 'his') but was woven into local *Tjukurrpa* stories and ritual practices as if it had always been there. This is a good example of how a historical event, namely the establishment of Yagga Yagga, has prompted the transformation of the forms of permanence. By his actions and intimacy with the *Tjukurrpa* realm, Tjampitjin validated a few families' right to stay in Yagga Yagga and, on a larger scale, wove Yagga Yagga into the regional initiation and ritual networks. From that point on, Yagga Yagga was in 'business.' Yagga Yagga is more than an example of something 'assimilated to the preexisting forms,' as Myers has suggested (1986a: 53), to the extent that the act of interpretation (and transformation) is a creative and innovative one.

The case of Yagga Yagga does not represent a departure from the rule. The 'openness' of mythical tracks is inherent in Western Desert sociality and is a way to validate (or integrate) territorial claims, alliance relationships, or ritual exchanges. In the Western Desert, we could hypothesize that the ideological discourse over the permanent and unchanging character of the Law has always served both to hide and to balance the necessity of structural openness in a region of great spatial mobility.[26] While such an innovative process may seem to originate from one person only, in fact it always operates in the name of a collectivity. In stating that such revelations come 'from *Tjukurrpa*,' it is not that the Aborigines refuse to recognize human creative action but that they refuse to credit one single individual with the creative and transformative process. Knowledgable people such as Tjampitjin participate actively and creatively in the production and regeneration of the sociocosmic environment through a basis of a shared identity and responsibility with others, acting as intermediaries between the ancestral realm and the ongoing present.

Even if they are ideologically rooted in a mythical space-time that seems to transcend history, ancestral itineraries are the very space where local historicity is recorded. It is precisely in that tension and dialectic between continuity and change in the forms of permanence that human action and intervention come into play. In Western Desert Aboriginal consciousness, ancestrality, the mythical landscape, and local historicity are closely intertwined. In relation to the local discourse that underlines the unchanging character of forms of permanence, some authors have suggested that Australian Aborigines ignore history (Lévi-Strauss 1962: 310), or else that they want to assimilate events through a sort of denial of their contingent or factual character (Sahlins 1985: xii), making them 'cold' or 'prescriptive.' What these interpretations fail to take into consideration is the meaning and the value granted to events and places, as well as the interplay between the human and the ancestral realms. It is not the contingent character and temporal reference of the event that stimulate Aboriginal imagination and interest but its relation to place and to an ancestral order that is coeval with the social order and the ongoing present, in a world that is forever unfolding and open to revelation.

As a complex of meanings and dimensions embedded in a single word, *Tjukurrpa* brings together the creative and generative essence of the universe that animates all forms and makes them consubstantial; it is the mythical space-time where the nomadic protagonists devised all rules and practices that became the Law; it is the mythical itineraries and sites that were named and shaped by these ancestral beings and that circumscribe social spaces of belonging and responsibility. *Tjukurrpa*, as a cosmological order and mythopoesis, is the basis upon which political, ritual, and territorial matters are orchestrated and negotiated. *Tjukurrpa* also unites the Laws of constraint, convention, and permanence, as well as those of negotiation, metamorphosis, and transformation. It is in the dynamic relationship – indeed, even in the tension – among these realities that the structural openness of ancestral itineraries manifests itself and that local historicity, strategy, and creativity are expressed. *Tjukurrpa* is an epistemology and an ontology of a relational nature in which knowledge of the world is inseparable from experience in the world.

Local knowledge, experiences, memories, and historicities are grounded in places. These places are pregnant with meaning and emergent possibilities. They are the source of Kukatja sociality and of one's identity and bodiliness. One's country is never conceived as a bounded area but as a set of places itself connected to another set of places, and so on. Named places and the networks they form are the 'gardens' of the nomads, shaped and transformed by both ancestral and human actions. The metaphor of the garden is appropriate here, since, like any garden, these sites must be tended, cared for, and, when necessary, transformed. This is in fact the object of human actions, realizations, and interactions related to the mythical landscape. In Kukatja ontology, human beings are an integral part of a sociocosmic environment that is forever unfolding and revealing itself through webs of agencies and networks of social relationships that also include non-human beings, ancestors, and named places that are endowed with personhood. Human actions and realizations, like hunting and gathering activities, ritual performances, or dreams, are part of this process of unfolding.

Chapter 3

Sociality, Mobility, and Composite Identity

Tjukurrpa itineraries, with their delineated segments and networks of sites, represent the main structuring elements that ground and inform Western Desert sociality, identity, and sense of self. In this chapter, I look more closely at the complexity of social morphology and at the different variables and processes through which the linguistic, territorial, residential, and ritual modes of social groupings are formed and transformed. The sociality of Western Desert groups cannot be satisfactorily analysed if one assumes that it is based on rigid structures. The degree of flexibility and of personal choice available must also be considered.

Following in the steps of authors such as R. Berndt, Myers, and Tonkinson, I stress the aspects of flexibility, fluidity, mobility, and thus negotiability with regard to the various social groupings and modes of belonging, without neglecting the rules and constraints of the Law. In the Western Desert, as elsewhere, the Aborigines 'play with boundaries, contexts and identities' (Rose 1992: 224), but always in a most serious manner and in keeping with the Law. The most appropriate way to understand the social morphology of the Western Desert is to approach it from the personal perspective (Myers 1986a). The articulation between egocentric and sociocentric dimensions of the different social groupings along with the aspects of openness and flexibility allow us to glimpse the sociocultural dynamic in all its complexity and to highlight the degree of personal choice and of strategic moves within the established social rules. What I call the 'personal configuration of belonging' is a composite of complex and dynamic social relationships among people, and among people, places, and ancestors.

Language Groups

It has been argued by a great majority of authors that the language group does not adequately render the Aboriginal affiliations to land. The language group does not represent a bounded social, linguistic, or even territorial entity. Although it is possible to identify one given language group within a certain geographic area, none can be delimited in any precise or final way. This is very true of Western Desert language group labels, such as Kukatja, Walmatjari, or Pintupi. R. Berndt (1959) was the first to demonstrate the inadequacy of the concept of the 'tribe' when applied to Western Desert social morphology, as it generally implies a territory and a population that can be easily pinpointed. This observation exorcised a classic paradigm of anthropology that was an obstacle to our understanding of Western Desert sociality. Instead, Berndt presented the Western Desert peoples as a 'broad cultural bloc' that includes a number of more or less bounded and overlapping dialectal (and territorial) units, each of which can be associated with a series of local sites (R. Berndt 1976).

It should be stressed that it is only recently – that is, since first contact – and within the context of more settled community life, that language group labels have taken on a more permanent character. In discussing the Pintupi, Myers wrote, 'Even their name is an artifact imposed on them by changing conditions. Though known in the area where they came to live as 'Pintupi,' most say they never used this label to refer to themselves before contacts with Whites. While they speak the same language, with some dialectical differences, the people called the Pintupi do not represent a single social entity, neither as a tribe, nor as a language group' (1986a: 28). Tonkinson made similar observations about the Mardu, who now live at Jigalong (1991: 66–7). Both authors demonstrated the primacy of country, as a cluster of sites along *Tjukurrpa* itineraries, in defining local identity. My own observations in the Wirrimanu area corroborate this conclusion.

The Aborigines now living in Wirrimanu are said to represent a wide variety of linguistic and territorial origins – Kukatja, Walmatjari, Ngarti, Pintupi, Mandiltjarra, Wangkatjunga, Warlpiri, and Tjaru. Only since the Aborigines' sedentarization, and through their relations with the *Kartiya*, have these names taken on a finality that they never had in the era of traditional nomadism. This became clear to me when I felt the uneasiness of the elders in referring to their affiliations to specific language groups. They were more inclined to name their country of origin and the sites with which they were intimately linked, rather than to refer to a larger group unit that meant little to them. Even today, Aborigines rarely define themselves as belonging to a language group; rather, reference is made to places, to countries, to the *Tjukurrpa* tracks with which they are associated, or to elders, living or deceased, who are likely to be known. In interpersonal relationships, membership in a language group is of little significance. A person remains a stranger as long as the local territorial (and thus ancestral) anchorage remains unspecified. It seems that, traditionally, such labels were used in order to identify and roughly situate distant groups with whom relations were infrequent. Kukatja, for instance, derives from the word *kuka* (meat) and means approximately 'those who give meat,' while Wangkatjunga means 'those who speak frankly,' and Pintupi means 'very good.' The possibility that terms like these have acquired a certain permanence since sedentarization but had other meanings in previous times cannot be rejected either (see also Merlan 1981). The possibility also that one name has been retained instead of another can only be due to a combination of circumstances. According to one man in Wirrimanu, all the inhabitants of the Western Desert speak 'the same language'; then he added, 'they are same but different.'

When I asked about the similarities and the differences between the language groups, my friends would always insist that they are 'all one company,' they are all *walytja*. *Walytja* means 'relatives,' and in some contexts it includes all those with whom one has a sense of identity and relatedness. *Walytja* are those who share a common ancestrality of related *Tjukurrpa* itineraries and Laws that criss-cross the Western Desert. The concept of *walytja* implies a deep sense of shared identity and responsibility towards the land. Such an inclusive representation of social relationships favours an openness to the outside world and is an element of nomadic reality, particularly in desert areas. A shared identity based on a common ancestrality explains how participants in Wirrimanu initiation ceremonies can come from as far as Jigalong, Lagrange, Fitzroy Crossing, Lajamanu, Yuendumu, or Kintore. This shared identity does not exclude the fact that at another level every person claims his or her particular affiliation to specific countries as a series of local sites. The coexistence of these two realities is not contradictory but shows how *Tjukurrpa* spatial stories connect people of different, and at times distant (language) groups, while always stressing local affiliations and responsibilities.

It is possible to map the territorial distribution of linguistic and cultural entities in the Western Desert (see map 2), as long as we remain aware of the limits and distortions of such mapping.[1] While such maps might be meaningful from a Western point of view, or prove useful for ethnological inquiry, they are inadequate to render the manifold qualities and aspects of Aboriginal reality, composite identity, and relationships to places. As soon as we move 'closer to the ground,' mapping becomes not only inadequate but also irrelevant. This difficulty in representation can be explained by five main variables that are inherent to Western Desert social morphology. First, the spatial distribution of language groups is never clearly circumscribed, since they overlap in several places. Second, mythical itineraries generally extend beyond a given linguistic (or dialectal) constituency, thus creating common allegiances and a sense of shared identity between people from different areas. Third, the personal configurations of ancestral connections, or one's composite identity, include affiliations to different *Tjukurrpa* (or segments of them) that are usually distributed across several regional and linguistic areas. A fourth factor is that a country (*ngurra*) is delimited on the basis of the local group (see below), not the language group, and a single linguistic entity necessarily includes several local groups. A fifth variable is the remarkable mobility of families during the epoch of traditional nomadism and also the necessity to abandon certain areas at certain times – for example, during prolonged droughts. All these factors are inconsistent with the concept of fixed territorial boundaries based on linguistic appellations.

The matter of affiliation to land ought to be approached not in relation to language groups and their territorial distribution but in relation to the areas of responsibility marked out by *Tjukurrpa* segments. The example of Lappi Lappi illustrates how it is possible for one major site, or mythical segment, to be claimed by peoples who have become identified with different language groups. Located on the edge of Lake Hazlett, Lappi Lappi is a permanent water-hole and used to be an important gathering place for bands that came from all over a vast region at the end of the dry season. As we have seen in the previous chapter, Lappi Lappi is one of the dwelling places of the Rainbow Snake. Myers and Clark (1983) identify the site as being in Pintupi country. I visited the site with a group of men and women from Wirrimanu in 1987, and all of them located it as being in Warlpiri-Ngarti country.[2] Upon returning to Wirrimanu, some people who had not been able to join our expedition reproached us for having visited the site without their permission;[3] according to them, Lappi Lappi lies in Kukatja country. If all those concerned are right about their respective claims, the case of Lappi Lappi demonstrates the interpenetration of different language groups' territories over the same geographic region. This geographic overlap shows that language groups are ineffectual when it comes to establishing the real foundations of belonging to, and responsibility for, a given country. It shows just how problematic and ambiguous current land claims and issues of 'traditional ownership' of *Tjukurrpa* sites can be, if they are approached only via regional linguistic entities.

Not only is it extremely difficult to map the spatial distribution of a language group in a precise way, but the matter is complicated by individual affiliations to different language groups. In Wirrimanu and Yagga Yagga, most people could claim affiliation to at least two language groups, sometimes more. The following examples illustrate this reality and allow us to glimpse the networks of ancestral connections from an individual perspective.

Tjapangarti, one of the founders of the Yagga Yagga outstation, was the liaison between the families and the government and oil companies. Conceived at Emily Spring in Ngarti country, he claimed this affiliation when some Ngartis from Ringer Soak objected to having the man's extended family settle in Yagga Yagga, because they allegedly lacked a true affiliation to the site (see chapter 2). In other contexts, he would emphasize his Kukatja origin and affiliation to Mungkayi, his father's country. On the basis of language group labels, the man is Ngarti and Kukatja.

Tjampitjin, his brother-in-law, was the elder who dreamed the new segment for Yagga Yagga. He was conceived and born in the Lake Mackay area, which was his mother's and father's country. Lake Mackay is usually identified as Pintupi in its southern region, as Warlpiri to the north-east, and as Kukatja to the north-west. It is an area where different regional identities overlap and where several major *Tjukurrpa* itineraries cross paths. On the basis of language-group labels alone, this man had a manifold configuration: his mother was 'from Warlpiri side'; his father was 'from Pintupi side'; he was himself conceived around Alec Ross Range, and he married a woman from Mungkayi, which is generally regarded to be in Kukatja country (except for the northern part, which is is identified as Ngarti). As a young man, Tjampitjin travelled extensively through all of these countries and thus became acquainted with their respective Laws. However, and like most people of his generation, Tjampitjin always refused to identify himself as Pintupi, Kukatja, or Warlpiri, something he could very well have done. Instead, he kept playing on the ambiguity of such names, considering that these were somewhat irrelevant in defining his networks of ancestral connections and responsibilities. All his life, he deeply longed to return to his country, Tjikarri, which remained the focal place of his identity.

Another example is that of Nungurrayi, who died in 1997. Her country of origin, Yikarra, lies between Kiwirrkura and the Canning Stock Route. She claimed a mixed descent, Pintupi and Mandiltjarra. Her life's itinerary brought her to the Balgo mission as a young woman. Her second husband, with whom she lived all of her adult life, identified himself as Walmatjari-Wangkatjunga. Depending on the contexts, and having acquired a fair knowledge of the Law of her husband's country, she could invoke any one of these four regional identities. Though she left her birth country at a fairly young age, she never denied her first identity and recalled all the places where she had camped as a child with her family, as well as the *Tjukurrpa* stories around Yikarra. A final example of multiple affiliations on the basis of language group labels comes from a Ngarti-Walmatjari man: he was Ngarti both through his father, who came from a place on the northeast side of Mungkayi, and through his conception site, Ngantalarra; he was Walmatjari through his mother, who came from Lake Gregory (Paruku). Sometimes he called himself Ngantalarra, after his place of conception. Simply naming himself in this way was enough for everyone to know his ancestral connection, and identification with a larger regional entity therefore became pointless.

One man who was listing, on the basis of language-group labels, the double or triple affiliation of some of the elders in Wirrimanu finished by saying, 'We are all mixed.' These mixed affiliations do not apply only to those living in Wirrimanu. When Warlpiri people from Lajamanu and Yuendumu came to Wirrimanu to visit relatives or to participate in a ceremony, they explained how they were either Warlpiri-Tjaru, Warlpiri-Ngarti, or Warlpiri-Kukatja, depending on their birthplace or conception site and the respective countries of their four grandparents.

In view of this, most of the people now known as Kukatja are of mixed descent, being either Kukatja-Ngarti, Kukatja-Walmatjari, Kukatja-Wangkatjunga, Kukatja-Warlpiri, or Kukatja-Pintupi.[4] It also goes without saying that most people in Wirrimanu are fluent in at least two languages (or dialects). This illustrates the flexibility of the language-group entities by demonstrating how they overlap, not only spatially, but also in terms of membership. To sum up: identification by language groups alone is barely relevant to Western Desert Aborigines because people's identity and sense of belonging are rather grounded in local *Tjukurrpa* paths and their various segments.

Sharing Countries and Personal Configurations of Belonging

The concept of the 'local group' is better than that of the language group for rendering Aboriginal affiliations to land and their sense of belonging to and responsibility for a country. The people identifying with a local group at a given moment of time and for a particular area are the guardians of that country. They are the custodians of the mythic, ritual, and esoteric knowledge attached to that country, knowledge that is held in the form of songs, dances, designs, and ritual objects. The local group is definitely not a residential group; rather, it is a group of guardians of the mytho-ritual knowledge associated with a country, as a *Tjukurrpa* expression. A local group's country, its area of responsibility (its 'estate'; Stanner 1965), exists as a series of sites along a mythic pathway created by one or a group of ancestral beings in the course of their travels. (This does not exclude the fact that the country may also carry the traces and narratives of other ancestral beings.) A country is more or less bounded by, though it may overlaps with, countries of neighbouring local groups.

The local group represents a more or less bounded territorial and ritual entity; it is not a 'corporate group.' As Myers and others have emphasized, claiming a right to a country can sometimes be the subject of intense negotiation. In the same way, delimiting a country and establishing responsibility for it can also give rise to litigation between members of different local groups. Not only is the membership of local groups fluid, but the spatial distribution of countries overlaps, and these factors render irrelevant any attempt to try to trace exclusive borders.

The Aborigines often say that they are 'holding the country' or 'looking after country.' These expressions do not convey any meaning of 'ownership' as private property in the Western sense. Western 'ownership' of land runs counter to local ontology. Rather, these expressions convey a sense of responsibility towards the land as a sentient entity to which Aborigines are intrinsically linked and towards the production and renewal of the vital essences (*kuruwarri*) bequeathed to particular places by the ancestors. The Aborigines feel responsible for these places with respect to each other, to members of other local groups, and to the ancestors, and for those who are yet to be born 'from' it. One's country is not a mere surface to be occupied, utilized, and owned; rather, it is a place of dwelling, remembering, relating, and becoming.

As regards Western Desert social morphology, R. Berndt (1972, 1976), Tonkinson (1991), and Meggitt (1962a) define the local group ('local descent group') as a unit that is essentially patrilineal. More recent research by Myers and Clark (1983) and Myers (1986a; he calls it the 'landowning group'), as well as my own observations in the Wirrimanu area, found that while patrilineal descent is indeed an important criterion in the composition of the local group, there are other variables that confer on a person the right to and responsibility for a given country. The membership in a local group must not be approached solely through descent.[5] There are numerous criteria that allow a person to claim an attachment (and a right) to a country and access to the associated mythic and ritual knowledge. It is possible for every individual to claim several local group allegiances at once and therefore attachments to those respective countries; this explains the composite character of personal identity.

Myers lists ten criteria for the Pintupi that can justify personal affiliation or claim to a country. I observed the same variables functioning in Wirrimanu, and therefore I cite Myers's list. If place A is situated along a *Tjukurrpa* track, any of the following variables may constitute reasons for claiming that country as one's own :

1 conception at place A;
2 conception at place B made by and/or identified with the same Dreaming [*Tjukurrpa*] as A;
3 conception at place B whose Dreaming is associated mythologically with The Dreaming at A (the story lines cross);
4 initiation at A (for a male);
5 birth at A;
6 father conceived at A or conditions 2–5 true for father;
7 mother conceived at A or conditions 2, 3, or 5 true for mother;
8 'grandparents' ... conceived at A or conditions 2–5 true;
9 residence around A;
10 death of a close relative at or near A.

(Myers 1986a: 129–30)

All these criteria can lead to a person's identification with a given country. I would also add that they are valid for men and women alike – even for point 4, initiation at A. Some female elders at Wirri-manu claimed a connection to the country where they underwent either perforation of the nasal septum or pectoral scarification, both of which are forms of initiation to the Law of a country. With these crite-ria, we see again the primacy of place, and of events that occurred in places, in defining one's composite identity.

The site of conception, the place where the mother realizes she is pregnant, is of particular importance in defining one's identity and sense of self.[6] The child is the incarnation of the ancestral being who has named the site in question; (s)he is a living expression of that *Tjukurrpa*. For example, in the 1980s, a child was 'conceived' during the enactment of the *Wati Kutjarra* (the Two Initiated Men) ritual at the site of Ngarili near Wirrimanu. He was born with the index and mid-dle fingers of his right hand stuck together, which was interpreted as a sign of the *Wati Kutjarra*. He is one of the manifestations of the *Wati Kutjarra* and is bearer and eventually caretaker of their ancestral essence. The constant identification of the living with *Tjukurrpa* ances-tors is significant in several respects. First, it signals the dimension of immanence of *Tjukurrpa* and its ongoing actualization and embodi-ment in life today. Second, the establishment of a common basis of identification with this primordial principle enriches personal experi-ence and provides a sense of self on a collective level. Finally, in some cases it can offer relevant reference points with regard to the relation between myth and historicity discussed in the previous chapter.

As a general rule, Aborigines develop and for the most part maintain intimate relationships – even if at a distance – with the country associ-ated with their site of conception and with their father's and mother's countries. Based on the criteria listed above, a person can also claim affiliations to other countries and the right to the ritual knowledge of several different local groups, though one does not necessarily develop all of these. It depends, among other things, on one's life course, places of residence, spouse, or, and particularly in today's context, the dis-tance to the claimed sites. These factors, along with the low density of population in the Western Desert, mean that the number of people who actually claim responsibility to the fullest extent for the Law of a coun-try always remains manageable. No matter how attachment to a coun-try is justified, there is a deep sense of shared identity with and responsibility towards the land as a whole and as ancestral expression.

It is possible to distinguish different degrees of relationship to and intimacy with a country. It depends if one is identified with a country upon birth, either through the place of conception or through maternal or paternal affiliation, or if one becomes identified with a country in the course of his or her life. In all cases, it also depends on the degree of (ritual) interest the person will demonstrate towards the country and its ancestral essence. Belonging to a country – and having such a claim recognized by others – implies, among other things, that once a man is fully initiated into the Law of the country, he has access to all its sacred-secret places and matters. He can also narrate the stories of that country and, in appropriate contexts, relate the esoteric masculine versions without fear of reprisal, as long as he has undergone the necessary stages of initiation and has reached a dignified age and a level of maturity in keeping with the nature of *Tjukurrpa* secrets. If there are no equivalent initiation ceremonies for women, it is age, (ritual) knowledge, and maturity that give them the right to tell the story of their country freely and fully, at least in their female versions.

Let us look at the example of the country of local group X, along *Tjukurrpa* pathway A. Individuals from the local group X, the people responsible for the country and its associated mytho-ritual knowledge, can participate, to varying degrees, in the rituals and also have access to the knowledge associated with groups and countries elsewhere along pathway A. A few individuals can even claim allegiance in full to these other countries. The people affiliated to the local groups along pathway A can also participate, again in varying degrees, in the mytho-ritual knowledge of local groups along *Tjukurrpa* pathway B, and vice versa, if it happens that pathways A and B are connected in some way and if their respective narratives (and songs) recount such a connection. In the case where the two itineraries cross paths, the areas of responsibility of the local groups concerned clearly overlap. Nevertheless, they are distinct, in that one group is caretaker of the knowledge bequeathed by *Tjukurrpa* being A, and the other group is caretaker of the knowledge bequeathed by *Tjukurrpa* being B. Members of each of the local groups will perform their own ritual sequences in celebrating the country.

In the case where all the members of a local group have disappeared, responsibility for their country would be transferred to a group whose country overlapped with theirs; or, if there were no neighbouring local groups, to one that was a caretaker of sites along the same *Tjukurrpa* itinerary. This transmission can occur without a hitch, or it can cause numerous disputes and negotiations between local groups if members disagree over the responsibility for the vacant area. In the late 1980s, this happened for the site of Lappi Lappi. All the custodians of that country who could claim close ancestral connections to this site on the pathway of *Warnayarra* (Rainbow Snake) had passed away. Negotiations took place between members of various local groups – then living in different settlements – over who would take responsibility for Lappi Lappi. Some of the people involved claimed affiliation to it through conception near Lappi Lappi, or by paternal or maternal affiliation to neighbouring countries of Lappi Lappi that were identified with different *Tjukurrpa* pathways. Others were caretakers of countries situated at the far western end of the *Warnayarra* pathway, in the region of Mungkayi, in Kukatja territory. Some others were responsible for the knowledge linked to the eastern sections of the *Warnayarra* pathway, in Warlpiri territory. All their claims were valid, based on ancestral knowledge as well as age-old occupation of the region. Many people felt responsible for this permanent water-hole because their parents and grandparents had used the site before the migrations to various settlements and the place was still permeated with their presence. Moreover, some of the relatives of the claimant groups had died at or near Lappi Lappi (criterion 10 of Myers). These negotiations took place in the late 1980s. I left the area before the issue was resolved.

At the narrative level, there are two ways in which a person can describe a country of belonging: one can name the series of places in reference either to the remembered human pathways and camps (*ngurra*), or one can name the *Tjukurrpa* itineraries and related campsites of the ancestors (*ngurra*). Both namings are always told as a story (*wangka*). In the first case, the speaker may list a series of places that, in traditional times and over a seasonal cycle, were visited by one's family and where they used to establish their camps (*ngurra*) for varying periods of time. It is a practice of remembering the land, its resources, and one's deceased relatives. The second way to describe one's country is in relation to *Tjukurrpa* pathways and *ngurra* of the ancestors.

When the Aborigines list the *Tjukurrpa* places that make up their country of belonging – or one of their countries of belonging – they usually name around ten places, and thus mark out the area of responsibility of their local group. The greater one's territorial and ritual knowledge and experience, the longer one's list is likely to be, and the greater the chances are that it will include sites for which responsibility lies with other local groups. For example, one man named sites along the *Marlu* (Kangaroo) itinerary between Tjalyirr (in the Lake Gregory area, the home country of his mother) and Karntawarra (in the region of Mungkayi, his father's country), a region to which he felt particularly attached; he refused to name any sites beyond those (even though he might have known them). Another man, the son of *Murtikarlka*, the hunter who had followed *Marlu* from north to south, listed approximately 100 sites along this same itinerary, from Halls Creek (and regions farther north) south to the region of Kiwirrkura, in Pintupi country. The naming of sites is always a political act.

In all cases of naming (and describing) their country, people's real knowledge of the country and their identity within the group, as well as the public knowledge recognized by all other members, provide markers that enable a person to judge how far he or she is allowed to go in the naming of sites. Generally, people will speak only of the pathway segment that is intrinsic to their identity and for which they feel responsible. But with increasing maturity and as the years of ritual participation add up, they may be able to name and tell of more sites along a mythic itinerary. One may even speak of sites that come under the custody of other local groups. However, each person must respect the superior jurisdiction of other local groups over their own segments of the pathway by not divulging the esoteric elements associated with these other segments.

In Western Desert sociality, no two persons have the same configuration of belonging. Two full brothers, for example, would have different conception and birth sites and different attachments to other countries through marriage. Their life trajectories on the ritual and residential levels would also likely differ. Thus, each person emerges from *Tjukurrpa* born of essences of the ancestors left along the ancestral routes and grows up in a world that gives him or her a configuration of belonging, of rights and responsibilities, that is never identical to anyone else's. The configuration of belonging as well as the relations of intimacy with ancestral beings stimulate a sense of responsibility for and creative engagement with the land and constituents of the world.

As I have tried to demonstrate, several factors make it difficult to delineate in any precise way the physical area of responsibility (and mytho-ritual custody) of a local group and its membership. These factors include the frequent overlap between the countries of neighbouring local groups; the unclaimed status of several countries because of current conditions of settlement that tend to separate people from their ancestral territories; and, finally, the composite identity of individuals

and the possibility that they may identify with several different countries. No doubt, the Aborigines play on this flexibility and ambiguity
that constitute undeniable dimensions of their sociality and politics
(and poetics) of culture.

The local group is not a residential group. In a traditional context,
the people could move freely through their country, while respecting
its sacred places, but they were never obliged actually to live there.
A condition of residence would have been inconsistent with their
nomadic way of life. In the same way that members of a local group
don't necessarily live in their country, they don't necessarily live
together, either. In today's context, for example, the main custodians of
a given country often live in different communities, in Wirrimanu,
Fitzroy Crossing, Christmas Creek, and so on. Nevertheless, even at a
great distance, individuals remain responsible for their country, the
place where in the time of traditional nomadism they would have
lived at least periodically. I was told that at the beginning of the mission, several elders, when faced with the impossibility of returning to
their countries from time to time, died from not being able to bond
again with the ancestral essences of their identity. Some provoked their
own deaths by singing certain specific verses of their country. Their
spirits (*kurrunpa*) returned to the place thus sung and merged with the
Tjukurrpa essence of which they were an embodiment.

Sharing Camps

Radcliffe-Brown defined the residential group – the traditional 'band' –
as a basically patrilineal and patrilocal unit, at once a 'land-utilizing
group' and a 'land-owning group.' Several researchers have since
helped to explode those classical paradigms by presenting interpretations of the residential group that are closer to Aboriginal reality (Hiatt
1962; Meggitt 1962a; Myers 1982, 1986a).[7] For the Warlpiri, Meggitt
noted that besides ties of blood and marriage, other variables, such as
friendship or ritual obligation, may prompt people to share camps for
a time (1962a: 51). Myers offers a similar description of the Pintupi
when he writes that residential groups 'are bilateral, composition actualized from numerous organizational categories, including kinsmen,
affines, and ritual partners' (1982: 181). In the region of Jigalong, Tonkinson observed the same thing. The accounts of the elders of Wirrimanu, who had lived the first part of their lives in the desert, support
these three authors' remarks. The residential group consists of the peo-

ple who may decide to share camps at a given time and space. It is a unit that is flexible. While it is no longer possible to observe the formation and transformation of such groups in a traditional setting, I have chosen to present the outstation of Yagga Yagga in its very beginning as an example of a residential group.

In 1987–8, about thirty people lived at Yagga Yagga. This is certainly a larger number of people than the traditional 'band' would have had; although, in the period of traditional nomadism, it possibly could represent the annual gathering of families around a major source of water at the end of the dry season. The Yagga Yagga outstation is also a good example of how a large residential group can comprise men and women derived from different local groups. Below is a list of the various camps of the outstation (numbered from 1 to 10), and their members. Two men, brothers-in-law and the main protagonists of the outstation, have already been mentioned in the previous chapter: Moora Tjapangarti, a Kukatja/Ngarti, then in his forties, and Sunfly Tjampitjin, a prominent Law man, a Kukatja/Pintupi/Warlpiri from Murungpa (Alec Ross Range), then in his sixties. Tjapangarti's father, Wanmall Tjapanangka, who died at the old mission, was from Mungkayi (Stansmore Range). Among Wanmall's children (he had two wives), four were living at Yagga Yagga with their old mother. Tjampitjin's father, Marrakurru Tjangala, was from the Lake Mackay area.

1 Sunfly Tjampitjin (a ritual leader), his second wife, Bye Bye Napangarti (Wanmall's daughter), about twenty years his junior, and two of their five children. Napangarti's ancestral connections were all in the Mungkayi area.
2 Moora Tjapangarti, his wife, Nampitjin, and their three children. Nampitjin was Walmatjari. She was conceived near Billiluna; her mother's country was Paruku (Lake Gregory), and her father came from around the Canning Stock Route.
3 Galova Tjapangarti, Moora's elder brother, his wife, Nungurrayi, and their eight children. A prominent Law man, Galova was also the first chairman of Yagga Yagga, a position he held for a number of years. He claimed affiliations to Yunpu (from his mother), Lintapurru (from his father), and Piparr. His wife came from the Canning Stock Route region.
4 Jimmy Flatnose Tjampitjin (a ritual leader), his wife, Njamme Napangarti (Wanmall's daughter), and their eight children. Jimmy

Tjampitjin was one of the main custodians for Piparr. He had also a number of children from a previous marriage, some of whom came to live at Yagga Yagga in the 1990s. Njamme Napangarti's conception site was Kunakurlu, forty kilometres south of Yagga Yagga.

5 Yundu Tjampitjin, Sunfly's brother, and his partner, Balba Napangarti. Balba was from Yunpu, in Kukatja/Wangkatjunga country; Yundu came from the Lake Mackay area. Balba was Sunfly's first wife; she was childless. As for Yundu, he was first married to another of Wanmall's daughters, Linda Napangarti. They had a child together before she decided to leave him for Jimmy Flatnose's brother (who died in the early 1980s).

6 Bandji Napurrula, Wanmall's wife (Moora, Galova, and Bye Bye's mother), then the oldest inhabitant of Yagga Yagga. Yunpu was one of her main ancestral connections.

7 Sunfly's brother, Sam Tjampitjin, a widower (he had no children).

8 Moora's mother-in-law, Elsie Nungurrayi, and her two husbands. Quite an unusual situation, this woman was living with her two husbands: an elderly man, father of her children, and a younger husband. Her first husband, Kanarri Tjangala, was Walmatjari. They had lived at Fitzroy Crossing for a number of years. Tjangala accepted his wife's second union, but according to the Law he could have opposed it if he had wished to.

9 Nanyuma Napurrula, the younger sister of Bandji, and her second husband, Bob Dingle (his mother was Sunfly's sister). She was Kukatja/Wangkatjunga, claiming affiliations with Yunpu and Mungkayi; he was Kukatja/Pintupi, from the Lake Mackay area. Both were very active in ritual matters. They had one daughter together, and other children from their first unions.

10 Mutji Tjangala, his wife, and their six boys. Mutji's wife was Nungurrayi's half-sister (camp 3). Born near the Canning Stock Route, Mutji also had close connections with the country south of Mungkayi towards Lake Mackay. His wife and her half-sister had lost their parents quite young. They had not maintained real ties with their own country near the Canning Stock Route, and so they strongly identified with the countries of their respective husbands.

The composition of the residential groups may be highly flexible, but it is not chaotic, given the complexity of the underlying social, ritual, and territorial principles. Within this framework, each person has his or her own rights and responsibilities and can find his or her own place (Tonkinson 1991). The question of one's choice is also certainly not to be downplayed here. Myers (1982) underscores the importance of personal choice in the ever-changing make-up of the residential group. All the same, a personal decision must be approved by the other members of the residential unit before it can take effect. This was the case at Yagga Yagga, where permission to come to the outstation, while usually granted, had to be formally requested.

Over the 1990s, the population of Yagga Yagga grew steadily. It fluctuates now from 100 to 250 people, depending on the circumstances. While most of the founding elders have died, the initial families are still living there. Now married, their children share their time among Yagga Yagga, Wirrimanu, and Mulan, while others move between Yagga Yagga and their spouses' settlements (Lajamanu, Yuendumu, Fitzroy Crossing, Kiwirrkura, or elsewhere).

While the people living at Yagga Yagga (for varying periods of time) may identify themselves with different countries (and different local groups), they consider themselves as *walytja* (relatives or 'all one company'). Some are linked to Walkarli, Yunpu, Kutal, or even the Canning Stock Route to the west; others to the Piparr area or to Lake Mackay to the south and south-east; some to Lappi Lappi country to the east; and still others to Mungkayi, or places closer to Yagga Yagga, such as Ngantalarra. While each man and woman has a personal configuration of belonging, in terms of attachments to and responsibilities towards specific sites, they share a common ancestrality to the main *Tjukurrpa* itineraries of this vast area: the various *Tingarri* expressions, the *Wati Kutjarra, Marlu, Warnayarra,* and a few others. Each local group is in turn responsible for segments along these major long pathways and for shorter *Tjukurrpa* tracks.

This flexibility in composition of the residential groups of today was also a feature during their travels in traditional times. Since the residential group was made up of people from several different local groups, the group had access to all its members' respective countries. In case of need, they also had access to the countries of all the people who might possibly choose to join the group for a while.[8] During the course of their travels, there was usually at least one person who could claim an affiliation to the country being crossed. Sunfly Tjampitjin, his brothers, Jimmy Flatnose, Bandji, Balba, Nanyuma, or even Bye Bye (as a young girl) knew all the countries mentioned above because they had travelled through them in the 1940s and 1950s, and even, some of them, the 1960s, as they accompanied their parents, grandparents, aunts, or uncles. For example, in the old days, Wanmall's family from the Mungkayi area would travel to the south and south-east around Lake Mackay and sometimes beyond; to the west as far as the Canning Stock Route; towards the east to Lake White, Lake Dennis, and beyond; and to the north beyond Lake Gregory.[9] All these countries were familiar to Bye Bye's father, who had visited them for economic, ritual, or personal purposes, either with his family, on his own, or with other initiated men. Both men and women knew the water sources, the flora and fauna, and the *Tjukurrpa* stories of all the sites along their route; women and children, though, had to avoid the vicinity of sacred-secret masculine sites (each local group's country having at least one of these). Some people, particularly men, travelled more extensively and knew the most distant territories better than others.

There is an element that is essential to an adequate understanding of traditional Australian nomadic reality. In the Western Desert, mere ecological constraints were by no means the only things that deter-mined the itineraries of families over the seasonal cycles. Although the families' journeys across the land were planned in part in relation to their quest for food and resources, cyclical initiation ceremonies and ritual exchanges, as well as funerary rites, represented additional rea-sons to travel. Myers explains this reality as follows: 'Pintupi did not simply move to where the food was, but rather scheduled their move-ment so as to use available resources in pursuit of their own social values – to initiate a boy or to exchange ceremonies' (1986a: 292).

These elements still motivate travel in present-day nomadism. Although redefined in the contemporary context, nomadism is still pivotal to the Aboriginal way of being and way of relating to the world, to such an extent that most people seem to be on the move all the time. In fact, none of the inhabitants of Yagga Yagga reside there on a permanent basis. The various familial, social, and ritual obligations of adult men and women frequently lead them to relocate to other communities for periods of time that can range from a few days to a few weeks, or even a few months. The motivations are varied: a group of people may depart for Lajamanu to attend mourning rites; another group may decide to visit their relatives at Nyiirpi (a community south of Yuendumu) for a few weeks; others may go to Halls Creek, or some-times as far as Alice Springs, for a few days' or weeks' binge; others may go to a church meeting in Broome, or a cultural meeting in Kununurra, and so on. All year long, groups of men and women leave Wirrimanu, Yagga Yagga, and Mulan temporarily in order to take part in ritual exchanges (these were frequent in the 1980s but became less common in the 1990s), mourning rites, or initiation ceremonies. The latter take place annually between October and March and lead to such large movements of people that Wirrimanu and Yagga Yagga some-times seem deserted – unless, of course, the ceremonies are taking place in one of these places (see chapter 6). Such mobility is also present within the settlement itself, and even more so in a large place like Wirrimanu. Individuals and families frequently shift camps, mov-ing from one house to another, again for various reasons: the death of a relative (see below), to avoid an unwanted neighbour, to join relatives, or simply in order to occupy a more suitable living space for a while.

Likewise, people from neighbouring communities, such as Mulan, Wirrimanu, Ringer Soak, Kiwirrkura, Lajamanu, or Fitzroy Crossing, may come to live in Yagga Yagga for a period of time. They may be rel-atives, ritual partners, or people who are linked to the surrounding countries in one way or another. The visitors might be elders who come to discuss the preparation of initiation ceremonies with the men of Yagga Yagga. Or they may have just come to see friends, or to bond with the region again and to go hunting and gathering. As a rule, visi-tors have to announce their arrival beforehand. This is an informal pro-cedure but none the less an important one. Some visitors are men or women in mourning, usually from Wirrimanu or Mulan, who come to stay for a while at Yagga Yagga. Ancestral Law decrees that a deceased person's camp and its immediate surroundings should be abandoned for several months. When someone dies, not only does the person's camp become a forbidden place to close relatives and friends, but his or her name must not be uttered for at least two years, and for a longer period when the deceased was an influential Law man or woman. The term *kumuntjayi* is used to refer to the deceased as well as anyone who has the same or a similar name. The sites and the ancestral being to which he or she was intimately related also become *kumuntjayi*; the country of origin is referred to as *kumuntjayi*. While today it is the camp (or house) of the deceased that is deserted, traditionally some sites were not visited for nearly two years following the death of their custodian. For instance, after the death of one of their sons, one of the core families of Yagga Yagga went back to live in Wirrimanu for two years.

Closer to the 'Skin'

In the Wirrimanu area, the eight-subsection system is another structur-ing principle that is pivotal to Aboriginal sociality and relationship to land.[10] It is a sociocentric system of classifying the world in social and ritual terms. This system is superimposed on the kinship system and provides a classificatory order that encompasses everything that exists: *Tjukurrpa* beings, human beings, *Tjukurrpa* segments, celestial bodies, named places, animals, plants, natural elements, and camp dogs, as well as non-Aborigines involved in lasting relationships with Aborigines.

Unlike kinship terms, that are defined from the standpoint of ego, these eight social and ritual categories are sociocentric in nature. They establish an exhaustive classification of everything that exists and a universal system of identification. Subsections are, in Meggitt's words, 'modes of classifying the world in social and ritual terms,' or in other words, 'schematic categories of cosmic classification' (1966b: 177). At a supraregional level, the subsection system organizes and facilitates relations among people who may be strangers to one another. The system can therefore be seen as another example of a structuring principle that favours an openness towards the outside world beyond local and regional limits.

I myself was incorporated within the classificatory system and became identified with the napangarti subsection while living in Wirrimanu in 1980. This followed my adoption by three Napangarti with whom I had been working; I was adopted as their classificatory younger sister and mother of their children. From then on, not only was my presence in the community made more meaningful, but I now was able to relate to other members of the community on Aboriginal terms.[11]

The following diagram shows the eight subsections and the manifold relations between these:

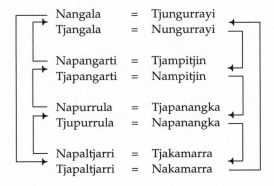

The terms beginning with the letters 'Tj' designate the masculine element, and those beginning with 'N' the feminine element. The 'equal' sign (=) represents matrimonial unions; and the arrows link the subsections of the mother and her children. The diagram can be read in the following manner: A woman from the napangarti subsection will marry a man from the tjampitjin subsection; their children's subsections will be tjangala (for their sons) and nangala (for their daughters). A tjangala man will marry a nungurrayi woman, and their children will belong to the tjampitjin and nampitjin subsections. For men, a subsection therefore recurs in alternate generations: a man is of the same subsection as his paternal grandfather. There are similarly recurrent matrilineal cycles in the system.

This system of classification offers a summary of kinship terms, but it is far from exhaustive in that respect. Thus, if a napangarti woman marries a tjampitjin, she cannot marry just any tjampitjin, since this subsection includes not only the preferred spouse, her second-degree crossed cousin (her mother's mother's brother's daughter's son), but also her father's mother's brother as well as her son's son, kin categories that are forbidden to be spouses. Similarly, the mother-in-law taboo between, for example, a tjampitjin and a napurrula, does not apply to all the women of the napurrula subsection but only to those who are in a potential mother-in-law relationship with the man (cf Hiatt 1984; Glowczewski and Pradelles de Latour 1987). The subsections therefore signify more than matrimonial categories.

The Aborigines use the English term 'skin' to refer to the subsection to which they belong. Thus, people will ask, 'What is your skin?' It is as if one could read in this expression a metaphor of the skin as an outer envelope that wraps up a multitude of interrelated elements. One could even push the metaphor farther and say that, as the skin is the point where the human being and the physical environment meet, so the subsection is the point where the social actor and his or her sociocosmic environment meet, since the subsection defines, according to the context, each person's place and role. One's 'skin' becomes a metaphor for the embodiment of manifold social relationships. The *Tjukurrpa* segments and the sites along these are also part of the subsection system, since places have a 'skin,' which is something else they share with humans. The subsection system is another way by which the 'bodies' of the land, the ancestors, and humans are connected.

As a general rule, people call each other by their subsection name. However, there is also the alternative option of calling others by kinship terms. This avoids the use of personal names that are considered rather intimate. It also reminds people that they are maturing in a world of relationships where each person defines himself or herself in relation to others and to the environment, and therefore should act accordingly. Everyone is socialized within the subsection system from a very early age. Through this system, the child learns whom to respect, whom to avoid, and whom to ask for food or other needs. For instance, one day a four-year-old boy of the tjapaltjarri subsection refused to get out of the car because of the presence of an adult woman of the nakamarra subsection, who was in a spouse relationship with him. The boy was clearly frightened, though his mother tried to soothe his fear by telling him that by the time he became of a marriageable age the woman would be far too old for him. Another mother explained to her five-year-old daughter the different subsections of a group of people who had just arrived from Jigalong so that the girl would know how to act with each of them.

As an all-encompassing principle, the subsection system becomes fully relevant when it is applied to the *Tjukurrpa* segments, the ancestral beings, and their respective rituals. The eight subsections are divided into patrimoieties, which provide a framework from which the responsibility for organizing and performing rituals can be established.

Patrimoiety 1:

Tjangala ———	Tjampitjin
(Nangala)	(Nampitjin)
Tjupurrula ———	Tjakamarra
(Napurrula)	(Nakamarra)

Patrimoiety 2:

Tjanpangarti ———	Tjapanangka
(Napangarti)	(Napanangka)
Tjapaltjarri ———	Tjungurrayi
(Napaltjarri)	(Nungurrayi)

The line (———) indicates a father (father's sister)/son (daughter) relationship. In the Wirrimanu region, the patrimoieties are not named, and they are exogamous. A man must marry a woman from the opposite patrimoiety if he wants his children to be in the same patrimoiety as he is. This is particularly important for sons during initiation. An example of these patrimoiety relations would be a tjapanangka male and his napanangka sister being in the same patrimoiety as their father (a tjapangarti) and their paternal aunt (a napangarti). Their mother's mother's brother, a tjungurrayi, would also be from the same patrimoiety. Their mother, a nampitjin, and their maternal uncle, a tjampitjin, would be from the other patrimoiety. A man belongs to the same patrimoiety as his mother-in-law.

All the sites of a *Tjukurrpa* segment are identified with a father (father's sister)/son (daughter) couple – that is, they are attributed to one patrimoiety or the other. Along the *Warnayarra* pathway, the country of Lappi Lappi is the responsibility of the tjapaltjarri-napaltjarri/tjungurrayi-nungurrayi dyad. At the westernmost point of this pathway, the site of Runpurntu in the Mungkayi region is also attributed to the tjapaltjarri-napaltjarri/tjungurrayi-nungurrayi dyad. The same goes for all the other sites along this pathway. The *Marwuntu* pathway, associated with *Luurn* (Kingfisher), and all the sites along it are identified with the dyad tjangala-nangala/tjampitjin-nampitjin. The *Tjukurrpa* ancestors, their corresponding segments, sites, and mytho-ritual bodies of knowledge are identified with one or the other of the patrimoieties. The patrimoieties establish a very important structural division that is particularly effective when it comes to the care of the countries and their associated rituals. This division splits the ritual community into two distinct but complementary entities: the *kirda* and the *kurdungurlu*. The members of one patrimoiety will be *kirda* (or *wapirra*) for a given country. In Aboriginal English, *kirda* means 'boss' or 'owner'; the *kirda* for a given country are, as they say, 'from father side.' The *kirda* thus legitimate their affiliation to a local group and to its corresponding country and rituals by the paternal side. The tjapaltjarri-napaltjarri/tjungurrayi-nungurrayi couple is *kirda* for the country of Lappi Lappi. The members of the opposite patrimoiety are *kurdungurlu* for this place. The Aborigines translate *kurdungurlu* into English as 'worker' or 'policeman.' The *kurdungurlu* legitimate their affiliation to a local group and its corresponding country and rituals through the maternal side (Bell 1993; Dussart 2000; Glowczewski 1991).

A man is *kirda* for the country of his father and his father's father, and its corresponding rituals. His children and his sons' children will also be *kirda* for this country. The same man will be *kurdungurlu* for his mother's country and his father's mother's country. He is also *kurdungurlu* for his wife's country, in that he belongs to the other patrimoiety.

A woman is *kirda* for the country of her father and her father's father. Her children will be *kurdungurlu* for that country. She is *kurdungurlu* for her mother's and her maternal uncle's country, and for her husband's country. The local group is therefore made up of bilateral relations. To take Lappi Lappi as an example again, the tjapaltjarri-napaltjarri/tjungurrayi-nungurrayi and the tjapanangka-napanangka subsections are *kirda* for the country. And because they belong to the opposite patrimoiety and trace their affiliation to the site 'through the mother,' the children of napaltjarri and nungurrayi women, who are respectively tjupurrula-napurrula and tjampitjin-nampitjin, are *kurdungurlu* for Lappi Lappi country. It follows that each person is *kirda* for some countries and *kurdungurlu* for others.

There is no hierarchical difference between *kirda* and *kurdungurlu*. Both are 'holding the country' in question, and the participation and responsibility of both are necessary for the proper upkeep of the country and the correct organization and performance of its rituals. Members of both patrimoieties have rights to the site and its rituals, and in these the roles of *kirda* and *kurdungurlu* are complementary and reciprocal (Myers 1986a: 148). The participation of members from both *kirda* and *kurdungurlu* is a *sine qua non* for the accomplishment of the ritual sequences linked to a given country. The *kirda* are responsible for incarnating, through song and dance, the mythic heroes associated with the country and for painting ritual objects when the ritual sequences are performed. The *kurdungurlu* guard the ritual objects, prepare any food required, and verify that the ritual is performed correctly, sequence after sequence, which is where their title of 'policeman' comes from. They can also sing and dance. Only when both groups are represented can a ritual properly take place.

Depending on the personal configuration of belonging, a person can act as *kirda* for some rituals and as *kurdungurlu* for others. When one claims an affiliation to a local group's country and mytho-ritual knowledge, it is always done either as *kirda* or *kurdungurlu*. This structural division of ritual practice has the further advantage of allowing all individuals, even those from distant regions, the chance to participate in any ritual. The role that they may play and the actions that they must either undertake or avoid are determined by the subsection to which they belong. Through this structural division, strangers and visitors can be integrated into the ritual activities of a given region, even if they have no affiliation to the country and the ancestral being that are being celebrated. No one is excluded from ritual performances and, consequently, those who participate in a country's ritual are not necessarily descendants of that place (Myers 1986a: 149).

Now that the relevance of the subsection classificatory system in sharing territorial and ritual responsibilities has been outlined, I would like to draw attention to the aspect of flexibility reflected in certain strategic practices, something that has rarely been referred to in the anthropological literature. The aspect in question is the possibility, one that occurs relatively frequently, of belonging to two subsections. This is the case for children of semi-regular or utterly irregular unions, and for those whose mother or father belongs to two different subsections. The decisional process behind the assignment of a subsection highlights several important points. The main concern is that children should belong to the same patrimoiety as their father, to ensure their full social inclusion and participation in rituals within the local group. The choice of the subsection that will prevail – which does not necessarily lead to the rejection of the other – is generally the task of close kin. As an adult, the person will be able to affirm his or her dual affiliation, depending on need and context. Ethnographic observation of this particular situation brings to light all of the complexities, subtleties, and tactics that can arise in the empirical application of such a classificatory system.

Three cases observed in the region of Wirrimanu serve to illustrate this. The first occurred during the first half of the twentieth century. Tjapaltjarri had three wives, two nakamarra and a nampitjin. A union between crossed cousins, in this case a tjapaltjarri and a nampitjin, is permissible and even relatively frequent. The spouses are of opposing patrimoieties, as they should be. The children born to Tjapaltjarri and his nakamarra wives belonged to the subsection tjungurrayi/nungurrayi. The woman who related this story to me was born from the union between Tjapaltjarri and Nampitjin. The system therefore gave her the option of belonging to two subsections: nungurrayi through her father, or napanangka through her mother. As a nubile girl, she was 'taken' by a man much older than she, a tjupurrula. It is uncertain whether she had been betrothed to him by her parents according to the rules, or whether the man carried her off; nevertheless, because she was also napanangka through her mother, her union with a tjupurrula was regular. This man's first wife was a napanangka, and from their union was born a nakamarra. My friend gave birth to a boy who belonged to the subsections tjakamarra and tjampitjin, because she was napanangka and nungurrayi. The tjupurrula husband was killed in the bush by a man of the same subsection who coveted his first wife, Napanangka; she joined him with her nakamarra daughter, and together they had more children. As a young widow, my friend was 'given' to her second husband, whose subsection seems to be so ambiguous that nobody dares make a clear pronouncement on the subject. Whatever the case may be, my friend, who had been mainly a napanangka during the first part of her life, describes herself today essentially as a nungurrayi (which is justified through her father, who was a tjapaltjarri). The son from her first marriage with Tjupurrula and those from her second marriage are tjampitjin, although occasionally, in certain contexts, they define themselves as tjakamarra.

A more recent example illustrates some of the complications that irregular marriages can lead to. There was a union between a nungurrayi and a tjapangarti, two subsections that are in a mother-in-law/son-in-law relationship with each other. Traditionally, such a union would have been difficult to accept, and the group would probably have put an end to it by killing one or both of the transgressors. Shortly after their marriage – which, as it happens, was Balgo's first Catholic wedding in the 1970s – the couple had to flee the elders' wrath by going into exile for some time. The union was finally accepted, or near enough, when the couple's first child was born. With the additional help of protection from the superintendent, Father Hevern, the couple were able to return to Balgo, and they now have nine children. Through their mother's subsection, the children should be tjampitjin/nampitjin. But this affiliation would place them in the opposite patri-moiety to that of their tjapangarti father. So the children 'follow their father' and belong to the tjapanangka/napanangka subsections. In this case, there is no question of the children claiming two subsections: their nungurrayi mother has never insisted that they keep even a vague affiliation with the tjampitjin/nampitjin subsection. By partici-pating in an out-of-order union, she had to accept some compromises. Furthermore, Nungurrayi had lost her parents when she was very young, and she has few links to her original family, country, and local group – and with the rituals that concern her directly. It is not surpris-ing that she has never insisted that her children keep up a second sub-section affiliation; besides, she would have received very little support for this idea from the elders.

The third case differs from the first two in that it involves the alloca-tion of a subsection that was not already acquired by descent. Such cases are, in fact, very rare. In the mid-1980s, Nungurrayi, the woman from the last example, gave birth to twin girls. A young childless couple offered to adopt one of the twins in the hope that she would attract other *murrungkurr* (tree spirits, at times referred to as spirit-children) to them. Since she already had seven children, Nungurrayi accepted the proposition. The biological parents of the twin are of the subsection nungurrayi/tjapangarti and, as I have explained, their children are tjapanangka/napanangka. The adoptive parents of the twin are nakamarra/tjapaltjarri. Negotiations took place in 1987 to change the little girl's subsection from napanangka to nungurrayi. She will always have the option, depending on her life trajectory and circumstances, of claiming one or the other of these subsections, but it is likely that nungurrayi will be the primary affiliation. When I knew her, she had two names: her adoptive father's late mother's name, and the name Yagga Yagga, so that she wouldn't forget her connection with the country where she was conceived.

Double subsection affiliations are not particularly rare. Marriages between first-degree crossed cousins (classificatory) are relatively frequent, as with the first example. A nangala who married a tjapanangka is in a similar situation. Their son is both tjapaltjarri and tjapangarti, but identifies himself most often as tjapaltjarri. Double affiliations don't really pose much problem, because usually the children belong to their father's patrimoiety. The more delicate cases are those that arise from irregular marriages, such as the union between two elders of Mulan, a nampitjin and a tjakamarra. Their son is both tjapanangka and tjupurrula. In this case, the mother, who is very involved in her country's ritual activities, wanted her son to keep his double subsection so that he could fully participate in the knowledge of his maternal country as *kurdungurlu*.

These examples show that real circumstances may require people to play with – or even play against – the system. Deviations and anomalies are inevitable; they have always existed and are by no means a consequence of colonization or imposed sedentarization. Several of the cases of irregular unions observed around Wirrimanu date from before the mission time, which proves that these are not a result of settlement. Some transgressors lost their lives, others were spared, and still others were allowed to continue their union in peace. All eventualities are possible, although each transgression of the Ancestral Law is generally punished in one way or another. The end result of unions such as these depends, in part, on the capacity of the people concerned to negotiate their choice and have it accepted on a collective basis. To the extent that they understand their 'model of reality,' Aborigines may interpret it or even occasionally manipulate it in order to satisfy both collective social requirements and personal desires. Negotiation is always possible. When such a need for negotiation arises, the couple concerned must be able to rely upon close relatives, and also must be able to support their claim with a thorough and confident knowledge of *Tjukurrpa* discourse and narratives, and examples of certain mythic episodes. I mean not episodes in which transgressor-heroes meet their deaths, but episodes such as the one in which the *Wati Kutjarra* incited people into irregular marriages.

Humans, non-humans, ancestral beings, territorial spaces, places, and ritual objects are included in the eight-subsection system. Far from being closed, this system integrates the most disparate elements, frequently including foreign ones – such as the majority of *Kartiya* who live for extended periods with the Aborigines – by identifying them with one of the eight subsections. By valuing inclusion more than exclusion, the system allows an openness towards the exterior and considerably broadens the scope of sociality by offering a means to extend and create relationships with new people, places, and ancestors. Not only does such a system present us with a universal complex of classification that can embrace everything that exists, it also confirms the networks of relations and responsibilities that endure between people and their social and cosmological environment, and that are intrinsic to the individual's identity and being.

This chapter has examined a number of interrelated aspects of Western Desert sociality and affiliations to land that demonstrate that the nomadic life of the Kukatja and their neighbours could not reproduce itself within closed and rigid frameworks. The degree of choice, variation, and flexibility in the spatio-temporal formation and transformation of different social groupings confirms the existence of a dialectic between the dimensions of autonomy and relatedness so eloquently demonstrated by Myers (1986a). Flexibility refers to the pragmatics of personal choice in the process of (trans)formation of various kinds of social groupings. The Aborigines are aware that the operational value of the established rules varies with context and with each person's ability to (re)interpret or (re)negotiate them. This is an intrinsic dimension of local knowledge. Myers has aptly expressed this in the following manner: 'As with relations to land, a negotiated quality characterizes much of Pintupi social life. Relationships among people are not totally "given" in the defining rules of landownership, residence or kinship. Instead, relationships must be worked out in a variety of social processes' (1986a: 159). Furthermore, the personal configuration of belonging, along with the non-finality of the *Tjukurrpa* itineraries, stimulates the creative participation of all members of society, because each person feels duly responsible, to varying degrees, for the *Tjukurrpa* essence of which he or she is an expression.

The various criteria that legitimize one's affiliation to not only one but several countries and their corresponding bodies of ritual knowledge are ideal examples of the need for openness in Western Desert sociality. Three points are particularly pertinent. First, when families used to move across vast territories with a low population density, the personal configurations of belonging, along with the networks of ancestral connections, ensured that each person had at least minor rights and claims to all the countries and places travelled through. Second, both traditionally and today, that composite identity increases the chances that all countries and all the *Tjukurrpa* segments would be claimed and held under the responsibility of a local group at any given time or place. An unclaimed country has a negative effect on all the local groups in an area. If it ever happened that the ritual and mythic knowledge linked with the country in question were lost, the vital essences of the country could not be renewed until a process of (re)discovery took place. Third, thanks to the configurations of belonging, each person acts as a kind of 'mediator,' sharing in the sacred knowledge of different local groups while at the same time respecting others' jurisdictions (Turner 1987). The best image to convey the multifaceted reality of social groupings and affiliations to land in the Western Desert is a series of concentric circles linked by paths that inherently connect people, places, and ancestors (see the first illustration in the photo section). The metaphor of the rhizome, that I have presented already with regard to the interconnected *Tjukurrpa* segments is also appropriate to convey such a reality.

It is important at this point to reflect further on the local notion of the person, as composite, 'dividual,' and permeable.[12] The Aboriginal person is not thought to be 'individual,' that is an indivisible and bounded unity, but is seen rather as a composite of intrinsic and reciprocal relationships among people, places, and ancestors; the person, human and non-human, in short, is a node within a nexus of relationships. These relationships are intrinsic rather than extrinsic and account for the dividual and divisible quality of the person. Ancestors and humans are 'divisible' in the sense also that their actions, objects, body parts, or bodily fluids contain the whole of their essence and link them to complex and dynamic networks. On account of *Tjukurrpa*, we have seen how all beings are consubstantial, and that all forms are permeable – hence the value granted to metamorphosis. This aspect of permeability accounts for different forms of exchanges among sentient agents, be they rocks, birds, humans, or ancestors. This permeability allows for communication and exchange of information between human and non-human agents. As a sentient entity, the landscape is receptive and thus responsive to human presence. As people move across the land, walking or driving, they literally engage in a dialogue with the various constituents of the land.

Chapter 4

Ways of Being, Relating, and Knowing

While being a hierarchically superior value, *Tjukurrpa* is immanent rather than transcendent; it is 'everywhen,' and its manifestations are part of daily life. *Tjukurrpa* represents a realm of action, a mode of experience, and a state of being that are coeval and consubstantial with the human realm. Ancestral essences and presences are embodied within the land as a sentient entity, and may interact and interfere with humans in their day-to-day lives.

In the Kukatja world, the manifold dimensions of relatedness among humans, and again among them, the land, and the ancestral order, are further expressed by the interaction and interplay among the different realms of locally recognized events and modes of experience: namely, the realms of everyday life, dreams, and *Tjukurrpa*. Although the Kukatja distinguish clearly among these orders of reality and realms of action, they do not establish any absolute division among them. These modes of experience are coexistent, and their ontological boundaries are permeable. To interpret an event or confirm the truth of her experience, a person may make reference to one or more of these realms of action.

The *Tjukurrpa* stories about ancestral performances and events are open to contextual and personal interpretations. They offer an almost inexhaustible source of knowledge, information, and imaginary on which the Aborigines can draw during their search for meaning, or to validate certain actions. Alongside the *Tjukurrpa* stories (and songs), which have a particular status, dream stories and stories of everyday life also offer a rich avenue for a better understanding of how the Kukatja and neighbouring groups conceive the interplay among dreams, everyday life, and the ancestral realm, and how in turn they may interpret and objectify events and personal experiences. In the Kukatja world, being and knowing always entail a relation (and thus a sense of responsibility) between humans, as well as between them and ancestral and non-human constituents of the dwelt-in world. In their daily engagement with the world, whatever is perceived and felt through any of the senses, whatever is experienced, whatever is dreamt is able to enhance their knowledge of the world, their understanding of the moment. Dreams and dreaming, to which I will now turn, are necessary to understand the intimate and reciprocal relations between humans and ancestors, and also, along with rituals, are a privileged medium of communication between these two modes of being.

Kapukurri and *Tjukurrpa*

Language groups in the Wirrimanu area use the term *kapukurri* (or simply *kapu*) or, less regularly, the term *winkirrpa*, to refer to dreams and dreaming. They might say, for example, *'Kapukurringkarna nyangu'* ('I saw it in a dream') (Valiquette 1993: 19).[1] Here, I explore some of the relationships between *Tjukurrpa* and *kapukurri* as two modes of experience and knowledge. While the *Tjukurrpa* and the dream realms are closely related, they nevertheless represent two levels of structurally distinct reality and experience; while they are not interchangeable, they are ontologically and epistemologically entwined. As modes of experience and ways of knowing, they both are inscribed in local theories of action (human, non-human, and ancestral) and are called upon to witness in the interpretation of events. They also share the same aesthetic and underlying narrative structure. As narratives and as experiences, *Tjukurrpa* and *kapukurri* are presented and received as *mularrpa* (true one). They are true, not in the sense of an absolute Truth but as true ways of knowing and relating to the world.

One of the ways to explore the relationship between *Tjukurrpa* and *kapukurri* is to look first at the different attitudes my companions adopted whenever I questioned them about *kapukurri* stories or about their own dream experiences. It took me a while to understand that such questions were inappropriate; very seldom do Aborigines ask others what they have dreamt the night before. In fact, among them, I seemed to be the only one to ask such questions in a straightforward manner. I realized later that this was a clear instance of 'symbolic violence' (Hastrup 1995: 142). This made me feel awful at times, even though my friends always did their best to make me feel comfortable.

My questions were often met by complete silence, or by expressions of puzzlement, amazement, or uneasiness. This was not out of lack of interest on their part – quite the contrary, as I was soon to learn. In the course of time, I understood that their initial responses reflected one important aspect of the dream realm; that is, its intimate relationship with *Tjukurrpa*. Dreams and dreaming are very serious matters that are not to be shared just anywhere or anyhow, or with just anybody.

My friends were accustomed to the *Kartiya*'s often alien or unexpected desires or requests. Some people expressed amazement at my interest in *kapukurri* stories, while others remained puzzled. Conscious that the *Kartiya* tend to use the same word, 'dreaming,' for both the dream experience and the *Tjukurrpa* realm, and accustomed to seeing them more interested in the latter, some thought that I had mistaken these two orders of reality. This became clear to me on the day that Napanangka went through the trouble of explaining the difference between *Tjukurrpa* and *kapukurri*. Though wishing to satisfy my request for *kapukurri* stories, she choose instead to tell me a *Tjukurrpa* story from her mother's country, Tjalyirr, on the northern edge of Lake Gregory. In this narrative, the mythical heroes have a dream that warns them of a coming danger.

> **Narrative 1** Two *maparn* [medicine men] were camping at Tjalyirr. In the morning, one of them recounted his dream from the night before. He had seen an old couple that they knew; the woman was preparing some damper [unleavened bread] from local seeds and poisoning it with the intention to weaken a young man. They killed him and ate him. Immediately after recounting the dream, both *maparn* stood up, took their spears, and decided to go after the couple. The old woman had told the old man to hide in a cave nearby while she went hunting for wallaby. Coming to the cave, the *maparn* gathered some spinifex [spiky desert grass] and laid it in front of the entrance, yelling at the old man 'Get up, get up, old man.' They set fire to the spinifex, and that was the end of the old man. They then went after the old woman and killed her.

Tjukurrpa stories such as this one in which the mythical heroes have dreams are quite frequent. They confirm that dreaming is a mode of experience and knowledge that the ancestors share with humans. Very often, when I asked the adults or the elders about their dream experiences, following, for example, a trip made to a site of significance, they would often choose rather to tell me a *Tjukurrpa* story about the place visited or about their country. It was as if, in the absence of a *kapukurri* story, there remained the more permanent realm of *Tjukurrpa*. These narratives, at least in their public versions, are always readily available and more easily communicated.

The attitude of the younger people, with their initial refusal to talk about dreams or to share their dream stories with me, is also significant. Some of the answers I received included, 'You should ask the old people, they know,' or 'The old people, they know how to dream, they know about dreams.' These comments express a connection among dreams, knowledge, and knowledgable persons. I also received similar answers whenever I asked them about *Tjukurrpa* stories of their country; even though they had heard these stories in their public versions, time and time again, they would immediately refer me to older relatives. Occasionally, younger people told me dream stories but only those heard from their parents or grandparents – there again, narratives that were already circulating within the public domain. I am not implying here that people are frightened of dreams, or frightened to talk about them, or that all dreams have a serious, dangerous, or sacred character. It is, rather, that in the dream sphere, as in the ritual sphere, the right to speech and the right to knowledge are gradually acquired and recognized through one's own engagement and participation in the world as a hunter, a forager, a ritual partner, a dreamer, or as kin.

The sign language of the Balgo area evokes the close relationship between dreaming and *Tjukurrpa*. The same sign is used to refer to both: the index and the middle fingers (right hand) are joined side by side and slapped two or three times in a repetitive manner on the top of the left wrist. Nungurrayi showed me a second sign, more recent and less widespread, that refers solely to dream experiences and narratives: the contour of a movie screen. She told me that in dreams she looks at her spirit travelling 'like in a picture' (see below).

Another way to explore the close relationship between *Tjukurrpa* and *kapukurri* is to examine local dream theories. For the Kukatja and neighbouring groups, a dream occurs while a person is asleep, when the *kurrunpa* (what we would usually translate as one's spirit) leaves the body to pursue various experiences and encounters. The *kurrunpa* relates to cognition, volition, and the expression of emotions (Peile 1997: 94). *Kurrunpa* also refers to the life essence and the vital forces;[2] whenever a person is sick or feels weak from exhaustion or lack of water or food, his or her spirit is also affected. *Kurrunpa* is associated with the *tjurni* (the abdominal area, the stomach, or sometimes the uterus), which is the seat of certain emotions: namely, anxiety, happiness, and sorrow (ibid.: 63). The *tjurni* is also associated with *maparn* (medicine man) power. For the Kukatja, there is a close relationship between dream experiences, knowledge, emotion, well-being, and strength (or power). For the Kukatja, there are two interrelated senses used in the acquisition of knowledge and understanding; in both cases, *kurrunpa* is the active agent. First, the ears function as the organ of thought (*kulila*) and are used to acquire knowledge through listening to others and to stories. Finding me one day in a thoughtful mood, a woman said to me, 'I look inside your ears to see what you are thinking.' In the waking state, the ear acts as the receptor of thought and understanding. Another such receptor is the *tjurni*, as the source of emotion and *maparn* power, the point from which the *kurrunpa* departs for dream experiences. While in the dream state, the *tjurni* acts as the receptor of knowledge. 'Openness' (*tintirrpuwa*, 'being open') is a fundamental quality in this state and can readily be seen as one's receptive, sensitive, and communicative skills. The term *tirintjarrpa*, meaning 'going right through,' is also used here; it refers to the permeability between one's bodily-self and the surrounding environment. Those who can 'open' their ears are said to be more suited to acquire knowledge and understanding; in a similar manner, a good dreamer is usually a person who knows how to 'open' his or her *tjurni*. An elderly woman said about her son, 'He is a good dreamer, he is open [showing her abdominal area].' In such cases, one's *kurrunpa* is knowledgable.[3] We find also this concept of 'openness' of the umbilical area in some of the healing rituals performed by the women. They use massage to help men or women who feel anxious. The massage is accompanied by healing songs and designs painted on the belly, and is focused on the abdominal area. It is performed mostly by pressing on the navel with the thumbs or the hands, and then in a repeated gesture of 'opening' up the *tjurni*.[4] This process of massaging and singing makes one's *kurrunpa* 'light again.'

The vital forces and the *maparn* forces are both located in the *tjurni*. *Maparn* refers both to the person who holds magical and healing powers and to the essences and the objects of their power. It should be stressed that the elders, all those men and women who are well versed in ritual matters and who have mastered the *Tjukurrpa* narratives, have developed, to varying degrees, their *maparn* power; very few, though, act as *maparn*, medicine (wo)men. In brief, someone who can 'open' his or her ears, or 'open' his or her abdominal area, has a power to relate to the world and will no doubt become a knowledgable person – a Law man or a Law woman. As knowledgable persons, the elders are usually, but not necessarily, seen as good dreamers.

Sign language[5] can also indicate the receptors of knowledge and the source of *maparn* powers. When one wishes to refer to understanding, memory, to a lack of these, or to a silly person, then the forefinger is pointed towards the ear (rather than the head, as we would do) in a rotating movement. To refer to the *maparn* drawing from his magical power to thwart some malevolent spirits, the right hand, partly closed as if to grasp something, makes a rotating movement on the umbilical area, as if to open it, extract the *maparn* forces, then pretend to send it in the direction from which the threat is coming.

Nungurrayi, an aboriginal friend, now deceased, taught me much about local dream theories and used many analogies to help me understand how she perceived and experienced dreams. She was a prolific dreamer who drew from her own experiences and 'metaphorical imagination' (Lakoff and Johnson 1980: 231) in order to engage in an intercultural dialogue and communicate to me the nature of these experiences. To help me understand the dream experiences as a 'voyage,' a 'journey' of one's *kurrunpa* (spirit) out of the body, she said once that 'it is the spirit that goes on walkabout.' On another occasion, she said that in dreams her '*kurrunpa* travels everywhere, like the Holy Spirit.' In another example, she said: 'When we are dreaming, we are thinking, we are feeling with our *tjurni*, we look at our spirit going away, like in a picture.' This aspect of travelling while dreaming is widespread, even to the extent that dream narratives usually specified the place where the dream action actually occurred (see chapter 5). This reinforces the importance of place in Aboriginal experiences and interpretations of events. Furthermore, this aspect of the travelling spirit, as detachable from the body, is another dimension of the 'dividual' person discussed previously.

Following on the analogical mode, Nungurrayi also compared dreams to 'telegrams.' In one of her dreams, she had witnessed a quarrel in Kiwirrkura, a settlement where many of her relatives lived. The dream left her with a strong feeling of discomfort and apprehension. A few days later, visitors brought news of a violent quarrel that had occurred in Kiwirrkura. As she recalled that experience, she said that dreams are like 'telegrams'; they are able to inform the dreamer and the community of events that have occurred or that will occur. On another occasion, Nungurrayi was feeling sick and was searching, in her dreams, for a healing sign. She explained to me then how *kapukurri* can be used as 'X-rays,' and added, 'We've got our own X-rays,' meaning that a sick person may observe the inside of her body and act upon it while dreaming. This is a skill that she had slowly developed over her life, and while she readily agreed that not everybody could do it, it was nevertheless a shared understanding and part of local knowledge about dreaming. These few analogies reveal the many potentialities associated with dream experiences, both as a way of knowing and relating and as a field of action.

Another quality granted to the dream experience, and related to the aspect of 'openness' and of the travelling spirit, is its 'permeability'; that is, a dream is not exclusive to the dreamer. This permeability implies that other dreamers can penetrate one's dream, at times unbeknownst to the dreamer, and that communication can occur between two or more dreamers. There were also cases where, as dreamers dreamed, they decided to enter another person's dream, attracted by the action occurring in the dream setting. Local epistemology recognizes and values interpersonal communication in dreams. This permeability and communicative potential of the dream state can be seen in the following example. Nungurrayi, who was well versed in ritual matters, told me one morning how in the previous night's dream she had been singing some sacred-secret men's songs. Aware that the men who were sleeping in nearby camps could hear her in their own dreams, she took great care to sing very softly. It was not so much because she feared that the men would reprimand her for singing their sacred-secret songs but rather to show her respect towards the sacred knowledge under their responsibility, and also to avoid having younger (and uninitiated) dreamers hear the songs.

Another form of this permeability of dreams is the 'shared dream.' In the Wirrimanu area, it was not uncommon for two individuals to share the same dream. Both dreamers usually would share the same camp overnight and would find themselves in the same dream setting and action.[6] In one example of this, two elderly sisters, two napanangkas, while sharing the same camp overnight, had the same dream. This occurred during a women's ritual gathering at Paruku (Lake Gregory) in 1988 that lasted for three days (see chapter 6). In the morning of the second day, the two women recounted how they had each found themselves in the same dream setting where two *Mungamunga, Tjukurrpa* women, had come to visit them. The *Mungamunga* had come to express their disapproval of some ritual sequences from the *Mina Mina* (see chapter 6) that the women had staged the day before. The *Mungamunga* did not know that particular *Mina Mina*, and they wanted some other songs performed. One of the dreamers added that the *Mungamunga* were 'real jealous mob.' It must also be mentioned that the day before, while on the ceremonial grounds, a few women had felt the presence of these ancestral women. No one questioned the authenticity of either experience. For the dreamers, their dream encounter became a rather strong argument to stage ritual sequences from their own country.

Tonkinson (1970) has given, for the Mardudjara (or Mardu) living at Jigalong, several examples of such 'shared dreams.' These include how the medicine man can travel with less experienced (and less knowledgable) people in their dream travels to their country and protect them from malevolent spirits. Similarly, Nungurrayi, who was suffering from severe headaches and wished to be cured by a *maparn* from Kiwirrkura, told me how they had both met in a dream and he had then performed a healing ritual on her. This permeability of the dream state also accounts for a higher receptivity to others in the dream state. Love-magic songs are used to influence the dreamer while in this state of heightened receptivity. The beloved will hear the suitor's love song in his or her dreams and be attracted to the singer. There is, however, a counterpart to the permeability and receptivity of the dream state: that is the vulnerability of the dreamer's spirit, particularly of younger ones, and the possibility that sorcerers or malevolent spirits could choose that moment to induce sickness or to cast a spell.

Because of these aspects of permeability and receptivity while dreaming, one's spirit is able to gain knowledge in the dream state. Knowledge is used here in a very broad sense: that is, knowledge about the land in terms of hunting and gathering resources; knowledge about specific sites to which the dreamer is related; knowledge about the well-being of relatives living in other communities; or sacred knowledge, as revealed in dreams by *Tjukurrpa* beings or dead relatives. Conversely, dreams can also be a means to steal knowledge, particularly sacred knowledge, songs, or designs. A knowledgable person can use the medium of dreams to gain access to knowledge otherwise concealed from him or her.[7]

Dreams and dreaming, as we are starting to see, are a privileged space-time that allows access to the *Tjukurrpa* realm. They are a medium of communication with the ancestral beings and the deceased relatives, both of whom can only be seen in dreams (though one can feel their presence in the waking state). At the same time, dreams and dreaming are a mode of experience that can be narrated and interpreted with no connotation whatsoever to the *Tjukurrpa* realm (see chapter 5). The distinction between dreams from *Tjukurrpa* and 'ordinary' dreams is not always obvious. Some dreams, such as those in which a dreamer encounters a *Tjukurrpa* being, are easily identified as *tjukurrmaninpa*. This expression means 'I had a dream,' and indicates clearly that the dream is linked to the *Tjukurrpa* realm. But not all dreams are so readily identified. The following dream narrative testifies to such uncertainty. It was told to me by Tjampitjin, who was well versed in ritual matters and renowned over a vast area.

> **Narrative 2** Tjampitjin is walking on the spinifex plain. Seeing a sand dune, he decides to walk towards it. He climbs on top of it, looking for a suitable place to establish his camp for the night. He realizes then that the dune forms a circle with a depression in the centre; it is as round as a dam [cattle hole]. He walks down into the middle of the circle to establish his camp. He makes a windbreak to protect himself. He lies down and, looking above, realizes that the sky is black. He keeps on looking and wonders about this blackness, repeating to himself, 'All black? All black?' He decides at once to leave the place, carrying his spears with him.

This dream left Tjampitjin quite puzzled. Upon narrating it in the morning, he repeated on many occasions, '*Kapukurri*, little bit *Tjukurrpa*.' Without any noticeable *Tjukurrpa* sign, the overall atmosphere of the dream and the feeling that it left him with made him think that his dream could contain a message 'from *Tjukurrpa*.' He was not certain how he should interpret the blackness of the sky, as a good or a bad omen. In the days following his dream, he still could not make sense of it in a satisfying manner. Vivid dreams that leave such a strong impression on the dreamer usually are kept in mind, in the hope that some future event might clarify their meaning.

Dreaming, far from being a private and inner experience, is directed outwards, allowing one's spirit to open up to the world, a world, however, inhabited by powerful beings and entities whose motivations are not always clear or benign. The following three dream experiences and narratives will clarify further the coeval nature between humans and ancestors, and the way they might, at times, engage in intimate relationships with one another. The first one of these *kapukurri* stories was told to me by Napangarti, an elderly woman who has been blind for most of her adult life. Like all women of her age group, she was very active in the ritual sphere. Furthermore, and in spite of her blindness, she was amazingly skilful at digging into the sandy soil and sensing *karnti* (desert yams), *tjirrilpatja* (pencil yams), or any other tubers; in a gathering party, she was often the one who would collect the greatest number. Napangarti lived with Tjampitjin, the brother of her first husband (who was still alive at the time and living with his younger wife). The day before the dream, a party of about twenty men, women, and children from Yagga Yagga had driven to Walkarli, some fifty kilomtres to the south-west of Yagga Yagga, to hunt kangaroos. Walkarli is one of the dwelling places (*ngurra*) of the *Kanaputa*, Digging Sticks Women, from *Tjukurrpa*.

> **Narrative 3** That night, the blind woman was visited in her dream by two of the *Kanaputa* of the nakamarra subsection. These *Tjukurrpa* women called out to Napangarti saying, 'Might be our man you are with?' The women started growling at her, they were 'jealous over Tjampitjin.' Napangarti refused to comply with their requests and told them to go away.

As she explained afterwards, the *Kanaputa* (who are often identified with the *Mungamunga*) are 'real jealous mob.' Though she said it was 'just a dream,' Napangarti seemed nevertheless proud that the *Kanaputa* had shown an interest in her *nyupa* (spouse), proud, too, that she had succeeded in confronting them. Aware of the magical powers of these ancestral women, the dreamer did not let herself be intimidated or frightened by their loving desires. Knowledgable in ritual matters and in the *Tjukurrpa* realm, Napangarti had previously encountered ancestral beings while dreaming. She would usually approach them, at least in certain contexts, with all the self-assurance and strength of a Law woman.

From childhood onwards, each person becomes permeated, to varying degrees, by the events and gendered characters of the mythical landscape, mostly those associated with one's ancestral connections. This is done mainly through stories and ritual performances, but also through travelling across the land. It is far more than simply a cognitive matter. The person's sense of self, experiences, and life itineraries (and responsibilities) unfold in close relationships with such connections. Individuals can develop a high level of empathy with particular ancestral characters. Their dreams are also impregnated with such events and characters. The next example testifies again to the interplay between the *Tjukurrpa* and the human realms, with dreams as mediators. It too was narrated by Napangarti. The dream occurred, as she says, 'long time ago' (which could mean anytime from her childhood onwards), and Napangarti had since inserted it into her own version and understanding of Yunpu, one of her main ancestral connections. Yunpu is associated with the cannibals (*kunatarkaratja*); they were eating the people of the area until the *Wati Kutjarra* confronted them (see chapter 2).

> **Narrative 4** In her version of Yunpu, Napangarti tells how she found one day a lone cannibal child and decided to take him with her [Napangarti is childless, though she brought up the eldest daughter of her first husband's second wife]. Worrying about the lost child, the *Yunpu* started to look for him and finally found him at Napangarti's camp. In their anger and in order to punish her, they beat her back black and blue.

When Napangarti first told me that story, she did not mention that it came from a dream. I thought it was an episode of that *Tjukurrpa* with which she directly identified herself, as Aborigines often do when they refer to some ancestor in the first person. It was upon hearing other versions of Yunpu from other people that I realized that this episode of the lost child was absent. Some time later, when I asked her again about her story, she specified that it came from a dream, and added that since that event she periodically suffers from very painful backaches. On the basis of local knowledge, her experience and narrative are true (*mularrpa*), and they are moreover an integral element of her life (hi)story. This example is also revealing on another level. The relation that Napangarti established between her body pains and an encounter with some ancestral beings is not unusual: one's bodily-self is permeable and vulnerable to the actions and moods of human and non-human agents.

The following example was narrated by Nungurrayi, the elderly woman who used analogies to help me understand the dream experience. This dream occurred in the early 1980s while she was travelling to Jigalong for initiation ceremonies. One night, along their way, they camped near a site associated with the *Yunpu*, the cannibals. It is said that at that place everyone should remain silent in order not to disturb the *Yunpu* or arouse their anger. That night, she had the following dream:

Narrative 5 My spirit [*kurrunpa*] been walking to secret place, women's Dreaming. I came across a little boy, like Tjangala [she is referring to my son, then three years old], but skinny one. I hear like an engine, like powerhouse [she imitates the sound of a running engine]. Then, I see lights: red, yellow, and purple. That little boy been pinched me on the thigh, to attract my attention. Then, he takes me by the hand to a group of old women and men. They are sitting down. That little boy, like a witch, real skinny one. He changed into a rock, right there in front of me. I sat with the old people.

For her, there was no doubt that her dream was 'from *Tjukurrpa*.' The metamorphosis of the young boy into a rock is a convincing element, but also the strong excitement she felt while dreaming and upon waking up was another proof. The elders in the dream entrusted her with relevant pieces of information that she chose not to share with me. Like other dreamers, Nungurrayi stored, within her vast repertoire of remembered dreams, the dream experiences that had left her with rather strong impressions. She said: 'I like keeping in my mind a little while. The dream gets clearer.' When I asked her how she managed to remember so many dream experiences and narratives, she simply answered, 'I open my ears, long way.'

The following example reveals the strong interplay between the *Tjukurrpa* and the dream realms. In September 1987, my husband, our son, and I went on a bush trip to Lappi Lappi with two anthropologists from the Central Land Council (Alice Springs) and a group of elderly men and women from Wirrimanu and Yagga Yagga. Even though it was a permanent rock hole and an important meeting place traditionally, Lappi Lappi had seldom been visited since the establishment of the mission. We arrived there on the third night of our travels. The elders, however, refused to establish the camp near the rock hole, frightened by the possible visit of *Warnayarra*, the Rainbow Snake, while dreaming. Because they had not visited the site for many years, the elders were not certain what to expect from *Warnayarra*. They feared that he (or some of the deceased relatives who now dwell there) might have wanted, as they said, 'to make humbug for [them] not having look properly after the place.' Tjupurrula, a respected Law man, who was the only one in the group with close ancestral connections to the site of Lappi Lappi, decided to protect the others' sleep by remaining awake overnight, singing to the Rainbow Snake and to the spirits of deceased relatives who dwell in the area.

Dreaming of Conception and Death

The close relationship between the ancestral and the dream realms is also explicit in the local theories of conception. In the Western Desert, as in many other parts of Aboriginal Australia, the dream is perceived as a transitional space-time, and is the necessary medium for the passage of the spirit-child from *Tjukurrpa* to the human realm at conception, and vice versa at death. In local representations and discourses, it is said that the child has been 'dreamt' or has been 'found.' These terms refer to the process of conception, where the spirit-child makes its presence known through a dream and then comes into physical contact with the mother and enters her body to take on a human form. This process is reversed at death for the return from the human realm to the *Tjukurrpa*. After a death, close relatives often confirm that they were informed of an impending death through a dream. At both conception and death we see how dreams prefigure significant events, and at the same time are a space-time that allows a transformation (or passage) from one state of being to another.

Saying that the child has been 'found' or 'dreamt' means that his or her incarnation and passage from *Tjukurrpa* to the human realm has been accomplished, after a process of metamorphosis, or a series of these (see below). The dream appears as an intermediary in human socialization. This is a universal theory in Australia, one that is amply documented in the ethnographic literature.[8] Australian Aboriginal theories of conception have given rise to many debates and misunderstandings among scholars, stemming mostly from the social-evolutionist perspective and from modern Western science, which stresses only the biological aspects of reproduction and denies the (co)existence of all other logic. Local conception theories were, more often than not, interpreted as Aboriginal ignorance of physiological paternity. After Warner, Meggitt (1962a: 273) rightly noted that, depending on the context and the informant, the Aborigines would refer either to the sexual act or to the action of the *kuruwarri* (spirit-children). Leach (1966) tried to end this decades-long debate by stressing the 'logical structuration' and the 'theological subtlety' of Australian Aboriginal conception theories. Tonkinson (1978) has admirably fleshed out the question by demonstrating how at Jigalong, for example, the elders seemed strongly inclined to want to ignore physiological paternity. According to him, and following the local dominant theories, physiological paternity is to some extent 'superficial,' even 'contradictory,' considering the sociological and ideological necessity of a conception through the action of the spirit-children.

The Aborigines' recognition of a cosmological explanation of conception does not deny the recognition of a biological one; it simply suggests that the first is far more important than the second in establishing one's being-in-the-world, identity, and networks of social and ritual relationships and responsibilities. In local ontology, such recognition confirms Aborigines' interest in and personal relationship with ancestrality as a generative force, rather than solely a matter of descent. Napangarti, mother of eight, told me about how and in which country she had 'dreamt' each of her children; every conception story is an important part of one's life (hi)story. At the end of these eight stories, I asked her, with all the zeal but also the ignorance of the ethnographer, how one could 'dream' a child. Astonished by my ignorance but nevertheless sympathetic, she whispered in my ear that I simply had to sleep next to my husband, 'on the same pillow.' I should mention that young mothers in Wirrimanu now use modern contraceptive methods; but this does not prevent them from continuing to have a conception story for each child, a story that confirms the child's incarnation from *Tjukurrpa*. I will now turn to the process of transformation (and metamorphosis) of the spirit-child from *Tjukurrpa*, and the associated conception stories.

In the Western Desert, the site of conception, the place where the spirit-child entered the mother's body (or, in other words, the country where the mother first experienced morning sickness), is a nodal element in one's personal configuration of belonging (see chapter 3; see also Peterson 1972; Myers 1986a; Merlan 1986). Each child is the living, actual expression of the *Tjukurrpa* being (and essence) dwelling at the site where the child was 'found.' As an adult, that person will become the custodian of the Law pertaining to that site, along with the other countries that are part of his or her own personal configuration of belonging.

In local representations and discourses, a dream is necessary to validate or confirm the passage of the spirit-child from the ancestral realm to the human realm. It is through dreams that the spirit-children announce their intention to take on a human form. The dream allows the process of metamorphosis to occur, even though such a dream might go unnoticed or unrecorded by the parents and close relatives. Outside the dream realm, prior to or during the first stages of pregnancy, the spirit-child will adopt different forms (an animal, a plant, or a natural element). It is often described as a trickster who enjoys teasing his or her future relatives. The permeability and transience of all forms, be they human, non-human, or ancestral, account for this aspect of metamorphosis.

The *Tjukurrpa* of the site of conception must be distinguished from the mediator of conception, the *tjarriny*, to which I will now turn. Kaberry (1938: 280) and Tonkinson (1991: 80) translate *tjarriny* (*djerin* or *jarrin*) by 'conception totem.' I prefer to use the expression 'mediator' or 'agent' of conception. In its widest sense, *tjarriny* refers to the process of conception itself; more precisely, it refers to the form of the animal, plant, or natural element that the spirit-child had momentarily taken before coming into contact with the mother, following the announcement of its arrival through a dream or some unusual event. In some cases, the *tjarriny* and the *Tjukurrpa* of conception may be identical. For example, at a site along the ancestral pathway of *Karnti* (Yam Man) where there are yams growing, the spirit-child can momentarily take the form of a yam, which the mother then ingests. The yam will be the *tjarriny* of the child-to-be, while at the same time the child will be the incarnation of *Karnti*. Usually, though, the *tjarriny* and the *Tjukurrpa* of conception are different, as testified by all the examples gathered in the Wirrimanu area (see also R. Berndt 1976: 144; Tonkinson 1991: 81). A person does not maintain any specific relation or obligation towards his or her mediator of conception, except sometimes for an emotional bond.

The *tjarriny* is relevant only in that it allows one to retrace the process of metamorphosis of the spirit-child and to identify the site of conception. While the dream is the liminal space-time that validates the passage from *Tjukurrpa* to the human realm, the process of conception also brings into play an unusual event that occurred during waking. The local theory of conception demonstrates the junction of the dream realm, the *Tjukurrpa*, and the waking world, and allows us to see how these modes of experience and realms of action interact, intertwine, and are manifested in one's own life. The spirit-child is from *Tjukurrpa*, 'dreamed' of by the mother, the father, or a close relative, and momentarily takes different forms in order to come in contact with the mother in waking life, usually through ingestion, but also through touching or seeing. Any body marks on the newborn offer indicators or proofs for the identification or confirmation of suspected forms of the *tjarriny*.

Whenever a woman becomes aware of her pregnancy, she will recall, with the help of her husband and close relatives (usually female), peculiar events that have occurred recently, such as hunted game that had unusual behaviour, a plant with an unusual shape, a dream, or some food ingested that made her sick. The parents, often with the help of close relatives, are responsible for retracing the thread of events linked to the conception of their child, understood here as a passage from *Tjukurrpa* and a transformation. They must identify the *tjarriny* and the site of conception. To do so, they recall recent unusual events and their dreams. The story of conception they construct is not only an integral element in the child's life history; it also confirms his or her intimate relation with the ancestral realm. It goes without saying that the identification of the *tjarriny* of the child-to-be and the site of conception are of a sociopolitical nature, although this does not exclude elements of a more contextual or emotional nature. The narrative (re)construction that retraces the process of transformation of the spirit-child and the conception is irremediably linked to an experience, usually an unusual event that occurred in early pregnancy. It is not necessarily a dream experience. In the stories that recall the process of conception of their children, some parents may include a dream experience: either the mother, the father, or a close relative has heard the child calling out in a dream, or, after eating some bush food that made her sick, the mother saw in a dream the spirit-child. Such mention of a dream experience appears more like a narrative convention. Whenever a dream does occur during pregnancy, one that can be interpreted as a dream of conception, it becomes a welcome addition to the story of conception, but it is not necessary. In their narrative, the majority of parents put more emphasis on events that occurred during the waking state rather than on a dream experience. The following examples of conception stories will clarify this.

In the mid-1980s, Nungurrayi gave birth to twin girls. With the help of her sister, husband, and sisters-in-law, she recalled the thread of events that accounted for the various metamorphoses of the spirit-children in the early stages of the pregnancy. One day as they were 'out bush' some twenty kilometres north-east of Wirrimanu, the sister and her two sisters-in-law found two yams (*karnti*) in the same hole, close together. That same day, in the same area, the group found two blue-tongue lizards and some particularly big bush onions (*tjunta*). Afterwards, the party came to the conclusion that these three cases were the spirit-children of the twin girls taking different forms. Some time later, still early in the pregnancy, one of Nungurrayi's sisters-in-law was digging for yams and felt something right behind her back. She turned around and there was a snake, which looked at her before crawling away. In the afternoon, Nungurrayi's nephew was bitten by that same snake. The father of the boy succeeded in sucking out the venom; the boy could have become quite sick but, as they explained, it was only the twins who wanted to play a trick on their cousin. The mother added that, to this day, the twins keep on teasing him. This narrative demonstrates how the spirit-child can adopt different forms over the course of pregnancy and go through a series of metamorphoses. The spirit-child here, as is often the case, is presented as a trickster, teasing and playing tricks on its future relatives.

Another example is the conception story of Nungurrayi's son. He was born in the mid-1970s, during the period when the people of Balgo were acquiring the *Tjulurru*, a travelling cult that came from communities to the west (see chapter 6). One morning when Nungurrayi was having a shower, she saw Cowboy, one of the figures of the *Tjulurru*, in the doorframe. She described him as wearing a black hat, a blue shirt, and white pants. She shook her head so as to make the image go away, but Cowboy remained in the same place. After that encounter, she had her first morning sickness. A few days later, her husband went hunting and killed a bush turkey. The spirit-child, who had first taken the form of Cowboy, had now transformed itself into a bush turkey. The latter is the *tjarriny* of her son, who holds a specific relation with the *Tjulurru*, his *Tjukurrpa* of conception.

The following conception story was told to me by Napurrula and her classificatory sister. One day, at Balgo, they were searching in the bundle of cult objects for a mother-of-pearl shell from Broome, an important object of ritual exchange. They found the shell, but discovered huddled up inside it a blue-tongue lizard (*lungkurta*) and her babies. Carefully putting them aside, they washed the shell and put it in their bag. That afternoon, the classificatory sister dreamed of a little child, and said to the child 'I am your mother.' The child answered 'No, you are not my mother. I am still looking for her.' Upon awakening, the dreamer told Napurrula that a spirit-child was searching for her. Napurrula gave birth to her fifth child, whose *tjarriny* is the blue-tongue lizard and whose *Tjukurrpa* of conception is the ancestor identified with the ritual object.

Another example is that of Nakamarra, who had 'gone bush' for a few days with her husband, their two children, and a few relatives. Along their way, they stopped to do some hunting. At that time a snake slipped, without their knowledge, underneath the car frame.

That night at their camp, the snake came out of its hiding place and curled up next to its future father. In the morning, when the children discovered the snake, they started to tease it with a stick. The snake became quite annoyed and tried to bite them. Nakamarra got hold of a stick and prepared to hit the snake, with the intention of killing it; as she did so, it inclined its head as if to better accept the blow, as in a communicative gesture. A few days later, when Nakamarra experienced her first morning sickness, she knew the snake was the spirit-child of her child-to-be.

Another conception example is that of a lone cloud, shaped 'just like a *murrungkurr*' (often used to refer to the spirit-child). It was seen by many people at Wirrimanu the same day a boy was born at Christmas Creek. The close relatives concluded that the cloud, the child's *tjarriny*, was from Kutal. The child's father and mother had affiliations with the site of Kutal (a rainmaking site) and its surrounding countries; the child was therefore an incarnation of Kutal as well as a future custodian of that site.

An element that is rather frequent in narratives about conception relates to how the spirit-child, seen in the form of an animal, suddenly disappears, not to be seen again. Nakamarra, the mother, was playing cards at the Balgo Homestead (Ngulipi). From the corner of her eye, she noticed something on the rock walls of the house and thought that it was a rope. She looked more closely and saw a poisonous black snake lifting its head. She jumped up quickly and joined the others in searching for it; but the snake was not to be found. As Nakamarra said, 'It just vanished.' The following day, they went hunting. Seeing a kangaroo, two of the men started shooting at it. Somehow, the kangaroo dodged all the bullets and kept on standing there. Nakamarra's brother finally shot him dead. The snake and the kangaroo were later interpreted to be the transient forms of her son-to-be. Another narrative element that is recurrent in conception stories tells how the spirit-child, embodied as an animal that has been killed, shrinks in the heat of the fire. As the game cooks on the fire, it gradually loses 'all its fat,' becoming 'all skinny one.' In such cases, the mother will know that this is her child-to-be and may refuse to eat it, knowing that she might become sick from it.

We see from these different conception stories that, during pregnancy and up until birth, the spirit-child can continue to adopt different forms and metamorphose at will. It is as if it is neither completely human nor completely from *Tjukurrpa*, but rather in a liminal state of being. The spirit-child and the many forms it may take during the process are definitively agents that intentionally interact with humans. It is through the Aboriginal engagement with the land as a sentient entity, and through daily interactions with non-human agencies, that the conception, the passage from *Tjukurrpa* to the human realm, is made possible. Far from being passive, the parents have the responsibility to be receptive to surrounding signs and to recall, confirm, and locate the process of transformation of the spirit-child into the human realm; they are guided by criteria of a contextual, mythological, sociopolitical, and emotional nature.

In the context of settlement life, the opportunities for the parents to select a conception site for their children are fewer than in the past (see also Bell 1993: 143). In order to establish a belonging to and a set of rights for their children at Wirrimanu, the parents tended to select the *Tjukurrpa* associated with the site of the settlement. This was a strategic choice on their part. A number of the local children now have as their *Tjukurrpa* of conception either Kingfisher (*Luurn*) or the Two Initiated Men (*Wati Kutjarra*). There are two creeks running past the community, dry for most of the year: the one to the east is associated with Kingfisher (and the *Marwuntu*), the one to the west (just behind the men's ceremonial hut) is associated with the Two Initiated Men. Spirit-children were left at the creeks by these ancestors and can therefore be found there. Even when the *Tjukurrpa* of conception are located in other countries, the children still have an interest in the above *Tjukurrpa* and some rights to these Laws through their residence at Wirrimanu. The same kind of choice occurred after the establishment of Yagga Yagga for the children conceived in that country or surrounding ones.

Some parents still seek, however, to diversify the *Tjukurrpa* of conception of their children for the sake of enlarging the child's configuration of belonging, and to ensure the (re)production of networks of territorial and social affiliations. Napangarti was proud to tell me that every one of her eight children was 'dreamed' in a country other than Wirrimanu, either while she was 'out bush' with her husband and relatives, or while she was visiting relatives or participating in a ceremony in another community. Napangarti was not an exception. As we have seen, the Aborigines at Wirrimanu and Yagga Yagga like to travel. They regularly go 'out bush' for hunting and gathering trips, or travel to other communities for personal, ritual, or mourning purposes. While a woman is pregnant, each one of the countries crossed can become the site of conception of the child.

Anthropologists have put much emphasis on the role granted to the dream realm in the Aboriginal theory of conception, but none, at least to my knowledge, has ever mentioned the same discursive and ideological reference in the case of death.[9] Whenever a death occurred at Wirrimanu or a neighbouring settlement, someone, usually a close relative of the deceased, would say that she or he had dreamt it. Such dreams are as meaningful as those that announce a conception, because they allow and validate the return to and merging of the person's *kurrunpa* (spirit) with *Tjukurrpa*. The dream appears as a transitional space-time that accounts for a transformation, a passage from one state of being to another, as it does at conception. The dream of death usually occurs prior to the death, but the dreamer usually conceals it, unsure or unaware of its meaning, until the announcement of the death. Then and only then – that is, after the event – is the meaning of the dream confirmed. In most cases, it was another deceased relative who had announced the death in a dream; in other cases, an element in the dream that had remained unexplained became meaningful for the dreamer upon hearing of the death.

After hearing the news of the death of one of her male relative from Kiwirrkura, Nungurrayi recalled the following dream from a few weeks earlier:

Narrative 6 'I am going to sleep. Some people from Narangtjatu [a place on the Canning Stock Route] had been lighting fire. There is smoke and I am just watching. Then, I am singing out [calling out], long way. I start walking. From there, I look around. I see a tree and a stick been spinning, spinning, spinning, like willy-willy [small tornado]. I tell the others not to look. The light from that fire is coming close up now.

Though Nungurrayi felt that the spinning stick was certainly the sign of something, she remained unaware of its meaning until learning of the death. At that moment, she knew that the dream was a prelude to the event. While a close relative is more liable to act as the receptor of such a dream, to some extent it can be anyone who was acquainted with the deceased. Certain dreams explicitly portray the death of someone known to the dreamer. In such cases, as if to brush aside any sense of fatalism, I have seen people interpret the dream as allegory, not literally. Often, then, the dream is interpreted in a classificatory manner. A young woman, for example, dreamt the death of a close tjampitjin relative; the elder to whom she recounted her dream told her that it might concern anyone from the tjapanangka subsection and belonging to the other patrimoiety. But maybe he was just trying to soothe her anxiety. With death, as with conception, the dream plays an active part in the flow of events, in the unfolding of reality. The high frequency of dreams in references to a death suggests that, more than simply announcing the event, dreams *allow* the passage from the human realm to the ancestral realm. This is in accordance with the knowledge that at death one's spirit usually returns to one's country and joins or merges with the ancestral essences of the area. It is through dreams that ancestral beings or deceased relatives communicate the news of an impending birth or death. In both cases, the dream appears as the witness and the space-time of the passage from one realm to the other. In theory, if not in fact, the dream confirms a conception or a death.

Neighbouring Others

The ancestors are not the only non-human agents who inhabit the land and coexist with humans. Other categories of 'neighbouring others'[10] also appear in local narratives and are involved in everyday events. These are, among others, the *murrungkurr*, the *pamarr karatja*, the *wanya*, the *Walawalarra*, and the *Mungamunga* (as groups of ancestral women), as well as two recent added figures, the Cowboy and the Three Ks. Coeval with humans, and part of Kukatja sociality, these neighbouring others are tangled in local historicity and subject to transformation. Some of these categories of beings and characters may become obsolete over time, while new ones may appear. With the exception of the *Walawalarra* and the *Mungamunga*, they are rarely, if ever, identified with particular places or ancestral itineraries. Narratives told about these 'hidden others' allowed me to outline their physical traits, personalities, and motivations, and the contexts of encounters with humans, including dreaming.

Murrungkurr is usually translated by the Aborigines as the 'little people' or 'little fellows.' The *murrungkurr* are usually described as dwarfs.[11] They live mostly in trees,[12] and on a few occasions my Aboriginal companions pointed out groups of trees, some with excrescences on their trunks, as the *ngurra* (camps) of *murrungkurr*. Their favourite foods are *karnti* (desert yams) and bush honey. According to some people, the *murrungkurr* tend 'gardens' of these, and whoever gets too close puts themselves in danger. There is a messenger bird that warns humans of the proximity of these gardens; one then knows to keep away or to take another route. The *murrungkurr* usually have beards, which testifies to their old age and confers upon them the status of elders. In light of their personalities, their small stature, their beards and their preference for tree dwelling, the *murrungkurr* can easily be compared to gnomes.

The *murrungkurr* are sometimes identified with the spirit-children (*kuruwarri*), and in some contexts the two are synonymous. In this case, it is said that the *murrungkurr* live in water points or river beds. Napurrula told me that one of the manifestations of the Rainbow Snake living along Sturt Creek and around the community of Billiluna carries *murrungkurr* on his back, which he leaves at various water points while travelling along. At one such place she 'found' the spirit-child of her daughter. When identified as spirit-children, the *murrungkurr* can metamorphose at will. Such identification of the *murrungkurr* with the spirit-children appears also in the following dream narrative told by Nungurrayi, a mother of nine children, who had been sterilized at Derby hospital after her last childbirth:

> **Narrative 7** One night, as she was sleeping, an old *murrungkurr* came to visit and see if she had milk. She felt his beard on her chest and breast. But she knew that she had no more milk and that the little man would find nothing. She woke up with a start, searching everywhere for that *murrungkurr*, but in vain. Her mother-in-law, who was sleeping nearby, had heard the visitor but had not seen him.[13]

The personalities of the *murrungkurr* are complex and multifaceted. They, like the spirit-children, are tricksters and are responsible for acts with a whole range of intentions and motivations, at times divergent ones. Whenever an object disappears in one of the camps, it is said that it is an act of the *murrungkurr*, who have come to take it more often to tease than out of meanness. Sometimes, they might even return the stolen object! By accusing the *murrungkurr*, people can avoid calling one of their relatives the offender. When it is a hat or a bag of flour or sugar that has been stolen, the offence is of course minor; it is another matter when it is a sacred object that has disappeared. The *murrungkurr* can also act as *maparn* (medicine men), and sometimes a recovery from illness is attributed to their healing powers. They can also induce sickness. Tjapangarti, from Yagga Yagga, was one of their victims.

Narrative 8 Tjapangarti dreamed that he was collecting some wild honey, probably in one of the *murrungkurr*'s 'gardens.' As soon as they saw him, they started to hit him. Tjapangarti woke up at once. The next morning, in such pain from a backache, he had to be transported to the regional hospital in Derby.

Tjapangarti's dream experience and encounter with the *murrungkurr* is, as he said, *mularrpa* (true one); it draws from a collective representation that is open to interpretation. It would be both hasty and incorrect to establish a general relation of the type 'dreaming of the *murrungkurr* causes backaches.' If we recall Napangarti's narrative (narrative 4), her backaches were the outcome of a dream encounter with the cannibals (*Yunpu*). These narratives are interesting in that they establish a relation between a dream experience (and an encounter with a non-human other) and a physical ailment.

As elders and *maparn*, the *murrungkurr* are also known to be well versed in ritual matters. The following dream of Napangarti, the blind woman (see narratives 3 and 4), is an example of this:

Narrative 9 Napangarti was visited one night, in her dream, by two 'little people' with beards. They had come to teach her new songs and dances in relation to a ritual associated with her country. Seeing that she was blind, the *murrungkurr* decided that it was not worthwhile and turned back. She called them back, but in vain.

The *pamarr karatja* are a group of 'neighbouring others' referred to less frequently than the *murrungkurr*. Often portrayed as women with very long hair, they resemble human beings except that their bodies are covered with stones (*pamarr*) that glow in the night. The younger Aborigines often like to imagine them covered with precious stones, such as diamonds or opals; this may be out of their understanding of (and puzzlement at) the *Kartiya*'s desire for these. In more recent descriptions, they wear long white dresses rather than stones. According to some people, they can only be seen at night, while a number of other narratives testify to their appearances during the day. The *pamarr karatja* are cave dwellers. My friends insisted also on the fact that they speak all Aboriginal languages. Unlike humans, they never lack *kuka* (meat) and *kalyu* (water), both of which they store up in abundance. During traditional times, it is said, they used to give assistance to people in need.

Their favourite foods are the *muntunyapa* (python), the *tjapiyinti* (possum), and the *tjilkamarta* (echidna).

Like the *murrungkurr,* the *pamarr karatja*'s relationship with humans is rather ambiguous, and can be either positive or negative. The *pamarr karatja* can provoke accidents (in today's context, events such as car accidents) or frighten people; on the other hand, they might decide to favour a group with a good hunt or help to release a vehicle stuck in the sand. In their feminine form, the *pamarr karatja* are often described as seductresses, of whom men should beware. In this aspect of their personality they are like the *Mungamunga* (see below), with whom they are often associated. Other narratives identify them with the *kunatar karatja*, which are cannibals or a kind of witches. According to some people, the *pamarr karatja* protect the sleep of humans. In this form, they are called *mungayagga* (silence of the night). However, one should always beware of them, because the *pamarr karatja* may try to steal children at night from the camps or to seduce a lone male.

The *Walawalarra* and the *Mungamunga* are groups of ancestral women who travel across the land and underground and periodically make their presence known. During my fieldwork, they manifested themselves on a few occasions and were referred to quite frequently. While the *Walawalarra* and the *Mungamunga* are closely related, they can be distinguished by their respective geographical origin. The *Walawalarra* come from Pitjantjatjarra country, to the south, whereas the *Mungamunga* originated in northern regions (C. Berndt 1950; R. Berndt 1970; Reay 1970; Dussart 2000; Glowczewski 1991; Rose 1992). They are identified with different mythical itineraries and rituals. The *Walawalarra*, along with the travelling cult ritual cycle that bears their name (also called the 'Bush Way'), were introduced to the Wirrimanu area in the late 1970s and early 1980s (see chapter 6). The *Mungamunga* have been present in the ritual life and the mythical landscape of the area since the 1950s (R. Berndt 1970). Sometimes, both are identified with the *Kanaputa*, the Digging Sticks Women.

In the Wave Hill area, according to C. Berndt, the *Mungamunga* are young women identified with the 'Old Woman,' a major mythical figure in northern regions (1950: 31). At Yarrilin, the *Mungamunga* 'do not give birth' and 'stay young and lovely forever, roaming this earth at will' (Rose 1992: 95–6). At Yuendumu, a Warlpiri community, the *Mungamunga* are depicted as young and fat ancestral women with shiny skin (Dussart 2000: 151). In all cases, the *Mungamunga* usually appear to humans in dreams, where they reveal new songs, dances, or designs. In the Balgo area, according to R. Berndt, the *Mungamunga* are the daughters of the *Kanaputa*, the Digging Sticks Women. Only one person described them like this,[14] while the others described the *Mungamunga* and the *Walawalarra* as adult and mature women well versed in ritual matters, endowed with strong magical powers, and who refuse men's company and advances. Generally, the *Mungamunga* and the *Walawalarra* are described as wearing the *yinpintji*, a ceremonial band made from threads of spun hair (usually human), strung with the non-edible beans of the *kumpupanu* tree, and worn around the head and the forearms. They have long hair, long underarm and pubic hair, as well as a long clitoris. They are usually encountered in groups of two.

During my main periods of fieldwork in the 1980s, there were frequent narratives of encounters with these *Tjukurrpa* women; at the same time, the local women were involved in major ritual exchanges with women of neighbouring communities. As sequences of the *Walawalarra* cycle (or 'Bush Way') were performed on a regular basis, it was understandable that the *Walawalarra* themselves were attracted to the ceremonial site; they heard the songs or felt, while underground, the stamping of the dancing feet. The *Walawalarra* and the *Mungamunga* would make their presence known through dreams (see the example of the 'shared dream' given earlier). While only seen in dreams, they can manifest their presence by other means, either by giving a slap on someone's shoulder, by singing, or by making the wind blow.

The two following narratives tell of encounters with the *Walawalarra*. The first one was told to me by an elderly napanangka, one of four sisters who were senior custodians of the *Walawalarra* cycle at Wirrimanu. While we were translating the songs associated with the ritual, she explained to me the recent origin of two of the songs. She told me about her brother, Tjapanangka, and the experience he had had a few years earlier as he was living at Yuendumu. Tjapanangka, now deceased, had lived in Balgo for many years (I had met him during my first stay) before going to Yuendumu. He was widely renowned for his ritual knowledge and *maparn* power.

Narrative 10 The old Tjapanangka was having one day a heated dispute with his younger wife. He threw a few boomerangs at her, which she dodged. As he was picking up his boomerangs, two *Walawalarra* came and carried him away in the air, from Yuendumu all the way to Karrinyarra, a hill in the direction of Kintore. In order to punish him for his behaviour, they did not let him rest: for days, they made him walk through the bush, with only short periods to rest under small bushes offering little shade. During that time, in Yuendumu, his wife and relatives searched everywhere for him, but Tjapanangka had disappeared. The *Walawalarra* kept him for many days; in the end, they gave him two songs for him to give to the women. Tjapanangka's relatives finally found him a few days later while searching for him in the bush, by himself.

Although the narrator did not mention it, this event could be derived from a dream experience, because it is usually through dreams that the ancestors reveal new ritual knowledge. The songs that were given to Tjapanangka have since then been included in the *Walawalarra* cycle. This narrative is also instructive in that it demonstrates, first, the revelation (and innovation) of sacred knowledge, and how an individual experience can contribute to enriching an already-existing ritual corpus (see chapter 6). Second, we see how men can contribute new ritual sequences to the women's rituals, and vice versa. And finally, in this narrative, as in the following one, the *Walawalarra* are presented as the protectors of women.

Narrative 11 In the early 1980s, a party of men and women were returning to Balgo after a few days at Papunya. The women had received a *kuturu* [ceremonial pole] associated with the *Walawalarra* cycle, which the Papunya women were in the process of exchanging with the Balgo women. They had stopped at Rabbit Flat, a service station and a bar on the Tanami Road, on the way to Balgo. After a few hours there, one of the men took the *kuturu*, which had been carefully wrapped in cloth, and hit his two wives, two Napanangkas who were the main guardians of the *Walawalarra* cycle. That night, the *Walawalarra* came to visit him in his dreams. He woke up the next morning with a swollen foot, and as soon as they arrived in Balgo, he had to be flown to the Derby hospital.

Most likely the man was drunk (though no mention was made of it in the narrative) when he handled the *kuturu*, otherwise he would have kept away from the sacred object belonging to the women, knowing well that he would be liable to attract the wrath of the ancestral women. This narrative confirms the power of the *Walawalarra* and through them the women's own power. I would also add that this narrative is similar to previous ones in that a physical ailment is attributed to a dream encounter with ancestral beings.

The following narrative presents another category of beings, the *wanya*. In the Wirrimanu area, *wanya* is a generic term that applies to evil spirits or malevolent sorcerers. They are spirits or humans who have temporarily become invisible; they are never described physically, unless they have temporarily taken the form of an animal. They are ill-disposed towards humans. They may or may not leave footprints on the ground. They are often identified with the 'feather foot,' those sorcerers who wear emu-feather sandals to avoid leaving tracks. Although the Aborigines are masters in the art of track reading, the *wanya* can still evade discovery, and it is impossible to identify them. As a general rule, the *wanya* are humans (or their spirits) who have temporarily made themselves invisible; one can sense their presence, but cannot see them. The *wanya* are often thought to be sorcerers from neighbouring communities who have come in a disguised form to cast a spell upon someone. The *wanya* are a temporary state of being, rather than a category of beings. Many elders in Wirrimanu and Yagga Yagga, both men and women, told of personal encounters with *wanya*, in which they either succeeded in killing (the men would kill them with their spears), escaping from, or scaring away the *wanya*.

Napanangka, the eldest of the four sisters mentioned earlier, was a prominent Law woman who told me of a few instances where she and her companions had to deal with the *wanya*. These events occurred in the 1970s, while she was living at Papunya, during a performance by the women of the 'Bush Way' or *Walawalarra* ritual that was later exchanged with the women of the Wirrimanu area. As a site of women's Law, the ceremonial ground is strictly forbidden to men. The narratives of the encounters with the *wanya* told by Napanangka all share a similar underlying structure. The following example is representative:

Narrative 12 It was the middle of the day and a group of women had gathered at the ceremonial ground, on the outskirts of Papunya, to stage some sequences of the *Walawalarra* cycle. Napanangka left the group for a few moments to urinate. At that moment, she caught sight of the hair of a *wanya* who was hiding behind some bushes spying on the women. Rejoining the group, she warned the other women of the *wanya*'s presence. They said among themselves, 'Look, there is a black dog spying on us.' They dared not say, 'Look, there is a man,' otherwise he might have run away. The women formed a line and started dancing in a circle and singing songs from the *Walawalarra*. The man [*wanya*] got up, he was staggering, made dizzy by the songs. He walked away with difficulty, and the women never saw him again.

In this narrative, as in other ones, the *wanya* are men, either strangers or foreign sorcerers, curious about the women's Law. In each case, the women cannot or prefer not to identify them. In other versions, the *wanya* are not only rendered dizzy by the dances and the songs, they are also hunted down by the *Walawalarra*, who then punish them by either beating or killing them. Such narratives, along with the previous ones of the *Walawalarra*, confirm the ancestral power of the *Walawalarra*, and through them, the women's own (ritual) powers. Another interesting aspect of the narrative presented above is its resemblance to the *Tjukurrpa* stories of the ancestral women (the *Kanaputa* or the *Mungamunga*), who, as they travel over the country dancing and performing ceremonies, are more often than not followed and spied on by men who try either to seduce them or to steal the sacred and powerful objects from them.

Two more recently introduced figures are the Cowboy and the Three Ks. While the Cowboy is representative of the Aborigines' contact history with the *Kartiya*, the Three Ks portray a facet of their current relations with the *Kartiya*. From the contact period onwards, the Cowboy played an important role in the lives and worlds of local Aborigines while they worked on cattle or mission stations. A number of women's love songs, which I had heard from the elders, were about seducing Aboriginal cowboys. It is no wonder that John Wayne's characters in Western movies have caught the local imagination. In the Wirrimanu area, the Aborigines drew John Wayne's heroic cowboy character out of the movie screen and have incorporated him into the local mythology, into the local scene and flow of events. This local appropriation of an introduced figure, which is almost an irony of colonial history, is most salient in their interpretation of the *Tjulurru*, an important travelling cult that was introduced to the Balgo area in the 1970s (see chapter 6). The Cowboy has two manifestations, the 'good' Cowboy, personified by John Wayne, and the 'bad' one. I will examine here the latter. Cowboy is usually described as a tall man mounted upon a horse (either black or white), wearing a hat (also black or white), with a gun at his belt, and smoking a cigarette. According to some people, John Wayne killed him, although he (or his spirit) still inhabits the region. During the 1980s, his manifestations were rather frequent. Whenever he is seen mounted upon a white horse (or wearing a white hat), it is usually the sign of a forthcoming accident; mounted upon a black horse (or wearing a black hat), it announces a death.

Napangarti, who was then in her mid-twenties, told me of a personal experience that occurred during her initiation to the *Tjulurru*. Two camps had been established at the outskirts of the community, one each for the men and the women respectively. During the initiation to the *Tjulurru*, the novices are forbidden to talk among themselves and must remain silent. If necessary, they can whisper to the adults and elders who accompany and instruct them during their initiation.

> **Narrative 13** One afternoon, during the seclusion period, Napangarti had gone to sleep under the shade of a tree. Before doing so, she noticed an axe had been stored in the branches over her head, something not unusual. While she did not appreciate the axe hanging above her head, she went to sleep anyway. She then had a dream where she saw the Cowboy mounted on his white horse. When she woke up, she found a bullet of a .22 in her hands. She immediately told her dream experience to her mother and a few elders. Later that day, her mother's sister had to be flown to Derby hospital and her father also got sick; both recovered in the following days. As for the bullet, her narrative was received and taken at face value, and even more so during the initiation to the *Tjulurru*, where it is expected that Cowboy will manifest himself in a convincing manner. The young woman, one of the very few of her generation deeply involved in women's ritual business, had gained respect and acquired some status as a Law woman, partly by demonstrating, through her dream narrative and encounter, her knowledge and understanding of the *Tjulurru*.

As a general rule, seeing Cowboy, either during the waking state or in a dream, is perceived as a bad omen. On a few occasions, when remembering car accidents they had had over the years,[15] my friends would often mention that, just prior to the unfortunate event, they had caught sight of Cowboy, mounted on his white horse. On the other hand, Cowboy can also give a helping hand. Napangarti told me of one such instance. One day as she was travelling with some of her relatives along the Tanami Road, their car broke down. They had no water, a situation that can be problematic in the hot season. They had been searching around for a water point for a few hours when she saw Cowboy some distance away. She grew worried over his presence, fearing that he might bring some trouble. But her grandmother reassured her at once, stating that Cowboy had come to guide them to some soak water, which they found not long after. What at first aroused a negative feeling, sighting Cowboy, is turned around by the elder into a positive event. Though the Kukatja world is filled with malevolent spirits and revengeful sorcerers, though they live in a harsh environment, though many stories have dramatic and fearful overtones to them, it must be said that the Kukatja rarely indulge in fear or frighten themselves over bad omens. Fatalism is rejected. Whenever someone is frightened or anxious, there will always be an adult or an elder trying to reassure them.

The other figures of recent introduction are the Three Ks. I first heard stories about them during a short stay in the area in 1998. The Three Ks are *Kartiya* men, very tall and strong and with tattoos on their arms; according to some people, they drive around in blue cars and usually in groups of six. Like the *wanya*, their intentions towards humans are malevolent. They are most often identified with town settings, where they drive around with the sole intention of chasing Aboriginal people leaving bars late at night. It is said that they beat, mutilate, and even kill their victims on the outskirts of town. Recently, according to some, they have started driving from Alice Springs along the Tanami Road and have been seen around nearby outstations and even in the vicinity of Wirrimanu. Many stories about the Three Ks were told at night time, about how they had mutilated or killed someone from a neighbouring community. Not only were these narratives received as *mularrpa* (that is, as true), they are in today's context relevant to certain aspects of the relationship between the Aborigines and the *Kartiya*. To a great degree, the frightening stories of the Three Ks have supplanted the narratives of other frightening figures such as the *wanya* or the *pamarr karatja*. They have also replaced the stories about the malevolent Cowboy, who had been a dominant figure during the 1980s while the *Tjulurru* was very important in local ritual life. Unlike the *wanya*, the Three Ks leave their tracks behind them, and whenever we happened to come across unidentified vehicle tracks while on our way to an outstation or driving around for hunting or gathering purposes, it was not long before someone would suspect the presence of the Three Ks.

Whenever I asked my friends the meaning and origin of the name 'Three Ks,' they shrugged their shoulders in ignorance. I then asked an Aboriginal friend in Alice Springs, a Warlpiri woman from Yuendumu, and she laughed at me for not knowing that the term is in fact derived from the Ku Klux Klan. She said that the Aborigines in Balgo would probably not have known about the Ku Klux Klan, and that the term

'Three Ks,' and stories about them, had been circulating in Alice Springs for the last few years. My friend was quite surprised that the stories about the Three Ks had already travelled through the Tanami all the way to Balgo. From her point of view, these stories had a beneficial effect on some of her relatives visiting from Yuendumu, who now preferred to stay home rather than hang around the bars until late at night.

An element about these narratives that captures my attention (and my imagination) is the fact that these *Kartiya* men were thought to be the associates of Pauline Hanson, the founding president of the One Nation Party. I was even told that the Three Ks had been trained by Pauline Hanson[16] to attack Aboriginal people and kill them; this tale represented their interpretation of Hanson's right-wing discourse. Stories of the Three Ks certainly portray an important dimension of the present-day experiences and sufferings of the Aborigines, including alcohol abuse and its violent and often fatal outcomes: fights outside bars or car accidents. The narratives of the Three Ks, in one facet, are evocative of Aboriginal drinking cultures. On the other hand, they can also be read as an Aboriginal statement, if not an icon, of the nature of the relationship between the Aborigines and the *Kartiya*. These narratives are in sharp contrast to the national discourse over 'reconciliation' that dominated the Australian public arena in the 1990s.[17] Taken together, these two narratives, one of reconciliation and the other of the Three Ks, coexist in the reality of today's Australia, but issue from two different worlds that are in sharp contrast to each other. The 'optimism of the rhetoric' of reconciliation (Mulgan 1998: 180) or the right-wing discourse can receive unexpected readings when they are heard on television by a campfire in the Gibson Desert. As John Wayne's local appropriation represented an irony of colonial history, the Three Ks represent one of the ironies and paradoxes of so-called postcolonialism.

The narratives of personal experiences and encounters with the *murrungkurr*, the *pamarr karatja*, the *Walawalarra* and *Mungamunga*, the *wanya*, the Cowboy, and the Three Ks – as well as all the ancestors who dwell in specific places or keep travelling over the land – show that these 'neighbouring others,' and agencies, are contextually referred to in the interpretation of events. They exist on their own and make themselves known to humans when they wish. Local descriptions of them may vary, even to a significant degree, depending on the narrators' age groups, gender, ritual affiliations, or involvement with Christianity.

Another major figure in the Western Desert, and also widespread in northern regions, is the Rainbow Snake, known in the area as *Warna-yarra*. The Rainbow Snake can manifest itself in various forms. One example occurred in November 1987, while the people of Wirrimanu and Yagga Yagga gathered at Mulan in preparation for initiation ceremonies. One afternoon, a man who had been sick for some time (he had just come back from a Perth hospital) died in his sleep. His death caused no surprise whatsoever, because the man had been suspected for some time of having killed, by sorcery, a young man from a northern community. It was well known that the relatives of the victim had thrown his clothes into the waters of Mistake Creek, one of the *ngurra* of the Rainbow Snake. Smelling the odour of the murderer, *Warnayarra* had travelled south to provoke the death of the older man. That afternoon, in Mulan, many people had recognized in the shape of the clouds the presence of the Rainbow Snake. Nobody, with the exception of his two wives, mourned the man.

Through the narration of events and of personal experiences presented in this chapter, we have approached not so much a different world-view as a different way of being-in-the-world and a different way of interacting with the constituents of the dwelt-in world. We have seen how the Kukatja and neighbouring groups are 'governed by a different rationality' (Hastrup 1995: 73), a different objectivity. The *Tjukurrpa* and the immediate present are not categories of 'time,' 'events,' and 'actions' that are mutually exclusive, as some authors have suggested. *Tjukurrpa* does not represent solely an ancestral past that accounts for the present; it is also a 'socially acknowledged mode of experience in the immediate present' (Dubinskas and Traweek 1984: 24) that permeates the aesthetics and politics of everyday life. Ancestors, the spirits of deceased relatives, the 'neighbouring others,' and the living are all present in the world at the same moment. The 'invisibility' of the first three does not make them unreal; they can be seen in dreams and can manifest themselves in a visible form when they wish. In our attempt to understand local theories of actions and modes of interpreting events, it is inappropriate to work on a dualistic basis; for the Kukatja, there are no absolute divisions between the visible and the invisible, the real and the imaginary, the present and the ancestral past. Rather, the different realms of action and states of being feed into and inform one another. Among the *Tjukurrpa*, the dream realm, and everyday life there is continual exchange and a permeability of borders. The permeability of all forms and the permeability of the body of the land and the human body are part of the mediation process. All that there is – be it an ancestor, a woman, a spirit-child, a breeze, an ant, a bullock, or a rock, as sentient agents – all are engaged together in the unfolding of reality.

Such engagement requires, as we have seen, that one's bodily-self be 'open' to the world, receptive to its signs and permeable to its various manifestations (including malevolent ones, such as acts of sorcery that consist of piercing one's body with magical objects; acts that knowledgable people will usually be able to counteract). The local notion of power is understood as the ability to relate to the world, and to know it following intimate, and at times frightening, experiences with its many entities, rather than as having power over fellow beings, human or non-human (excluding acts of sorcery).

The Aborigines play with the (ontological) ambiguity between the realms of action and the modes of experience during their narration of events and personal experiences. In a similar manner, while interpreting an event, they may draw from the interrelation of the realms of action. In the contextual interpretation of events and experiences, personal motivation and improvisation are listened to and respected, although this does not mean that they cannot be contested and negotiated; their degree of validity and credibility may vary from one person to another.

Daily activities such as walking and leaving tracks on the ground, sensing the wind entering one's body, poking into a goanna hole, digging into the ground in search of tubers, and dreaming of one's country, as well as ritual activities such as dancing, singing, and painting, are all ways of knowing the world and relating to it. These activities, though, may have different meanings and outputs in different contexts and places. When it is said that some rocks at Kutal are the ears of the ancestors that dwell there, this should be understood in a literal sense and not as a metaphor. The consubstantiality and permeability of forms account for the exchange of substance and information among all objects and beings existing in all the possible realms of Kukatja reality. This information may be contextually interpreted by the Aborigines and made meaningful, but it is rarely done in a definite and closed manner.

Chapter 5

The Social Setting of Dreams and Dreaming

'We've been listening *kapukurri*. Sometimes bad news coming, We'll know then. Old people, they tell us these stories all right. From long time, we've been listening *kapukurri*, from grandmother, grandfather, auntie ...'
(Napangarti, Yagga Yagga)

The cultural system of dreams and dreaming, in its essential correlation to *Tjukurrpa*, was introduced in the preceding chapter, though not in its complete form. Dreams and dreaming appear as a realm of action and a mode of experience that are distinct from, although related to, the ancestral realm. The local theories of dreams and dreaming are closely related to the local notion of the person as a permeable, composite, and 'dividual' being. In this chapter, I examine dreams and dreaming as a meaningful realm of experience in daily Aboriginal life: the themes of dreams, their contexts of narration, and local ways in which dreams are shared and interpreted – the whole socialization process of the dream experience. In a sociality where the epistemology of dreams is tightly bound to the cosmology, and where dreams are often referred to in various contexts, I have chosen to concentrate not only on the content of dreams (taken alone, they would have been reduced to simple 'objects'), but also on the multifaceted potentialities of the realm of dreams and dreaming, at both the discursive and the pragmatic level. Analysing the various stages of the social setting of dreams in this fashion should fill a gap in the existing anthropological literature on this topic. Although anthropologists have recognized the innovative and mediating value of dreams in Aboriginal sociocultural dynamics, they have failed to comprehensively consider the place that dreams and dreaming occupy in Aboriginal sociality; nor have they mapped out the parameters of this realm of experience. It is essential to develop an overall picture of the dream process in the sociocultural dynamics of the Western Desert Aborigines before one can proceed to analyse dreams as ancestral revelations. Both dreams and revelations play an important role in the structural transformation of the ancestral inscription of the land, the *Tjukurrpa* pathways, and in the mytho-ritual creativity of contemporary groups (see chapter 6).

Dream Themes and Interpretations

In the Wirrimanu area, people do not recognize, in any explicit manner, different categories of dreams. The same term, *kapukurri*, is used to refer to all dreams. The comments and qualifications that accompanied the narration of dreams allowed me, however, to identify the main themes of *kapukurri*, as well as the contexts in which they apply. These themes that I have identified from a vast repertoire of dream stories are based more on the contextual scope of the dreams than on their actual content. Overall, they offer a guide to the vast and varied field of dream experiences and discourses experienced by the Kukatja and neighbouring groups.

One type of dream was called *wuunpa kapukurri* by one elderly woman, which she translated as 'shadow dream.' These are the dreams that are forgotten upon waking or that are judged to be insignificant. They are the least important dreams: they are forgotten or barely remembered; they make a weak impression on the dreamer or are considered of little importance; they are not worth sharing because they have no apparent contextual meaning; or they simply cannot be turned into a decent story. At the same time, this kind of dream is not entirely irrelevant: it shows that even in this society where the dream experience is highly valued, it is agreed that dreams may happen independently of anyone's will and do not necessarily have to be shared or given a meaning.

Another type of dreams are those linked somehow to the flow of events. They are the most frequently referred to in local discourse and are the object of more sustained social interest. These are the dreams that may announce an event that will happen, or an event that has already happened elsewhere. These message-bearing dreams apply to a range of contexts, including the following: dreams linked to foraging activities and game or plant resources on the land; dreams that announce a forthcoming visit from a relative or a stranger – and in the latter case, whether the visit is with good or bad intentions. Some dreams presage a possible danger or unfortunate event (witchcraft, conflict, and accidents); others point to an unexpected or unhappy event in the countryside or in another settlement, one that the people will only find out about afterwards. Other dreams may inform about the state of being of specific sites such as the dwelling places of ancestors and deceased relatives. Finally, there are dreams that announce a birth or a death, as discussed in the previous chapter. These constitute a theme in themselves, given that they confirm the metamorphosis and the passage from the *Tjukurrpa* realm to the human realm through conception or, conversely, a return to the *Tjukurrpa* realm through death.

In some respects, dreams that foresee an event or reflect an event that has already happened dominate dream discourse and interpretation. Dream interpretation is often done *a posteriori*, that is, after the occurrence of the announced event. A dream offers clues, allowing an idiosyncratic explanation to be developed, and it is never considered a definitive interpretation until confirmed by the foreseen event. One could almost say that in Western Desert logic, all unexpected events and all events involving a transition or a transformation are first manifested through dreams, sometimes as an expression of *Tjukurrpa*, before they occur in everyday life. This is a dominant characteristic of discourses on dreams and dreaming. Whenever an unexpected or unusual event occurs, be it happy or unfortunate, there is usually someone who says that they had dreamt it (or had been informed about it in a dream), either a few days, a few weeks, or even a few months before. Dreams are often seen as a prelude to significant or peculiar events, even though they may only be understood after the event actually occurred. Often someone will say, 'I knew it, I've been dreaming.' Obviously, it is difficult, if not impossible, to know whether there really was a *kapukurri* linked to the event, but this hardly matters; what counts is that such a. discourse is socially important.

Dream experience is not only an integral part of human and mythic action; it is also necessary to the day-to-day flow of events. In the Kukatja world, the activity of dreaming is as valued as the dream content. Even though the dream realm plays an active part in the flow of events and in the unfolding of reality, it does so without carrying any sense of fate or determinism. This last remark is most relevant in that it stresses the fact that the Aborigines' overall attitude towards dreams and dreaming is one of flexibility and openness. I always felt that they approached dreams as a kind of game, at certain times a most serious and sacred game, while at other times quite playfully.

A major dream theme relates to foraging activities and to resources available on the land. With hunting and gathering, it is preferable to dream of the sought-after game or plant beforehand; the expedition will be more fruitful because of it. One day a group of women had pursued a huge water goanna in vain for several hours, following its tracks along a dry creek bed, to the south of the old mission. When night fell, as we were driving back to Wirrimanu, they promised to continue their search the next day and told each other that they should dream of the animal that night in order to ensure a successful hunt. The next day they were successful in their pursuit (although an unsuccessful hunt would have been surprising since they had already identified the territory of the coveted game very well). One morning at Yagga Yagga, while sitting around the campfire, a man told everyone that he had dreamt about big fat yams. Even though it was rather early in the season (the end of May), the women set off into the bush, but with little conviction, to see if the yams were ripe enough. They weren't, so the dream had turned out to be irrelevant. In other cases, when people came back empty-handed from hunting or foraging, I heard them say, as if to console themselves, 'nothing – no dreams, that's why.' Such a remark attests to the integration of dreams and dreaming into the everyday flow of events and to the value of their collective appropriation. According to local discourse, though it is preferable for the sought-after game or plant to appear first in a dream, it is far from being a *sine qua non*. Moreover, such a dream appearance is often recognized only *a posteriori*, after the hunting or gathering trip, provided that it was successful.

People occasionally adapt their dream stories to the realities they encounter during their waking state, and may adapt these realities to their dreams. It is almost like a game in a world where dream facts and everyday facts are inscribed upon each other, and stem from the same theory of action. One woman told me of a dream in which she unearthed a handful of *kumpupanu* (inedible orange-coloured beans that are strung on spun hair strings and used in the fabrication of ritual objects) under the sand in a dry riverbed. The next morning, she found in the root of a bush a number of *lukurti* (highly appreciated edible larva). She corrected her dream story then, saying that it must have been *lukurti* in her dream and not *kumpupanu* as she had previously thought. Here again we see the close relationship between dream experiences and foraging experiences. It also demonstrates the element of play, because the dreamer adapted her dream to what actually took place. This is indeed playful, since it hardly needs to be spelled out that the Aborigines are well aware that successful hunting and gathering demands a thorough knowledge of the land, the seasons, and the available resources. When the facts corroborate a dream, or conversely when a dream corroborates the facts, it proves the integration of dreams with the flow of events. The dream can stimulate the hunt, though it is not necessary for a good hunt, even if discourse sometimes seems to suggest that the right dreams are a *sine qua non* of successful hunting. Hunting and gathering activities occurred very frequently in the dream stories of the adults and elders who had lived a nomadic life before the mission was established and who regularly continued to perform and spend time at these activities. This type of dream does not necessarily predict a good or bad hunt, but it usually provides a good story, and good entertainment. The Aborigines do not necessarily interpret a dream, unless future events evoke the dream's relevance to the dreamer.

Another aspect worth considering is the correlation between dreaming, both as a human action and a way of relating to the world, and land resources. Povinelli (1993a: 152–60; 1995) has demonstrated, among the Belyuen Aborigines (Northern Territory), how the land, elements of the landscape, and named places, as embodiments of ancestral essences and presence, are sensitive and responsive to the immediate by-products of human hunting activity, such as sweat and speech. This observation also applies to dreams and dreaming, as human products and human activity. Therefore, when people dream of their country or of specific sites, when they hunt and gather there, or when, before going to sleep, they express their intention to travel to their country while dreaming (either simply to visit a specific area or to meet dead relatives), they show not only that they are caring for their country, but also that they are contributing to the well-being of that country and to the regeneration of local resources (in their intrinsically linked cosmological and physical dimensions). Napangarti, a middle-aged woman, expressed a good illustration of this. While talking of the plant resources of her country, Mungkayi, she said, 'This is good country, we are good dreamers.' Obviously, she is not implying that dreaming itself is the source of the production and the regeneration of local resources, but that dreaming is a way of thinking, caring, feeling, and relating to the country, as a series of places that are sensitive to humans' attention, and that, in return, the country might respond positively. This example also demonstrates the permeability and consubstantiality between the bodily-self (that is, the person) and the landscape, as sentient agents who engage together in reciprocal relationships (Poirier 2004).

Gathering, along with hunting small game, are principally (but not exclusively) women's activities, and are the predominant themes in the four following dreams. The first two were dreamt by Napangarti, who is from Yagga Yagga. The first was narrated early one morning, while sitting around the campfire, to her husband, her sister, and myself.[1]

Narrative 14 That *nyinytjirri* [rough-tailed lizard] been walking. I've been tracking him in a log. I see the tail. I pull him out by the tail and hit him on my digging stick. Then I see another one. I pull him out and hit him. In another log, a small log, another rough-tailed, but no tail. Too much in a small log, big mob, and no tail again. I've been track him in spinifex. These two fellows been going in hole now (might be husband and wife). No tail. I get them. I show to the old man [her husband] and say 'Look, no tail.' I see a place cleaned by a rough-tailed. I got one *kurrkati* [a sand goanna]. Looking up a tree now, *walakari* tree [supplejack][2] for good firewood. It's getting cold now. The old man wants to cut it. I've been tell him 'Too big that tree, leave it.' Napangarti [her sister] been coming from other hunting. 'What have you got?' she's been ask. 'Big mob rough-tailed and one goanna. What have you got?' Nothing, old man and me [her sister's husband] got nothing.' [The dreamer] 'Maybe we can cook them here.' We cook and eat them there. We going back to Yagga Yagga now. Finish now that story.

A few days later, when I asked her what this dream meant, Napangarti told it to me again, but with more precision. She also accompanied her narrative with a graphic design on the sandy ground that showed the respective location of the spinifex bushes, hollow logs, and trees that appeared in her dream, and the animal tracks. The dreamer and her group didn't necessarily wish to interpret this dream. This dream made a good story (*palya wangka*); not only did some of the lizards have no tail, which is quite unusual, but even then, Napangarti succeeded in catching them. It must also be said that Napangarti is one of the best small-game hunters in the whole region and rarely returns to camp empty-handed. Furthermore, the listeners were glad that the hunt was successful and hoped that it boded well for the days to come.

Because the dream occurred in late June, at the beginning of the dry (and cold) season in the Western Desert, when the lizards and snakes hibernate until the next wet season, it is unlikely that the dream was concerned directly with the hunt for lizards.

Narrative 15 We've been go to hill place, east of Yagga Yagga. Looking for something around. These men [referring to her husband and his brother] are with me. These men been climbing up. That snake saw them. Biggest snake, *muntunya* [python, edible snake]. Good dream. That snake went in the cave. Men been coming, looking inside and wondering, 'Where has he gone?' I've been coming. Lighting fires all the way [so as to force the snake out of his hiding place]. I've been walking little way. I saw snake in the spinifex, another one snake. Lighting fire again. Following him in the hole. I've been chasing him. Nothing. I asked the men about that other snake in the hole. Nothing. I've been frightened. I've been go now.

The dreamer made one comment about this dream. Impressed by the size of the first snake, she said that it was a 'good dream' (*palya kapu-kurri*), and hoped that it boded well for future hunts (for snakes or anything else).

The next two examples were dreamt by Nungurrayi, the woman who used analogies to help me understand the manifold potentialities of dream experiences (chapter 4).

Narrative 16 I've been climb up. Three fellows are with me. Tjakamarra been leading. Two women are with him. We come to a first rock hole. There is water inside. The hole covered up with spinifex. I've tried to pull it. Too hard. I walk there to another rock hole [she draws on the ground two circles representing the rock holes]. Water inside. Covered up with spinifex all the same. I come down little way. Big mob *lukararra* [a type of sedge grass, edible seeds]. I sing out to the others. From there, we climb up. *Lukararra* everywhere, black and white ones.

Narrative 17 I tell you real story from last night. *Kapukurri*. I'm following tracks, *tjalapa* tracks [great desert skink]. I come to his hole. I've been pushing, digging. I've been get up now. Another hole. [She is drawing on the ground.] Spinifex here, and holes, here and here. I've been miss him, here on the right side. I go back the other hole and catch him by the head. From there, plenty women been start. They look like Warlpiri side. They want to cover up their camping place. I've been ask, 'Who are these women?' Four women been walking behind. We are standing up, hands on hips, waiting for these women to come back. These women been come back now. They are changed into sheep now. They make sounds like sheep. People never come up, only sheep been come up. Good story that one.

Nungurrayi did not interpret these two dreams for me; like Napangarti, she just told them to anyone who wanted to listen to 'good stories.' This does not mean that she did not have an interpretation for herself. The two narratives were accompanied by sand drawings, indicating the main features of the dreams. In the first dream, the *lukararra* seeds that she finds in great quantities are (or at least used to be) highly prized. Along with other types of grass seeds, they were an important food during the dry season and were made into unleavened bread.[3] The seeds are usually gathered at the entrance to ant holes,[4] then cleaned in a wooden dish, ground, mixed with water, made into a flat bread, and cooked in ashes. The dream occurred in early June, at the beginning of the *lukararra* season. Napangarti and Nungurrayi were prolific dreamers and, like others, they seemed to store up their dreams until they could be told at an appropriate moment. While they didn't necessarily give explanations for their dreams, they knew that the stories could be meaningful for some listeners or might possibly be relevant to future events.

The following dream is grouped under dreams that carry a message. This dream foresaw a coming event but was remembered and interpreted as such only after the event had happened. It was told to me by Napurrula who dreamt it while she was participating in women's rituals at Ringer Soak, a neighbouring community.

Narrative 18 The dreamer sees two men, strangers, coming towards her. They tell her to get up, which she does. She then sees an enormous snake climb up a tree. It comes back down and goes towards a nearby water-hole. She follows it and kills it.

The woman would surely have forgotten this *kapukurri* if she hadn't been asked, a few days later, to kill a snake seen at the water-hole near the camps. At the moment the dream is actually dreamt, it is usually impossible for the dreamer to know if it contains a relevant message or not. It is only when a related incident occurs that the dream experience is remembered, shared (unless it has already been shared), interpreted, and woven into the fabric of everyday events.

A dream can tell of an event that has already happened in another place. This was the case for a woman who dreamt of her classificatory brother from Kiwirrkura.

> **Narrative 19** Two fellows [referring here to her classificatory brother and his horse] been riding, coming in the bottom camp. The man is kicking kids and people, and the horse is running around everywhere. Myself and everybody we are walking west. The man is climbing up the window of a house trying to get to the people inside.

The day after this *kapukurri*, she learnt that her brother had started a big fight at Kiwirrkura a few days previously. Often, after a fight between two or more people, or after an accident, someone says that they were told about the event in a dream. It is not necessary for the dream to match the event in every respect, or vice versa; just a few details suffice to establish a relationship between the two facts.

The dream of the angry horseman brings us to another dream theme, which features battles or conflicts of interest between two or more people. The following dream, told by the blind female elder of Yagga Yagga (see narratives 3 and 4), is representative of this theme.

> **Narrative 20** Some people want to pierce a man's thigh with a *wurrum-puru* [a spear with a flat head]. The argument started because he coveted a married woman. The man runs to take refuge in the dreamer's camp [at the top camp in Balgo]; one of his pursuers catches up with him and throws a spear at him, cutting open his thigh. The dreamer cries and hits her head to show her distress. A general battle follows. Spears are thrown, thighs are pierced. Then, finally, the combatants sit down. But the hunted man gets up, looking for a fight again. The dreamer tries to stop him. At this point she wakes up, frightened, and looks all around her, shaken by this experience. She added: 'I thought they were fighting for real, but only a dream.'

Dreams of meeting long-dead relatives are another major theme. The deceased relatives that one might encounter in dreams are now identi-fied and united with *Tjukurrpa*, and often bear messages. Such dreams are generally welcomed for this reason, and also because it is enjoyable to be with loved ones. It is usually a pleasant experience, in which the dreamer may talk, hunt, or sing with the dead. A few people, particularly elders, told me about dream experiences in which they found themselves in such company, going hunting with them, or sharing their camp in specific sites in the land, or carrying out ritual sequences with them. One woman told me about a dream where she found herself on the site of the old mission, visiting different camps where the living and the dead were side by side; she shared their camp-fire and talked with them. She added: 'Poor bugger [fellow], all family belong us.' When she told this *kapukurri* to her husband, he envied her for it – as she said, 'Tjampitjin been craving for that *kapukurri*' – since he too would have loved to have been with his classificatory mothers and aunts again in such a dream. The dead relatives, re-identified with *Tjukurrpa*, can bring a message to the living about a death or an accident soon to happen. Yet I have never heard anyone describe such experiences as being unpleasant or frightening. In such cases, it was the news of the event that was received as unpleasant, not the encounter itself. In 1998, a young man told me how his deceased father had come to him in a dream to pass on his *maparn* powers.

Some dreams are related to illness. These dreams are generally interpreted after the illness manifests itself. The case of illness is the only time, except perhaps for periods of initiation, when a person will be explicitly asked to share his or her dreams with the *maparn* (medicine man) and the elders because of the link between illness and dream. Certain dream experiences contain signs that allow an ill person, the person's kin, or the *maparn* to identify the origin of the illness. The illness can be caused by some wrong done during a dream dreamt by either the ill person or his or her close relatives or friends, or it can be caused by a curse cast in a dream by sorcerers from other regions. In this type of dream, we see how the dreaming *kurrunpa* is permeable to ill intentions from outside the dreamer. The interpretation of the dream, if any, is fairly open. It takes into account, to varying degrees, the dream's content, the dreamer's social and territorial configuration, the dreamer's actions and those of his or her kin, the community's overall circumstances, and even relations with other communities. Moreover, the root of the illness may be a dream (see chapter 4, narratives 4, 8, and 11), just as a dream may be the ideal way to cure an illness, through utilizing the clues given in the dream about the origin of the illness.

Obviously, it is not only through dreams that the causes of the illness are sought. No aspect of the victim's and his or her kin's relationship with the social and cosmological environment is overlooked. When people are trying to discover the why and how of an illness (or a death), or trying to figure out reasons for an attack of witchcraft, many diverse theories and interpretations are developed (Reid 1983). The actions of the victim and of the family, in both their waking and dream states, are scrutinized. The victim's relationship to places, people, or objects that pertain to *Tjukurrpa,* along with their respect (or disrespect) for the Law, are also examined. *Tjukurrpa* places, ancestors, or members of neighbouring local groups that might have been offended by the victim's words or actions are identified. If the Law has been contravened, not only the well-being of the perpetrator is at stake, but also that of all his or her network of relationships, including named places.

Sometimes it is impossible to reach agreement on the precise cause of an illness. The process of speculation and linking of cause and effect allows people to evaluate a situation that may affect not only the victim but also other members of his or her entourage, and sometimes the whole community. In such a dwelt-in world, where all elements and constituents are inherently linked to each other, and where events are 'rhythmed' within a relational and process-oriented mode (rather than a linear one), a person's actions and words may have repercussions upon the entire social group and environment, even years later. This search for an explanation of illness reveals the role played by the idiosyncratic attitudes towards the cultural world of signs and the existence of a context-sensitive local schema for understanding events and relations that may exist between these. Social, political, ritual, and cosmological aspects are all taken into consideration. In the case of an accident or sudden death, all those closely linked to the victim feel that they have a responsibility to participate in the process of investigation and interpretation of the events.

In the previous chapter, I examined how dreams are perceived and experienced as a journey, as the wanderings of one's spirit out of the body (as a characteristic of the 'dividual' person). Journeys to precise places in the territory while dreaming, premeditated or otherwise, represent another important theme of dreams in the Western Desert. As a general rule, when a dream is told, an effort is always made to locate the exact site of the dream's action. This desire to find geographical landmarks is explained by the primordial value of places in one's composite identity and ancestral connections, and by Aboriginal 'spatial ontology.' The dreamer, sometimes with the help of friends and kin, tries to identify the site visited during the *kapukurri* through specific clues or vague impressions left by the dream. It is rare that dream narratives do not specify the scene of the action. The theme of travelling to one's country is particularly frequent in the elders' dream stories. Such journeys can be premeditated, in the case where the person expresses the desire to travel to a certain place before going to sleep. The two following dreams, though, had their geographic location established afterwards. Napangarti, an adult woman from Yagga Yagga, concluded that during the night she had been to Kutal, south-west of Yagga Yagga. Kutal is one of the *ngurra* of the Rainbow Snake and is also the ancestral country of the rainmaker, a Walmatjari man from Balgo who is the dreamer's classificatory brother. The dreamer's own country is Mungkayi, but she knows Kutal through a visit there the previous year, when she stayed several days with a group of people to do the rainmaking ritual.

> **Narrative 21** In her dream, Kutal has been changed. She sees hills that seem to have been formed by a mechanical crane. She is with her husband and the rainmaker. The sand they are walking on is very hard. They continue walking, going round the hills until they come to a particular place [a sand drawing accompanied this narrative] from which they survey the surroundings. They retrace their steps and then return again to the same place. At this point, the hills start to shake and shake and shake. The three people start to run and run and run. A huge snake shining like metal comes out of its den. They take shelter on the other side of a hill, and she thinks she recognizes one of the hills near Balgo.

The dreamer and her husband link this dream with another one that she had had the year before at Kutal itself, while they were there for the rainmaking ceremony.

> **Narrative 22** At Kutal, she sees the snake come out of his den. He has a white head. The dead ancestors have made him come out of his shelter and have forced open his mouth. While one of them holds the snake by the throat, the others set about pulling his teeth out, one by one.

These two narratives suggested to the dreamer and her husband that the Rainbow Snake may have temporarily or permanently left Kutal, which would be disastrous, not only for the rainmaker and his relatives, but for the whole community. In narrative 21, two major clues indicated to the dreamer that she was in Kutal: the presence of the rainmaker and that of the mythic Snake. Oil companies explored in the region of Kutal in the early 1980s. The site has since become a major concern for its traditional caretakers. They have undertaken proceedings to protect the site from all future exploration. In times less dangerous for Kutal – that is, if the oil companies were not present – the dream might have been interpreted differently, or even identified with a different *ngurra* of the Rainbow Snake, another place where he might also surface.

The site of the following dream experience was also established after the fact. It was dreamt by the same woman.

> **Narrative 23** While she is hunting small game, the dreamer sees the tracks of a snake. She starts to follow them and she finds herself in front of a huge snake with green and yellow spots [she points out that it is not edible]. The snake hides in a tree. The dreamer's dog, her faithful companion and an excellent hunter, manages to take the snake's head in his mouth and kills it. The woman is proud of her dog and praises him for a long time.

The unusual colour of the snake led Napangarti to suppose that it might be a snake from Talapunta, a place about thirty kilometres south of Yagga Yagga and part of her configuration of belonging. The *Tjukurrpa* story tells of a terrible battle between snakes that took place at Talapunta; they came from all directions and were of all different types. Her dream experience at Talapunta made her think that someone must have recently thought or talked about the place. This explanation reinforces the idea that dreams are particularly permeable to outside influences, a realm (and a state of being) of increased receptivity to others' thoughts or spoken words. The following example, too, can be explained by the permeability of dreams; at the same time, it relates to a dream journey.

> **Narrative 24** People been come from Kiwirrkura with a round plane like a boat. No wings on that plane. Plenty women, only women. That plane been land now, other side Mulan, at the Business camp [ceremonial ground]. From there, six women been come out. Napurrula, Napaltjarri, all come out of the plane [she named the six women]. They take branches from a tree and start walking towards that place, waving the branches [a rite performed whenever one approaches a ceremonial ground for the first time]. Walking that way now to the women's bough shed. Real one this story, *mularrpa* [true one]. Their spirit travelling.

Because of her dream, Nungurrayi knew that these Kiwirrkura women (their spirits) had travelled to Mulan while dreaming; in her own dream, she had met them at the ceremonial ground. This occurred in November of 1987, and the initiation ceremonies were soon to be held at Mulan. Because of a phone call a few days earlier, she knew that some of these women wished to travel to Mulan to participate in the ceremonies, in the flesh, not just in the dream state.

In the case of dream journeys, sometimes the dreamer cannot identify the exact location of the dream, as the following narrative from Nungurrayi demonstrates.

Narrative 25 Nungurrayi is walking across the spinifex plains accompanied by another person [?]. She climbs to the top of a sand dune and sees in the distance a windmill and a few makeshift camps. She reaches them, but there's nobody there. The windmill is turning and the water tank is overflowing. She follows some tracks and realizes that some people came to fetch water recently. She continues to walk and comes to a group of women sitting down. Farther on, a White man is also sitting on the ground. Nungurrayi approaches the women and introduces herself, saying her name.

The dreamer knows that that night she had travelled southwards, a 'long way south,' and that she had met people whom she had never seen before. But since she had never been to that place, it was impossible for her to identify its location precisely.

As stated above, journeys undertaken in a dream can be premeditated. This type of travel in a dream is easily identified because it follows an explicit intention that the dreamer formulates beforehand. People can dream with the specific goal of visiting their countries of belonging to bond with a particular place or to converse with the *Tjukurrpa* being or a deceased relative that dwells there.[5] A dreamer can also decide to visit close kin who reside in another settlement, mostly if they are worrying about them. For example, an elderly woman who had heard from a visitor that her son had just left the hospital (he had kidney disease), decided to visit and meet him at Lajamanu (where he lived) in her dream. Another woman, while in a dream, went to Kiwirrkura to consult with a respected *maparn* who was also a relative of hers. Tjampitjin, one of the elders of Yagga Yagga, told me that a few decades ago, when he was guarding sheep alone near the old mission, witches attacked him. They had come from the south-west and spirited away his kidney fat, which is where the life force is stored. The man fell seriously ill for several weeks; according to a missionary, he was in a comatose state. Then one day, he travelled in his dreams to the witches' country (apparently to Jigalong) in order to get back what they had taken away from him.[6] He recovered quickly after that dream, and left the old mission for a few months to live in his country. This dream experience represents the positive outcome of an illness identified through a dream experience. After that dream, Tjampitjin's own *maparn* power, and his knowledge of the world, improved significantly.

Premeditated dream journeys are not the sole prerogative of men, as Elkin (1977) and others would suggest. In the Wirrimanu area, women too, at least the elders, can travel at will during their *kapukurri*. Accomplished Law men and women who have acquired a certain mastery of and intimate relationships with the ancestral realm are capable of guiding their dream travels, and of 'opening' their *tjurni* to let their spirit 'go on walkabout.' They are also more skilful not only at interpreting the meaning of dreams but also at confronting any dangers that they may encounter during their dream journeys.

Some dreamers don't hesitate to interpret their most striking dreams when they understand the immediate meaning. The following dream by Tjampitjin was told to me by his wife, while he was next to us cleaning a kangaroo that the young men had killed the previous day.

> **Narrative 26** Tjampitjin been tracking for snake, inside spinifex. That snake been come out, long one, nice colours on it. That snake been chasing that old man now, up the tree. The two of them are climbing up a tree. The old man been frightened. Wake up now.

Tjampitjin then stoically interpreted this dream for me by stating that his wife had left her bag of ritual objects inside the house that night (rather than in the women's house or at the women's ceremonial ground). He also mentioned the intense feeling of unease that the dream had left, but concluded that the colours of the snake seen in his dream would be a good inspiration for his next acrylic painting.[7] We see here how a nightmare can be turned into an aesthetically inspiring experience.

Dreams can also portray ritual sequences and performances. This occurs most often, but not exclusively, during initiation or ceremonial times.[8] Men and women, young and old, told me of dream experiences in which known ritual sequences, songs, or dances were acted out. This is a quite widespread theme of dreams. These dream ritual sequences may differ in some aspects from what the dreamer already knows, but this does not necessarily give rise to ritual transformations or innovations in the performed sequence.[9] Rather, these dreams are seen as a source of entertainment; or they may possibly transmit a message but one that has nothing to do with the ritual domain. The following dream was dreamt by a young woman, then in her twenties, who was an assiduous participant in public and women's rituals. The sequence that occurred in her dream was inspired by the *Warkaya* ritual, a public ceremony.[10] In her dream, the men are sitting in a group, with their backs turned to the group of women. Her dream story, and especially her clumsiness in recreating the dance sequence, made her mother and the other women roar with laughter as they listened.

> **Narrative 27** One man, with a loincloth and red paint on him, gets up and instead of dancing that way [she draws here on the ground] like they do in *Warkaya*, starts dancing towards the women. His hands behind his back, dancing two feet together, dancing women way. The women get up and start dancing same way, towards him. They all go back to their place. Then the women tell me, 'It's your turn now.' One man gets up and starts dancing towards the women. I get up. At first, I can't dance. I have a cramp in my leg. As I get closer to the man, in the middle, my cramp goes and I dance all right now.

Nungurrayi explained the next dream of ritual healing with this comment: 'Spirit going around to that Business place because he likes it.'

> **Narrative 28** I had good dream last night. We've been start that Toyota. Napanangka, Nampitjin [a White woman then working on the women's project], and other women going bush to that Business place [women's ceremonial ground]. We've been bring one boy with us to make him better [meaning that they are going to conduct a healing ritual on him]. One woman, that Napanangka, painting herself with *karntawarra* [yellow ochre] and *karltji* [white ochre]. Two other Napanangka playing around, painting themselves. I've been asking, 'What are you doing? When are we gonna start?' We've been singing secret way now [she sings a few song lines]. That song belong us, all the Nungurrayi, Napaltjarri, Napangarti, Napanangka [patrimoiety]. That *Mungamunga* been looking. Making tea now.

The different themes discussed so far, in addition to those presented in the previous chapter, underline the richness and extent of the local discourses on dreams and the various contexts to which they apply. Not all dream themes have been included. Among those left out, mainly because there were not enough ethnographic examples collected, are dreams with a sexual content and those that include *Kartiya* (White people). I was told only a few dreams that involved *Kartiya*. One women, a mother of eight who was often short of money, told me about a couple of dreams she had had where she was 'growling' at the office staff who refused to give her the 'kid's money.' The following narrative by Nungurrayi is by far the most representative of dreams involving *Kartiya*.

> **Narrative 29** Napurrula and Napangarti [two elders] been sitting outside their bough shed at the top camp. I've been made *kumpu* [urine] outside the camp. Napurrula is not happy and growling at me. I said to her 'I am sister-in-law [*mantirri*] to you. I've been lose your kin brother, Tjupurrula' [referring here to her first husband who was killed in the bush a few decades earlier]. Napangarti been talk for me and help me. From there, I've been sit down, like in a meeting. A policeman is there, holding a piece of paper. I ask him where he comes from. He says, 'I've been come from Darwin.' I told him, 'I've been see your place. If you come here, don't ever question us. This is our place.'

The dream left Nungurrayi with a strong feeling of unease, and she added 'no good that dream.' Not only did it start with an argument with Napurrula, with whom she usually had very good relations, but the arrival of the policeman (with a piece of paper) could mean that one of her sons or some of her relatives were in for some trouble, or had been 'humbugging,' farther north. In the local system of dream interpretation, I have not encountered any dream signs that have fixed meanings;[11] any sign can be read as a good or a bad omen, depending on the context. The intratextual, contextual, and intertextual levels are all consulted in dream interpretation. Unless a dream has left a vivid or unpleasant impression, rarely do people seek to interpret their dreams upon awakening. As a rule, Kukatja dream interpretation is flexible and open to multiple readings, depending on the context and current events, as well as the impression made on the dreamer by the dream. Dream narratives are essentially open, and there is much room for individual and contextual interpretations.

Whenever an interpretation is suggested, it is seldom assumed to be immediately true; only future events may eventually confirm its accuracy. Rarely do dream narratives and interpretations carry a sense of fate or determinism.

There are personal differences in attitudes towards dream signs. For example, when Tjapangarti affirms that to dream of *murrungkurr* provokes backache, this is an explanation that comes from a personal experience (narrative 8), but he does not generalize this to cover the entire group, only his own dream experience. The interpretation given of his dream is none the less taken to be true (*mularrpa*); it is understood by everyone, it stems from common local knowledge, and no one would deny or contradict the man's explanation. Aboriginal dream signs are not fixed in any kind of grid of dream interpretation, as is the case in other cultural dream theories and settings. Rather, the individuals, through their own life experiences (and personalities), develop their own personal language of dream signs.

For the Kukatja, a dream sign or, for that matter, any other sign, is never good or bad on its own. It can be either, depending on the context in which it is perceived and how it relates to the flow of events at the moment. For example, one night in Yagga Yagga, an old woman fell seriously ill. We were all very worried because there was no nurse available and the two-way radio was out of order. Accompanied by the woman's son and two of her daughters-in-law, my husband drove her in haste to the Balgo clinic, 100 kilometres away. Along the way, they saw a particularly brilliant shooting star. One of the daughters-in-law told me the next morning that upon seeing the shooting star, she had feared the worst. But when the old woman began to recover, she concluded that the shooting star had been a good omen. On another occasion, a man concluded that seeing a shooting star had confirmed the news heard the previous morning on the radio about an aeroplane accident near Alice Springs in which two men died.

In a world of relationships where anything can become meaningful (a common Aboriginal expression is 'might be something'), nothing is ignored. To some extent, we could say that the Aborigines are always involved in 'reading' signs that continuously present themselves, not only in dreams but also in the waking state. Here are a few examples. Upon seeing a tiny solitary cloud in the west one noontime, an elder told me that it was surely a sign from the Rainbow Snake telling of some trouble in a community to the west. I have already mentioned that a dream can announce the forthcoming visit of a relative. Other signs during waking, such as sneezing or yawning, or a tingling in certain parts of the body, can also predict a visit from one's kin. Furthermore, some bodily sensations, such as throbbing, soreness, or clicking of specific parts, may indicate that the person is thinking or worrying about some relative, or, conversely, that some relative is thinking or worrying about the person; or it could be the sign of the impending arrival of some relative from another community (Peile 1997: 90–1): Here are a few further examples drawn from Peile: 'A noise or whistling in a person's ears indicates that person is thinking of their elder brother ... If a person has an itchy feeling in the head, he is worrying about his *yumari* (mother-in-law). When a man has a throbbing in his penis, he is worrying about his *tjamurti* – this term refers to any man participating in his initiation. When a woman has a throbbing feeling in her breasts, she is anxious about her son or daughter' (ibid.: 90–1). These examples reinforce the intrinsic character of one's composite of relationships. Such bodily signs correspond to the notion of 'shared identity': interpretation of the signs allows one to be reminded of their relations to others.

People do not look for signs in any explicit way, but they engage in being receptive to all the actual and possible expressions and manifestations of their environment: physical, social, and cosmological. This gives a density of experience and interpretation that draws on the various interrelated levels of reality (dreaming, waking, and ancestral). Each of these levels is woven into the fabric of everyday events and contributes to the unfolding of reality. As Povinelli has correctly noted for the Belyuen people, 'Just as the country (or the sentient landscape) is constantly emitting signs, so people are constantly displaying their prowess or clumsiness in interpreting them' (1993b: 692). The dream realm is exempt from the constraints of time and space, and is perceived in the Western Desert as the ideal field for one's spirit to go on walkabout. By extension, it is also a propitious place for communication, encounter, and interaction with all beings and agencies. The majority of dream narratives reinforce the idea that dreams are a place of increased receptivity. Dreams of encountering *Tjukurrpa* beings or deceased relatives, 'shared dreams,' dreams that bear a message, these all attest to the greater communicative permeability that occurs during dream experiences. In narrative 23, the dreamer's remark that her dream at Talapunta suggested that someone might have thought about that place reinforces the idea of increased sensitivity to others' thoughts when one is dreaming. But such sensitivity is not limited only to the dream experience; one's bodily-self is constantly receptive to signs that may (or may not) be noticed and interpreted.

Several interpretations of dreams present the dreamer as an intermediary, the agent who receives a message or lives an experience that can then become meaningful to others. Messages received in this way can be linked, as with narratives 21 and 22, to important cosmological, social, and familial issues. Dreams and dreaming are valued not so much for what they have to say about the dreamer but for what they are capable of saying to the dreamer about his or her surroundings. Dream experiences are valued as a barometer of the state of the relationships between humans and between humans and their physical and sociocosmic environment. It is in this sense that they are acts of communication with the world, acts of opening up to the world.

Sharing Dreams and Learning Dream Language

Surprisingly, even though dreams and dreaming are highly valued in local discourses and practices, the Aborigines do not systematically share their dreams. Quite the contrary. Out of respect for the other's autonomy, or so I guess, people rarely ask what was dreamt the night before. Until I realized it was improper, I was the only one to ask such questions. Only in cases of illness or crisis do elders or medicine men ask the people concerned to share their dreams. Otherwise, it is up to individuals themselves to decide whether or not they wish to share their dreams; this depends on the dream content, on their mood, the context, the emotional impression left by the dream, or the dream's narrative value. In spite of this, it is quite frequent for people to share their dreams, usually while around the campfire when relatives and friends have gathered for morning tea.

The telling of the dream may vary considerably, depending on the audience and the context of narration, the dreamer, and the dream's content. Dreams are frequently told to spouses or camp companions in the morning. When, for one reason or another, the *kapukurri* is considered to be relevant, or simply entertaining (a far from negligible factor), it is told to close friends and relatives, usually in an informal context and without the explicit intention of gathering comments about it or suggestions for an interpretation. If the dream seems to convey a message of broader scope, or if it has troubled the dreamer, then care is taken to let the elders know about it. Modes and frequency of sharing dreams vary according to individuals. Some people take pleasure in telling their dreams, whereas others are more reticent about it. Just as not everyone dreams with the same degree of intensity, not everyone gives the domain of dreams the same value or depth of significance. Some people like to retell their own *kapukurri* or those of others that they have heard over the months, even over the years, and to reflect upon their content. These people are looking for dreams that they consider, as one man put it once, 'as sweet as tea.' They seem to cultivate their memory for dreams, because dreams may shed light on the day-to-day flow of events. At the same time, dreams sharpen people's capacity for interpretation and understanding.

In contrast to welcoming dreams in their forms as messages or as just 'good stories' to share, other people prefer dreamless nights (or avoid speaking about their dreams), thereby reducing the risk of receiving bad news or of having dangerous encounters (with a sorcerer or a malevolent spirit). One can hear two opposite remarks: 'Good night last night, no dream,' or 'I had a bad night, I did not go dreaming.' While some people are apprehensive about getting bad news in a dream, others are forever scrutinizing the horizon of their dreams, looking for different experiences or relevant messages. The two attitudes correspond to different personal dispositions and are not contradictory; rather, each person recognizes in his or her own way the mediating, communicative value and potential of dreaming.

It is rarely asked if someone has dreamt the night before. Usually, it is the dreamer's decision to tell a dream or not. Most dreams are not heard beyond the private sphere. They are told only to the spouse or to close friends, either with the aim of clarifying their meaning or, more often, as a good story (*palya wangka*). Dreams that are infused with a sense of coming from *Tjukurrpa*, or that are considered particularly relevant or troubling, or that predict an unfortunate event for the dreamer, the dreamer's kin, or the community, are first shared with close relatives (and friends) and then with some elders, usually within quite a short time.

Dream narratives usually begin by specifying temporal and spatial references: where and when the dream occurred and who was sharing the camp at the time of the dream. It might have occurred at various points in time: last night, a few days ago, when such-and-such a ceremony was going on, before the rainy season, or even 'when I was a child.' Temporal references can, at times, be precise to the point of including the time of the day or night when the dream occurred: at daybreak, during an afternoon nap, at midnight, or in the middle of the night. The spatial coordinates of the sleeper at the time of dreaming are just as precise: the dreamer will give the exact site of the camp, whether it was within the community or on a journey in the bush, and sometimes even the body's orientation along the four cardinal points. This attention to detailed spatio-temporal factors attests to the continual importance for nomads of situating themselves in a clearly positioned field. These temporal and spatial specifications may also help in the interpretation of the dream by giving precise information about the dreamer's immediate surroundings.

Not all dreams can be shared with everyone. Some dreams that are secret in character and emanate from *Tjukurrpa* (or leave the dreamer with such an impression) are told first to the elders. If it is appropriate, then they may be divulged to a wider audience. This is especially true for the case of revelatory dreams. If there is uncertainty about the real scope of the dreamt message, it can happen that the dreamer decides not to broadcast the experience. This is what happened with narratives 21 and 22, which left the dreamer and her husband afraid that the Rainbow Snake would desert Kutal. They judged it better not to inform the rainmaker about the dreams, so as not to worry him needlessly; they also lowered the risk of creating a stir in the community. However, if other relevant signs had appeared afterwards, then they would have shared these two dreams and their ideas about them.

Conversely, other dream experiences that are bad omens have to be made public, if the elders decide so. This happened to a young woman who had a traumatic dream. In it, two strangers (unknown sorcerers) pierced her body with sharpened bones that had harmful powers, which was a clear act of sorcery. As soon as she woke up, she told her brother about her *kapukurri* (her father was away at the time), so that he could inform the elders about it. They agreed that the dream should be told in the camps and made public. In the event of any real intention of witchcraft, the attackers would be prevented from going ahead with their project once they realized that many people knew about it. This public broadcast of the dream also had the effect of easing the young woman's fears. A similar example occurred during a soccer game at Wirrimanu in 1998. Many people from Mulan, Yagga Yagga, and Wirrimanu had gathered at the oval for the match. A young man who had been quite sick for several weeks had dreamt the night before that he had been a victim of sorcery. His relatives decided to take the opportunity of the gathering that day to recount the dream, in the hope of causing the sorcerers to back off.

I have already mentioned that not all dreams are interpreted. Sharing a dream can nevertheless indicate the dreamer's desire for explanation. The following example is significant here. One day, as I was driving to Mulan with a group of people for initiation ceremonies, a woman told us about the dream she had had the night before:

Narrative 30 Several road trains [these are used for transporting livestock] are driving slowly, one behind the other. They manoeuvre to form a circle. A group of women whom the dreamer knows find themselves sitting in the middle of the circle. They panic a bit and try to get out. Finally, they find a gap between two road trains. Then, they walk to a creek flowing with water. There are some people on the other side. A child swims across. The dreamer must cross but is afraid of drowning, because she does not know how to swim. Finally, she gets across and is very proud of herself.

This narrative drew a comment from another woman. She suggested that the road trains were the ritual convoy that was due to arrive from Christmas Creek, and for which they had been waiting impatiently for several days. The actual convoy was made up of several trucks and cars driving along slowly in single file; it was bringing back a young novice to Mulan for the final stage of his initiation.

Analysing the social setting of dreams and how they are shared demonstrates the relevance of investigating the cultural process of learning the language of dreams. In the Wirrimanu area, although the children are not systematically encouraged to share their dreams, they are none the less sensitized to this mode of discourse and experience at a very young age. They learn to consider it as an integral part of their overall experience and relation to the world. Dreams and dreaming are a true part of the world, just as are the ancestral beings and their embodiment within a sentient landscape, or malevolent spirits and sorcerers, or dramatic narratives and rituals. Through regularly hearing adults and elders telling their dreams or bringing the realm of dreams into the waking world, children are sensitized to dreams at a very early age. This listening is a major part of the process of learning dream discourse and practice. Children are not asked to share their dreams; rather, it is left to them to take the initiative when they feel the need, after a troubling dream, for instance.

Infants and children are considered to have quite an intense dream life, even though they may not yet be able to share it. It is intense to the extent that it is sometimes thought to influence events. The following example points to the relevance attributed to children's dream activity. A group of people from Yuendumu had been visiting some relatives at Wirrimanu. As they were getting ready to depart for another community to participate in some ceremonies, their car broke down. For two days, the young men tried to repair it. On the third day, they finally succeeded in fixing it. As the engine started running again, the wife of one of the men pointed to her toddler and said, 'Might be that Tjangala had a dream about that car and saw it working properly.' As none of the adults present had come forward to recall a dream in relation to the happy event, she concluded that the child must have dreamt it. The purpose was not to bring attention to the child, but to bring dreaming into the flow of events; the dream itself became part of the event, a prelude to a happy ending, even though no one recalled such a dream. I don't wish to imply that dreams are predictive of the future; if that were so, people would put far more energy into the interpretation of their dreams. Rather, it demonstrates the necessity of bringing the dream realm into relation with the flow of daily events.

Learning the language of dreams, like learning the language of *Tjukurrpa* and of rituals, is spread out over a whole lifetime. Dream experiences can serve as triggers or stimuli to the attainment of a different ritual or social status. In the Western Desert, dreams are not an essential condition of passing from one stage of initiation to the next, as they are in some North American Amerindian societies. However, they can help accelerate the passage to a higher level of knowledge, or reinforce the credibility of a status or degree of respect already acquired. The three examples that follow illustrate the way in which the dream experience appears to be a way of passing from one social or ritual status to another. The first dream concerns a young mother, about fifteen years old, who received a visit from the *Mungamunga* in a dream. After this experience, the elders invited her to participate in the women's rituals. Given the present-day context, in which participating in ritual life is more a question of personal choice than it used to be, the young woman could have ignored her dream and refused the invitation. But she decided to join in with female ritual activities. She would receive instruction in them gradually over the years; at Wirrimanu, at any rate, she was the youngest participant.

The second example is of a woman then in her late twenties who had been participating in women's rituals for about five years. She explained to me that her active interest in them dated from the day she

recovered her health after a group of elderly women carried out a healing ritual on her – a ritual that had been taught to the women by the
Walawalarra. During my stay in 1987, she had a dream in which the
Mungamunga gave her a song linked to the *Mina Mina* ritual; this is also
the name of a country to the east of Wirrimanu, in Warlpiri territory,
which was her mother and her mother's mother's country. Her revelation was integrated with the ritual in question. Furthermore, her experience meant that she was given the chance to do body paintings on the
other women during ritual gatherings and performances, something
she had not been allowed to do until then. The third example was told
to me by a highly respected Law woman. She explained that when she
was barely five years old, a dragonfly told her in a dream that she
would be a great Law woman. It was as if this childhood experience
gave greater credibility to the status, authority, and (magical) power
that she had later acquired over her lifetime.

There is in Aboriginal socialization and sociality a universal factor in
the process of learning and acquiring knowledge, be it social norms,
mythic and ritual content and meaning, foraging activities, or dream
practice: children and young people rarely ask in any explicit way how
and why things are. Learning is based on listening, observing, imitat-
ing, and doing; a question asked rarely receives an explicit answer.
Often, young people expressed their astonishment upon hearing my
son, then aged three, endlessly asking the why about things. Some rep-
rimanded him, telling him that it would be better if he talked less and
listened more. Adults and elders never answer a question directly, but
rather in a roundabout way or by analogy, often through a story. This
helps explain the common practice of retelling dreams or mythic segments instead of trying to explain or grasp their possible meaning.[12]
The Aborigines are more concerned with the performing of things than
with their 'meaning,' which is another difference between a relational
epistemology and a modernist one. Furthermore, by leaving things
open, or leading people towards other paths of reflection, this attitude
to the process of understanding and transmitting knowledge helps to
develop people's imagination as well as their faculties of interpretation
and analogy – and surely their patience, too. Even as it transmits the
intransigent, permanent nature of the Law, the spoken word of the
elders also leaves a freedom of choice where autonomy can then be
expressed. Their spoken word is not therefore authoritarian.

Another current practice in the process of socialization consists of
inducing fear. Most narrative constructions contain elements that aim

to make people scared and/or to make them laugh. Aborigines take pleasure in inducing fear in others, and even go so far as to frighten themselves. This is a game that adults particularly play with the younger ones. It can be understood as a form of learning in which men and women from a very young age must gradually learn to control their fear and to deal with it positively, even creatively. They all manage to achieve this, to varying degrees. When confronted with ancestral forces and malevolent spirits or beings, some people feel more confident whereas others, usually the younger ones, are still fearful. Before initiation periods, to give the novices a foretaste of what awaits them, elders often take a malicious pleasure in instilling fear in young boys. This is done more in a spirit of fun, but without denying the gravity and necessity of the rite of passage. The mastery and the discipline acquired during initiation strengthens their personal autonomy, which can potentially form human beings of 'high degree.'[13]

This practice of inducing fear appears to be both a necessity and something of a social play (and drama) in a sociality in which people must learn not to fear things that may seem to be out of their control. It has the aim of increasing their knowledge and autonomy. Learning to deal positively and creatively with one's dream experiences, and with the nightmarish elements that they may contain, is something that the elders try to foster in the young. The world of the Kukatja is filled with malevolent spirits, vengeful sorcerers, and powerful ancestral beings who can also all be encountered in dreams. Learning to meet these beings face to face, either in dreams or in waking life, and also learning to deal positively with one's own fears, are surely important aspects in the process of socialization among the Kukatja.

The response towards what we call nightmares – no distinct term exists in Kukatja – depends on personal variables, although there are notable differences between age groups on this matter. As a general rule, younger people tend to react to traumatic dreams with fear and vulnerability. Though they may have known since an early age how to 'open' their abdominal area, they do not yet possess the skill and self-assurance of the elders. The latter have learnt, over the course of various initiation ordeals and with increased familiarity with the ancestral realm, to develop a more positive, even stoical approach towards the traumatic experiences that dreams sometimes have in store for us. This is the effective result of a cultural project that aims at making human beings of 'high degree,' who are autonomous and yet engaged in and part of networks of sharing relationships. Once they have attained this level, it is easier to adopt a more detached attitude to even the most nightmarish *kapukurri*. The majority of adults and elders do not let themselves be easily frightened or intimidated by dream experiences. Some even say that all dreams are good (*palya*).

It took me a while to understand why dreams, from the moment one chose to share them, were generally qualified either as 'good dreams' (*palya kapukurri*) or 'good stories' (*palya wangka*). Even after listening to the most frightening nightmares (dream narratives that finish with something like 'I was frightened. I woke up' are not rare), someone in the audience would often say, 'Good story, this one.' I think that this is explained by the fact that in societies of oral tradition any story (and dream stories are no exception) has entertainment value. But there is more to it. A story carries its share of cognitive value, informative potential, and aesthetic flavour, as well as its own truth (*mularrpa*). In fact, dreams are 'good' because they are capable of informing one about past, current, or future events that may concern either the dreamer, his or her close relatives, the community, or the sentient places; they may also shed light on the state of the relationships between humans and ancestors. Even a dream that leaves a very negative or frightening impression on the dreamer might, upon awakening, be viewed positively for its informative, curative, or aesthetic potential or value. This is the case for narrative 26, whose nightmarish aspect becomes almost insignificant, and is then recuperated for artistic purposes. Another example is that of an elder whose dream ended with him falling into a bottomless pit. This experience certainly frightened him, but he concluded that it was nevertheless a 'good dream' (*palya kapukurri*), because perhaps it was warning him of malevolent intentions or slander directed towards him. The suggested explanation once again presents the dream realm as a space-time of increased receptivity and interpersonal communication.

When the more vulnerable or less experienced dreamers have traumatic dreams, people usually try to allay their fears. My husband, for example, had a dream a few months after our arrival at Yagga Yagga that frightened him considerably. It should be pointed out first that upon our arrival there, Alan (Tjampitjin) began to take part in hunting activities with the men; he rapidly acquired quite a good knowledge of the territory and an expertise of which everyone was proud. He regularly went hunting large game with the young men, and they rarely came back empty-handed.[14] He told his dream to two adult women of Yagga Yagga.

Narrative 31 The dreamer is driving his four-wheel-drive vehicle on the track that leads to Kunakurlu, a hunting territory to the south of Yagga Yagga that he knows very well because he has hunted there often. He stops his vehicle and notices that he is surrounded by many kangaroos. They are watching him. He quickly aims his gun but all he can see in his line of sight is the threatening eye of a kangaroo. It is as if this eye was invading him. The dreamer is frightened and wakes up.

This dream drew some interesting comments. First, after Tjampitjin insisted on the anxiety he had felt, the older of the two listeners said simply, 'Then, you woke up. Kangaroos were not there any more. You saw it was a dream.' These comforting words, far from undermining the dream's value, try to lessen fearful and often fruitless reactions by searching instead for a relevant explanation, which works at different levels depending on the people. Second, the two listeners exclaimed that it was a good dream (*palya kapukurri*) and a good story (*palya wangka*), and that it was a 'true' experience ('*mularrpa* that one, real true one'). The experience and the story are true because of the intensity of feeling they evoked. By extension, they must contain a 'true' message from which the dreamer will benefit if he examines the dream. On this point, however, the listeners chose not to express an opinion. Third and finally, one of them brought up the idea that if I (the dreamer's wife) became pregnant, the kangaroo might be the child's *tjarriny* (conception mediator). In similar ways, listeners make different comments in an attempt to diminish the negative effects of traumatic dreams, and always with the final objective of adequately invoking the dream's message. Young dreamers will then be all the more inclined to familiarize themselves with this mode of experience.

The fear that surrounds all that is *tarruku* (secret-sacred) is an integral part of the learning process and of the hierarchical relationship between the initiated and the uninitiated. Such a relationship needs to be understood in its progressive and therefore alterable aspects: the uninitiated will one day become novices, then initiates, and finally elders. Although initiation ceremonies for young girls do not exist as such, girls are nevertheless 'initiated' into the Law of their country and that of the travelling cults, such as the *Tjulurru* and the *Walawalarra*. Their learning process and integration into ritual activities also unfolds gradually. Young people know that they must comply with the elders' authority if they wish one day to be able to express themselves openly in public or develop *maparn* forces. In the Western Desert, there is no status from which some people are irremediably excluded for life. The learning process that allows gradual acquisition of sacred knowledge is accessible to all, within the limits set by configurations of belonging and local jurisdictions. In this sense, the thesis of gerontocracy is inadequate, as is any that tries to establish an irremediable hierarchy between the initiated and the uninitiated. Development of the character occurs, boundaries will be crossed, as long as they are not transgressed, in the proper times and places as decreed by the Law or one's ability to negotiate it (Poirier 2001).

From childhood on through to old age, there is definitely a progression in learning the language and the experience of dreams. This gradual learning process is tightly intertwined with an ever-deepening comprehension of *Tjukurrpa*, which is acquired through increasing participation in the ritual sphere, but also through an increasing understanding of the relationships among the ancestral, dream, and waking realms. Dream activity contributes to the growth of understanding and self-discipline of a person in the same way that other fields of action and experience do. Through the years, and over the course of their own life itinerary and experiences, people will develop their own dream language and a personal relationship and self-assurance in dealing with this realm of action, to varying degrees. Most elders, having cultivated their intimacy and ease with *Tjukurrpa* discourse and practice, have acquired this kind of self-mastery. I will now use the specific dream activities of two elders, a woman and a man, as examples to demonstrate the high degree of learning that is implied (and generally desired) in dreaming.

Nungurrayi used analogies to help me grasp the diversity and scope of the dream realm (see chapter 4). Like the majority of elders, she was highly versed in the ritual sphere and had a very esoteric personality. Nungurrayi was a prolific dreamer and took my interest in dreams very seriously; she often shared her dreams with me. She suffered from terrible migraines caused by wounds to the head that she had inflicted upon herself during the mourning ceremonies for her son. She was on medication but, unsatisfied with the results, she regularly consulted the *maparn* of the region, preferably those from Kiwirrkura, whom she trusted deeply. She attempted a definitive cure through the medium of her dreams. During my stay, she told me about four of her introspective dreams (she used the expression 'X-ray') through which she hoped, if not to cure her migraines, then at least to alleviate them. The following dream turned out to be the most efficient from a therapeutic point of view.

> **Narrative 32** A group of people, the majority of whom are known to the dreamer, form a circle. She walks towards them and enters the middle of the circle. A *maparn* from Balgo, Tjupurrula, who is closely related to the *maparn* from Kiwirrkura, tries to take something out of her forehead. The people scatter. She tries to call them back and cries, 'It's nothing, you can come back!' Then she feels something inside her head; a [tiny] kangaroo comes out of her forehead, sits on her head, and scratches it. She grabs him and wrings his neck.

She declared herself to be so satisfied with this dream that she didn't complain of any migraines during the days that followed. Nungurrayi would dwell upon her dreams regularly, searching for aid and knowledge for herself and for her entourage, and she was able to move through this dream state with great ease. Moreover, since her legs were half-crippled, she enjoyed being able to walk normally in her dreams. When one of her sons was hospitalized at Derby for kidney stones, each night's dreams brought her more information about his condition. Like other elders who have learnt how to converse with their dreams, Nungurrayi had developed her own dream language.

The next dream concerns the rainmaker, Nungurrayi's husband, who was of mixed origin, Walmatjari-Wangkatjunga. His country of belonging – which was also his conception site and his father's country – was Kutal, *ngurra* of the Rainbow Snake. When he felt the need, the rainmaker used his dreams to visit Kutal.[15] These dream journeys happened in two stages. First, the rainmaker expressed his intention to visit his country before going to sleep. His father (or other deceased relatives whose spirits now live at Kutal) would hear him and draw him and push him towards Kutal, 'like the wind.' Once he had arrived at Kutal, he would take in his hands a sacred object (talking to an uninitiated person such as myself, he preferred not to name it) that was always kept at the place and without which he could not address the mythic Snake (also called the 'old man').[16] The second stage of the journey then began, and the rainmaker and Kutal, for this is one of the public names of the Rainbow Snake, travelled through the air to different places of the territory that the rainmaker would usually wish to visit. When they returned to Kutal, the sacred object was put back where it belongs, the Snake went back into his *ngurra*, and the rain-maker went back into his dream, which took him back to his camp. The next day was devoted to resting.

In the mid-1980s, when the monsoon was late in coming, the rain-maker went to visit Kutal in a dream. When he arrived, he realized to his great distress that the sacred object had disappeared and that he now had no means of conversing with the Snake. When he returned to his camp, he felt seriously ill, since the very essence of his identity had been profoundly damaged. He suspected that the elders of one of the neighbouring communities had gone to Kutal, while in their dream state, and had taken the object. His classificatory brother went on a dream journey to Kutal in order to look for more clues, and there he noticed a new heap of sand. Upon returning from his dream journey, as he woke up, he told the rainmaker about what he had seen. The rainmaker went back to Kutal by dream the following night. When he saw the mound of sand, he unearthed (the term 'unlocked' was used) the sacred object from it. A few days later, the rains finally arrived. Once he got his health back he visited the neighbouring community to reprimand those whom he suspected of burying the sacred object and 'locking up' communication with Kutal.

In the cultural context of the Western Desert, this elder's dream dis-course and practice flowed from his configuration of belonging and ancestral identity, and from an overall process of knowledge acquisi-tion. Since childhood, the rainmaker had heard the elders tell of jour-neys undertaken in dreams or *Tjukurrpa* stories in which the heroes (often identified with living or dead relatives) travelled through the sky 'like the wind.' These narratives of true experiences would have shaped his own experience and imagination. Furthermore, the rain-maker knew Kutal to its smallest physical detail, because he had lived there periodically with his parents when he was young, and since then had returned upon a few occasions. The rainmaker also knew that he was born of Kutal and that the spirit-child of which he was the incar-nation had lived in the country before he was conceived; when he died, his spirit, like those of his father and grandfather, would return to the same place. In this world of immanence and shared dwelling, his being participates in Kutal's existence and well-being: the two are con-substantial, each existing as part of the other. These were realities that he had embodied since early childhood. Furthermore, he knew how to dream; the elders had taught him to cultivate this mode of experience and not to fear its various manifestations. He had developed a self-control and a sharp sense of self-discipline as well as a relationship with his bodily-self that enabled his spirit to slip out of it more easily.

A good dreamer, like a skilful hunter or dancer, is respected and listened to in Aboriginal society, but doesn't explicitly have greater decision-making power within the group. It is the realm and activities of dreaming as a whole that are valued. A woman remarked one day that 'We, the people of Yagga Yagga, are always dreaming.' She was therefore enhancing the value of both her group and the act of dreaming. This remark, too, is parallel with the enthusiastically expressed vaunting of the abundance of the animal and plant resources in one's own country. In a society in which dreaming is perceived as a fundamental force, constantly called upon, it is obvious that some people seek to delve into it further than others, though rarely on their own behalf. The skills needed for dreaming are transmitted to the young by example, through the sharing of dream stories and the omnipresent discourse on dreaming. Each person must learn to 'open' up his ears to develop listening and memory, open up her umbilical area to become sensitive to dreaming and ancestral forces, and become able to receive knowledge and increase understanding. Dreaming is a personal discipline that is only collectively validated, however, through its influence on and contribution to a person's social, territorial, and cosmological connections.

'This one true story': The Weight of *Mularrpa*

It has long been asserted that stories and storytelling play a prominent role in the process of socialization, possibly more so in societies of oral tradition (Goody 1977, 1979; Eggan 1972), in the embodiment, understanding, and experience of one's world, and in the expression of local historicities and memories (Rosaldo 1980). In a number of hunting and gathering societies, 'many sorts of knowledge are acquired through hearing the dramatized story of a day's event rather than in a directly didactic learning context' (Biesele 1986: 163). It is probably through stories and through the art of storytelling that the poetics, politics, and dynamics of a culture are most closely intertwined. The anthropological and interpretative potentials of stories and storytelling are almost inexhaustible. For the ethnographer, the narrated event, the narrative event, and the various narrative forms all offer a ground for making sense of local processes of interpretation. Furthermore, what is at stake in the narrative dimension is 'the ontological and the epistemological status of the narrated events themselves' (Bauman 1986: 5). The epistemological characteristic of a narrative tradition gives an understanding of the philosophy of the real, of the status of the imaginary (and imagination), and of the local notion of truth. Such epistemologies are always attributable to a specific rationality and cultural objectivity. I will now turn my attention to the status of 'stories' (*wangka*) and their intrinsic quality of truth (*mularrpa*) in the Kukatja world, as well as to what they might reveal about the interplay between different modes of experience.

The primary role and status of *Tjukurrpa* stories (*turlku*, in their sacred and sung forms), as mythical narratives (re)creating the travels and actions of the ancestral beings across the land, have for long been in the foreground in our understanding of Australian Aboriginal sociality, mythopoesis, and politics. Myers proposed in that respect a most appropriate metaphor of 'country as story' (Myers 1986a: 59). Among the place, the experience, and the story, none of these dominate; they are constructed and given meaning in a dialogical mode, partly inspired by pre-existing places, experiences, events, and stories. As a narrative form, the *Tjukurrpa* stories are easily identifiable. As we have already seen, the right not only to know but to tell these stories, even in their public form, is restricted by questions of age and gender and by one's ancestral connections. Although such emphasis on *Tjukurrpa* stories is necessary, other existing narrative forms and the epistemological and ontological status and values of the narrative dimension itself should not be neglected.

In Kukatja, the term *wangka*, used as a noun, means word, language, voice, speech, or noise and sound; as a verb, it means talking, speaking, saying, or making sound or noise. In Aboriginal English and in reference to narratives, no matter what the narrative form, the Aborigines use the word 'story' for *wangka*. The term *wangka* ('story') is applied to a whole range of narrative forms, contexts, and situations. This translation of *wangka* as a story is evocative of an attitude towards speech and the spoken word where (re)description and interpretation are intertwined and indissociable.[17] Whether it is the narrative of a personal experience, the dramatization of a daily event, or the transmission of a particular body of knowledge, all are 'stories' (*wangka*): they are narrative constructions that draw from the context of the moment and from the knowledge, motivations, and imagination of the narrator. The expression 'Let me tell you a story now' (*Watjalatju wangka*, or, *Wangkananku watjalkunangku*) can then be followed by a narrative of a past event, a dream narrative, the narration of a *Tjukurrpa* episode, the naming of places in the narrator's country, or the listing of edible plants. As Rosaldo observed among the Ilongot, 'any kind of information ... can be encoded in this flexible cultural form' (1980: 16). In order to sustain the truth value and authenticity of the experience or event narrated or the knowledge transmitted, the teller will end a story with either of the two following expressions: *palya wangka* (good story) or *mularrpa wangka* (true story).

A pivotal aspect of Western Desert narration is that there does not exist any category of fictional narrative (see also Myers 1986a: 49): there is no absolute epistemological distinction between fiction and (re)description, between false and true, or between real and unreal. Whatever the narrative, whether it be the dramatization of a daily event, a dream experience, or an encounter with a *wanya* (malevolent spirit) in the waking state, it is usually taken at face value and received as *mularrpa* (true). Upon hearing these stories, the Aborigines do not measure the amount of (re)description and the amount of personal fantasy, improvisation, and interpretation contributed by the teller. Rather, the narrative is received as true (*mularrpa*) for its potential for meaning and for generating sense. It is the informative and aesthetic potential of the narrated (and narrative) event, the fact that it might 'generate sense for circumstances beyond the story itself' (Biesele 1986: 161), that is received as *mularrpa*.

The following example will clarify this further. A few people from Yagga Yagga had gone to Wirrimanu to attend a meeting with some government officials. The subject of the meeting was funding from the Community Development Employment Projects (CDEP) program. That night, those who had remained in Yagga Yagga wanted to hear the various versions of the event. They listened to each story (*wangka*) of the event without trying to measure the respective degrees of truth. On the contrary, each version was received as *mularrpa* in terms of the individual experiences and interpretations of the meeting. No one felt the need – as we would generally do in the West – to establish whether one version was closer to the facts than others, just as no one sought to impose, at least not in an authoritative manner, his or her own version of the event. This attitude comes from a dimension of social relations that has been underscored by a number of authors: namely, the respect for individual perceptions, along with the desire to avoid confrontation, when possible. Drawing from his experiences in Central Australia Aboriginal communities, Liberman wrote, 'Despite the recurring conflicts of camp life, there is nothing quite so distinctive about their ordinary lives as the ways they are able to enjoy each other's presence without a deluge of dissonant pressures arising from egoistic competition' (1985: 5). He called this quality 'congenial fellowship.' Among the Pintupi, Myers has noted a similar attitude, which he links to the dimension of shared identity (and relatedness) and to the fact that they are all *walytja* ('all one mob').[18]

I think, however, that this example should be taken a step farther. What was being discussed was not the meeting as an 'objective' fact that could be described independently of one's relation to and understanding of it, but rather how each participant related to the event, and how each of their respective narratives would in turn inform those in the audience. Each participant's experience and story of the event were part of the event itself and contributed to its making and unfolding. In that sense, they were taken to be 'true' and worthwhile. This demonstrates an attitude towards reality that includes, respects, and is open to each person's interpretation. It allows one to ponder over and to realize the truth of the multifaceted aspects of the event, as experienced.

Many types of narrated events and experiences reveal and evoke a local epistemology (and objectivity) that does not establish any absolute division between true and false, between real and unreal, or between the visible and the invisible (whatever is not seen can have other perceptual and tangible manifestations and is part of reality). When a man returns to the camp after his hunt and declares that he has killed a *wanya* (malevolent spirit) with his spear, everyone listens to his story with great interest. When a young man comes back from Halls Creek after three days of heavy drinking and is dizzy, confused, and hears the *Mungamunga* singing, the women fear that these ancestral women may harm him further, so they conduct a healing ritual on him. After a serious car accident, when a man declares that he saw Cowboy mounted on his white horse, there is no doubt that his story is *mularrpa*. When a young man reports having seen a *murrungkurr* (one of the little people, often identified with the spirit-children) wearing a red cloth near the clinic building, his relatives interpret it as a sign of an impending pregnancy for his wife. Such narratives of personal experiences and encounters are received as *mularrpa*, not only because these 'neighbouring others' are intrinsic to the Kukatja world and to local interpretations of events, but also because one's experiences and feelings are valued and respected. This does not mean that one's interpretation cannot be contested, or further verification sought.[19] The audience is very aware that individual stories are impregnated with the personal fantasy and interpretation of the narrator, but this, far from lessening the truth value of the experience, only enhances it. No matter what the story, such events and their interpretations may inform people about a current situation, as well as enhance local knowledge of the moment.[20]

It was during 1988, while living at Yagga Yagga, then only a small outstation, that I came to appreciate the values and status of stories and storytelling in the world of the Kukatja. At night-time, when we gathered around the camp-fire, stories ranging from hilarious to frightening were told by the adults and the elders as the younger ones listened. An element of these narrative events that attracted my attention was the creative and open way in which the stories followed each other. One story (or some of its elements) would suggest another story to one of the listeners, and story would follow story. During such storytelling events, a dream narrative could be followed by a *Tjukurrpa* episode, which would then be followed by a story about the feat of some deceased relative, and so on. The reasons that might initiate such narrative choices were manifold, but usually they sought to give meaning to and make sense of a current event: the prolonged illness of a relative, a death, a recent car accident, a violent fight between two young women over a man, queries over unusual climatic conditions, or simply the successful or unsuccessful day's hunt. These animated evening narratives usually went far beyond the initial queries of those present, and all usually learned and gained something from them.

During these narrative events, as stories followed upon each other, different realms of action and modes of experience (*Tjukurrpa*, dreams, and daily life) as well as different spatial and temporal referents were included in the narration.Considering the complexity of the interplay among the different realms of action, it was at times difficult for me to distinguish the context of the action narrated (whether it was a dream, a myth, or the dramatization of a daily event), because the narrators would not necessarily specify what the realm of action was. Apart from the *Tjukurrpa* stories or the dream narratives that were usually, but not necessarily, clearly identified, it was not always clear to me to which realm of action the narrator was referring. This difficulty in the identification of the realm of action made it impossible to establish a typology of the stories. In the Kukatja narrative tradition, we have not only the different narrative forms (dreams, myths, anecdotes, dramatizations of daily events, etc.), but also narrated events and experiences in which the different realms of action intersect with one another. This is the case, for example, with narratives 4 and 11 where the ancestral realm, the dream, and the waking state are integrated to make an interpretation of an illness. In their narratives, the way in which the Aborigines play with the interrelation and ambiguities among these different realms is itself a very creative one. In storytelling, the creative and subtle interweaving of the different realms of action – *Tjukurrpa*, *kapukurri*, and daily life – is particularly present in the stories told about the feats of elders, deceased or living. These narratives are especially meaningful in the way they tend to identify these elders, men and women, with *Tjukurrpa* beings, or the way they draw a close affinity between them. Through these stories, we develop a better understanding of the Kukatja conception of the interplay between the human and the ancestral realms. The knowledge and understanding that the elders have acquired through their life experiences allow them to demonstrate a high level of reciprocity and intimacy with the ancestral agencies. In these narratives, some men and women are represented (or present themselves) as personas endowed with magical and ancestral powers; the element of metamorphosis (or that of invisibility) is also present, and spatio-temporal constraints are eliminated. The following narratives are particularly revealing. They portray Napanangka, a prominent Law woman, whose knowledge and power were recognized far beyond Wirrimanu, where she lived during the 1980s. While I often sat in her camp to listen to her stories, the following tales were told to me by two younger women. Each of the versions of narrative 33 was told to the narrators by Napanangka when they were young women, not yet married.

Narrative 33a Napanangka, then a nubile young girl, was travelling with her sister. Two men, two *maparn*, were secretly following them, wanting to have sexual intercourse with them. But Napanangka knew that she was spied on; like the two men and in spite of her young age, she had already acquired some magical powers. She carried around her neck a dilly-bag.[21] As night came, she made her camp with her sister, lit a fire, and built a windbreak. She lay still with her dilly-bag around her neck and held in her hands two magical sticks she had made, upon which she had engraved sacred designs. She started singing, and as she did so, she sank into the ground, becoming invisible. Only her dilly-bag could be seen. The two men came closer, but by then the fire had diminished and they could not see very well. Napanangka chose at that moment to reappear, and with her two magical sticks she pierced their eyes and killed them.

One can see these two men today at the place where the event occurred because they were changed into two termite mounds.

Narrative 33b Napanangka, then a nubile young girl, came back one day from a day's hunting and gathering to find that her relatives had decided to move to another place without waiting for her. She only had to follow their tracks in order to rejoin them, and she could see their fire in the far distance. She started walking. Some time later, while she was resting, she inadvertently dropped her dilly-bag; as she picked it up, she saw that two men were following her. In her bag, she was carrying threads of spun hair as well as two magical sticks that she had inherited from her mother's mother. With the help of the magical sticks, she buried herself in the ground, only letting her head out; it was, in fact, quicksand. As they approached, the two men sank into the quicksand. Napanangka then got out and resumed her walk, thinking that from then on she would never be afraid.

There is a strong resemblance between these two versions of Napanangka's story (and experience) and those of the *Tjukurrpa*. Napanangka presents herself as someone endowed with magical powers, just like the ancestral beings. In fact, she does more than identify herself with these, she becomes one through the help of powerful objects that she has inherited through the maternal line, according to one version. Other elements are found in common with *Tjukurrpa* narratives: the theme of the couple (two *maparn* or two sisters [narrative 33a] travelling together); the two men who metamorphosed into termite mounds and became permanent features of the landscape; a man chasing after a woman (or a group of them) in order to have sex with her. In spite of the minor differences between the two versions, they share a similar underlying structure and convey the same messages. Napanangka presents herself in such a way in order to make a strong and positive impression on the young women, teaching them to have confidence in themselves and their own potential powers and to not fear the *maparn* power but try rather to master such powers, just as she had. These narratives convey also a strong statement about the relationship between men and women, and confirm the powers of women.

The following narrative, again about Napanangka, was told to me by one of the previous narrators. She did not remember all the details of the story, which Napanangka had told her only once and many years earlier.

Narrative 34 Napanangka was chased by a *Kartiya* man [the reason was not specified]. In order to escape from him, Napanangka metamorphosed into a bird. She then perched on the top of a tree, next to a water-hole where the *Kartiya* had stopped with his camels. From there, she poisoned the water and the man died.

The presence of the camels in the story tells us that it may have occurred in either the 1940s or the 1950s, when caravans were still being used in some desert areas; Napanangka would have been a young woman then. In this narrative, as in the previous ones, Napanangka presents herself as endowed with ancestral powers. Just like a *Tjukurrpa* being, she has the skill to metamorphose at will. In the Western Desert, as elsewhere in Australia,[22] the theme of metamorphosis is a recurring one. According to local conception theories, humans come into being through the metamorphoses of the spirit-children. We can't reduce this theme to a mere figure of speech or even to an element within a symbolic system, though the relevance of these are not to be downplayed. The theme of metamorphosis reveals some of the principal elements of the local ontology, mainly in terms of the permeable and transient character of all forms (human, non-human, or ancestral), and at the same time reinforces the idea of consubstantiality among all forms. It also reveals the level of empathy with the ancestral order that a person may develop over the course of his or her life. Furthermore, while most Aborigines may agree that metamorphosis might not occur in ordinary waking life, it does occur in the *Tjukurrpa* and the dream realms. The three modes of experience are coeval and interconnected, and Napanangka's experiences and narratives are therefore *mularrpa*.

A multifaceted epistemology underlies the two previous narratives, while they are ambiguous ontologically. There are a number of hypotheses that might explain these stories. First, these stories may both dramatize a lived experience and also draw from the collective imaginary and from the *Tjukurrpa* itinerary associated with the place where the event actually occurred. They may also derive from a purely *Tjukurrpa* story of an ancestral woman with which Napanangka identifies herself; this sort of narrative is fairly frequent whenever Aborigines recount events and actions from *Tjukurrpa*. A third hypothesis is that Napanangka recounted a story that she herself had heard as a child, a story with which she had chosen to identify herself. Finally, the stories could stem from a dream experience. Whatever the case, not only are the stories received as *mularrpa*, but the narrators (Napanangka and the young women) did not feel the need to specify the origin of the narratives – that is, from which realm of reality they came. Contrary to Western epistemology, Aboriginal epistemology is not concerned with the absolute demarcation between different levels of reality. In fact, Napanangka creatively uses the interplay and underlying ambiguity between the levels of action and modes of experience to stage her own performance and demonstrate her powers as human and suprahuman female persona. Is she not inviting the young women to cultivate such powers as well?

The following narrative shares certain similarities with the previous ones. Two elderly women told it to me in 1988, on the same day, but independently of each other. That day, a few people in Wirrimanu had seen in the shapes of the cloud a man sitting, legs crossed. It is this sighting that prompted the women to tell me the following story.

Narrative 35 Before mission time, a Pintupi man of the tjangala subsection killed a male relative of the two narrators. The deceased had to be revenged. Three men [the fathers of some men living in Wirrimanu at the time of the narration] proposed to go after him. Their wives suggested that they chase him during the night, but the men chose instead to wait until morning. They tracked him, found him, and speared him. At the moment that they killed him, a huge noise [like a jet plane, added one of the narrators] was heard. At midday, the wives saw the smoke of the bush fire lit by their husbands indicating the place where they had killed Tjangala. But in the smoke of the bush fire, they also saw Tjangala, with his arms and legs crossed, and fists closed.

Ever since that day, as a reminder of that event, Tjangala would periodically appear either in the smoke of a bush fire or in the clouds. For some reason, he and the circumstances of his death were not forgotten by the local collective memory. Narratives about the feats of living or deceased relatives or one's identification to the ancestral realm are not unusual in the Wirrimanu area. These stories make sense within the local philosophy of the real, in a world that unfolds and reveals itself through the interplay among *Tjukurrpa*, everyday life, dreams, and their manifold expressions, and through the actions, motivations, and improvisations of humans, ancestors, and non-human agents.

Stories in Aboriginal society, as a flexible cultural form, have another component that is integral to the narrative event: their graphic expression. In the Wirrimanu area, the oral tradition and the process of knowledge transmission necessarily have a graphic counterpart. I have already mentioned (see chapter 2) that there exist a number of sacred designs (*kuruwarri*) for ancestral itineraries and named places that are reproduced in ritual contexts either on the ground, on the body (with ground ochre mixed with animal fat or, more recently, cooking oil), or on ritual objects. These *kuruwarri* designs are not just simple representations of ancestral beings and actions, they are also another of their manifestations, and are bearers of their essences and powers. They link in an intrinsic and intimate way the ancestors, the bodily-self, and the land (or ground). The paintings themselves and the act of painting are ways of knowing and relating to the ancestral order. In a ritual context, painting, singing, and dancing are forms of total engagement and empathy with the ancestral order.[23]

Besides the ritual *kuruwarri* designs, there are also the more public graphic forms. In fact, most narratives, whether of a day's hunt or event, a past event, a dream, or the transmission of specific foraging skills, are accompanied by drawings in the sand. They are an integral dimension of the narrative event and 'important channels for handing down basic cultural information' (Watson 1997: 109). These sand drawings represent the main elements of the story narrated.[24] Watson describes this practice as 'opening up the skin of the body of the land.' Somehow, the narrated event must be imprinted on the ground, even temporarily, just as the ancestors have inscribed the ground and the landscape. As soon as the story is over, however, the narrator erases the drawing (usually with a gentle gesture of the hand), in case someone passing by later misinterprets it. No mark or imprint on the ground should be left for the watchful eye of a person who might be tempted to interpret the drawing out of the control of the narrator.

Bodily marks and scars (*kumurlpa*) of various origins are another form of such inscription. Just as the ground is marked and inscribed through the actions of human, non-human, and ancestral agents, so is one's body. To some extent, every person carries the permanent inscriptions of meaningful events and experiences that stand out as landmarks in his own life (hi)story. This scarring can happen for a variety of reasons. There are the initiation marks: the piercing of the nasal septum and scars across the chest that most elders in Wirrimanu, both male and female, had. There are also the various wound marks left by spears, boomerangs, or fighting sticks following fights or the settling of scores. Some of these occur over issues regarding the Law. Others are of a more personal nature and may have occurred between men, between women, between husband and wife, or between relatives. There are the wounds that are self-inflicted during mourning rituals ('sorry business'): close male relatives of the deceased pierce their thighs with spears, while the female relatives injure their heads with stones or other heavy objects. Some people have inscribed their conception marks on their bodies, to testify to their passage from *Tjukurrpa* to the human realm. A spirit-child, for example, had taken the form of a kangaroo eaten by his future mother; since birth, the boy has had on his shoulder blade the mark left by the spear his father used to kill the kangaroo. Each of these scars can give rise to narratives relating to significant events in the person's life. We can say, too, that one's life (hi)story could be retraced and told using the bodily marks and scars as a starting point. The body and the land both appear as 'open texts,' over which are written the results of meaningful actions, events, and experiences.

In the Western Desert, dreaming is regarded as a real experience and as a realm that mediates between the human realm and the spoken word of the ancestors. It is also the favoured time-space of all transformations, a place for increased receptivity, a prelude to life and death, and an essential link in the chain of all events. A dream does not belong to the dreamer alone, and it is rarely thought to be knowledge solely for the dreamer. Rather, the dreamers tend to consider themselves as messengers or witnesses to something that can, when shared, become meaningful and relevant to others. Dreams and dreaming constitute potential sources of information that can contribute as much to everyday life as they can to major social, territorial, and cosmological issues. In other words, dreams and dreaming are ways of knowing the world and relating to it.

An essential thread of this chapter was not only to present the main themes of dreams but also to look at the degree of openness and flexibility in the interpretation of dreams. As a rule, Kukatja dream interpretation is flexible and open to multiple readings, depending on the context, current events, and the impression made on the dreamer by the dream. Unless a dream has left a vivid or unpleasant impression, people rarely interpret their dreams upon awakening, and when a dream is recounted, most listeners are content to have heard a 'good story.' Whenever an interpretation is suggested, however, it is rarely assumed to be true at the immediate moment, and there may be sev-

eral interpretations; eventually, future events may confirm an interpretation's accuracy. The comments given following a dream story rarely
constitute an end of the dream interpretation. Often, a dream is
remembered and retold when it can meaningfully shed light on certain
facts, or can otherwise be integrated into the flow of events at that
moment. Because there are no official dream interpreters and no fixed
grid of dream interpretation, and because the dreamers and their listeners usually prefer not to give a definitive interpretation of a dream,
each person's perception and understanding are respected. The intratextual, contextual, and intertextual dimensions are all put into motion
in the process of searching for the meaning of a strong dream. For all
these reasons, dream narratives and interpretations rarely carry a sense
of fate or determinism. The following statement by Povinelli provides
a delightful analogy for the interpretation of dreams: 'As things are
happening, women collect, so to speak, a basketful of potential signs
and wait for events down the track to indicate which ones to keep'
(1993b: 692).

What possibly might be seen, at first, as a lack of interest in dream
interpretation reveals, on closer examination, another local reality – the
paramount role of the action of dreaming itself in one's life itinerary
and in the unfolding of reality. Primacy is given to the activity of
dreaming – as a means to know the world and to relate to it – over the
dream content or dreams simply as 'objects' (or products of the mind,
as in the dominant dream theories of the West). The activity of dreaming, like other human (and non-human) actions within the world
(walking, talking, hunting, or singing), is a highly valued thread in the
dynamic reproduction and transformation of networks of shared relationships or connections that are at the same time social, territorial,
and ancestral. This attitude towards dreaming conveys the manifold
potentialities of dreams and dreaming, as events, as actions, as experiences, and as narratives.

In such a world of relationships, the interpretations of events,
dreams, experiences, or stories can draw from a combination of
sources: mythical, historical, social, contextual, or personal. Here is a
world where anything may constitute a sign or say something about
the state of the relationships between humans, and between humans
the surrounding 'others,' and the sentient landscape. 'Might be something,' as the Aborigines usually express it. The form of a cloud, the
song of a bird, the direction of the wind, the marks on a stone, the tick-
ling sensation on one's body, or a dream are all capable of suggesting

information to whomever is willing to listen or note them and decipher them within the framework of cultural idioms. The interpretations are done with a touch of improvisation and with reference to a whole series of mythical, contextual, and personal variables that also include the anthropologist's presence.

This hermeneutic of everyday life is open, multivocal, and negotiable; at times, it is most serious and sacred, while at other times it is quite playful. It is a way of being-in-the-world that is primarily dialogic (in Bakhtin's sense, 1990), and a mode of dwelling within the world and engaging with a sentient landscape. This constant linking of different elements, constituents, and realms is in itself an act of creativity. As Breton remarked about New Guinean societies, we here are dealing with 'a world of open signs' (Breton 1989: 269–74). I would also add that among the Kukatja, signs seldom stand alone; nor do they have fixed meanings. The interpretation of signs 'is not a matter of construction but of engagement' (Ingold 1996: 121). They are the products or manifestations of actions or messages sent by human, non-human, or ancestral agencies. In Kukatja ontology and epistemology, dreaming is a way to relate, a way to gain knowledge (or to steal sacred knowledge), and one of the means by which humans engage with and dwell within the world, a world that is not given once and for all but is emergent. A world, furthermore, in which ritual knowledge, activities, and exchanges play a paramount role.

Chapter 6

Ritual Vitality and Mobility

In the Kukatja world, the relations between the immanence of the ancestral order and the mediating role of dreams on the one hand, and the flexibility and openness of the social morphology on the other, find their ultimate expression in the domain of ritual forms and practices. Rituals and the ancestral actions and itineraries that they express are manifestations of the permanence of the ancestral order. They are also dynamic in that they are transformed over time and across space, either through the reinterpretation of existing elements, or by the insertion of new elements prompted and inspired by local events of various scopes and characters. In this way, the dynamics of the mytho-ritual sphere present a major stage for the reproduction of the social and cosmological environment and for the inscription of local historicity and identity. Ritual forms and performances (singing, dancing, painting) are also probably the most salient expressions of the interplay between human and ancestral actions and of their intersubjective and embodied character.

The dynamics of the mytho-ritual sphere stem from three interdependent factors. First, rituals are the expression of ancestral itineraries that are open, not only at their extremities, but also at each named site. Consequently, these itineraries are subject to additions, transformations, and reinterpretations according to events and sociopolitical conjunctures (see chapter 2). As a result, the pathways and their corresponding rituals are never quite 'finished.' Second, certain mytho-ritual complexes or sequences are 'nomadic,' in that they must travel, usually over traditionally defined routes of exchange. Over the course of these exchanges, the nomadic rituals, as travelling cults or travelling *turlku* (songs), undergo local reinterpretations of varying scope. The third factor linked with Western Desert mytho-ritual dynamics concerns the revelation by the ancestors or deceased relatives of new elements that were until then concealed from humans. These new sequences are almost exclusively revealed by dreaming, a realm of action through which the spoken words of the ancestors are mediated. Moreover, the role of dreams in revealing cultural innovations represents the fifth aspect in the process of dream socialization that I discussed in the Introduction.

In the analysis of such ritual and mythical innovation, it is appropriate to make a distinction between the role of dreams as a privileged medium of the ancestral spoken word rooted in local discourses and the role of personal and collective knowledge, creativity, and strategy. In other words, there is a difference between the ancestral agency manifested by dreams on the one hand and human agency on the other. The latter, though, in terms of human creative and innovative potential, is usually denied in local discourses. Indeed, the anthropologist ought not to let herself be seduced by the dominant discourse in which dreams are presented as the unique source of regeneration and validation of sacred knowledge. It goes without saying that after experiencing a dream revelation, the dreamer and his or her group, as interpreters of the revelation who are conscious of the needs and expectations of the time, are in a position to creatively and strategically orchestrate the material received in the dream. The mythical territorial reinscription and ritual transformation that may result from the revelation then become a means of expression of local (and regional) politics and historicity.

Ritual Vitality[1]

For the Kukatja and neighbouring groups, the ritual dimension is a basic expression of sociality, inasmuch as places and ancestors are intrinsic to their sociality. Myers has eloquently demonstrated how the Pintupi, southern neighbours of the Kukatja, traditionally 'did not simply move to where the food was, but rather scheduled their movements so as to use available resources in pursuit of their own social values – to initiate a boy or to exchange ceremonies' (1986a: 292). In the contemporary context, this essential trait of Western Desert nomadism has been maintained. Thus, journeys are made throughout the year for initiation rites,[2] ritual exchanges, and mourning or funerary rites, and may involve a greater or smaller number of people depending on the occasion.

In a general way, the ritual domain conveys various dimensions of Aboriginal reality. It expresses territorial spaces and ancestral connections, and everyone's responsibilities towards these; it strengthens the links between local groups that are more or less distant and reinforces exchange networks; it is a major ground for the expression of Aboriginal aesthetics; and finally, it offers a schema of meaning and action that enriches experience and knowledge. The preceding analysis of different modes of experience and realms of action (see chapter 4) shows that ritual activity seems to be the most complete realm, one that simultaneously includes components that emanate from *Tjukurrpa*, the realm of dreams, and the waking state. As one elder put it, ritual is '*mularrpa* [true] proper *Tjukurrpa*.'

Australian Aborigines often translate the ensemble of ritual activities by the term 'business.' By extension, the elders are called 'business men' and 'business women' and are responsible for the realization of the ancestral order, as well as for enforcing respect for the Law. These terms furthermore link ritual to major territorial, social, and political issues that engage each individual personally because of his or her configuration of belonging. Ritual 'business' is intrinsically bound up with the land and the ancestral pathways that cross it. Ritual gatherings also offer a place for meetings and discussions between the members of different local groups who are the caretakers of countries for themselves, their neighbours, and the ancestors. As a place for exchanges and alliances, 'business' legitimates belonging and ensures the reproduction of the ancestors' world as well as the social and cultural dynamic. Since 'business' is a generic term, there are different ritual categories. Among these, I have selected for discussion the *Yawulyu*, a category of women's rituals, and the initiation ceremonies. Since they entail long journeys, the latter involve extensive participation and cooperation among several local groups over a vast area.

Yawulyu

The *Yawulyu* certainly represent the most important category of women's rituals for the Aboriginal groups of the desert and some northern regions.[3] They can sometimes express rites associated with a whole mythic pathway, or sometimes just a segment of it, and they define the ritual 'ownership' and responsibility of women towards a given country. Some *Yawulyu* sequences define the women's participation in the initiation ceremonies. *Yawulyu* rituals are always performed

during the boys' initiation, and they represent one of the women's contributions to the passage of their son, brother, son-in-law, or nephew
into manhood. At other times, the women may decide to perform
Yawulyu sequences for various other reasons: for healing or love-magic
purposes, to soothe the atmosphere in the community after a major
fight or conflict, or to feel closer to their country. But it can also be that
they just feel like dancing and singing, or being in the company of the
Mungamunga or the other *Tjukurrpa* heroines celebrated. These mythic
women, too, can express their desire for some *Yawulyu* sequences to be
performed, through a dream given to a woman (or a man). Though
Yawulyu is always a serious business, its performances are also a form
of entertainment and a forum for socialization, to use Dussart's expression here.

In the Wirrimanu area, the performances of *Yawulyu* sequences are
not as frequent as in other settlements, such as Yuendumu (Dussart
2000). It is not because the local repertory of rituals is less extensive –
far from it. Rather, at Yuendumu, the Northern Territory Land Rights
Act (1976) has allowed Aborigines to become actively involved in the
process of land claims. It was partly through performing the *Yawulyu*
sequences associated with their countries that the women from
Yuendumu justified their rights of 'ownership' of land to the non-
Aboriginal authorities. The second reason is probably related to the
absence of *jilimi* in the Wirrimanu area. A *jilimi* is a women's-only
camp that is established within a community. Widows, young single
women, or women who are fleeing an unwanted or violent husband
usually live there. *Jilimi* are common in Warlpiri communities (Warrabri, Lajamanu, or Yuendumu), and obviously their presence stimulates
the practice of *Yawulyu* rituals (Bell 1993; Glowczewski 1991; Dussart
2000).

A *Yawulyu* ritual, like any Aboriginal ritual, is based upon the narratives of a mythic itinerary. It is composed of numerous sequences, each
of which relates the actions of the male or female ancestral beings
in particular named places. Each ritual sequence includes graphic
designs, dances, and songs. The body paintings and sacred objects
associated with a *Yawulyu* ritual carry the vital essence (*kuruwarri*) of
the *Tjukurrpa* being celebrated. The distribution of participants' roles
and tasks follows the *kirda-kurdungurlu* division (boss, owner/man-
ager, and policeman) discussed in chapter 3. The women of Balgo,
Mulan, and Yagga Yagga are the guardians of several *Yawulyu* and are
familiar with those of other regions. I will describe here briefly the

most important *Yawulyu* for their region: the *Tjiparri, Mina Mina, Innin-garra*, and *Ngantalarra (Wati Kutjarra)*.

The *Tjiparri* is thought to be the oldest *Yawulyu* in the area. In the women's words, '*Tjiparri*, mother for all *Yawulyu*,' 'proper long time, first one into this place, like mother to other songs,' or 'real old one that *Tjiparri*, underneath one.' It is said to have originated in the Lake Mackay area, and before mission time it was in the custody of three sisters of the nungurrayi subsection. When the eldest of these died in the bush, she transmitted it to her younger sisters. Before the youngest sister died, she handed responsibility for the *Tjiparri* to her daughter, a nampitjin who, during the 1980s, lived mostly in Mulan. One of the female elders was convinced that the eldest sister (the mother of a respected Law man who died in the mid-1990s) received this *Yawulyu* in a dream, 'long time ago in the bush,' but others disagree, preferring to attribute its origin to *Tjukurrpa*. In the *Tjiparri*, the nangala-nampitjin-napurrula-nakamarra subsections are *kirda* (bosses), while the napangarti-napanangka-napaltjarri-nungurrayi subsections are *kur-dungurlu*. Both groups do the dances.

Tjiparri is also the name for the Sturt Creek mallee, a type of eucalyptus whose fruits have a medicinal value. Its leaves are used frequently as a medicinal smoke for different purposes, such as strengthening a newborn child or anyone who feels weak, or for soothing menstrual pain. The *Tjiparri* ritual sequences are performed on various occasions, including during the boys' initiation. It expresses both the women's resignation at losing their children and their contribution to the crucial passage of the boys from childhood to manhood. The *Tjiparri* sequences are also done in other contexts: as healing songs, love-magic songs, for the young girls' passage to womanhood (when their menstrual periods arrive), and to aid women's fertility.

The mythic narrative of the *Tjiparri* traces the journey of the *Nangala Kutjarra* (Two Nangalas) who set out from the Lake Mackay region at Tjikarri. They then journeyed north and north-west to the regions of Rapi (Lake White) and Mungkayi (Stansmore Range), before rejoining the underworld east of the Stansmore Range. The male version of *Tji-parri* is different: it says that, near Mungkayi, the *Nangala Kutjarra* climbed up a sand dune and turned into the Rainbow Snake. In any case, their journey does not end there, because it then blends with the pathway of another group of *Tjukurrpa* women, the *Kungkayunti*, who travelled south to Pintupi country, to a place called Marapinti (nose-peg), west of Kiwirrkura.[4] In the course of their journey, the *Nangala*

Kutjarra established their camps at different places and performed numerous actions. Among the songs that I have heard are the following: they gathered bush raisins, and later bush tobacco; they crawled underground like goannas, fleeing a bush fire; they tied their long hair in a bundle on the top of their head (*muli-muli*); they made a long thread of spun human hair (one of the sacred objects used today in some sequences of the *Tjiparri*) that they dipped in their urine (women's urine being symbolically and therapeutically more powerful than men's); at another place, they sat face to face and looked at their swollen bellies (in the words of one woman: 'two fellows been getting headache, two fellows' bellies getting bigger, blood running'). Like other female ancestors, the *Nangala Kutjarra* have strong magical powers and avoid the company of men.

Unlike the *Tjiparri*, the *Yawulyu* of *Mina Mina* did not originate in the Wirrimanu area, but is rather of Warlpiri origin and is strongly connected to the initiation of boys. The *Mina Mina* is a major song cycle; today it is narrated and performed in the Warlpiri communities of Yuendumu and Lajamanu, as well as in Wirrimanu, Yagga Yagga, and Mulan (i.e., caretakers for this *Yawulyu* live today in these communities). In the Wirrimanu area, in the 1980s and 1990s, four sisters of the napanangka subsection and with Warlpiri/Ngarti affiliations (and Kukatja affiliations for some of them) were the main custodians of the *Mina Mina*. From what I was told, the eldest received the ritual from her older brother many years earlier, while they were living in Papunya. It seems that Tjapanangka, the brother, had a dream about the *Mina Mina*. Since it was a *Yawulyu*, he transmitted the *Mina Mina* to his sister, Napanangka. She brought the ritual with her when she came to live at Balgo with her sisters and their families in the late 1970s. Because it generally involves important social and political issues, the process of transmitting any ritual is much more complex than these brief comments suggest. The explanations given by Napanangka about the transmission of this cycle none the less reveal some of the elements of the process, such as dreaming a revelation that can justify transmission of rituals.

The mythic pathway of *Mina Mina* has links with the *Mungamunga*. The site of Mina Mina is situated to the south-east of Balgo, at a water point between the Inningarra Range and Lappi Lappi, and it straddles both Warlpiri and Ngarti country. It is also known as Kanakulagnu, from the term *kana*, 'digging stick.' The site of Mina Mina was traditionally an important initiation site for the local groups of that region;

it is close to a water-hole known as Kimayi. The narrative recounts the journey and deeds of a group of *Tjukurrpa* women who behaved like men and were the guardians of the ritual's power, and of how they lost this power to the men after being cleverly tricked by a man from the tjakamarra subsection.[5] Here are a few excerpts from Napangarti's account of the story:

> All the women been travelling, hunting like men. Those women used to act like the men, telling men what to do (get water, make fire). They used to hit them when the men did not listen. Those *Mungamunga* had their spears and boomerangs. The men had *luwantja* [wooden dish used by women] and were getting bush tucker [at this point, the narrator and the other women present roar with laughter]. One old man, Tjakamarra, was coming and saw all the women dressed like men in business time. He asked one of the men what was happening. He told him: women's *tarruku* [sacred-secret]. That Tjakamarra pulled all the branches from the *warakatji* [snake vine] and dried them in the sun. After eating, the women were resting with their husbands. Men and women were sleeping together. That Tjakamarra had made the women feel no good. He threw dried vine [*ngalyipi*, a generic term for vine woven into rope] at them. He made like a cowboy's rope and threw it at the women. Those women got no good. They have lost all their sacred things. Those *Mungamunga* kept travelling long way.

After losing their sacred objects, the *Mungamunga* travelled towards the east, well beyond Warlpiri territory and, according to some women, as far as the Mount Isa region in Queensland. They have been living in this distant place ever since, their gaze always turned westward towards their country, Mina Mina. When they die, the *kirda* of the Mina Mina join the other *Mungamunga* off in this distant region.

The napangarti-napanangka-napaltjarri-nungurrayi subsections are *kirda* for this *Yawulyu*, while the nangala-nampitjin-napurrula-naka-marra subsections are *kurdungurlu*. As with the *Tjiparri*, the women perform the *Mina Mina* ritual sequences during a boys' initiation period; the choice of the *Yawulyu* performed depends on the boys' own ancestral connections. At one initiation ceremony in which I partici-pated in January 1988, the women performed the following *Mina Mina* songs and ritual sequences: the episode with the vine; the mother-in-law making and presenting the hair belt (*nanpa*) to the young initiate; the men and women from *Tjukurrpa* bringing the boy to Kanakulagnu;

the *Mungamunga* poking the ground with their digging sticks (*kana*) and moving around in the sand; the *Mungamunga* mocking the corella bird when it moves its neck while eating worms. There were also some songs that referred to the *kurrkapi*, the desert oak[6] and some episodes that referred to the Mythic Snake or to the women's sacred pole (*kuturu*). Most of the body paintings for the *Mina Mina* pictured vegetable foods; one of these was the *puluntari*, a kind of truffle.

There is also a male ritual repertoire linked to the mythic narrative of the Mina Mina country. Some of these sequences were performed in Balgo in 1988, after there had been a conflict between a young woman, Napangarti, and her classificatory father, Tjapanangka (her deceased father's younger brother). The night before, while drunk, Napangarti had violently struck Tjapanangka. In order to compensate for this affront and re-establish respect, Tjapanangka chose to perform in public a few of the sequences from the male repertory of the *Mina Mina*.

Since the beginning of the 1980s, the *Inningarra Yawulyu* has enjoyed a vibrant renewal. The site of Inningarra, which is in the Northern Territory near the chain of mountains of the same name, had not been visited for about thirty years. Then, in 1982, a group of men and women from Balgo, Ringer Soak, and Lajamanu went there, accompanied by the anthropologist Fred Myers. The trip was a part of a land-claims process that was underway, and the trip's goal was to map the mythic pathways and major sites of the region (Myers and Clark 1983). One night while they were camping near Inningarra, a female elder was visited in her sleep by the *Mungamunga*, who told her things that had been partly forgotten, particularly some of the songs, drawings, and dances of the *Inningarra Yawulyu*. This led to an immediate revival of the ritual, and to renewed performances. In 1992, the land claim ended positively and an outstation was established soon afterwards near what used to be the Mongrel Down cattle station.

The *Inningarra Yawulyu* is part of a *Tingarri* itinerary. The site of Inningarra is in fact situated on a *Tingarri* initiation pathway that links it to the site of Ngantalarra, in the south-west (see below). The mythic narrative tells how a group of men and women accompanying the novices stopped at Karliyaka, where they met a group from another *Tingarri*. Great ceremonies were being celebrated at Karliyaka when a bush fire came from the east, from Warlukurluangu, causing them to flee to Inningarra (Myers and Clark 1983: 16–18). Mostly women of Ngarti/Warlpiri descent hold this *Yawulyu*.

Another important *Yawulyu* is the *Ngantalarra Yawulyu*, about the travels and deeds of the *Wati Kutjarra*, the Two Initiated Men (see chapter 2). The site of Ngantalarra is in Ngarti country and located along the *Tingarri* itinerary that joins it with Karliyaka and Inningarra. At Ngantalarra, the *Wati Kutjarra* participated in the initiation ceremonies of the *Tingarri* group. The different sequences of this *Yawulyu* refer to places in the vicinity of Ngantalarra, including Kunakurlu, where they killed a kangaroo; Nampurrungu, where the two men fled from the *wanya*, guided by the nighthawk; Karntawarra, where they painted themselves with yellow ochre (*karntawarra*); Marrapri, the place where they pierced their septa; and Nakarra Nakarra, where a group of ancestral women ran away from them, towards the west. Watson (1996: 116) identifies these ancestral women as the Seven Sisters, fleeing from their 'wrong skin' lovers.[7] In the ritual sequences of this *Yawulyu*, women dancers act out the roles of the *Wati Kutjarra* and the ancestral women. As with the *Inningarra Yawulyu*, the napurrula-nakamarra-nangala-nampitjin subsections are *kirda*, and the other patrimoiety is *kurdungurlu*. The custodians of the *Ngantalarra Yawulyu* (or *Nakarra Nakarra* song cycle) are mostly, but not essentially, of Kukatja and Ngarti descent. The *Wati Kutjarra* itinerary, as a major song cycle of the area, includes a ritual corpus for the women and another one for the men.

Tjiparri, Mina Mina, Inningarra, and *Ngantalarra* are the main *Yawulyu* of which the women of the Wirrimanu area are currently the guardians. Personal networks of ancestral connections and configurations of territorial belonging give each woman access to other *Yawulyu* under the custody of women established in other communities, such as Christmas Creek, Ringer Soak, Kiwirrkura, Lajamanu, or Yuendumu. When *Yawulyu* rituals are performed, those who are *kirda* usually are responsible for preparing the ritual objects, painting the sacred boards (*yukurrukurru*) and the ceremonial pole (*kuturu*), and daubing the bundles of hair-string with a mixture of oil and ochre, among other tasks. Women who hold the rights of a particular song cycle (and its associated sites), either as *kirda* or *kurdungurlu*, initiate and conduct the body painting, singing, and dancing. Participation in these rituals is open to all the women in the region and beyond, since the division of tasks during the ritual among the eight subsections either as *kirda* or *kurdungurlu* gives each woman access to all the *Yawulyu* being performed. *Yawulyu* ritual knowledge, practice, and experience confirm, ground, and express the women's responsibilities for and rights to the country and to the reproduction of the sociocosmic environment. The complexity and density of the narratives and songs give room for idiosyncratic interpretations. The ambiguity that often underlies the meanings of the songs, and even at times the ambiguity in the identity of the ancestral characters involved, offers a ground for discussions and negotiations between local groups and between women and men.

One woman distinguished two categories of *Yawulyu*, the 'private ones' and the 'dreamed ones' (*kapukurri Yawulyu*). While the recognition of such a distinction did not seem widespread among the women, the distinction itself conveys an intrinsic reality of mytho-ritual dynamics. The 'private' *Yawulyu* corpuses, which include those mentioned above, have been transmitted for several generations. The women of today remember seeing their mothers and grandmothers performing them, and learned them from the earlier generations. That long-term collective recognition, performance, and transmission seem to be what distinguish a private *Yawulyu* from a dreamed *Yawulyu*. A *kapukurri Yawulyu* is a new work that usually seems to develop from a series of dreams that occur over an extended period. At first it is dreamt by just one woman; then other women dreamers (and occasionally men dreamers) will help to enrich the number of songs and ritual sequences in it, and refine the new corpus. Following a process of collective recognition and elaboration, a dreamed *Yawulyu* may possibly, but not necessarily, become an integral element of the region's mytho-ritual baggage. Such a song cycle could eventually be transmitted to the daughters, nieces, and granddaughters of the first dreamer, and they would then become the main caretakers of the ritual. Since a *Yawulyu* is a manifestation of a mythic itinerary or of a particular segment of it, the result would be the enrichment of the mythical landscape of the region.

Once the process of collective elaboration and recognition and the test of transmission are underway, a dreamed *Yawulyu* can acquire the status of a private *Yawulyu*. This transition is not necessarily automatic, since the collective recognition of the dreamed *Yawulyu* depends on several factors, including, among other things, the personality of the dreamer, her strength of negotiation and persuasion, the interest of her relatives in learning and 'holding' the new *Yawulyu*, various contextual social and political factors, and the relevance of the narrative thread, on a collective level, with respect to the pre-existing *Tjukurrpa* corpuses. A present-day example will illustrate the passage from a 'dreamed' to a 'private' *Yawulyu*.

Nampitjin, a Walmatjari elder who lived at Mulan, is at the origin of a *kapukurri Yawulyu* that took form during the 1980s. In July 1987, I had the chance to witness some of the sequences of this new ritual during a gathering at Lake Gregory attended by more than 200 women from various communities.[8] For several years, Nampitjin had been elaborating this *Yawulyu*, which she had received from *Tjukurrpa* beings, sequence by sequence, while dreaming. It is understood that if a body of ritual is dreamed, there must necessarily be a new mythic segment to match it. This one is said to begin in the region of Lappi Lappi, where Pelican (*Walanypa*) and the Two Nangalas (*Nangala Kutjarra*) lived together. They decided to leave this region and travelled northward until they reached the edge of Sturt Creek, which they then followed south, passing through Caranya, Billiluna, and finally Paruku (Lake Gregory). Most of the songs of this cycle refer to the country (the 'milky water,' the creeks, and bird life) along Sturt Creek from Billiluna down to Lake Gregory.

This new segment reflects the life trajectory of Nampitjin, who was in her seventies when I met her in the late 1980s. As a child, she had lived in the Lake Gregory region, and had travelled farther east and south-east, at times all the way to the Lappi Lappi area. While she was still a young girl, she journeyed north with her family and lived at various cattle stations along Sturt Creek, such as Caranya and Billiluna, before settling at Mulan, her country. The *Yawulyu* that she has developed is an amalgamation of her own life trajectory with her knowledge of an already existing *Tjukurrpa*. The *Nangala Kutjarra* involved in the song cycle belong to the original group of *Tjukurrpa* women, the *Kanaputa*, who left the region of Lake Mackay after the mythic fire of the *Tingarri*.

Nampitjin's *kapukurri Yawulyu* will probably pass the test of collective recognition and be transmitted as a private *Yawulyu*, and eventually be inserted into the ensemble of permanent rituals. There are several reasons why I expect this to be so. Nampitjin's life trajectory echoes those of several women of her generation who left the desert at a young age to live on cattle stations farther north. The narrative thread of the new *Yawulyu* expresses a shared world and historic reality, and many women easily identify with it. This new mytho-ritual corpus confirms and inscribes on the land a relatively recent collective experience and memory. By 1987, the women of Mulan, Balgo, and Yagga Yagga were already familiar with this dreamed *Yawulyu*. During my stay (1987–8), another Law woman of the nungurrayi subsection enriched it further by contributing a few songs to the initial corpus, as well as a new body painting and a dance, all of which she had received in dreams. Furthermore, a few young women from Mulan who were close relatives of Nampitjin already knew the songs and the different ritual sequences well and were more than willing to take over responsibility for the ritual when she passed away. The process of transmission was already underway. Moreover, the fact that sequences from the new song cycle had been presented at the Lake Gregory gathering demonstrates that this 'dreamed' ritual had reached an important phase in the process of regional collective recognition. As it gradually becomes more and more integrated into the women's ritual activities in the region, this 'dreamed' *Yawulyu* will most likely become a 'private' *Yawulyu*. If that happens, the women will eventually deny that it ever came from a series of dreams, and will instead insist, as they do for the *Tjiparri*, that it comes from *Tjukurrpa* and that it has always been a part of the forms of permanence. All references to specific times and people at the origin of this *Yawulyu* and its corresponding mythic segment will be denied, and then simply forgotten.

In any given region, over time, some *Yawulyu* corpuses fall out of use, usually when the custodians have died without transmitting their knowledge, while new ones emerge and other older ones are given new meanings as they undergo a process of reinterpretation and transformation. This is typical of the ritual dynamic, which ceaselessly adapts to historic contexts and events in order to express, at a given time and as adequately as possible, the world, the experiences, the aesthetics, and the sociopolitical configurations of a given group, at a local level as well as a regional one.

Initiation Ceremonies

In the Western Desert, the *Tingarri* pathways reflect the initiation ceremonies of the boys. Men and women re-enact today what ancestral men and women experienced and performed in the space-time of *Tjukurrpa*. At Balgo, the *Tingarri* is often a synonym of *Tjukurrpa*, but while *Tjukurrpa* represents the Law in a broader sense, the *Tingarri* is specifically the Law concerning the initiation of young boys and their passage to manhood. The narratives linked to the *Tingarri* itineraries recount the travels of ancestral novices accompanied by their elders, as well as the different stages of initiation they underwent. They also tell of the women who gathered not far away, preparing food for those who were undergoing and overseeing the initiation. At the same time, these ancestral women performed their own ritual sequences and lived their own adventures. These initiatory itineraries usually extended over long distances and were spun from the deeds and encounters with other *Tjukurrpa* beings. One recurrent symbolic element of the *Tingarri* epics is the bush fire, which forced the novices and initiators to flee the initiation sites, and which even killed a few of them. The fire is simultaneously a destructive and a regenerative force.

Today in the Gibson Desert, the organization, enactment, and different stages of the initiation ceremonies, taken as a whole, are relatively similar from one language group to another (Myers 1986a: 228–33). As for the specific *Tjukurrpa* celebrated and the ritual sequences performed at the initiations by men and women, they vary according to the novices' configuration of belonging and the local groups involved. The initiation period offers the novices the opportunity to familiarize themselves with the Law and to discover some of its sacred-secret matters, to meet elders from other communities in order to broaden their knowledge, and to learn from them the *Tjukurrpa* corpuses of their own specific configuration of belonging. The boys' initiations are the ceremonies that involve the greatest number of people, assembling together from over the greatest distances for the longest periods of time. An extensive network of relationships spread over a vast area of land links the members of various local groups, now established in different settlements, who are all affiliated to the *Tingarri* of the Western Desert. The initiations are also an occasion to conclude matrimonial alliances, negotiate ritual exchanges, and discuss matters of all kinds, including political and land issues. An intensely excited atmosphere reigns from November to March, the period during which the ceremonies take place.

As a woman, uninitiated into the men's Law, I focused my research on the journeys undertaken in the present-day context for the initiation ceremonies, rather than on the description of the ceremonies as such. Here I present journeys taken during the year 1987–8, and attempt to give the perspectives of the communities concerned (Wirrimanu, Mulan, and Yagga Yagga). These voyages demonstrate the scope and dynamism of the networks of participation in initiation ceremonies. The men and women of the Wirrimanu area do not bear the sole responsibility for initiating their young boys in Ancestral Law; instead it is a communal effort involving members of local groups living in other settlements, even far distant ones.

In mid-November 1987, a boy about twelve years old from Billiluna was 'seized' and taken to Mulan, where he was isolated for two weeks in the men's initiation camp, set up especially for this purpose on the outskirts of the community in the bush. After this period of seclusion, during which the novice (*malulu*) received instruction in the secrets of the Law, he was returned to Billiluna to undergo the final stages of his initiation. The English expression 'to finish him' is often used to refer to the final stages of the circumcision ritual. At the same time, the elders of Balgo isolated several of their young men aged eighteen to twenty in their secluded camp for another step of their initiation into the Law. A short while later, a delegation of elders from Christmas Creek, a Walmatjari community in the Kimberley, 'seized' a young tjungurrayi from Mulan and took him to their place in order to isolate him for a few weeks in the men's camp.

At the end of November, men, women, and children from Balgo and Yagga Yagga joined those from Mulan to wait at Mulan for the arrival of the ritual convoy that would bring back the young tjungurrayi from Christmas Creek. For several days, people waited stoically. The heat was intense, and the temperature oscillated between forty and fifty degrees Centigrade. Two bough sheds were put up for the occasion, about 100 metres apart, one for the women, one for the men, on the southern edge of the settlement. During the day, the men came and went between their bough shed and their secluded camp, which was built about 300 metres farther out in the bush, away from the eyes of women and children. The women waited sitting under their shelter. They painted *Tjukurrpa* motifs on each other's chests and sang *Yawulyu* verses; every now and then they danced. In the evening, the men, women, and children would get together in the space that separated the two bough sheds. Sitting in a semicircle, the men sang verses relating to the initiatory complex while the women danced behind them. On this occasion, particular attention was paid to the novices' mothers' dances, and even more to the dances of their real and classificatory sisters.

Finally one morning, a delegation from Noonkanbah and Christmas Creek arrived, bringing a young tjakamarra to Mulan to be sequestered in the men's camp. A welcoming ceremony for the novice (*malulu*) took place before his isolation period. A group of men sat between the two bough sheds and were soon joined by several women. Two elders led Tjakamarra towards them. His body was coated with a mix of oil and ochre, and he wore a red ceremonial headband and a belt of hair-string at his waist, the *naanpa*. He would wear the *naanpa* throughout the initiatory period; it is a distinctive mark of his *malulu* status. A classificatory brother lifted him onto his shoulders and took him around the seated group. The old men and women took Tjakamarra on their laps, each in turn, before he was led off to the seclusion camp.

Two days later, the eagerly awaited young tjungurrayi finally returned, accompanied by nearly 200 men, women, and children from Christmas Creek, Looma, and Noonkanbah. Next morning, the hosts, both men and women, gathered near the bough sheds. The women had to keep their heads low when the male visitors led Tjungurrayi to the front of the group. As they passed, they threw branches (*tjalyirr*) on the people who were seated. The novice sat on the lap of each of the elders in turn, his torso and waist encircled by belts of hair-string. Then all the men went off to the isolated initiation camp. All the women gathered under their shelter to sing and paint their bodies. They performed some of the sequences from one of their *Yawulyu*. Next to the shelter, the real and classificatory sisters of the novice, the nungurrayi, started cooking, a task for which they alone were responsible. They prepared dozens of dampers (flat bread cooked in hot ashes), huge quantities of tea, and the meat from a bullock from Mulan's cattle, killed that very morning. A few hours later, the nungurrayi set down the food, halfway between their shelter and the men's shelter. They divided the food into two parts, one for each patrimoiety. The women and children then had to turn away, not looking under any circumstances at the men as they arrived from their camp, painted and dancing. The men each took their share of food and sat under the men's shelter. The women and children then were able to look at them; the men returned to their seclusion camp soon afterwards. In the evening, everyone met for songs and dances that recreated episodes from the *Tingarri* epics. The next day at dawn, after a call to meeting, the men gathered in their isolated camp where they spent the rest of the day. On the second evening, Tjungurrayi was circumcised, where no woman could spy upon the event. During the two days of this initiation, ceremonies mourning the death of a Balgo man a few days earlier were interspersed with the celebrations. For this occasion, the real and classificatory wives of the deceased had their faces and torsos painted white with kaolin.

In mid-December, it is the turn of the people from Mulan, Balgo, and Yagga Yagga to take to the road and travel to Christmas Creek in order to bring young Tjakamarra back home for the final stages of his initiation. The ritual convoy, made up of a dozen trucks and as many cars, carries more than 200 people. On the first evening, camp is set up near Christmas Creek. Next morning at dawn the men, still hidden away from the women and the uninitiated, paint themselves. When the convoy gathers together again, it makes its way slowly to the community. The men march in front, in tight formation, each carrying a branch (*tjalyirr*) that he has torn off along the way. They surround young Tjakamarra. Men and women from Christmas Creek are gathered near the bough sheds built for the occasion. Tjakamarra is introduced to the elders in the customary manner and then taken away by the men to the seclusion camp. The ceremonies end two days later, and the convoy returns to Balgo.

At the end of December, two youths from Mulan are initiated at Balgo, and several families from Mulan come to live there for the occasion. At the ceremonial site in the 'bottom camp,' two bough sheds are put up. The first morning, the women gather around the cult objects belonging to the *Mina Mina Yawulyu*. The *kirda* daub the bundles of hair-string with oil and ochre and draw the ritual boards. They sing a few verses and dance some of the sequences of *Mina Mina*, to give the novices strength for their upcoming ordeal. The real and classificatory sisters of the novices cook for everyone. The women continue to sing their songs and perform some of the sequences from other *Yawulyu* throughout the afternoon. As they did at Mulan and Christmas Creek, the men present some of the public sequences of the *Tjukurrpa* with which the novices are closely affiliated.

The next day, the women wait underneath their bough shed most of the day while the men are away at the seclusion camp. Just before sundown, the women and children are called to approach the seclusion camp, and the young *malulu* are presented. The men and women sit on the ground in two separate groups. They gather according to the generational moieties: Tjampitjin/Nampitjin – Tjanpangarti/Napangarti – Tjakamarra/Nakamarra – Tjapaltjarri/Napaltjarri; and Tjapanangka/Napanangka – Tjupurrula/Napurrula – Tjangala/Nangala – Tjungurrayi/Nungurrayi. Then a few women from each of the subsections disappear into the bush with the men and the novices, while the rest of the women and children hurry back to the camps. At the circumcision site, the men sing to accompany the dances of the real and classificatory sisters of the *malulu*. A few young boys, about ten years old, are thrown up into the air and then caught again, to symbolize their future initiation. The young boys and the women are then asked to leave the site so that the circumcision can take place.

In mid-January, initiation activities become even more intense. At Balgo's seclusion camp there are three boys: a tjampitjin from Turkey Creek, a tjangala from Kiwirrkura, and a tjapaltjarri from the Balgo homestead. A convoy leaves for Christmas Creek in order to bring back a young tjapaltjarri. At the end of January, a hundred or so men, women, and children from Balgo, Mulan, and Yagga Yagga set out for the Pintupi community of Kintore. They are returning the young tjangala to his people, and they will wait there for the Pintupi novices to return from their instruction and seclusion period in Amata (an Aboriginal settlement in the northern part of South Australia). They return to Balgo three weeks later, somewhat disappointed, since the convoy from Amata never arrived with their boys.

During this period, initiation ceremonies continue at Mulan where a boy has returned after a few weeks' seclusion at Kununurra (a mainly Kuruntji community to the north). The last stages of his initiation take place at Mulan. During this event, a delegation of elders from Ringer Soak (a Ngarti community) comes to tell the people of Balgo that they will be entrusting three young boys to them for the next month. They will be isolated and instructed in the Law concerning *Luurn* (King-fisher Man). In mid-February, another boy from Mulan is 'seized.' He will be sent by plane either to Christmas Creek or to Lagrange, on the West Coast. At the beginning of March, a convoy from Balgo, Mulan, and Yagga Yagga sets out for Ringer Soak to return the three *malulu* to their own community.

The initiation ceremonies begin in November and continue until March, and sometimes even April. Each year, the journeys undertaken and the communities involved vary. In October 1980, during my first visit, the people of Balgo hosted a convoy that brought young novices from Jigalong. Then in December, an impressive convoy of families from Yuendumu, Lajamanu, Balgo, Mulan, and Christmas Creek trav-elled nearly 3000 kilometres to Jigalong in order to return the *malulu* to their own community for the final stages of their initiation rites. The initiation periods are marked by great excitement, and everyone feels involved. Often the novices, children, and young women are fearful during the initiation season, since it is the most *tarruku* (secret-sacred) event possible and they are not certain what to do or what to expect. The adult and elderly women, for their part, know very well their responsibilities; women usually start participating actively in the initi-ation ceremonies after their first pregnancy. During this period, they spend days and weeks under their bough shed, patiently waiting for the *malulu* to come back, painting each other's chests, and singing and dancing *Yawulyu* sequences to help strengthen the novices during this crucial rite of passage, from which they will emerge as men, *wati*.

Year after year, the initiation ceremonies mobilize people from distant regions. Journeys to participate in such events are on a regional or even a supra-regional scale, and they consolidate the networks of belonging for numerous local groups who share affiliations to and responsibilities for the Western Desert *Tjukurrpa* pathways. Contemporary networks of participation in initiation ceremonies reflect those of the traditional era when novices were required to visit, on foot, the sometimes very distant countries of affiliated local groups. At certain times, all the bands from a vast area gathered together at a given place in order to hold ceremonies concluding the initiation.

Nomadic Rituals and Travelling *Turlku*

'They cannot stay in one place, they must keep going.'

(Napangarti, Balgo)

The circulation and exchange of rituals are essential features of Australian Aboriginal sociality. The topic has been dealt with by various authors in relation to the major mytho-ritual complexes and travelling cults such as the *Kunapipi* (R. Berndt 1951), the *Gadjari* (Meggitt 1966a), the *Worgaia* (Petri and Petri-Odermann 1970; Akerman 1979; Kolig 1981) and, more recently, the *Tjulurru* (Kolig 1979; Glowczewski 1983; Myers n.d.). More recently, Swain (1993) has published a comprehensive and detailed analysis of travelling cults and cosmological innovation, particularly in the northern regions. While these authors have provided invaluable and extensive descriptions of the rituals themselves, they have given little attention to the processes and modalities of exchange.[9] The exchange of mytho-ritual complexes between neighbouring groups, the reality of the 'travelling *turlku*' (ritual songs), which circulate over wide stretches of land and follow the traditional trade routes, has been a continuous practice in Aboriginal Australia[10] since before contact with the *Kartiya*. Travelling cults can be held by only one group at a time and must eventually be given up and taught to a new group in exchange for another.

There is no doubt that the pace of exchange has increased over the course of the twentieth century, particularly in the northern and desert regions. The colonial encounter, the changing conditions of life, the

greater mobility of groups and individuals, and the varying and complex expressions of accommodation and resistance to White society's
law (including Christianity) are among the main factors that have stimulated cosmological innovation, as well as the emergence of new cults,
with their eventual spread over wide areas. Prior to the colonial
encounter, rituals and songs travelled as objects of exchange, and they
contributed to maintaining interconnections and alliance networks
between groups of different cultural areas (without denying local variations and interpretations), while stimulating ongoing local cultural
and ritual renewal. I discuss next three important mytho-ritual corpuses that have undergone such a process of exchange and transmission since the 1950s, and whose respective travelling routes have
crossed Balgo.

The *Tjulurru* is a travelling cult that has been widely documented
and analysed in the anthropological literature,[11] but there remain
many unresolved questions about its historical and semantic complexity. I feel it is important to mention the *Tjulurru*, at least briefly, because
it impregnated the reality of the Balgo mob significantly from the mid-
1970s to the mid-1980s. I then discuss in greater detail two women's
rituals that were exchanged for each other, as well as their respective
travel routes and their modalities of exchange. This transfer of mytho-
ritual corpuses and knowledge underlines their value as exchange
objects. I call these rituals 'nomadic' as well, because, as my friend
Napangarti expressed it, 'they cannot stay in one place, they must keep
going.' The expression of 'travelling *turlku*' that was used by Moyle's
informants in Balgo is also relevant here.

The exchange of travelling cults in Aboriginal culture represents an
ongoing process that involves the participation of various groups from
different cultural areas, and the fulfilment or the finishing of the cult's
exchange may take years, if not decades, to occur. Furthermore, these ritual exchanges contribute, at specific times, to enhancing the reputations
of particular groups and individuals. My emphasis here is on the mobility of the rituals and of the groups enacting the exchange, on certain
aspects of the modalities of exchange, and on the local interpretations
and transformations of the rituals, rather than on their content *per se*.

The exchange and circulation of rituals automatically raise the question of local appropriations and interpretations, particularly in relation
to the connections with the mythical landscape. A group may reinterpret the mythical narrative of a newly received ritual, or certain
sequences of it, modifying it to fit pre-existing land narratives and

ancestral connections of their area, and giving it a local flavour and identity. Such a process implies that ritual and mythic forms are 'open' to change, and that new sequences and elements can be added to an already existing corpus. As will be seen, these local interpretations and innovations are achieved without transforming the underlying and original structure of the rite itself.[12] They also illustrate the dialectic inherent in Western Desert sociality and ritual life between the principles of permanence and repetition and those of openness and transformation.

Tjulurru

The *Tjulurru* is a travelling cult that originated on the West Coast in the first half of the twentieth century.[13] According to Akerman (1979: 235), it began in the Pilbara area. At Balgo, people referred to the Port Hedland area, and to Lagrange and Broome, as being its area of origin. Whatever its exact time and site of origin, it has since then been travelling towards the east and south-east.[14] From Broome, it was given to the groups around the Fitzroy Crossing and Christmas Creek area (Kolig 1979; Akerman 1979) in the Kimberley. From there, it travelled south-east, first to Billiluna in the early 1970s, then on to Balgo. Most people in Balgo were initiated into the Law of the *Tjulurru* at Billiluna. In the late 1970s, the Balgo mob gave the *Tjulurru* to the Pintupi of Kintore and Papunya (Myers n.d.) and to the Warlpiri of Lajamanu and Yuendumu (Glowczewski 1983; Dussart 1988: 128). Since then the Warlpiri of Lajamanu have taught it to the Kurintji of Wave Hill (Glowczewski 1983: 13). From what I was told, the *Tjulurru* travelled to Warrabri, a Warlpiri community to the east, sometime during the 1980s; and the Pintupi have taught it to groups farther south.

The *Tjulurru* is known both as the 'Sleeping Business,' and as the 'Balgo Business.' It is as if the Balgo mob, the first desert people to receive the *Tjulurru*, had imprinted it in a particular way. I witnessed the *Tjulurru* performed at Balgo in 1980. The Balgo mob were very proud to have the *Tjulurru* and drew increased prestige and power from it. They were even, at the time, feared by neighbouring groups, particularly in Halls Creek, because of their close affinity with the *Tjulurru*. When I returned in 1987, a few people even expressed their deep sorrow that the *Tjulurru* had gone and that they had had to give it away. They regretted that the younger generations would never have the chance to be initiated into that Law unless they travelled to the

very distant communities where it was performed. But the long distances involved, and other obligations, usually prevented them from
being able to do so. This sorrow seemed to contrast with what others
have reported elsewhere (Glowczewski 1983: 14–15; Myers n.d.) with
regard to this cult. Some people at Papunya and Lajamanu refused to
be initiated into it because they considered the 'new Law' too dangerous, and chose instead to flee the place for a while. I have never
encountered this attitude in Balgo (which does not mean that it was
not present). Instead, in 1980, a few weeks prior to and after the staging of the *Tjulurru*, men and women were regularly and openly singing its songs at night around the camps. A special bond had evolved
between the *Tjulurru* and the Balgo and Mulan mobs, which might
possibly explain why it is called the Balgo Business.

The We could generalize and say that the *Tjulurru* expressed the Aborigines' response to their encounter and dealings with the White society's
law, and led to the redefinition of such relationships as those between:
Aborigines and Whites, men and women, and old and young.[15] As the
Worgaia did before it, the *Tjulurru* 'transcends local language and
mytho-ritual boundaries' (Akerman 1979: 240). It offers a unifying
principle from which emerges a pan-Aboriginal identity. As Swain
remarked, 'this is not a cult which passively unifies all people and all
places. Its pan-Aboriginal platform is conscriptive, and the locative
powers of the world are being absorbed into a new domain' (1993:
262). In Balgo, this was done by establishing a relation between the
power of the *Tjulurru* and that of the *Tingarri*, as the major Law in the
region. Traditionally, *Tingarri* itineraries crossed the Gibson Desert and
were known to the Walmatjari, Kukatja, and Pintupi alike, but since
the *Tjulurru*, they are now said to travel underground all the way to
Broome, 'all the way to salt water.' The creation of such a link between
the *Tjulurru* and the local mythical landscape and *Tingarri* actors and
events has given every individual the opportunity to identify with the
power of the *Tjulurru*, and with far-away people and places, without
denying their local ancestral connections. It also offered a new ritual
form to make sense of their changing world.

The ethnographic descriptions of the staging of the *Tjulurru* given by
Kolig (Fitzroy Crossing), Myers (Papunya), and Glowczewski (Lajamanu) are very similar to what I observed in October of 1980; the different sequences described by these authors were performed at Balgo
over the four consecutive days and nights of the ritual. This means that
over the course of its travels, the original form of the *Tjulurru* has

remained unchanged. There is, however, a difference in the local inter-pretations that varying groups have given to the major themes and fig-ures of the *Tjulurru*. This is understandable, considering that such travelling cults will be interpreted and adapted to local realities and Laws. We have also to take into account that the colonial history and experiences in the first half of the twentieth century for the Aboriginal groups of the West Coast and those of the Western Desert differ in some respects. The themes, for example, of shipwrecks or plane crashes (and bombings, during the Second World War) that were present in the initial versions of the *Tjulurru* were not part of the reality of the people in Balgo, and seem not to have been present in their ver-sion of it. Whenever I discussed the *Tjulurru* with them, or when we translated the songs from the *Tjulurru*, these themes were never men-tioned. While the Balgo mob did not have exactly the same reading of the *Tjulurru* as groups on the West Coast, no doubt, it spoke and appealed to them at some level, though in a slightly different manner.

The main themes of the *Tjulurru* cult present in all regional versions and accounts, including Balgo, are those of the 'prisoner,' the 'three male figures' (powerful *maparn*), and the 'bush fire.' During the enact-ment of the 'prisoner' theme, the novices to the cult are kept – and treated – like 'prisoners' in seclusion camps under the watchful eyes of 'policemen,' usually with one prison for the men and one for the women. During their period of seclusion, the novices are not allowed to talk and must 'keep their heads down.' They are fed by the 'police-men' and are asked to walk in lines through the bush to an unknown destination; they are asked also to sleep underneath their blankets – hence the name 'Sleeping Business.' In their accounts of the *Tjulurru*, the researchers mentioned above did not emphasize the relation between this aspect of the cult and the repression (and humiliation) that many Aborigines experienced a few decades earlier at the hands of *Kartiya* authorities. The themes of the 'prisoners' and the 'police-men' express the experiences that the Aborigines in the northern and desert regions underwent as prisoners, when they were chained by White police. The following excerpt about Broome from Ryder (1935) is revealing: 'Along the road, a group of Aboriginal prisoners is working under the supervision of policemen armed with rifles. The prisoners are coupled with chains and rods, just like the indigenous people in Congo.'[16] As mentioned in chapter 1, the people in Balgo strongly identified with this theme, because in the early years of the mission, some of them were chained and marched to the Halls Creek prison (then an unknown destination) by armed police. Some of the songs of the Balgo *Tjulurru* refer to 'chains' (and to being chained).

The three male figures that are dominant in the cult in all versions seem to have had a slightly different meaning in Balgo than elsewhere, where they were presented either as 'kings' or as 'demons.' In the Balgo version, these figures were definitively associated with the mythical Cowboy (see chapter 4),[17] and were presented as being powerful and dangerous. Some people even insisted that one of the cowboys was really John Wayne. During the last night of the performance, one of the cowboys kills the other two. This was said to be the act of John Wayne. The two other cowboys are said to be of Asian origin. Since about 1880, the Aboriginal groups in the Broome area had been in close contact with Chinese, Japanese, and Malaysians who had immigrated to Australia to participate in the pearling industry. One woman stated that these three figures were in fact the 'three shadows' of one powerful *maparn* (medicine man). While all the regional versions (and accounts) of the *Tjulurru* refer to an Asian (Malay, Chinese, or Japanese) presence or influence, their role in the elaboration and the narrative thread of the cult remains ambiguous.

As regards the theme of the 'bush fire,' in the Balgo version of the *Tjulurru*, it is said that in Broome, one *maparn* threw away his healing powers, which then turned into a huge bush fire. The songs then would make a close connection between that particular bush fire and other bush fires that occurred in desert area *Tingarri* events. As one elderly woman put it, 'That bush fire been cover up that *Tingarri*. Finish now that *Tingarri*. Start *Tjulurru*.'

The Balgo people learned the *Tjulurru* from the Kimberley groups in the early 1970s. They immediately started to teach and transfer it to the Warlpiri and the Pintupi; the teaching and transfer processes were finished by the early 1980s. Such an exchange implies that the receivers must give something to the givers; and in the case of a ritual exchange, money, blankets, and other such goods are far from sufficient. In exchange for the *Tjulurru*, the Warlpiri of Yuendumu gave the performance rights of the *Jardiwampa* ceremony (also called *Winparrku Turlku*) to the Balgo mob (Moyle 1979). Though the Lajamanu people had received the *Tjulurru* from Balgo in the late 1970s, their exchange payment had not yet been completed. In October of 1987, a group of men and women from Lajamanu came to teach the Balgo mob the last of the parts of one of their public ceremonies. The teaching process for this ritual had started a few years earlier, and this visit represented one of the final stages in giving the full performance rights to the Balgo people.

The ritual is linked with, among others, the *Tjukurrpa* of *Puluwanti* (a night bird, probably the owl) and was often called by that name. Other ancestral beings referred to in the ritual were the Snake and the Blanket Lizard. The tjapangarti/napangarti, tjapanangka/napanangka, tjapalt-jarri/napaltjarri, and tjungurrayi/nungurrayi are *kirda* for that ritual. Peterson had observed this ritual (*Buluwandi*) in Yuendumu during the 1960s and described it well.[18] What I observed in Balgo over that period of seven days included the main structural elements and ritual sequences presented by Peterson: the patrimoieties' respective roles and responsibilities, male and female participation, singing and dancing with the decorated shield and the ceremonial poles, the fire sequences, and the burning of the pubic hair. Men and women in Balgo established some connections between the *Puluwanti* and the *Worgaia* (*Wakaya*), a travelling cult that had passed through Balgo, heading from east to west, probably sometime in the 1960s (not long before the *Tjulurru*).[19] They had received it from the Warlpiri (of Lajamanu and/or Yuendumu) before giving it to the Christmas Creek and Fitzroy Crossing groups. We could infer from this close association between the *Puluwanti* and the *Worgaia* (itself associated with the *Kunapipi* and the *Kadjari*, see Swain 1993: 250), that these ceremonies might have originated from the same wider mytho-ritual complex and were being transmitted west by successive sections. As for the *Tjulurru*, no one knows where, when, and how it will end its travels.

One of the main differences between a travelling cult such as the *Tjulurru* and a 'travelling *turlku*' is that once the first is taught and transferred in completion to another community, those who gave it cannot stage it again in their own community. In the late 1980s, the only way that the people from the Balgo area could participate in the *Tjulurru* was to travel to the distant communities where it was being performed. The *Jardiwampa* or *Puluwanti* ceremonies are travelling *turlku*, and the right to perform them can be given (which implies a long teaching process of all the songs, dances, and designs) to new groups, while the ownership of the ceremony remains in the hands of the initial owners. However, both types of travelling rituals share a nomadic dimension that implies complex and reciprocal modalities of exchange.

Tjarada and Walawalarra

In March 1988, thirty women from Wirrimanu, Yagga Yagga, and Mulan travelled by plane to Kiwirrkura, a Pintupi community south of the Gibson Desert. This one-week visit was to be one of the last stages in a long process of ritual exchange that had been initiated a few years earlier. The visiting women were to give to the Pintupi women a *Tjarada*, a love-magic ritual that they had themselves received some fifteen years earlier from some northern communities. In exchange, and respecting the underlying principles of reciprocity, they were to receive from the Pintupi women the third, and final, part of a large ceremonial cycle called the *Walawalarra*, or 'Bush Way.' Originally from Pitjantjatjarra (and Luritja) country farther south, the Bush Way was given to the Pintupi women of Papunya during the late 1950s (or so I guess). Then, in the early 1980s, the first two parts of that particular ceremonial cycle were given to the Balgo and Mulan women. I shall now describe the two rituals, respecting the limits given to me by the women as to what may legitimately be revealed.

Tjarada

Catherine Berndt (1950) describes the *Tjarada* as a ritual category closely related to the *Yilpintji* (*Ilbindji*), which she calls 'love magic.' Without denying this one facet of the *Yilpintji*, Bell offers a more encompassing description: 'Love and sex are only aspects of *Yilpintji*, which encompasses the sweep of emotion and tension engendered by male-female relationships' (1993: 163). Payne presents *Yilpintji* knowledge in a similar manner, 'as a mechanism through which social and emotional balance is maintained in a community' (1989: 54). The Balgo women described the *Tjarada* received from the north as *Yilpintji*. However, a notable difference between the two is that the *Yilpintji* songs, dances, and designs, at least in the Balgo area, have male and female versions, whereas the *Tjarada* appears to be solely a women's concern. As a ritual category, the *Tjarada* is much more widespread in the northern areas where Berndt conducted her research (Kununurra, Turkey Creek, Wave Hill, Nicholson) than in the desert regions.[20] In fact, the *Tjarada* dealt with here is the only one I have ever seen (or heard of) performed by the women of the Balgo area.

Berndt's informants in the Wave Hill area classified the various *Tjarada* as either 'old' or 'new.' She does mention an old *Tjarada* that had been given to the groups of Ord River in the 1940s, and a 'new one' that had been created 'recently' – that is, sometime in the late 1940s (C. Berndt 1950: 31). A testimony to ritual dynamism, this distinction between old and new is still invoked today as new *Tjarada* emerge and others are traded away or locally transformed during the course of their circulation. The Turkey Creek women performed a few sequences of a new *Tjarada* in a rather imposing ritual gathering that took place on the shores of Lake Gregory in July 1987. By contrast, the one that I discuss here was regarded as an old *Tjarada*.

The women from Wirrimanu, Mulan, and Yagga Yagga who flew to Kiwirrkura in 1988 to teach and give a *Tjarada* to the Pintupi women had themselves received it fifteen or more years earlier from the northern communities. A couple of women in their forties told me that in their youth, while they were working on cattle stations in the north, they had observed this same ritual performed at Port Keats, Kununurra, and Wave Hill. Some of the women said that it came originally from Port Keats, while others insisted it came from Wave Hill or Nicholson. In any case, the *Tjarada* given to the Pintupi women in 1988 emerged in the Wave Hill region (or possibly farther north), and women from different groups may have participated in its elaboration.

The performance of the *Tjarada* that took place at Kiwirrkura occurred over a three-day period and conjured up an aura of love magic. The body paintings done during the ritual used essentially white ochre; in *Yawulyu* rituals and in the *Walawalarra*, red and yellow ochre are also used. *Tjarada* participants drew a series of white lines on their foreheads and chins and under their noses. While they were enacting the *Tjarada*, the women did not isolate themselves completely from the men, as they do when they perform sequences of the *Walawalarra* or the *Yawulyu*. They would settle some fifty metres away from the main camp, where the Kiwirrkura men could, without approaching, hear the songs if they wished. The sacred pole (*kuturu*) of the *Tjarada* was not identified with any particular subsection or patrimoiety during this ritual.

To my knowledge, the main difference between the exchanged *Tjarada* and other women's rituals were the sequences that conveyed a mocking atmosphere, which provoked roars of laughter from the participants.[21] During these particular sequences, women would either imitate a man or mimic an attempt to seduce him. Much more than with the other rituals that I witnessed, the *Tjarada* had a contemporary flavour to it: the sequences of humour portray aspects of recent contact history. For example, a dancer imitates a man shaving in front of a mirror (the accompanying commentary relates that the *Tjukurrpa* women desired him as soon as they saw him); or a man putting on his cowboy boots; or two dancers performing a sequence with a cowboy hat. These demonstrate the insertion of ritual sequences introduced since the contact period. Catherine Berndt (1950) mentions similar sequences, which she observed during the performance of this *Tjarada* at Wave Hill. Overall, though, the *Tjarada* conveys a serious, dramatically charged atmosphere, directly linked to the acts of the *Tjukurrpa* heroines associated with the ritual.

In comparing Berndt's descriptions of *Tjarada* with my own data, I find two major differences. First, in the Wave Hill area of the late 1940s, the heroines of the *Tjarada* are the *Mungamunga*,[22] while in the Balgo version of 1988 they have become the *Nangala Kutjarra*, two *Tjukurrpa* women of the nangala subsection. The ritual was often referred to as the *Nangala Kutjarra*. These heroines could belong to the *Mungamunga* category (see chapter 4), but the women of Wirrimanu never referred to them as *Mungamunga*. Second, according to Berndt, the *Tjarada* rituals she witnessed did not seem to correspond to any *Tjukurrpa* tracks, and had no specific geographically based narratives. In Balgo, the correspondence between a given ritual and a *Tjukurrpa* track is imperative. The *Tjarada* received from the north had therefore been assimilated – as would happen with any new or exchanged ritual or travelling cult like the *Tjulurru* – into the pre-existing land-based mythic forms of the area. The Balgo version has the *Nangala Kutjarra* starting their travels around Lake Mackay, at a site called Tjikarri (near Alec Ross Range), a place of great significance long before the *Tjarada* came to Balgo. A few songs in the *Tjarada* refer to the *Nangala Kutjarra* as passing through Tjikarri. They then travelled farther north around Lajamanu, Wave Hill, and finally into the Halls Creek area where, it is said, they completed their journey.[23] A further proof of recently added local innovations into this *Tjarada* is that the songs that refer to the site of Tjikarri are in Kukatja, whereas those received with the initial corpus from the northern communities are in Kurintji.

This local identification of the northern *Tjarada* with the site of Tjikarri and its associated ancestral beings, which the Balgo women initiated, has a political significance, since most of these women are able to trace an affiliation to this particular site (or related segments), as either *kirda* or *kurdungurlu*. Furthermore, the process of the identification of a relatively newly received ritual to a Kukatja site of local mythological significance is even easier to see when we bear in mind that in the local *Tjukurrpa* narrative, four ancestral women, not two, began their mythical travels at Tjikarri. According to this narrative, from Tjikarri two of the four heroines headed towards the Stansmore Range (Mungkayi). The *Yawulyu Tjiparri* (discussed earlier, and of

which some Balgo, Mulan, and Yagga Yagga women are the main custodians) recounts these two women's travels. The *Tjiparri* is an old
ritual; locally, it is said to be 'the mother of all *Yawulyu*.' The other two
Tjukurrpa women who set out from Tjikarri towards the north are the
heroines of the 'new' *Tjarada*.

   This assimilation of a ritual received from the north into a pre-existing *Tjukurrpa* narrative of the Gibson Desert illustrates very clearly the
process of significant local reinterpretation, innovation, and integration into the local mythology without denying the real origin of the ritual (in this case, Wave Hill) or its own underlying structure. The
Tjarada songs relating to the site of Tjikarri were revealed by the *Nangala Kutjarra* in dreams to a few Balgo and Mulan women. The assimilation of the received *Tjarada* into the mythic reality of the Wirrimanu
groups allowed them to give it a local feeling as well as facilitating its
regional insertion. This bears testimony to the spatio-temporal 'openness' and underlying potential for the transformation of mytho-ritual
forms. The connection of the *Tjarada* to the local mythology also carries
a political significance: the identification that they have established
between the two narratives is even more relevant when one bears in
mind that the two heroines of *Tjiparri* are closely connected to the
Kungkayunti, a group of *Tjukurrpa* women who travelled in Pintupi
country, farther south.[24] One can infer that eventually the Pintupi
women, since 1988 custodians of the *Tjarada*, will integrate it into some
of their own mythical tracks and narratives, without denying its northerly origin and the travels of its heroines from Tjikarri.

Walawalarra

   'This one big Law. Number one Business. You've got to remember this
   Law.'

                                                          (Napangarti, Mulan)

The *Walawalarra* are a category of *Tjukurrpa* women having many
physical and esoteric similarities to the *Mungamunga*.[25] Like the latter, they are said to be women of 'high degree,' with strong magical
powers; they have long hair and long pubic hair, and wear ceremonial regalia. They live on their own and avoid the company of men;
they like dancing and singing. They reveal in dreams new songs and
ritual sequences. In Balgo, the *Mungamunga* are distinguished from
the *Walawalarra* mainly by their geographical origin: the *Munga-*

munga are associated with the Warlpiri to the east, and with northern groups, while the *Walawalarra* are from the southern parts of the desert. The ceremonial cycle that I will briefly present here is called either the *Walawalarra* or the 'Bush Way.' It is highly valued by the women of the Balgo area, and feared by most men and young people. It originally came from the region of Amata, Ernabella, Ayers Rock, and Docker River, which are farther south in the Central Desert. A few of the songs of the cycle heard in the Wirrimanu area are still in the Luritja and Pitjantjatjarra languages. The performance of the whole ceremonial cycle goes on for five days. I was privileged to witness it in July of 1987, during the women's gathering at Lake Gregory that was mentioned earlier.

The *Walawalarra* is a women's ritual that is highly *tarruku* (sacred-secret).[26] Under no circumstances are men and children allowed near the ceremonial grounds. An elderly woman told me a few recent stories in which the *Walawalarra* reputedly punished men (either by killing them or by making them sick) who had tried to hear the songs connected with the ritual or to violate its sacred objects (narratives 11 and 12). Despite the prohibition on men's participation in the performances, some elderly men in Balgo (and other communities) do know some of the stories and songs related to the ritual. In fact, an old man of the tjapanangka subsection had received two new songs from the *Walawalarra*, which they wished him to transmit to the women (narrative 10). Children do not accompany the women to the ceremonial ground during the staging of the *Walawalarra*; the power of some songs could be harmful for them.

The *Walawalarra* is not considered to belong to the *Yawulyu* category. When I asked the women whether the *Walawalarra* was a *Yawulyu*, they would hesitate before answering: '*Yawulyu* and Bush Way are different'; or 'Bush Way, different way, coming from south'; or else, 'Doesn't look like *Yawulyu*.' One informant said that the *Walawalarra* was originally a *Yawulyu* and that it transformed eventually into the 'Bush Way.' One could infer from this last comment that when the initial owners of the *Walawalarra* decided to use that particular corpus as an object of exchange, it ceased to be identified with the *Yawulyu* category. As a travelling cult like the *Tjulurru*, the *Walawalarra* is acquired and given away through exchange, and today its mythical narratives cover wide stretches of land from the Pitjantjatjarra to the Pintupi countries. In contrast, a *Yawulyu* is inherited through the mother's or the father's line, tends to be held by the same group(s) over succeeding genera-

tions, and helps them in establishing their responsibility (and ownership) over a particular country.

The *Walawalarra* is composed of 'three mobs [sets] of songs': one
belongs to the Balgo (and Yagga Yagga) women, another to the Mulan
women, and the third to the Pintupi women of Kiwirrkura (and Kintore). The first two song series were given to the Balgo and Mulan
women in the early 1980s by women from Papunya. The third group of
songs, as already noted, was in the process of being passed on to the
Balgo, Yagga Yagga, and Mulan women by the women of Kiwirrkura,
in return for the *Tjarada*. Among the sacred objects of the *Walawalarra*
are three *kuturu* (ceremonial poles), one belonging to each of the communities mentioned above. The 'ownership' of the three poles and
associated songs are defined under the *kirda/kurdungurlu* division.
Only the *kirda* are authorized to dance with the pole and to drive it into
the ground at the beginning of the ritual performances;[27] they also
have the responsibility at the end to pull it out. The Balgo (and Yagga
Yagga) *kuturu* was associated with the napanangka/napangarti patrimoiety; the Mulan and Kiwirrkura (Kintore) poles were associated
with the other patrimoiety. Thus during performances of the *Walawalarra*, the same person can act as *kirda* for some parts of it, and *kurdungurlu* for others. It remains to be seen whether the *Walawalarra* is
indeed a 'trilogy.' If so, this would suggest a more permanent division
than one resulting merely from one stage in the process of exchange.

The mythical narrative of the cycle tells the story of two *Walawalarra*,
from the nangala and napanangka subsections (in a cross-cousin relationship such that each belongs to one patrimoiety).[28] They began their
journey in Pitjantjatjarra or Luritja country, to which a number of
sequences refer; they then travelled in Pintupi country and around
Kintore and Kiwirrkura. It seems that they finished their travels at
Winparrku, not far to the east of Kiwirrkura. Nevertheless, they keep
on travelling, even today, protecting women and going where there is
dancing. They generally signal their presence through dreams. The
possibility is not to be ruled out that their territorial inscriptions, in
terms of *Tjukurrpa* segments, could eventually be extended farther,
through dream revelations, closer to Kukatja country.

The songs of the *Walawalarra* cycle are countless. Through the years
some disappear into oblivion, while new ones emerge after dream revelations or unexpected experiences. During my first stay in Balgo in
1980–2, I taped performances of some *Walawalarra* sequences. When I
returned in 1987–8, I asked some of the women to listen to those tapes.

They realized then that they had in fact forgotten two songs. On the other hand, during my second stay, I collected six new song-lines and ritual sequences that had been given to women (and to the elderly man mentioned above) by the *Walawalarra*, mostly through dream experiences, in the intervening years. Here again, as for the *Tjarada*, we are witnessing the transformation of a mytho-ritual corpus by the people who, during a particular period at a particular place, hold custody over it.

The Process of Exchange

I will now reconstruct the respective routes, over the past thirty years or more, of the two nomadic rituals previously described, and their meeting and exchange in Balgo: the *Tjarada* originated in the north and is moving south, while the *Walawalarra* is travelling from the south to the north-west. I first became aware of this ritual exchange in September 1987, when seven Pintupi women from Kiwirrkura came by plane to Balgo. Over the period of one week they taught the land-based narrative and the ritual sequences linked to the third part of the *Walawalarra* to the Balgo and Yagga Yagga women. They also brought with them the ceremonial *kuturu*, but it was not to be finally given to the Balgo women until some subsequent occasion, when the whole learning process would be completed. During that week, practices were held every afternoon outside the main community, and well away from the men and children. On the final day, and this time not far from the camps, the Balgo and Yagga Yagga women performed for the Pintupi a few sequences of the *Tjarada* in order to start the return teaching process. The Pintupi women returned to Kiwirrkura with the recorded tapes that I had made of these sequences. It was agreed that, after the initiation ceremonies held between October and March, the Balgo, Yagga Yagga, and Mulan women would bring the *Tjarada* (and its associated sacred objects) to Kiwirrkura.

I have already mentioned that the *Tjarada* came to Balgo from the northern communities, and that by the late 1980s the women in the Balgo area had been its custodians for the last fifteen years or so. A woman currently in her late twenties saw the *Tjarada* performed in Balgo for the first time not long before her puberty. When the *Tjarada* was first given to the Balgo women, they were all living in one community. Later, the ownership of the *Tjarada* and the responsibility for its ritual sequences and objects was divided among three groups: the

Balgo and Yagga Yagga women, the Mulan women, and the Ringer Soak women. This division developed following the creation of outstations, and in two stages: first, with the establishment of Mulan sometime after 1975; and second, in the early 1980s when a few families left Balgo to settle in Ringer Soak (south of Halls Creek). When certain women decided to leave Balgo for the outstations, they probably wanted to maintain access to the *Tjarada*, and so negotiated to bring with them some of the ritual objects and sequences of the *Tjarada* to which they felt entitled. Today, this division of ownership of the *Tjarada* is respected. For example, the Balgo women refused to translate to me the *Tjarada* song-lines that came under the responsibility of the Mulan or Ringer Soak women.

Let us examine how and when the *Walawalarra* came to Balgo. It originated in the southern parts of the Central Desert, and was transmitted, according to my estimations, to the Papunya women in the 1950s or early 1960s. Papunya is a community consisting mostly of Pintupi, southern Warlpiri, and Luritja people. An elderly woman of the napanangka subsection, the main custodian of the *Walawalarra* cycle in Balgo, told me at great length how it was introduced into Papunya by their southern neighbours when she was still a young woman. In her story, she specified that the southern groups had travelled to Papunya by donkey and camel. This bit of historical detail suggests that the ceremonial cycle was brought to Papunya – or a neighbouring community – in the 1950s, or before. After the 1950s, the use of camels became obsolete. By the end of the 1970s, that same Napanangka had become a senior Law woman, and she and Nungur-rayi, a Law woman from Yuendumu, were responsible for teaching and transmitting the *Walawalarra* to the women of the Balgo area. Partly because of that, Napanangka decided to settle in Balgo. Over the years, she contributed to the enrichment of this ceremonial cycle by adding new songs and ritual sequences that were given to her, largely through her dreams (but also through some other experiences), by the *Walawalarra*.

In July 1981, during my first stay in Balgo, Napanangka, with a group of Papunya women, visited the community in order to teach the *Walawalarra*. The practices went on for four days on a ceremonial ground outside the community. The previous year (1980), a group of Balgo women had gone to Papunya in order to receive the *kuturu*, the ceremonial pole they reverently keep today, a symbol of their responsibility towards the *Walawalarra*. The third part of the ceremonial cycle remained in the hands of the Pintupi women. It was this final part (or 'mob of songs') that the women from the Balgo area prepared themselves to receive in 1988, in exchange for the *Tjarada*.

In March 1988, as had been agreed the previous September, thirty women from Balgo, Mulan, and Yagga Yagga flew to Kiwirrkura. Over three days they performed the *Tjarada*, teaching the Kiwirrkura women (and those who had come from Kintore) all the ritual sequences including the designs, the dances, and the songs. Every evening after sunset, the Pintupi women would in turn show their visitors a few songs linked with the third part of the *Walawalarra*. Finally in the early morning of the fourth day, the sacred objects of the *Tjarada*, consisting of hair strings, emu feathers, spears, two boomerangs, and a *kuturu*, were given to the Pintupi women, and with them, the complete responsibility for a ritual that had originated forty or so years earlier in the northerly regions. However, the whole process of exchange was not quite finished when we left Kiwirrkura: in the years to come, Ringer Soak women would have to travel to Kiwirrkura to transmit their part of the *Tjarada* knowledge and sacred objects. This was necessary before the Wirrimanu mob could have access to the third and final part of the *Walawalarra*.

Commenting on this particular cycle of ritual exchange, my friend Napangarti told me that on the day that the Balgo women were to receive a new ritual from the south, the *Walawalarra* cycle would have to be passed on (most likely to Christmas Creek in the Kimberley, a predominantly Walmatjari community), so that it could continue to travel towards the north-west. As for the Pintupi women, they would eventually transmit the *Tjarada* to their southern neighbours, the Pitjantjatjarra.

Nomadic rituals must keep on travelling, to reinforce sociopolitical bonds between neighbouring groups and to create new ones. At every stage in the process of exchange, the mytho-ritual corpus, be it a travelling cult or a 'travelling *turlku*,' undergoes local interpretations: the group that holds custody over it at a particular place in a particular time may add to its geographical narrative in order to fit it into pre-existing local forms of *Tjukurrpa*. This continually changing ritual body becomes a testament to cultural dynamism and to local (regional) historicity, and is done without ever denying the origin of the exchanged ritual, or the identity of its initial custodians. These realities are a fundamental principle of Aboriginal 'Business' and politics.

Creativity, Innovation, and Collective Issues

The dominant discourse in the Western Desert insists that all transformations of the forms of permanence are essentially initiated through dreaming, a medium that transmits the spoken word of the ancestors. The discourse stipulates that, during dreaming, *Tjukurrpa* beings and deceased relatives reveal to humans the content of mythic segments and ritual sequences that were, up until then, unknown, but that have always existed at a virtual level. Exempt from the constraints of space and time, the dreaming experience appears as the medium of contact between *Tjukurrpa* and the ongoing present. In order to remain faithful to Aboriginal perspective, it is therefore more correct to speak of revelation rather than innovation. Such revelation is proof of the reality of ancestral intervention in the ongoing present, and of the ancestor's embodiment in specific places; it is also proof of the ancestors' concern with human affairs. However, at the level of praxis, the value of personal creative and strategic contributions within the mytho-ritual dynamic must also be investigated, since it is these contributions that end up transforming the 'state of the world' on a collective level. It is in this way that the configuration of belonging and the immanence of *Tjukurrpa* offer each person the possibility of acting creatively, in the name of the Law and of the local group, by either adding or reinterpreting mytho-ritual components. This is assuming that the relevance of each rereading is recognized and validated by the whole group.

On an analytical level, there is a crucial distinction to be made between, on the one hand, dreaming as a place for revelation (and recognized as such in the social discourse), and on the other, the contribution made by creativity and strategy of people in the waking state to collective issues. Western Desert societies rely on this creativity of people, along with their understanding of *Tjukurrpa* matters and intimacy with some ancestral beings, in order to ensure the spatial and temporal renewal of the forms of permanence. We are therefore far from those 'prescriptive' societies where, according to Sahlins, everything consists of mere execution and repetition. We could argue, on the other hand, that even 'execution and repetition' in the ritual domain imply performative and aesthetic considerations, as well as a deep knowledge of the world in which such actions take place. In Aboriginal Australia, as anywhere else, any form of participation and engagement in the ritual sphere, or any other sphere, necessarily entails a performative dimension. At the same time, the denial by the Aborigines themselves of creative human action in favour of an ancestral intervention avoids the risk of overemphasizing the individual's importance and is consistent with a logic of shared identity and responsibility. It is also consistent with the notion that the person is one dynamic node within a network of intrinsic and manifold relationships among people, places, and ancestors.

As a general rule, such a process of creativity weaves together the aesthetic, political, social, and historical dimensions of collective expressions. Creation is sometimes spontaneous, as when it is received in dreams, and sometimes strategic, as when it is elaborated in the waking state with full consciousness of recent events and current collective needs. But more often than not, these two processes work in unison: a mytho-ritual element that is first perceived in a dream will afterwards be investigated, interpreted, and restructured by the dreamer and his or her close relatives. Thus, the revelation/innovation is unavoidably subjected to a process of collective recognition and elaboration before it is integrated into mytho-ritual practice. Once it is inserted into the forms of permanence, any personal or temporal (but not spatial) references will be forgotten, erased, or denied. This is an essential element of Aboriginal historicity and cosmocentric understanding of a world that is forever unfolding through the interaction among the ancestral order, the ongoing present, and the dream realm, and between human and non-human agencies. What appears as a denial of human creative action is rather a recognition that whatever happens is the outcome of an interplay among different agencies, realms of action, and modes of experience, with ancestrality as a hierarchically superior value.

The discourse that fixes dreaming as the medium of communication with the ancestors appears to an outsider to deny human creative participation. It coexists, however, with the cultural and social practices that ceaselessly stimulate the personal imagination and make use of its cognitive and creative potential for collective purposes. The different levels of mytho-ritual transformation and innovation, and the modalities of their insertion into *Tjukurrpa*, will emerge more clearly in the following examples.

Example 1

More than 200 women from various regions participated in the ritual gathering at Lake Gregory in July of 1987. While they were there, a new ritual sequence that originated in a dream was presented for the first time, a few weeks after its revelation. One afternoon, at the ceremonial ground, as the women were rubbing oil onto their bodies and painting sacred designs on each other in preparation for the *Walawalarra* dances, two women from Ringer Soak, Napangarti and Napurrula, of mixed Ngarti-Warlpiri origin, chose that moment to present a new sequence of a *Yawulyu* that fell under the guardianship of the women of Ringer Soak and Lajamanu. What first attracted my attention was the fact that not a single song was sung during the dance sequence. This silence was unusual, to say the least, since dances are always accompanied by songs. A murmur rumbled through those watching: '*kapukurri, kapukurri.*' The audience was pleased with the demonstration, which was an important step in the acceptance of the sequence into the *Yawulyu.*

Napangarti, a middle-aged woman, and one of the two dancers, explained to me how she had received this sequence in a dream. It was around noon and she was taking a nap in her camp at Ringer Soak. Her husband had lit a fire not far away, and the smoke woke up the *Mungamunga*, who visited Napangarti in her sleep. At the beginning of her dream, she saw two *Mungamunga* dancing towards her, then behind them she saw many more *Mungamunga*. They were dancing in twos towards a ceremonial pole driven into the ground. It was this same sequence that Napangarti and Napurrula reproduced in part at the gathering by the lake. Napangarti hadn't forgotten the songs that the *Mungamunga* were singing in her *kapukurri*, either. She added that this revelation came in fact from her father, a tjapanangka, because the songs received bore his personal name. As soon as she woke up, she shared her dream with one of the main custodians of the *Yawulyu*, a nampitjin. Since the latter wasn't at the Lake Gregory gathering, there was no one to sing the songs that accompanied the two dancers. It was nevertheless crucial to obtain some kind of collective recognition. As the Lake Gregory gathering offered an excellent forum for this, they decided to present just the dance by itself. Moreover, this public presentation bore witness to the future insertion of the dreamed sequence into the *Yawulyu*, which belonged to the women of Ringer Soak and Lajamanu.

This dream revelation leads to another point to consider: because the personal name of the dreamer's father appeared in the verses, he became by virtue of this fact fully identified with *Tjukurrpa*. It can be supposed that during his life, this man had earned the esteem of the community by his actions in general and his sustained participation in the sacred domain. To honour his memory, his children have inscribed his name in the *Tjukurrpa*. Any reference to the person who really lived will gradually fade, and his name will blend into the forms of permanence. This first example thus signifies the interweaving of dreaming, myth, and local historicity.

Example 2

Napangarti, then in her mid-twenties, was one of the few women of her generation who was very active in rituals. She received through a dream a new sequence for the *Mina Mina Yawulyu* (see above), a *Yawulyu* that she knew very well because she regularly participated in it. It was her first revelatory dream, and she was very proud of both her experience and her contribution. She told me that the night before, she had woken up at sunrise. She saw the first light of day, pulled the blankets over herself better, and went back to sleep. It was then that she saw some napangarti and some napanangka dancing, one behind the other, in a long line, like a snake. Each woman held two little sticks that she hit together and all of them had their heads turned, looking behind. This last detail recalls a part of the narrative where it is said that the *Mungamunga*, exiled to the east, are always looking westwards, to their Mina Mina country. The dreamer did not notice what designs were painted on the bodies of the dancers, but she did hear two verses sung by the *Mungamunga*. These verses named a place neighbouring Mina Mina and referred to the mythic Snake. As soon as she woke up, she told her mother and grandmother about her dream. She then went to the camp where four napanangka, the female caretakers of *Mina Mina,* were living with their families, and recounted the dream to them. The eldest of these was extremely satisfied with the dream and knew immediately where to situate this sequence into the *Mina Mina* narrative and into the performance of the ritual. According to her, it comes just before the sequence where the ceremonial pole (*kuturu*) is driven into the ground.

For Napangarti, this innovative contribution and its insertion into the pre-existing forms helped increase her participation in ritual activities. After this dream, the elders let her do body painting on the other women, a privilege that she had not yet received because of her youth. Her dream experience was fruitful and accorded her more respect, and one can assume that it encouraged Napangarti to keep up her active, creative participation in the mytho-ritual sphere. Indeed, this was possibly the elders' aim in greeting her dream so positively. It is usually more mature adults or elders, men and women, who are hosts to *Tjukurrpa* beings in dreamt revelations like this one. This is because they have both integrated the discourse of permanence and understand the possibility, sometimes presented as a necessity, of transforming ritual content and mythic pathways. Nevertheless, nothing in the Law prevents the creative participation of young people if they can demonstrate their interest and competence. Dreaming thus allows people to transcend, to a certain extent, the boundaries of the sacred and the boundaries between the initiated and the uninitiated, between young and old, and between women and men (Poirier 2001).

Example 3

Napanangka was the main guardian of the *Walawalarra* in Balgo before her death in the 1990s. She had significantly enriched this body of ritual knowledge through two new sequences, including songs and dances, that were revealed to her by the *Walawalarra* as she was returning from Alice Springs with a group from Balgo; they had been to hear Pope John Paul II.[29] Napanangka had very few ties to the Catholic church, and I doubt that she was baptized. She was already quite old in 1986 and travelled rarely, so for her the trip to Alice Springs was above all an unexpected opportunity to get together with relatives from near and far.

On the way back, while they were travelling through the Tanami region, she fell ill. The convoy interrupted its journey, and one vehicle was sent ahead to Balgo to fetch the nurse. During this halt, the old woman received a visit from the *Walawalarra* in a dream. The first verse that was revealed to her sings of people returning home, and mentions a hill on the route between Alice Springs and Yuendumu. Today, when the *Walawalarra* is performed at Wirrimanu, this song is used to call the women to the ceremonial ground. In a second dream, she saw two *Walawalarra* dancing, holding each other by their little fingers, and heard them singing a long song. This sequence has also been incorporated into the ritual in question.

It is significant that in the three examples above, each narrative features the intervention of an external element: the smoke from a fire lit by the husband; the first rays of light from the rising sun; and lastly, illness. Far from being trivial details, these elements constitute keys to understanding the process of creativity. First, it can be supposed that this kind of experience and narrative form implies light sleep rather than deep slumber, so that the dreamers could be in a state of semi-wakefulness and witness the elaboration of the ritual sequence not passively but actively. Second, the external elements seem to evoke a '*rêverie*,' in Bachelard's sense of the term, rather than a dream proper. Third, there is a dominant narrative form concerning the visit of *Tjukurrpa* beings or deceased relatives who make ritual revelations. It is often (although not always) said that the *Mungamunga* or others visit the dreamer at dawn, just before or just after first light. This may, of course, be an unimportant discursive element, but it is also highly likely that the Aborigines see this time of day as propitious for the greatest possible receptivity.[30] The same receptivity can be extended to sickness, another auspicious state for dream journeys, revelations, and encounters with *Tjukurrpa* beings and deceased relatives, and ultimately a period during which one acquires greater strength (*marrka*).

Example 4

This example concerns the sequences of the *Inningarra Yawulyu* that were revealed during a journey to Inningarra country by a group of men and women from Balgo and Lajamanu (see above) in 1982, nearly thirty years after they had last visited that country. I was told that Napurrula, a Balgo woman of Ngarti-Warlpiri origin who was directly affiliated to Inningarra country through her father, was visited by the *Mungamunga* in a dream and became the source of the new *Yawulyu* sequences. When I asked her, she denied this, and said that it was Nakamarra, her father's sister, then living at Lajamanu, who had received the dream visit and the revelation from the *Mungamunga*. This example is doubly pertinent in that it highlights the refusal to take the credit for, or to personalize, an innovation (revelation) to the ritual domain. It also confirms the concept of shared identity. Napurrula and her aunt, Nakamarra, both have definite claims to Inningarra country and to the *Tjukurrpa* segments that cross it. Both come from Inningarra country and were conceived there, and are included among the guardians of the country's vital essence. Neither feels the need to affirm her rights and responsibilities as *kirda* over the other, and neither thinks that it matters which of them served as the intermediary for the *Mungamunga* when they want to reveal the sequences of a *Yawulyu* that had been forgotten. It is possible, of course, that the two women both had the dreams, in which case this example could be related to the theme of the 'shared dream' (see chapter 4).

Examples 5 and 6

An event experienced during the waking state could possibly lead to the creation of new ritual songs and sequences. The journey to Kiwirrkura, mentioned above, was undertaken in order to transmit the *Tjarada* to Pintupi women, who in turn took the opportunity to show their hosts some more sequences in the third part of the Bush Way. One of the sequences had first appeared at Kiwirrkura itself, a few years beforehand. I was told that a group of Pintupi women had met up at Kiwirrkura to perform the *Walawalarra*. One evening, an elder's blankets caught fire because they had been left too close to the camp-fire. She tried in vain to stamp out the flames burning her few blankets; for her it was a terrible loss, and she was very upset (blankets are very often the only things a person owns, as well as being indispensable during the chilly desert nights). After this sad event, the *Walawalarra* brought her two sequences of dance and song that have since been integrated into the ritual. In one of them, the women imitate the elder trying desperately to stamp out the fire, and they sing about the loss of the blankets that have turned into ashes. Thus, the elder reinvested her particularly disappointing experience with creative worth. This contribution to the corpus was part of the knowledge that was transmitted to the women of the Wirrimanu region. This example also demonstrates how daily events, some of which may appear trivial to an outsider, may eventually find their way into the ritual domain.

Narrative no. 10 (see chapter 4) offers another example in which the reference to dreaming is not explicit. It tells the story of Tjapanangka, a highly respected Law man and *maparn* who was carried off by the *Walawalarra* after he tried to beat his wife. His family set out to look for him and only found him a few days later, alone and exhausted in the bush. Meanwhile, the *Walawalarra* had left him two songs about the country to which they had taken him, and had ordered him to transmit these to the women. The two new songs today form an integral part of the ritual in question. Here, in the absence of explicit references to dreaming, the discourse is identical, since any trace of personal creativity is still denied. It is effectively the *Walawalarra* who revealed the new songs.

Not all dream revelations have such positive outcomes, for a variety of reasons. Either the dreamer wakes abruptly before receiving the whole

238 A World of Relationships

revelation; or when the dreamer awakens, he or she forgets the relevant content; or the dreamt song is about a recent event (for example, a meteorite that fell near Jupiter Well, to the south, in 1987) but cannot be fitted into any existing mythic or ritual form; or else the dreamer or some elders decide that the new verse is not relevant because it is either incomplete or doesn't match the forms of permanence. So, the reception of new songs, designs, or other elements in dreams often involves its own share of trial and error.

All the examples of revelation/innovation discussed in this book, including the one about Yagga Yagga (see chapter 2), illustrate different levels or types of mytho-ritual transformations: the interpretation of historical events and encounters and their integration into pre-existing *Tjukurrpa* pathways (e.g. the *Tjulurru*); the addition of new segments along an itinerary in order to respond to historical contingencies (alliances, migrations, ritual exchanges, and so on) or the insertion of a new episode in the narrative thread of an ancestral itinerary for political, residential, or other reasons (e.g., Yagga Yagga); the creation from pre-existing segments of a new ritual or pathway that reflects the life story of a generation or at least of a group of individuals (e.g., the dreamt *Yawulyu*); the integration into the forms of permanence of a deceased relative who had a remarkable life, or of that person's exploits or experiences.

This underlying dynamic of change inherent in the mytho-ritual sphere thus raises the question of the historical duration of mythic itineraries and segments. According to Aboriginal discourses, new (revealed) knowledge has always existed in a virtual state and, over the course of events and the succession of new generations, the medium of dreams allows them to be 'unearthed' and actualized. In the Western Desert, it is a sociological necessity to attribute age-old, timeless qualities to the *Tjukurrpa* pathways, as if they had always immutably existed. However, we now know that new segments do appear following ritual exchanges, or in order to respond to collective issues and diverse conjunctures, or to introduce people or events of varying significance to the local mythical landscape and ritual corpus. Therefore, certain mythic itineraries or segments are relatively recent, while others are older. Nevertheless, the discourse about them remains the same: they all emanate from *Tjukurrpa*, as ancestral revelations. As soon as a person or event has merged with the ancestral order and is fully identified with it, any temporal reference attached to the person or event is erased. None the less, Aborigines do qualify certain *Tjukurrpa* or rituals as 'very old.'

The dream origin of mythical and ritual elements does not suffice, by itself, to validate their integration into the forms of permanence. These new elements must be subjected to a process of recognition by the Law men or Law women at a local and regional level. Once new elements are integrated into the pre-existing body of knowledge, after the dream material has been interpreted and restructured, all personal and temporal references in the material are negated – only their spatial inscriptions and ritual expressions are retained. Such double negation has long hidden from observers the dimensions that are dear to the Aborigines' sense of historicity, notably the *Tjukurrpa* pathways and different segments and associated rituals.

The main part of my fieldwork was conducted in the 1980s, at a time when the ritual renewal that began in the 1970s was still at the forefront of the people's preoccupations and interests. All year long, the Balgo mob, along with other Western Desert mobs, were intensely involved in ritual activities. As we have seen, these included the annual initiation ceremonies and the exchanges of travelling *turlku* and of major travelling cults. While the exchange of rituals and travelling *turlku* has always been part of Aboriginal reality (and sociality), the accessibility of modern means of transport and communication contributed to increase their frequency, scope, and range. Along with the outstation movement and the acrylic movement, the ritual activities offered a forum to express the specificity and the strength of their own ways, identities, and sociocosmic order, in reaction and resistance to the increasing pressures and demands from the *Kartiya* world. The overall atmosphere that prevailed then in Balgo was centred on ritual activities and responsibilities and offered an excellent climate for ritual and mythical innovations. In many ways, it stimulated the men and women who were actively involved in the Law into creative participation. While I agree that the ritual and mythical revelations (and innovations) may have been more frequent at that time than in traditional times – in any society, innovations are much more frequent in times of major social changes and crisis – the situation offered a favourable environment to understand better the social and cultural processes at work in the structural transformations of the Law and in the inscription and expression of an endogenous historicity.

The analysis of the dynamic dimension of mythic and ritual knowledge contributes to a better understanding of Western Desert sociality by revealing its intrinsic qualities of 'openness' and 'flexibility.' By 'openness,' I mean the ability of the ritual forms to accept either the reinterpretation of already existing elements or the addition of new ones. At the structural level, the quality of openness applies to ritual sequences and their associated *Tjukurrpa* tracks and segments. At the experiential level, it applies to the 'openness' of the bodily-self, in terms of one's increased receptivity, usually in the dream state, to the spoken word of the ancestors. The aspect of flexibility refers to the pragmatics of collective choice (in answering local politics and interests) and of personal creative potential in the process of rereading and reinterpreting the mytho-ritual corpus.

In the Wirrimanu area, the possibility of proposing a rereading of the existing *Tjukurrpa* forms or of adding new elements to these forms through the medium of dreams is available to all, in keeping with the individual's ancestral connections and configuration of belonging. We must distinguish, however, as Keesing has noted among the Kwaio, between the degrees in the levels of a person's sacred knowledge and his or her capacity to translate a creative experience into a public discourse (1982: 208–9). While every adult man and woman is able to narrate the *Tjukurrpa* stories linked to the lands of his or her configuration of belonging, and often beyond that, some people master the exegesis with greater subtlety and semantic depth, not so much by virtue of their social status but because of their own personal engagement with and interest in the ritual sphere and their intimacy with the *Tjukurrpa* realm.

In the ritual domain, the dialectic between permanence and transformation, between repetition and creativity, now appears more clearly. While Western Desert Aborigines proclaim the everlasting and unchanging character of ancestral itineraries and associated ritual performances, it is nevertheless within these that local and regional historicity are inscribed. The revelation and innovations at the origin of these transformations cannot be assigned to anyone – at least not for very long – avoiding the possibility of focusing too much on the individual – a focus that would not have much place or space for expression in Kukatja sociality anyway. In receiving and communicating the revealed knowledge, dreamers see themselves essentially as intermediaries for the *Tjukurrpa* ancestors (or deceased relatives). The creative and innovative aspect is somehow denied, with the revealed knowledge being seen as something that had always existed at the virtual level, or 'underground,' until its revelation. Unless one can observe the process of innovation 'in the making,' it is difficult, if not impossible, to evaluate the life span of any *Tjukurrpa* segment or ritual sequence.

Such a double denial of the personal creative contribution and of the temporal reference will eventually allow the new material to assume the forms of permanence. Once a segment or sequence is identified with the ancestral realm, temporal and individual references are usually erased from collective memory. As we have seen, such a process is grounded not so much in the denial of human creative abilities as in the recognition that the world is forever unfolding; it is the outcome of an interplay between different agencies, of the manifold and dynamic relationships among different constituents, human and other-than-human.

Conclusion: Ancestrality, Imaginary, and Historicity

In the preceding chapters, I have explored some facets of the dynamic relationships among people, places, and ancestors in Western Desert sociality, identity, and historicity in their structural, narrative, and experiential expressions. In an attempt to understand the world of the Kukatja and neighbouring groups, I have emphasized the following aspects of their reality: the immanent and coeval nature of *Tjukurrpa* as ancestrality; the permeable and flexible character of boundaries; the composite and dividual dimensions of the person; and, finally, the role of dreams and dreaming in the flow of everyday events and in the reinterpretation of forms of permanence. These are social and cultural values that have, somehow, endured to this day. Now irremediably entangled with *Kartiya* values, objects, and institutions, these Aboriginal realities have experienced major transformations and continue to be expressed in unexpected ways.

We can understand the reality of the relationships that are intrinsic to an Aboriginal way of being-in-the-world only when we seriously accept the fact that to them there are no concepts or categories of 'nature' or 'culture' (as we understand these in Western modern dualistic thought), nor is there a separation between the two. From an Aboriginal perspective, and from Aborigines' experience in the world, neither 'nature' nor the land are passive and without purpose, existing only as objects for human perception, mastery, and possession. On the contrary, the world as the Kukatja understand it exists and reveals itself through dynamic and manifold interactions and exchanges among different agencies, be they human, non-human, or ancestral; it is these interactions and exchanges that allow the world to generate itself and to unfold. To say that the 'mythical landscape' is a social construction imposed upon a unique and universal nature, or to reduce it to a system of mental representations, disempowers the land, the sentient places, and all the non-human agencies and discredits (or masks) the reality and value of exchanges between human and non-human agencies. In doing so, it denies the very reality and historicity of the Aborigines, and of how they actually engage and interact with the different constituents of the world.

The role of the landscape and of places in mediating between present experience and the ancestral order, between the contingent and the mythical, and between human and ancestral actions has been dealt with by a number of authors (Munn 1970, 1973; Myers 1986a; Morphy 1995; Rumsey 1994). In this process of mediation (and communication), and with respect to Aboriginal ontological and epistemological principles, we cannot downplay the fact that places, with their vegetable, animal, and mineral constituents, are the embodiment of ancestral actions and essences and can 'speak' to humans. Places and the sentient land can offer messages and novel information to those willing to listen, information that may influence important decisions, trigger processes of negotiation of varying scope, change the course of events, or be called upon in the interpretation of events. In waking, as in dreaming, the Aborigines can be receptive to these signs and messages, and they can engage in an ongoing dialogue with the various constituents of the world. At times, this communication can be informal and playful, while at other times it is very serious and sacred. The quality of openness, which can be applied to the body of the land as well as to the human bodily-self, has proved a valuable variable in the investigation of structural transformations of the ancestral itineraries and their associated rituals, as well as in the investigation of the avenues available for the expression of the individual's creative and interpretative skills.

Innovation, in terms of both the reinterpretation and the invention (as revelation) of mythical and ritual elements, does not occur less frequently among the Western Desert groups than in other parts of Aboriginal Australia, as Myers argues (1986a: 297); however, its novel character is more strongly denied here than elsewhere. In fact, I would argue that the innovation/revelation of mythical segments and ritual sequences is more frequent in the Western Desert (or at least in certain parts of it). This is most likely because of the flexibility of local group membership, its greater mobility, and also because these groups frequently have had to redefine and validate their connections to the land on the basis of the *Tjukurrpa* itineraries and segments. Both the transformations (in terms of reinterpreting existing bodies of mythical and ritual knowledge or adding new ones) and the creative work of the social actors are concealed by a local discourse that stresses the permanent and unchanging character of the ancestral order. Another local principle is that only dream revelations from the ancestors or deceased relatives can allow the state of the world to be transformed. What is often interpreted by anthropologists as a denial of human creative action seems rather to be seen by the Aborigines as 'work' – 'very hard work' indeed – that requires knowledge and skills of varying types, such as the ability to dream, to be receptive to ancestral messages and to decipher them, and to be well versed in current political and ritual matters. Such work, however, does not involve humans alone, as it is based upon and constructed from exchange and communication among different states of being and realms of action. Furthermore, from an Aboriginal perspective, and in reference to the rhizomatic and relational form of culture and being in the Kukatja world, it would seem improper and illogical to credit a single individual with an innovation.

Tjukurrpa is a fundamental reality that ensures the continuity of the world; it is also the space-time through which transformations are validated. Ancestrality conveys the sense of continuity and discontinuity (or rupture), of morality and transgression, and of permanence and transformation. It expresses, in a certain sense, the dialectics and paradoxes of human existence while maintaining the enchantment of the world. *Tjukurrpa* as the ancestral order, while a hierarchically superior value, does not exist beyond the individual. In its manifold expressions, *Tjukurrpa* is immanent and consubstantial with humans. The ancestral itineraries and the segments delineated along these itineraries are the 'gardens' of the nomad: they represent the complex networks of social, ritual, and territorial belonging and responsibilities. Like a 'garden,' they are cultivated, renewed, enriched, or left to lie fallow. Through the course of events – ritual exchanges, alliances, deaths of custodians, traditional and contemporary nomadism, singular events, births, dream revelations, and so on – the ancestral itineraries and associated rituals undergo reinterpretation and structural transformation of varying degrees. It is at this level that Aboriginal historicity is most fully expressed.

Without entering here into the decade-long debate on the distinction between history and myth, I hope to have demonstrated that from an Aboriginal perspective these categories and the distinctions between them are to some extent irrelevant – as are the nature-culture catego-ries and the distinction between them. It is not that they mix up the mythical and the historical, or confuse them (or stand 'above' them), or consider them to be one and the same. Rather, these categories do not exist, in and of themselves; in other words, Aboriginal Australians refuse the distinction. The mundane, the contingent, and the ancestral are articulated together and feed into one another; they participate together in the dynamic unfolding of the world. The contingent is at times likened to pre-existing structures, but such likening first requires a work of strategic interpretation – that is, human agency and knowl-edge – and second, it often serves to transform such ancestral struc-tures and inscriptions. Events, experiences, and narratives are made meaningful and interpreted partly by drawing from existing ancestral forms, idioms, agencies, and events; and, in turn, the ancestral forms are (re)read over the succeeding generations by feeding in historic, novel, and contingent events or characters. In such a world, where ancestrality and ancestors play an active role in the present unfolding of the world, social changes do not have the same meaning as they do in a world where Time and History are key embodied symbols, and where only humans are considered historical agents. The 'ethos of inclusivity' that Tonkinson and Tonkinson (2001) suggest for the social and territorial organization of Western Desert groups – in terms of the flexibility and permeability of boundaries, and of multiple affiliative criteria – can just as well be applied to the groups' understanding of historicity and change – an understanding that also includes places, ancestors, and dreams.

In the Western Desert, there is a clear relation between dreams and historicity – between dreaming and the 'historical' imagination and consciousness. This is true to the extent, first, that it is partly through dreams that the words of the ancestors are actualized, and second, that dreams and dreaming play an active role in the flow of events and in the unfolding of reality. Local 'historical' consciousness and imagina-tion necessarily consider the co-presence of human, non-human, and ancestral agencies, actions, needs, and desires in the land, and they are inspired by ancestral deeds and inscriptions grounded in the present and looking towards the future. I would also add that it is not suffi-cient, as Sahlins has argued, to study the structure *in* history, without also investigating the structure *as* history. Studying the structure as his-tory implies that we should further consider the ways in which social actors understand their roles in an ever-changing world, and the multifaceted social and cultural codes that operate in historical imagination. The Kukatja and their neighbours deny a historicity that is constrained by a unidirectional chronological order, and refuse to adopt a sense of history that claims to rise above the imaginary. Most importantly, they refuse to accept a sense of historicity that includes only humans, to the exclusion of all other agencies, forms, and beings. Ancestral and non-human agencies, as I hope I have demonstrated in this book, participate in and are a part of local historicity.

The examination of dreams and dreaming has proven to be a valuable avenue for exploring the Kukatja way of being in the world and relating to it. The dream narratives presented have shown how dreaming is a means of opening out to the world, a moment of greater receptivity and heightened communication (between humans, and among humans, places, and ancestors), and a place of pleasant, unpleasant, or dangerous encounters. The dominant Aboriginal theory about dreams and dreaming stands in logical continuity with their notion of personhood: as a composite of ancestral connections, as 'open' and permeable to the entourage, and as 'dividual.' While dreaming, the travelling spirit retains the subjectivity and the agency of the dreamer; the action of dreaming brings the dreamer (and his or her spirit) into relation with the social, physical, and cosmological environment. Such action has a real effect in the world. In today's context, for example, and as before, dream-spirit journeys allow the Aborigines to maintain attachment to far-away places to which they are connected (see also Tonkinson and Tonkinson 2001).

In Aboriginal Australia, dreams have aesthetic and pragmatic value, and the work and language of dreams are socially and creatively invested, on both an individual and a collective basis. As a general rule, however, the Aborigines do not seek at all costs to interpret their dreams, nor are they compelled to share them. Dreams that leave a strong impression on the dreamer (or on someone who has heard the narrative) might be 'stored' until they can be significantly connected with the course of events. The interpretation of a dream is dependent on a series of variables, at once social, cosmological, contextual, and personal. The dream is usually received as a 'good story' – a value that is not trivial in an oral tradition – that people share without necessarily seeking to unravel its meaning; but at the same time its narrative, aesthetic, and contextual value is not denied. Even the most frightening dreams have a 'flavour' and are received, at least by the elders, as good dreams. Dreams and dreaming are not understood or experienced as a repressed language or as something that would concern only the dreamer and his or her life history, but are regarded as an action in the world and a 'work' of communicative, and at times creative, expression.

As a realm of action and a mode of experiencing and knowing the world, dreams and dreaming thus have an ontological and epistemological status. In continuity with this observation, we have also seen – and I feel this is most significant – how the action of dreaming itself is, in many respects, more valued than the actual content of the dream. Like ancestrality, dreaming itself is an essential component of the flow of events and the unfolding of reality; it has the potential to act upon the world and to transform it, even when it is not directly acknowledged by humans. This is sufficient to give to dreams and dreaming a quality of 'trueness' (*mularrpa*). For the dream to be 'true,' in the sense of having a true effect on the world, there is no need for its content to receive a definitive interpretation. A dream, however, may communicate signs to the dreamer (pertaining to the conception of a child, an impending death, or any other event), and in doing so, it has indicated that the state of the world has changed. It may also transmit some knowledge that gives the dreamer and his or her entourage clues as to the interpretation of an event; or new knowledge may be revealed pertaining to existing mythical and ritual forms. The Kukatja adopt an attitude towards dreams and dreaming, and towards the work of interpretation in general, that we can qualify, once again, as open, flexible, and even playful. The widespread Aboriginal expression used for signs of all sorts, including dream signs, that they 'might be something,' reflects such an attitude, as well as the absence of any sense of fatalism and determinism in relation to dreams.

The Aborigines play with signs, events, and dreams in the same way that they 'play with boundaries, contexts and identities' (Rose 1992: 224), without challenging the fundamental and intrinsic relationships between the different forms and states of beings. Gadamer (1975) has explored play as a mode of being, and it seems appropriate here to define the way in which the Aborigines play with the interconnectedness of the realms of action, the states of being, and the modes of experience, of the ancestral, the mundane, and the dream realms. Play, as a mode of being-in-the-world, does indeed seem an appropriate way to describe the state of things, to the extent that it necessarily conveys an aesthetic and strategic (and thus political) dimension, and that 'play itself contains its own, even sacred, seriousness' (Gadamer 1975: 91). These worlds of 'open signs' are not constrained by any sense of closure. The intransigent character of Aboriginal Law is lessened by the dimensions of openness, flexibility, and negotiability that characterize the social, territorial, and ritual components of the Aborigines' world. This openness and space of negotiability grant everyone a 'freedom of decision, which at the same time is endangered and irrevocably limited' (ibid.: 95). At the narrative level and in the course of telling stories, people 'play' with the different realms of action by continuously merging them into the 'true' (*mularrpa*). The ritual performances are also somehow a 'transformation into true being' (ibid.: 101). Ultimately, *Tjukurrpa* represents the aesthetic play of local historicity – in other words, 'the infinite play of the world, the eternally self-creating work of art' (Schlegel, cited in Gadamer, ibid.: 94). From an Aboriginal perspective, however, and again in contrast to Western views, 'nature' and non-human others, far from being without purpose or intention, are active participants in this work, as are the ancestors; the intentions of these other 'players' are not, however, always known to the human participants. As we have seen in regard to the innovation of mythical and ritual elements and the structural transformation of ancestral forms, the person responsible for the innovation disappears, and 'the identity of the player does not continue to exist for anybody' (ibid.: 100). I would also add that the Aborigines are 'players' with infinite patience.

The metaphor of the rhizome discussed by Deleuze and Guattari (1987) has proven relevant in depicting a nomadic way of life (and mind). It has proven relevant in depicting the nature and extent of the networks of relatedness that include all the entities and agencies of the dwelt-in world, and that orchestrate the poetics and politics of the Kukatja and neighbouring groups. As we have seen, the description of the rhizome can be applied to the mythical itineraries and their segments, and to the way that they intersect with each other and are connected (or disconnected) while remaining autonomous, as they travel across the land, in the heavens, and underground. It can also apply to the notion of the person (human and non-human) as a composite of embodied and ancestral connections, of manifold and dynamic social relationships and responsibilities to other beings and places – each person being a node within a nexus of relationships, simultaneously autonomous and related to others, whether human, non-human, or ancestral. The dialectic between autonomy and relatedness that pervades the world of the Kukatja leaves ample room for negotiation.

The rhizomatic logic and rationale of relatedness that pervade the

Aboriginal world help us to understand some aspects of the contemporary reality of the Balgo mob. Among these aspects is the persistence of a nomadic way of life, where people seem to be constantly on the move, to and fro between the different communities, either to visit relatives and places, to participate in Aboriginal sports events or cultural meetings, to go on a drinking crawl, or for ritual and mourning purposes. Another aspect is the embodied character of the individual's network of social and ancestral connections and responsibilities, and how it may offer further keys to an understanding of the ongoing resistance of the Aborigines towards the spirit (and values) of capitalism and the 'monetisation of mind' (Sansom 1988: 159). All money and goods acquired individually – through, for example, the art market – are at once reinvested in social capital and relations. Although the Kukatja and their neighbours have appropriated for themselves, and included in their social and exchange networks, many of the objects and goods of White society, they have refused to adopt or to comply with the values of the society that produced these objects in the first place.

Among the many realities and expressions of differences that I have experienced with my Aboriginal friends, the one that perhaps astonished me most is their local resistance, in the sense both of the resistance (and persistence) of culture and of a culture of resistance (Sahlins 1993; T. Turner 1991). From the early contact period in the 1940s to this day, the people of Balgo have never responded in the way the White authorities expected or wanted them to. Like other groups in Aboriginal Australia, they have maintained confidence in their own Law and ways and have resisted the rape of their imaginary. Over the last decades, they have made use of novel opportunities and means to pursue their own agendas: to carry out their responsibilities towards their own sociocosmic order, to reproduce and transform their social and symbolic values and capital, and to redefine their manifold identities (in relation to kin, neighbouring groups, and their ancestral and territorial connections). This resistance and persistence have caused great despair, initially among missionaries, and more recently among government officials and representatives.

   In a liberal-democratic nation-state such as Australia, and in view of the current national policies towards Indigenous self-determination and the recognition of specific rights of Indigenous citizens, one of the questions that is often raised is how to 'accommodate' such differences, or what seems to most Euro-Australians to be a radical alterity. I will address these complex and difficult questions only briefly here, drawing from my own experiences with and observations of the people of Balgo. But first, I will address some more general issues.

In the 1960s, Australian Aborigines gained the same set of citizenship rights as non-Indigenous Australians. Since the Mabo High Court decision in 1992, and its enabling legislation, the Native Title Act (1993), Indigenous citizens have had distinctive rights recognized by the state. In this context, Peterson (1998) raises a crucial question, that of the recognition of membership in their own Indigenous social orders. This question requires closer examination, to the extent that such membership entails a set of responsibilities and values that find no room for expression within the concept of citizenship, at least as we usually define and understand it. On the one hand, the concept of citizenship stems from a world-view that is exclusive rather than inclusive; or, to use a classic distinction, it is a world-view that is anthropocentric rather than cosmocentric. Citizenship and civil rights include and involve only humans. By definition, non-humans, be they ancestors, places, animals, plants, or minerals, are excluded from the political arena and from local sociality. On the other hand, in Western ontology, the notion of person, as a conscious and intentional agency, is exclusive to humans only. As I have amply demonstrated in this book, this is not the case in Aboriginal ontology, where non-human and ancestral agencies are fully included in the social order and in local sociality and historicity. In view of such considerations, we can ask the following question: To what extent can the concept of citizenship conciliate Western and Indigenous ontologies and values without the dissolution of Indigenous values (and responsibilities) within a single hegemonic regime of values and moral code?

In view of these overall considerations, I would like to present a situation that I have witnessed during my last two visits to the Balgo area, in 1994 and 1998, a situation that I understand, like the stories about the Three Ks (see chapter 4), to be an expression of the irony and paradox of postcolonialism, or of a conflict of interests between local Aboriginal agendas and those of the state. In the 1990s, it would not be an exaggeration to say that the Native Title issue, in many respects, dominated relations between the Australian state and the Aborigines. For the Kukatja and neighbouring groups, it was their first opportunity to lodge a claim for their ancestral lands. Many people myself included, thought that the Native Title issue would immediately become a priority for them.

However, during my visit in 1998, I was astonished to realize that not only had the Kukatja not yet lodged their Native Title claim, but most of them barely knew about the issue or at least seemed to show little interest in it. Lest, I misunderstood, I am not saying that they found the Native Title issue irrelevant – though some of them might have – but that at the time they did not make it a priority; in other words, it was not at the forefront of their agendas. Considering the importance that the Native Title issue had acquired at the national level, and considering the timely efforts of anthropologists, lawyers, and legislative bodies, it seemed ironic and paradoxical to me that all these events had gone almost unnoticed in this part of Australia where the enactment and transmission of Ancestral Law and connections to the land were still a major concern. While most neighbouring Western Desert groups were already, albeit to varying degrees, involved in the Native Title issue, a whole series of local and contingent factors and events can be cited to explain the Kukatja's delay in lodging their claim. Among these was the lack of communication between the Kukatja and the legislative bodies, and the antagonistic power relations among young leaders. Additional considerations include the reticence and suspicion of the Kukatja and most Western Desert groups towards a White society that presents land tenure systems in terms of boundedness, fixity, and exclusive use, as well as their own understanding and conviction that these lands are already theirs under their own system of law: what is the point then of claiming them?

However, at the time, there was another factor that could help to account for the lack of local interest and involvement in the Native Title issue. All through the 1990s, in the Balgo area and far beyond, local agendas at the individual and collective levels were overwhelmed with a kind of 'work' and a set of responsibilities that appear, in this age of late modernity and neoliberal capitalism, rather 'unproductive' from the state's or the non-Aboriginal's point of view. These imperatives were for the people to mourn their dead, and to take the time to participate in lengthy mourning ceremonies, as a major responsibility towards their sociocosmic order. Since the Kukatja have been settled at Balgo, burials have been the responsibility of the local church authorities. But mourning ceremonies – what the Aborigines call, in English, a 'sorry business' or a 'sorry meeting' – still play a major role in local sociality, responsibility, and sense of being. During the 1980s, I took part in many 'sorry businesses' in Balgo and in neighbouring communities. However, it was during my visits in 1994 and 1998 that I was struck by the unusual number of deaths that had befallen small communities such as Balgo and Yagga Yagga. One 'sorry meeting' followed another; either someone in the community had died, or a group from Balgo and Yagga Yagga had to go to a neighbouring community (Billiluna, Yuendumu, Lajamanu, Kiwirrkura, or Christmas Creek) for a mourning rite. I spent those few months in 1994 and 1998 on the road, accompanying my friends to sorry businesses.

When news of a death is received – whether of someone in the community, someone from the community but who had been in the hospital, or a relative from another community – at once keening and wailing start in the camps. Mourning ceremonies can last for days, and even weeks, and usually involve a fair number of people. In order to express their grief over the loss of a relative, the deceased's close male and female relatives inflict injuries on themselves, sometimes quite severe ones. They also withdraw from the main camps to places where people come to cry with them; there, they wait for the arrival of relatives from neighbouring and distant communities without whom mourning ceremonies cannot be concluded. Mortuary rituals are an expression of their shared identity (Myers 1986a: 133–4). When the other participants arrive – sometimes days later – a ritualized 'sorry fight' takes place. Relatives from other communities, their chests and faces painted with white kaolin, pretend to attack the deceased's close relatives (with boomerangs). It is a way of expressing their grief over the close relatives' failure to look after the deceased properly. If the deceased was an elder, whether a man or a woman, a few hundred people will gather for the 'sorry business.' When the deceased is from another community, relatives from Balgo have to travel to that community.

I realized that my friends were constantly engaged in the 'sorry business' of death. All the different taboos following the death of a close relative, according to Ancestral Law, were present everywhere, at all times and in all contexts: taboos over the deceased's name, various food taboos for close male and female relatives, taboos over the camp or house that had to be abandoned after the death of one of its inhabitants, taboos over the sites to which the deceased was related, and, at times, taboos over some of the songs and ritual sequences that were the deceased person's responsibility.

All through the 1990s, mourning ceremonies strongly permeated the lives and agendas of the Balgo, Yagga Yagga, and Mulan mobs, leaving little time for dealing with the Native Title issue (itself rather time-consuming). But this raises another question, about the reason for so many deaths. There are several. First, there are those who simply die of old age. The generation of elders who died in the 1980s and 1990s were the men and women who had been born in the desert and had lived in a traditional and self-sufficient way in the bush. They were young adults when they first walked in from the desert with their parents, grandparents, aunts, and uncles to join the mission settlement. Over the following decades, they had strategically managed the co-existence of both laws. They had initiated the ritual renewal of the 1970s, under the constraints of the rules of the Balgo mission settlement. They had orchestrated and supervised the initiation ceremonies, the ritual exchanges, and the transmission of knowledge during the transition from nomadic hunter-gatherers, to settled workers, and then to semi-nomadic outstation residents.

The other types of deaths are much more disturbing, in many respects. Some deaths come prematurely as a result of poor health care or sanitation. But many more either are due to fights (usually around bars in townships farther north), or are the result of car accidents. Fatal car accidents as people drive back to the community (often under the influence of alcohol) have been increasing drastically over the last two decades. They usually involve young adult men, in their twenties and thirties; when they die, they leave behind young widows and children. Observers at places like Balgo will easily notice that there are very few men of that generation left alive. They were educated in the White society's school system, and some of them had acted, at one point, as Council chairmen. A few years prior to their tragic deaths, these young men had been initiated into and entrusted with the Ancestral Law, at a period in their lives when they are supposed to reaffirm their knowledge of their cultural world and become fully aware of their membership in their own social order – a membership and a social order that are not, however, fully recognized by mainstream society and in which they often find themselves marginalized, disempowered, and subject to racial discrimination. The ordeals they went through, as young initiates, in order to be recognized as full members of their sociocosmic order are in stark contrast to their status in mainstream society as second-class citizens. There is some truth in Cowlishaw's statement that 'There are few ways in which to be black and also to be fully connected to the modern world outside' (1999: 289).

These tragic deaths, along with an increase in violence at Balgo and a few recent suicides of young men, are a direct result of the clash between their rapidly changing world and the increasing pressures and demands from White society. To carry out their responsibilities towards their own social and ancestral order, and in order to maintain their manifold relationships, my friends chose to invest their time and energy in the 'sorry business' of death – so that the social networks could be reconnected and life could start anew. Mourning rituals are a means to convey the spirit of the deceased to his or her land of belonging, usually the site of conception; they are a part of the production and reproduction of the person's world. Furthermore, such ritual practices are 'proof' of an ancestral connection to the land, but one that is not acceptable within the requirements of the Native Title legislation.

In this age of globalization and late modernity, the neoliberal discourse around multiculturalism and 'the accommodation of differences' gives the impression that cultural differences are recognized and celebrated – as long as these differences do not go beyond 'a moral, national limit of tolerance' (Povinelli 1998: 578). The kind of cultural differences that are usually celebrated are 'more superficial cultural expressions which can be learned about and mimicked, or read and displayed, in ways that assert tolerance and also offer the stimulation of difference without disturbance' (Cowlishaw 1999: 296); in other words, differences that do not challenge the dominant social and moral order – the dominant society's epistemological and ontological principles. I would also add that I find such rhetoric on the 'accommodation of differences' somehow ironic and paradoxical, even disturbing, considering that since the early contact period, through colonial history, and up to the present day, Indigenous peoples throughout the world have done just that: they have 'accommodated' settler societies, state policies, and now the forces of globalization by adapting their social orders and cultural practices. They know, perhaps more than any other group, that such 'accommodation' entails major social and cultural reinterpretations and transformations. We should never downplay the fact that alongside the Indigenous experiences of suffering, alongside their dispossessions and disillusions, they have 'accommodated' changing conditions of existence and are expressing their contemporaneity (Poirier 2000) and coevalness (Fabian 1983) in unexpected and often highly creative ways.

In the Introduction to *Millennial Capitalism and the Culture of Neoliberalism*, Comaroff and Comaroff present the postmodern person as a subject made with objects (2001: 4); they add that 'citizenship is measured increasingly by the capacity to transact and consume' (ibid.: 16). In Aboriginal Australia, the person is a subject composed of relations

among human, non-human, and ancestral agencies; and it is the production and the reproduction of these relations that represent their
main responsibilities for their membership in their own social order. In
other words, if modernity means no longer interacting with ancestrality and with the spoken words of the ancestors, and if late modernity
means being a consumer citizen, then the Aborigines in Balgo have
chosen to be (or simply to remain) non-modern (in Latour's sense,
1993). They do express, however, their contemporaneity and coexistence with mainstream society by appropriating for themselves modern
means to pursue their own agendas and responsibilities towards their
own social and cosmological orders.

Notes

Introduction

1 See, among others, Myers (1986a), Morphy (1984, 1991), Rose (1992), Dussart (2000), Keen (1994), and Povinelli (1993a).

2 Among the works that focus on the relations between Aborigines and non-Aborigines (mostly in northern regions), see Trigger (1992), Merlan (1998), Povinelli (1993a), Cowlishaw (1999).

3 I would also add that their high level of confidence in the true value of their Law could partly explain the strength and the specific forms of their resistance to the Whites' social and moral codes.

4 Flexibility is not synonymous with 'fluidity' (Sutton 1999: 14), to the extent that structural flexibility always operates within the dictates of the Law and within the more systematic aspects of Aboriginal cultural and social life.

5 Sahlins's thesis (1981, 1985) on the relations between structures and events, between social actors and eventual cultural changes is most enlightening, even though he considers only 'exogenous' and 'extraordinary' events to support his demonstration. For fine ethnographic works that discuss the creative potential of cultural agents within the reproduction of the cosmological order, see Keesing (1982), Obeysekere (1981), Barth (1987).

6 The complex and dynamic relations among events and places have become quite explicit recently in Australian Aboriginal studies. See, among others, Merlan (1998), Myers (1986a), Povinelli (1993a), Rose (1992).

7 On the anthropological study of dreams and dreaming, see, among others, B. Tedlock, ed. (1987), O'Flaherty (1984), Jedrej and Shaw, eds (1992), Graham (1995), Parman (1991), Charuty, ed. (1996). I have dealt elsewhere with some of the difficulties in establishing a genuinely anthropological approach to dreams and dreaming (Poirier 1994, 1999).

8 On that specific aspect, see Keesing (1982), Brown (1987), Herdt (1987).

9 Roheim's work in Central Australia is one such example where he used a psychoanalytical grid to make sense of Aboriginal dream narratives (1988).

10 Bourguignon (1972, 1973, 1977), Burridge (1960), D'Andrade (1961), Devereux (1966), Eggan (1972), Hallowell (1966), Keesing (1982), Kilani (1983), Lincoln (1970), Obeyesekere (1981), O'Nell (1976), Roseman (1991), Stephen (1979, 1982), B. Tedlock (1992), Tylor (1958), Wallace (1956), to name but a few.

11 See C. Berndt (1950, 1965), Glowczewski (1989), Kolig (1980), Meggitt (1962a: 228), Munn (1986a), Tonkinson (1970), Dussart (2000), and Myers's mention of 'vision' (1986a: 53).

12 Sahlins reminds us that 'objectivity is culturally constituted, it is always a distinctive ontology' (1995: 169).

13 In her ground-breaking article, based upon her work among the Hagen of Papua New Guinea, Strathern (1980) was among the first authors to seriously question the nature/culture dichotomy as a universal category of thought. Since then, a whole series of works has been written precisely on this issue, which opens novel potential avenues of anthropological thought and ethnographic methodologies.

14 The term 'non-modern' refers to peoples who do not share, and who even resist, the dualistic, positivistic, and disembodied aspects of Cartesian (and modern Western) thought. It must be strongly distinguished from the expression 'pre-modern,' which was used to reflect and advocate an evolutionist and colonial perspective.

15 This echoes the work of Latour, among others, who has argued convincingly that our own 'modern' networks (including those of science) are 'simultaneously real, like nature, narrated, like discourse, and collective, like society' (1993: 6).

16 The question of ontologies is fundamental in ethnographic encounters and anthropology for two reasons: first, because it refers to 'being' and what members of a culture have to say about it, and second, because it is linked to knowledge and action. Furthermore, all ontologies are value-laden (Overing 1985: 7). For insightful discussions on the importance of considering local ontologies in ethnographic and anthropological inquiries, see Clammer, Poirier, and Schwimmer, eds (2004).

17 I cannot possibly recount the times my Aboriginal friends took me out into the bush for hunting and gathering activities during the three years I lived in the area. Furthermore, I always made sure my vehicle was available for the needs of those with whom I shared camp and their extended families: to fetch wood, for taking people out into the bush, or for travelling to more or

less distant communities (for mourning rituals, initiation ceremonies, ritual exchanges, or simply to visit relatives).

18 The redefinition of Australian Aborigines' nomadism since they have become sedentary is an issue that has not been sufficiently documented. To my knowledge, Young and Doohan (1989) are the only authors to analyse contemporary Aboriginal mobility (in Central Australia).

19 I find that while the concept of person has been extensively discussed in the anthropological literature on Melanesia and elsewhere, it has not been given equal attention in Australian Aboriginal studies. For Melanesia, see, for example, Strathern (1988, 1992), Wagner (1991), and Iteanu (1990); for South Asia, Marriott (1976).

20 I have borrowed the expression and the concept of 'dividual' from Marriott (1976) and Strathern (1988).

21 The concept of bodiliness (*corporéité* in French) refers to the socially informed body and to the 'intrinsically social character of the human body, in all its material, phenomenal, biological, psychological, social, and cultural dimensions' (T. Turner 1995: 145). See also Csordas (1990) on the concept of 'embodiment' where he links Bourdieu's theory of practice and Merleau-Ponty's phenomenology.

Chapter 1 A Place like Balgo: A Story of Accommodation, Resistance, and Misunderstandings

1 Rodman has argued how the multivocal dimension of place 'shapes and expresses polysemic meanings of place for different users,' while multi-locality conveys the idea that a single place may be experienced in different ways by different people (Rodman 1992: 647).

2 On the theorization of resistance, see Comaroff and Comaroff (1992) and Ortner (1995).

3 For subtle and insightful analyses of Aborigines' sense of place and relations with non-Aborigines in settled settings, see Sansom (1980) on 'fringe dwellers' in Darwin, Trigger (1992) on Doomadgee, and Merlan (1998) on the town of Katherine.

4 In Kukatja, *Kartiya* refers to a pale-skinned lizard – hence the choice of this word for the Whites. It refers also to white bands or stripes on a reptile (Valiquette 1993: 28).

5 Around the end of the nineteenth century, the Pallottines established mission settlements at Broome and Derby, Beagle Bay, and Lombadina, on the West Coast; then Balgo Hills in 1940 and Lagrange in 1958 (Durack 1969).

6 Long (1989) gives a detailed account of the various expeditions into Pintupi country up until the 1960s, and an overview of the movements of the Pintupi among the settlements, including Balgo.

7 For a brief account of the Catholic missionaries' practices, discourses, and attitudes in the Kimberley towards the Aborigines, see Alroe (1988).

8 On that episode of Aboriginal history in northern Australia, see Berndt and Berndt (1987), Rose (1992: 1–25).

9 According to Peterson, 'the receipt of full welfare payments in cash provided a more than adequate income for people to pursue indigenous agendas leaving people free to produce social and symbolic capital without the necessity for the great majority to be involved in any conventional productive activity' (1999: 853). This is what has been termed a 'welfare autonomy.' On this topic, see also Tonkinson about the Mardu at Jigalong (1991: 163–6).

10 As a general rule, in the Kimberley and elsewhere in Australia, Christianity, as Kolig has noted, 'has had little impact on Aborigines' (1989: 89), in comparison, for example, with other groups in Polynesia and Melanesia. See also Tonkinson about the Jigalong mob (1974).

11 Their refusal to convert to Catholicism did not mean that they did not appropriate, over the decades, some elements of Christian cosmology for their own Law. Such appropriation would require further analysis. During the early 1980s, some Aborigines in Balgo, mostly Walmatjari, talked of traces left in the desert by biblical ancestors such as Moses and Noah. On this topic, see also Kolig (1980).

12 This strategic change on the part of the Catholic church, not only in Balgo but all through the Kimberley, corresponded with the Second Vatican Council where 'a new concept of mission has been developed, one that gives greater recognition to the integrity of the people the Church seeks to missionize' (Alroe 1988: 37).

13 Father Peile lived in Balgo for twenty-five years until his death in 1989. During this time, he conducted insightful research into the Kukatja language and medical system (Peile 1997).

14 This spatial orientation in settlement contexts, one that attempts to maintain and affirm the link with each group's respective country, has been noted elsewhere. See Bell (1993: 74).

15 On a similar issue and from his analysis of Aboriginal and non-Aboriginal relations at Doomadgee, an Aboriginal community in north-west Queensland, Trigger made the following observation that would be relevant for Wirrimanu: 'tactical management of social distance from White society, on the part of structurally subordinate Aborigines, constitutes a non-trivial

form of resistance because its consequences are the denial of results sought by local White staff (and more generally by the Australian state)' (1992: 221).

16 On the issue of local councils and politics in Western Desert communities, see also Tonkinson (1991: 166–74) and Myers (1986a: 256–85).

17 In 1998, the Kukatja and other families linked to the Stansmore Range area (Mungkayi) had not yet submitted a Native Title claim under the Native Title Act. Without going into a detailed analysis, I can identify several different factors that explain this delay: misunderstanding or confusion over what is at issue; a lack of communication between the local people and the representative bodies; difficulties in finding a local leader who would act as spokesperson; the expression of a form of resistance towards an agenda they see designed, yet again, from the outside, and whose outcome is most uncertain.

18 In a similar manner, Mardu families from Jigalong and Pintupi families from Kiwirrkura have established small outstations farther into the desert. Also, the Mardu have established one at 33 Well on the Canning Stock Route (Tonkinson 1991: 174–82).

19 In Aboriginal Australia, whatever cash money is acquired through the art market, government benefits, card playing, or other means, is at once reinvested in social capital, in the production and the reproduction of social relations. In this way, Aborigines refuse to conform to the logic of capitalist consumption and offer a strong resistance to what Sansom has called the 'monetisation of mind' (1988: 159; Peterson 1999).

20 Indeed, and as Merlan has noticed for the Aborigines living at Katherine (Northern Territory), they 'tend not to comment on that situation or to have a distinctive vocabulary of inequality' (1998: 60).

Chapter 2 Ancestrality, Sentient Places, and Social Spaces

1 Strehlow (1968) and Roheim (1945) have also emphasized the notion of 'eternity' in their respective work on Central Desert groups.

2 In a comprehensive discussion of the expressions 'Dreamtime' and 'Dreaming,' Morphy writes, 'There has always been some discomfort with the term, and some reluctance to use it, because of an awareness of its limitations and of possible misleading connotations' (1997: 179).

3 In that respect and using a phenomenological approach, Tamisari's work (1998) among the Yolngu (Northeast Arnhem Land) on the relations between the body, the land, and the ancestors is also revealing about the embodiment of experience, of subjectivity and agency.

4 For an insightful discussion on the distinction between immanence and transcendence, see Augé (1982).

5 The concept of a linear time is partly suggested, however, in the way they now distinguish between their lives 'before' the mission, during the mission, and now.

6 While classical and positivist approaches in anthropology have tended to present hunters and gatherers as people who do not build, transform, or act upon the landscape, their own ontology seems, as Ingold has remarked, to assert the precise opposite, wherein 'form arises and is held in place within action; it is movement congealed' (1996: 146).

7 In the anthropological literature on Australian Aborigines, apart from blood, which is used extensively in ceremonial contexts, very little attention has been given to the corporeal fluids and their local symbolism and uses. See Peile (1997).

8 I use the term 'myth' (or mythical) inasmuch as the *Tjukurrpa* itineraries and the stories reporting them represent a collective reference in a given time and space. However, that wording should not exclude the fact that these 'mythical' tracks and stories are open to transformations and to different interpretations, and that idiosyncrasies or elements born out of other contexts of action can play a part in their formulation.

9 The yam (*karnti*), a widespread edible plant throughout the desert, is a good example of a rhizome.

10 Deleuze and Guattari write about what they call the 'principle of asignifying rupture' in the rhizome. It is relevant at this point to cite them at length: 'A rhizome may be broken, shattered at a given spot, but it will start again on one of its old lines, or on new lines ... Every rhizome contains lines of segmentarity according to which it is stratified, territorialized, organized, signified, attributed, etc., as well as lines of deterritorialization down which it constantly flees. There is a rupture in the rhizome whenever segmentary lines explode into a line of flight, but the line of flight is part of the rhizome. These lines always tie back to one another' (1987: 9). This description is relevant to the reality of the numerous segments of the ancestral itineraries in the Western Desert.

11 The debate over gender relationships in Aboriginal Australia has a long history in the anthropological literature. For the Kukatja and neighbouring groups, I have dealt elsewhere in more detail with the politics of ritual knowledge in relation to gender (Poirier 2001). See also, among others, Hamilton (1980), C. Berndt (1950, 1965, 1974), Bell (1993 [1983]), Dussart (2000), Glowczewski (1991), Merlan (1988, 1992).

12 Peile noted indeed that in Kukatja thought and local conceptions of the

body and good health, there is 'a total interaction between the wind, the spirit and the breath, the latter being perceived as a physical manifestation of the spirit within the body. The wind protects and nourishes the spirit and the breath inhabiting the human body ... and constitutes a permanent link with the ancestral realm' (Peile 1985, my translation). The wind is thus consubstantial with humans; they share the same ancestral essence.

13 Watson offers a detailed analysis of *Kuruwarri* designs and power for the women in the Wirrimanu area, in relation to women's rituals and relationship to land (1996).

14 R. Berndt has published some of his data on the region's mythical itineraries. Some sequences are described with relevant details, and the main *Tjukurrpa* beings mentioned here are featured in his writings (1970, 1972, 1976).

15 Myers (1986a: 239), as well as Mountford and Tonkinson (1969), mention the *Wati Kutjarra* in their respective writings about the Pintupi and the Mardu. The Berndts also have recorded several narratives about them from different Western Desert groups (Berndt and Berndt 1945, 1964, 1989).

16 Ngantalarra was an important gathering site for Ngarti, Kukatja, and Walmatjari families at the time of traditional nomadism. Initiation ceremonies were held there.

17 Watson (1996: 115–45) gives a detailed account of the events from *Tjukurrpa* that occurred at and around Ngantalarra and Nakarra Nakarra, and involving the *Wati Kutjarra* and the group of ancestral women.

18 *Murtikarlka* was the father of a man bearing the same name and now living in Wirrimanu. The nominal identification of an individual with a *Tjukurrpa* ancestor occurs frequently in groups of that region since each person is the incarnation of an ancestral entity associated with his or her conception site.

19 *Marrakurru* was the father of a Wirrimanu elder. His grandson, now deceased, also bore his name.

20 One dimension of these *Tingarri* cycles, often neglected in the literature and yet crucial from an Aboriginal perspective, are the groups of women (and children) who often accompany the men, either behind or to the side, and always keeping a reasonable distance so as not to be seen by the novices. Autonomous, they establish their own *ngurra*.

21 See R. Berndt (1970) for an account of *Tingarri* stories to the south of Wirrimanu; Myers (1986a) for the *Tingarri* stories in Pintupi country. See also Berndt and Berndt (1964).

22 Recorded at the end of the nineteenth century from the Gippsland groups, the Curr version (1886–7, vol. 3: 548) recounts that *Luurn* (*Loon*) saved the Aborigines from a flood caused by a frog. The Petri and Petri-Odermann

version (1970: 230) tells how *Luurn* (*Lun*) then led a group of novices to the south.

23 In the mid-1980s, when the Aborigines had to select a new name for their community in replacement of Balgo, they hesitated between two possibilities: Ngarili, a site identified with the *Wati Kutjarra*, or Wirrimanu, identified with *Luurn*. They opted for the latter.

24 Today, one of the final stages of initiation for the boys recreates this episode, where those yet to be initiated are thrown into the air.

25 This is a recurrent theme in Aboriginal mythology. Roheim mentions a similar narrative heard from Central Desert groups (1945: 139) where Snake smears his victims with saliva to make their ingestion easier. See also Hiatt (1975b).

26 At the discursive and ideological levels, the Western Desert people insist on the ever-existing and unchanging character of forms of permanence. Such a discourse has long hidden from the various observers not only the potential for transformation (though Spencer and Gillen in their time caught a glimpse of it [1899: 12–13]) but also its structural necessity in a region of great mobility such as the Western Desert.

Chapter 3 Sociality, Mobility, and Composite Identity

1 Recall the ontological difference, noted by de Certeau, between the map and the itinerary.

2 The expedition to Lappi Lappi was organized by the Central Land Council (CLC) at Alice Springs to map the significant sites in the region and to establish Aboriginal territorial rights in relation to future gold exploration. The two anthropologists from the CLC kindly allowed me and my family to join them.

3 Regarding the meaning of 'property' in Aboriginal Australia, Williams (1982) and Myers (1982) have already pointed out the importance attached to the 'right to be asked' when access to a country is desired in order to exploit its economic resources. Permission will generally be granted, but it is essential to formulate an explicit request for access.

4 In order to simplify these multiple affiliations, some people did at times use the name *Kutjanka* ('all the same'). It will be interesting to see if this name endures over time to the extent even of eventually eradicating all the others.

5 In his distinction between a genealogical and a relational model, Ingold offers some comments on the question of descent that I found most relevant for Western Desert reality. In a relational model, 'grandfathers are ancestors because they were there before you and because they guide you through

the world. In that sense you follow them. But you are not descended from them' (2000: 141) as would be claimed in a genealogical model.

6 The processes through which a child is 'dreamed' or 'found' will be discussed in more detail in chapter 5.

7 For a debate on the subject, see Hiatt (1966a and 1966b), Stanner (1965), Birdsell (1970), and Gumbert (1981). Equally relevant are the works of R. Berndt (1972, 1976), Tonkinson (1991), and Peterson (1972, 1975, 1986).

8 The near-reciprocity with regards to access to economic resources among the groups of the Western Desert has been discussed by R. Berndt (1972, 1976), Gould (1969), Tonkinson (1991) and Myers (1982, 1986a), among others.

9 R. Berndt (1976) estimates that the traditional band moved through and exploited an area (which Stanner defines as a 'range') of 240 to 320 square kilometres. Myers (1986a: 78) calculated a range of roughly 320 kilometres in every direction from the main water sources. These evaluations correspond to the accounts from elders in Wirrimanu.

10 The eight-subsection system apparently originated in the north and then spread gradually across the Western Desert in the 1930s (Berndt and Berndt 1964; Myers 1986a: 183).

11 When I went back to Wirrimanu in 1987 with my family, my husband was identified with the tjampitjin subsection and our son was tjangala.

12 While these aspects have been extensively discussed in the anthropological literature on Melanesia (see, among others, Strathern 1988; Iteanu 1990) and Southeast Asia (Marriott 1976), they have not been given equal attention in Australian Aboriginal literature.

Chapter 4 Ways of Being, Relating, and Knowing

1 Not all Aboriginal groups have a different word for dreams and dreaming. This is the case for the Arrernte (Strehlow 1968) and the Warlpiri (Dussart 2000; Glowczewski 1991). To indicate a dream experience, the Warlpiri use the expression *tjukurrmaninpa* ('I had a dream'), again testifying to the close relationship between dreams and *Tjukurrpa*.

2 The concept of *kurrunpa*, the spirit, is closer to the idea of an embodied mind than to that of a disembodied soul.

3 According to Peile, who conducted extensive linguistic studies among the Kukatja, 'cognition is seen as a quality of the spirit (*kurrunpa*) rather than something gained independently of the spirit, such as implied in the rationalistic European view of intellection' (1997: 94)

4 See also Watson (1996: 94) on how the body is 'opened up' through the process of painting in women's rituals.

5 In the Wirrimanu area, sign language is used frequently by men, women, and children. Among the Warlpiri (Kendon 1988), widows use sign language almost exclusively during a mourning period that varies from a few months to two years, and during which they are forbidden to talk. This rule does not exist among the Kukatja. Among them, one prominent man in the community who had been dumb since his childhood communicated through sign language; and most people could reciprocate. He was also a very good storyteller.

6 On the shared dream, see also Munn (1986a: 37–8).

7 See Watson for one such implication of this (1996: 55).

8 Strehlow (1968 [1947]), Ashley-Montagu (1937), Spencer and Gillen (1927), Warner (1958 [1937]), Tonkinson (1978, 1991), Kaberry (1938), Elkin (1967), Glowczewski (1991), to name but a few.

9 Tamisari (1998) also reports the existence of 'death signs' among the Yolngu (Northeast Arnhem Land).

10 This expression is borrowed from Bird-David (1999).

11 Mountford and Tonkinson (1969: 386) mentioned briefly the *mudinga*, among the Mardu at Jigalong (Western Desert); these are described as dwarves and could possibly be the local equivalent of the *murrungkurr*.

12 Valiquette translates the term *murrungkurr* as 'tree spirits' (1993: 121).

13 Peile offers a similar example: 'During a good dream, a good spirit (tree spirit, *murungkulypa*) stimulates the vagina and also the breasts' (1997: 118).

14 There can be no doubt that ancestors such as the *Mungamunga*, the Rainbow Snake, or the *Wati Kutjarra*, whose tracks exist over a wide area, have local and regional variations in the description and interpretation of itineraries.

15 In the last few decades, car accidents, with quite a few fatal ones, have become an integral part of collective memory and of contemporary life. These occur usually on the return trip from Halls Creek or Rabbit Flat, and because of drunk driving (though that is seldom mentioned in the narrative of the event).

16 In the years that I lived in the area, only two national political figures caught the attention (and the imagination) of local Aborigines. The first was Charles Perkins, then deputy in Canberra, whom some had met in Halls Creek during the presentation of the ATSIC reform in 1988. Local residents were curious that he was 'half-caste' and involved in the *Kartiya* world, and wondered to what extent they could trust him. The second was Pauline Hanson, whom they had seen on television. They interpreted her right-wing discourse and denial of Aboriginal rights as a desire to rid Australia of Aboriginal people. Still fresh in the local memory are the massacres

of Aborigines that occurred farther north in the first half of the twentieth century.

17 In 1991, a Council for Aboriginal Reconciliation was established at the national level and was very active in the public arena during the decade.

Chapter 5 The Social Setting of Dreams and Dreaming

1 Napangarti, her sister, and a few other women of the same age group, whose husbands were much older than they, often told me that they usually recounted their dreams first to their husbands.

2 Besides being used for firewood, the *walakari* tree has a number of other uses: 'The sweet white gum often found seeping from insect wounds in the trunk of this tree during spring is a favoured food. The bark is burnt and the ash mixed with (native) tobacco *pituri* to give it more tang or "bite." Boomerangs and small spears are sometimes made from its stems' (Valiquette 1993: 313). It is not that this information is necessarily relevant in the context of this dream; rather, I am presenting this information because Napangarti and those who listen to her dream narrative know this information about *walakari*.

3 When the season was right, these seeds, as well as different types of beans, could be stored in a hole covered with spinifex, for use in leaner times.

4 As one woman said, 'The ants, they know. They know we like the sweet taste of *lukararra*.'

5 On this topic, see also Tonkinson (1970) for examples of dream-spirit journeys by Jigalong men.

6 Other versions of the same event do not explicitly mention a dream experience. Rather, it is said that the ill man was looking at smoke from the fire when his spirit (*kurrunpa*) was transported to the witches' country.

7 Tjampitjin was, at that time and until his death in the mid-1990s, one of the best artists in the area; his paintings were highly prized on the national market.

8 R. Berndt has given a number of such examples (1951: 71–84).

9 In another theme of dreams, and certainly the most prestigious one for the dreamer, given its collective and cosmological impact, the dreamer receives from the ancestors or deceased relatives new mythico-ritual elements in the form of songs, dances, or designs. I will discuss these innovative dreams in the final chapter, relating them to the dimension of openness in the *Tjukurrpa* pathways and the ritual sphere.

10 The Warkaya ceremony, associated with the *Wampana* (Wallaby) *Tjukurrpa*, is closely related to the *Puluwanti* ceremony (Peterson 1970). Apparently,

the Balgo mob received it some time ago, wholly or in part from Lajamanu, in exchange for the *Tjulurru*. They have since transmitted it to the population of Christmas Creek.

11 According to Glowczewski (1989: 209–18), who worked at Lajamanu, seeing either a horse, a black dog, or a water buffalo in a dream presages an illness or an unfortunate event. In the Wirrimanu area, the majority of people prefer to make nuances by saying that these signs are 'sometime good, sometime no good,' depending on the context of the dream in which they appear, the dreamer, and the situation at the time. Thus, the few dreams of horses that I was told bear no signs of misfortune.

12 Reflecting upon the fact that the anthropologists never get a straightforward answer to their questions about the 'meaning' of myth, Stanner cited one of his informants: 'It is no good asking the old men why this and why that ...' (1966: 43n23). We see here the difference between the epistemology of the anthropologists (Western and modernist) and that of the Aborigines. For the Aborigines, a myth or a dream has no 'meaning' *per se*, but the telling, hearing, or performing of the myth (or dream) is itself a form of engagement with the world. The myth does not need to be grasped conceptually and appropriated symbolically to be meaningful; rather, it must be told, heard, and felt, allowing others to become involved in it rather than just observing it from the outside (Ingold 1996: 120–1).

13 With respect to the fear instilled in young novices in the northern regions, Stanner noted that, 'Full knowledge brought immense relief but I saw no signs of the cynicism one might have expected. Evidently the interior life is so deepened that the inculcation of fear comes to seem to them just and wise' (1966: 11).

14 Not only was his gun the only one in good working order at the time, but he was also the only person able to buy bullets. The Halls Creek police refused to give the Balgo Aborigines a gun licence, which is compulsory in order to buy bullets; they feared that the guns might be used for other purposes than hunting.

15 For similar examples, see Elkin (1977) and Tonkinson (1970).

16 More than just a simple representation, the object 'is' the ancestor in question; it is one of his manifestations and imbued with the ancestor's magical powers. See also Munn (1970).

17 It is relevant to refer to Ricoeur's hermeneutic where description and interpretation are two complementary and necessary acts in the process of understanding.

18 Myers's research on the emotions among the Pintupi is also relevant here (1979, 1988b).

19 For an insightful discussion on the interpretation of events and the construction of meaning at Yarralin, Northern Australia, see Rose (1992: 225–9).

20 Such an attitude shares some similarities with the 'experientialist alternative' proposed by Lakoff and Johnson. For example, 'From the experientialist perspective, truth depends on understanding, which emerges from functioning in the world. It is through such understanding that the experientialist alternative meets the objectivist's need for an account of truth. It is through the coherent structuring of experience that the experientialist alternative satisfies the subjectivist's need for personal meaning and significance' (1980: 230).

21 Made of vegetable fibres and used solely by women, the dilly-bag is usually found in northern regions. It is not found in the desert areas. Napanangka either borrowed this element in order to add it to her narrative, or else she had received such an object during a ritual exchange or during one of her trips to the northern communities.

22 In Stanner's words, 'The conception of a metamorphosis of animals into humans or humans into animals is of course at the very centre of aboriginal symbolism throughout Australia' (1966: 79).

23 Since the early 1980s, the acrylic movement in the Wirrimanu area has grown significantly. Aboriginal artists have begun to use the introduced materials (acrylic paints and canvases) to create a new form of art that still expresses their intrinsic relations to places and their responsibilities towards these places. Their art, which was essentially ephemeral, has now acquired a more permanent form. See Watson (1996) for a comprehensive history of the acrylic movement in the Wirrimanu area and an analysis of women's acrylic paintings; see also Poirier (1992a). See Myers (2002) for a comprehensive study of the acrylic movement in the Western Desert.

24 In her analysis of the iconography of women's public sand drawings in the Wirrimanu area, Watson distinguishes between two ways of creating sand drawings: *walkala*, drawing on the ground with the fingers, and *milpapungin*, beating the ground with a stick (1997).

Chapter 6 Ritual Vitality and Mobility

1 The rituals discussed in this chapter are those that I observed or that were described to me. It is by no means an exhaustive list of all the rituals that exist or that are known in the Wirrimanu area. My main sources of information in the ritual domain were mainly, but not exclusively, women, which is why I mainly discuss here women's ritual knowledge, understanding, and

responsibilities. In describing the rituals, I have respected their secret-sacred dimensions where people wished me to do so.

2 See also Peterson (2000).

3 For local descriptions and analysis of *Yawulyu* rituals, see, among others, C. Berndt (1950, 1965), Munn (1986a), Hamilton (1979), Bell (1993 [1983]), Glowczewski (1991), and Dussart (2000).

4 Moyle conducted research at Balgo and a Pintupi outstation in the 1970s, and mentioned a *Yawulyu* called *Kungkayunti* in the two communities without, however, mentioning the *Tjipari* (1979: 24). According to my information, it seems to be either the same ritual or two rituals linked to the same mythic pathway, which is an extensive one. The Kukatja and the Pintupi share a number of territorial and ritual affiliations and responsibilities. According to the explanations I was given by the women, there is a close link between the heroines of the *Tjipari* and the *Kungkayunti* (*kungka* being another word for women).

5 A Warlpiri woman from Lajamanu, of the napangarti subsection and belonging to that country, told the story of *Mina Mina* to Glowczewski (1988: 584–8).

6 The different parts of the desert oak (seeds, wood, bark, roots, etc.) are used for different purposes (Valiquette 1993: 55). These trees were referred to by the women as 'long trees'; at Mina Mina, their leaves are constantly moving with the wind and, according to one woman, sound like an airplane. Mina Mina means 'top of a tree' (Valiquette 1993: 95), though I did not find out from the women if this was also its ritual meaning.

7 Watson (1996) offers a detailed analysis of this *Yawulyu*, also identified as the Nakarra Nakarra song cycle (instead of Ngantalarra). The narratives and songs portray not only the *Wati Kutjarra*, but also their mother, the Seven Sisters, and their encounter with the *Wati Kutjarra*.

8 This six-day gathering had been suggested and sponsored by the Kimberley Law and Culture Center. The edges of Lake Gregory were chosen as the meeting place. More than 200 women came from Broome, Noonkanbah, Christmas Creek, Turkey Creek, Lajamanu, and other communities; ritual sequences from various song cycles were performed over the six days of the meeting.

9 Moyle noted that, in such ritual exchanges, the 'mechanics of the transaction' are rarely specified (1979: 60). He offered valuable data on one such process of exchange that occurred in the mid-1970s in Balgo. It concerned the giving of full performance rights for the *tjatiwanpa* or *winparrku tulku* ceremony to the Balgo mob by the Warlpiri of Yuendumu, apparently in exchange for the *Tjulurru* (ibid.: 60– 7).

10 See Micha (1970) for a bibliography of classic ethnographic accounts on the exchange and circulation of rituals (and cults).

11 See, more particularly, Kolig (1979), Glowczewski (1983), and Swain (1993: 252–64).

12 Meggitt (1966a) has discussed such a process for the *Gadjari* among the Warlpiri.

13 The exact time of its origin is unknown, though Glowczewski (1983: 7) noted that it was already being performed at Lagrange in the 1920s. According to Swain (1993: 252), the *Tjulurru* began in the late 1950s.

14 A few years earlier, the *Worgaia*, another major travelling cult, had followed the same exchange route but in the opposite direction, headed from east to west.

15 In his analysis of the 'Balgo Business,' Myers (n.d.) emphasizes how these relations are redefined in the ritual context.

16 'Le long de la route, un groupe de prisonniers aborigènes travaille surveillé par des policemen armés d'une carabine. Les prisonniers sont accouplés avec des chaînes et des barres, comme les indigènes du Congo' (Ryder 1935: 221–2).

17 Akerman mentions that, in the Kimberley area, the main figure of the *Tjulurru* is a man and his horses (1979: 241).

18 According to Peterson, the ceremony is associated with the northern Warlpiri of Lajamanu (1970: 201). *Puluwanti* corresponds also to the Fire Ceremony witnessed by Spencer and Gillen in 1901 among the Warramunga, eastern neighbours of the Warlpiri. The ceremony, therefore, is being traded along an east to north-west route.

19 Akerman noted that 'it is through Balgo that major religious cycles are said to be diffused into the Kimberley' (1979: 235).

20 Dussart, who studied extensively the women's rituals at Yuendumu, makes no mention of the *Tjarada*. Rose, though, mentions the *Tjarada* rituals performed at Yarralin (1992: 114)

21 Rose remarked that '*Jarata* rituals are both serious and playful' (1992: 114).

22 See also Rose (1992: 114).

23 This is comparable to the *Tjulurru*, when *Tingarri* itineraries and heroes are said to travel all the way to the West Coast, the place of origin of the cult.

24 Moyle observed the *Yawulyu Kunkayunti* performed at Balgo during the 1970s (1979: 23).

25 A woman commented that the *Walawalarra* have fair skin and are prettier than the *Mungamunga*.

26 It is probably this ritual (or parts of it) that Moyle observed in the late 1970s, first at the outstation of Kunkayunti, and then at Balgo the following

year. In view of the restricted sacred-secret aspect of this song series, the women asked him not to reveal the name of the ceremony (Moyle 1979: 24).

27 On the contrary, in the *Tjarada*, the *kurdungurlu* dance with the pole and then drive it into the ground.

28 In the more extensive classificatory manner, they can, at times, be considered as two sisters, the eldest and the youngest. In daily life, it is also frequent for cross-cousins to call each other sister.

29 In November of 1986, Pope John Paul II visited Alice Springs during his stay in Australia, in order to meet with Aboriginal groups from the surrounding regions.

30 For the Greeks, dreams that bore messages (*'les songes'*) were also experienced at dawn.

References

AGPS (Australian Government Publishing Service). 1987. *Return to Country: The Aboriginal Homeland Movement in Australia*. Canberra: Author.

Akerman, Kim. 1979. The Renascence of Aboriginal Law in the Kimberleys. In *Aborigines of the West: Their Past and Their Present*. Ed. R.M. Berndt and C.H. Berndt, 234–42. Nedlands: University of Western Australia Press.

Alroe, M.J. 1988. A Pygmalion Complex among Missionaries. The Catholic Case in the Kimberley. In *Aboriginal Australians and Christian Missions. Ethnographic and Historical Studies*. Ed. Tony Swain and Deborah B. Rose, 30–44. Bedford Park, SA: Australian Association for the Study of Religions.

Anderson, Christopher, and Françoise Dussart. 1988. Dreamings in Acrylic: Western Desert Art. In *Dreamings: The Art of Aboriginal Australia*. Ed. Peter Sutton, 89–142. New York: George Braziller Publishers.

Ashley-Montagu, M.F. 1937. *Coming into Being among the Australian Aborigines*. London: George Routledge and Sons Ltd.

Augé, Marc. 1982. *Génie du paganisme*. Paris: Gallimard.

– 1988. *Le dieux objet*. Paris: Flammarion.

Bakhtin, M.M. 1990. *The Dialogic Imagination*. Ed. M. Holquist. Austin: University of Texas Press.

Bardon, G. 1979. *Aboriginal Art of the Western Desert*. Adelaide: Rigby.

Barth, Frederik. 1987. *Cosmologies in the Making: A Generative Approach to Cultural Variation in Inner New-Guinea*. Cambridge: Cambridge University Press.

Basso, E.B. 1987. The Implications of a Progressive Theory of Dreaming. In *Dreaming: Anthropological and Psychological Interpretations*. Ed. Barbara Tedlock, 86–104. Cambridge: Cambridge University Press.

Bateson, Gregory. 1980. *Mind and Nature: A Necessary Unity*. New York: Bantam Books.

Bauman, R. 1986. *Story, Performance and Event*. Cambridge: Cambridge University Press.

Bell, Diane. 1993 [1983]. *Daughters of the Dreaming*. Minneapolis: University of Minnesota Press.

Bell, Diane, and Pam Ditton. 1980. *Law: The Old and the New.* Canberra: Aboriginal History (for Central Australian Aboriginal Legal Aid Service).

Berglund, A.I. 1976. *Zulu Thought-Patterns and Symbolism*. London: C. Hurst.

Berndt, Catherine. 1950. *Women's Changing Ceremonies in Northern Australia*. Paris: L'Homme 1.

– 1965. Women and the 'Secret Life.' In *Aboriginal Man in Australia*. Ed. Ronald Berndt and Catherine Berndt, 238–82. London: Angus and Robertson.

– 1974. Digging Sticks and Spears, or the Two-Sex Model. In *Women's Role in Aboriginal Society*, 2nd ed. Ed. Fay Gale, 39–48. Canberra: Australian Institute of Aboriginal Studies.

Berndt, Ronald. 1951. *Kunapipi*. Melbourne: F.W. Cheshire.

– 1959. The Concept of 'The Tribe' in the Western Desert of Australia. *Oceania* 30 (2): 82–107.

– 1970. Traditional Morality as Expressed through the Medium of an Australian Aboriginal Religion. In *Australian Aboriginal Anthropology*. Ed. Ronald Berndt, 216–47. Nedlands: University of Western Australia Press.

– 1972. The Walmadjeri and Gugadja. In *Hunters and Gatherers Today*. Ed. M.G. Bicchieri, 177–216. New York: Holt, Rinehart and Winston.

– 1976. Territoriality and the Problem of Demarcating Sociocultural Space. In *Tribes and Boundaries*. Ed. Nicolas Peterson, 133–61. Canberra: Australian National University Press.

Berndt, Ronald, ed. 1970. *Australian Aboriginal Anthropology*. Nedlands: University of Western Australia Press.

Berndt, Ronald, and Catherine Berndt. 1945. *A Preliminary Account of Fieldwork in the Ooldea Region*, South Australia. Sydney: Oceania.

– 1964. *The World of the First Australians*. Sydney: Ure Smith.

– 1987. *End of an Era: Aboriginal Labor in the Northern Territory*. Canberra: Australian Institute of Aboriginal Studies.

– 1989. *The Speaking Land: Myth and Story in Aboriginal Australia*. New York: Penguin Books.

Berndt, Ronald, and Catherine Berndt, eds. 1965. *Aboriginal Man in Australia*. London: Angus and Robertson.

– 1979. *Aborigines of the West. Their Past and Their Present*. Nedlands: University of Western Australia Press.

Biernoff, David. 1978. Safe and Dangerous Places. In *Australian Aboriginal Con-*

cepts. Ed. L.R. Hiatt, 93–105. Canberra: Australian Institute of Aboriginal Studies.

Biesele, Megan. 1986. How Hunter-Gatherers' Stories Make Sense: Semantics and Adaptation. *Cultural Anthropology*, 1: 157–70.

Bird-David, Nurit. 1999. Animism Revisited. *Current Anthropology*, 40, Supplement: S67–91.

Birdsell, J. 1970. Local Group Composition among the Australian Aborigines. A Critique of the Evidence from Fieldwork Conducted since 1930. *Current Anthropology*, 11: 115–42.

Bourdieu, Pierre. 1980. *Le sens pratique*. Paris: Les editions de Minuit.

Bourguignon, Erika. 1972. Dreams and Altered States of Consciousness in Anthropological Research. In *Psychological Anthropology*, 2nd ed. Ed. F.L.K. Hsu. Cambridge: Schenkman.

– 1973. *Religion, Altered States of Consciousness and Social Change*. Columbus: Ohio State University Press.

– 1977. Altered States of Consciousness, Myths and Rituals. In *Drugs, Rituals and Altered States of Consciousness*. Ed. B.M. Dutoit, 7–24. Rotterdam: A.A. Balkema.

Breton, S. 1989. *La masquarade des sexes: Fétichisme, inversion et travestissement rituels*. Paris: Calman-Levy.

Brown, M.F. 1987. Ropes of Sand: Order and Imagery in Aguaruna Dreams. In *Dreaming: Anthropological and Psychological Interpretations*. Ed. Barbara Tedlock, 154–70. Cambridge: Cambridge University Press.

Bruner, Edward. 1986. Experience and Its Expressions. In *The Anthropology of Experience*. Ed. Victor Turner and Edward Bruner, 3–30. Urbana: University of Illinois Press.

Buchler, I.R., and K. Maddock. 1978. *The Rainbow Serpent: A Chromatic Piece*. Chicago: Mouton Publishers.

Burridge, Kenelm. 1960. *Mambu: A Melanesian Millennium*. London: Methuen.

– 1973. *Encountering Aborigines*. New York: Pergamon Press.

Cane, Scott. 1984. *Desert Camps: A Case Study of Stone Artifacts and Aboriginal Behaviour in the Western Desert*. PhD diss., Australian National University, Canberra.

Cane, S., and O. Stanley. 1985. *Land Use and Resources in Desert Homelands*. Darwin: Australian National University (North Australia Research Unit).

Carnegie, David. 1898. *Spinifex and Sand*. London: C. Arthur Pearson Ltd.

Charuty, Giordana, ed. 1996. Rêver. *Terrain*, 26.

Clammer, John, Sylvie Poirier, and Eric Schwimmer, eds. 2004. *Figured Worlds: Ontological Obstacles in Intercultural Relations*. Toronto: University of Toronto Press.

Colby, B., J. Fernandez, and D.B. Kronenfeld. 1981. Towards a Convergence of Cognitive and Symbolic Anthropology. *American Ethnologist*, 8 (4): 422–50.

Comaroff, Jean, and John Comaroff, eds. 2000. *Millennial Capitalism and the Culture of Neoliberalism*. Durham, NC: Duke University Press.

Comaroff, John, and Jean Comaroff. 1992. *Ethnography and the Historical Imagination*. Boulder: Westview Press.

Coombs, H., B.G. Dexter, and L.R. Hiatt. 1982. The Outstation Movement in Aboriginal Australia. In *Politics and History in Band Societies*. Ed. Eleanor Leacock and Richard Lee, 427–39. Cambridge: Cambridge University Press.

Cowlishaw, Gillian. 1999. *Rednecks, Eggheads and Blackfellas*. Ann Arbor: The University of Michigan Press.

Csordas, T.J. 1990. Embodiment as a Paradigm for Anthropology. *Ethos*, 18(1): 5–47.

Curr, E. 1886–7. *The Australian Race: Its Origins, Languages, Customs, Places of Landing in Australia and the Routes by Which It Spreads Itself over the Continent*. Vol. 3. Melbourne: John Ferres.

D'Andrade, R.G. 1961. Anthropological Studies in Dreams. In *Psychological Anthropology*. Ed. F.L.K. Hsu, 296–332. Homewood: Dorsey.

Daniel, Valentine. 1984. *Fluid Signs: Being a Person the Tamil Way*. Berkeley: University of California Press.

de Certeau, Michel. 1984. *The Practice of Everyday Life*. Berkeley: University of California Press.

Deleuze, Gilles, and Félix Guattari. 1987. *A Thousand Plateaus: Capitalism and Schizophrenia*. Minneapolis: University of Minnesota Press.

Descola, Philippe, and Gísli Pálsson. 1996. Introduction. In *Nature and Society: Anthropological Perspectives*. Ed. Philippe Descola and Gísli Pálsson, 1–21. London: Routledge.

Detienne, Michel. 1981. *L'invention de la mythologie*. Paris: Gallimard.

Devereux, George. 1951. *Reality and Dream*. New York: International Universities Press.

– 1957. Dream Learning and Individual Ritual Differences in Mohave Shamanism. *American Anthropologist*, 59 (6): 177–98.

– 1966. Pathogenic Dreams in Non-Western Societies. In *The Dream and Human Societies*. Ed. G.E. von Grunebaum and Roger Caillois, 213–28. Berkeley: University of California Press.

Dubinskas, F., and S. Traweek. 1984. Closer to the Ground: A Reinterpretation of Warlpiri Iconography. *Man*, 19 (1): 15–31.

Dumont, Louis. 1966. *Homo Hierarchicus: Le système des castes et ses implications*. Paris: Gallimard.

- 1983. *Essais sur l'individualisme: Une perspective anthropologique sur l'idéologie moderne.* Paris: Editions du Seuil.

Durack, Mary. 1969. *The Rock and the Sand.* London: Constable.

Durkheim, Emile. 1960. *Les formes élémentaires de la vie religieuse: Le système totémique en Australie.* Paris: Presses Universitaires de France.

Dussart, Françoise. 1988. *Warlpiri Women's Yawulyu Ceremonies: A Forum for Socialization and Innovation.* PhD diss., Australian National University, Canberra.

- 2000. *The Politics of Ritual in an Aboriginal Settlement: Kinship, Knowledge, and the Currency of Knowledge.* Washington, DC: Smithsonian Institution Press.

Eggan, Dorothy. 1949. The Significance of Dreams for Anthropological Research. *American Anthropologist*, 51 (2): 177–98.

- 1952. The Manifest Content of Dreams: A Challenge to Social Science. *American Anthropologist*, 54 (4): 469–85.

- 1961. Dream Analysis. In *Studying Personality Cross-Culturally*. Ed. B. Kaplan, 551–78. Evanston, IL: Row and Peterson.

- 1966. Hopi Dreams in Cultural Perspective. In *The Dream and Human Societies*. Ed. G.E. von Grunebaum and Roger Caillois, 237–66. Berkeley: University of California Press.

- 1972 [1955]. The Personal Use of Myth in Dreams. In *Myth, a Symposium*. Ed. T.A. Sebeok, 107–21. Bloomington: Indiana University Press.

Elkin, A.P. 1967 [1938]. *Les Aborigènes australiens.* Paris: Gallimard.

- 1977 [1945]. *Aboriginal Men of High Degree.* Queensland: University of Queensland Press.

Ellen, Roy. 1996. Introduction. In *Redefining Nature: Ecology, Culture and Domestication*. Ed. Roy Ellen and Katsuyoshi Fukui, 1–36. Oxford: Berg.

Ellen, Roy, and Katsuyoshi Fukui, eds. 1996. *Redefining Nature: Ecology, Culture and Domestication.* Oxford: Berg.

Evans, C. 1983. *Landscapes of the Night: How and Why We Dream.* New York: Viking.

Fabian, Johannes. 1983. *Time and the Other: How Anthropology Makes Its Object.* New York: Columbia University Press.

Gadamer, Hans-Georg. 1975. *Truth and Method.* New York: The Seabury Press.

Geertz, Clifford. 1983. *Local Knowledge: Further Essays in Interpretative Anthropology.* New York: Basic Books.

Giddens, Anthony. 1987. *La constitution de la société: Éléments de la théorie de la structuration.* Paris: Presses Universitaires de France.

Glowczewski, Barbara. 1981. Affaire de femmes ou femmes d'affaires: Les Walpiri du Désert Central Australien. *Journal de la Société des Océanistes*, 70–1: 77–97.

- 1983. Manifestations symboliques d'une transition économique: Le 'juluru,' culte intertribal du 'cargo' (Australie occidentale et centrale). *L'Homme*, 23 (2): 7–35.
- 1988. *La loi du rêve. Approche topologique de l'organisation sociale et des cosmologies des Aborigènes australiens.* Thèse d'état ès-lettres et Sciences Humaines, Université de Paris, Paris.
- 1989. *Les rêveurs du désert: Aborigènes d'Australie.* Paris: Plon.
- 1991. *Du rêve à la loi chez les Aborigènes: Mythes, rites et organisation sociale en Australie.* Paris: Presses Universitaires de France.
Glowczewski, Barbara, ed. 1991. *Yapa: Peintres aborigènes de Balgo et Lajamanu.* Paris: Baudoin Lebon.
Glowczewski, Barbara, and C-H. Pradelles de Latour. 1987. La diagonale de la belle-mère. *L'Homme*, 27 (4): 27–53.
Goody, Jack. 1977. Mémoire et apprentissage dans les sociétés avec et sans écriture: La transmission du Bagre. *L'Homme*, 17 (1): 29–52.
- 1979. *La raison graphique: La domestication de la pensée sauvage.* Paris: Editions de Minuit.
Gould, Richard. 1969. *Yiwara: Foragers of the Australian Desert.* New York: Charles Scribner's Sons.
Graham, Laura. 1995. *Performing Dreams: Discourses of Immortality among the Xavante of Central Brazil.* Austin: University of Texas Press.
Grunebaum, G.E. von, and Roger Caillois, eds. 1966. *The Dream and Human Societies.* Berkeley: University of California Press.
Gumbert, M. 1981. Paradigm Lost: An Analysis of Anthropological Models and Their Effect on Aboriginal Land Rights. *Oceania*, 52 (2): 103–23.
Hallowell, A.I. 1966. The Role of Dreams in Ojibwa Culture. In *The Dream and Human Societies.* Ed. G.E. von Grunebaum and Roger Caillois, 267–92. Berkeley: University of California Press.
Hamilton, Annette. 1979. *Timeless Transformation: Women, Men, and History in the Australian Western Desert.* PhD diss., University of Sydney, Sydney.
- 1980. Dual Social Systems: Technology, Labor, and Women's Secret Rites in the Eastern Western Desert of Australia. *Oceania*, 51 (1): 4–19.
Hastrup, Kirsten. 1995. *A Passage to Anthropology: Between Experience and Theory.* London: Routledge.
Herdt, Gilbert. 1987. Selfhood and Discourse in Sambia Dream Sharing. In *Dreaming: Anthropological and Psychological Interpretations.* Ed. Barbara Tedlock, 55–85. Cambridge: Cambridge University Press.
Hiatt, L.R. 1962. Local Organisation among Australian Aborigines. *Oceania*, 32 (4): 267–86.
- 1966a. The Lost Horde. *Oceania*, 37 (2): 81–92.

- 1966b. Ownership and Use of Land among the Australian Aborigines. In *Man, the Hunter*. Eds. Richard Lee and I. DeVore, 99–102. Chicago: Aldine.
- 1975a. Introduction. In *Australian Aboriginal Mythology*. Ed. L.R. Hiatt, 1–23. Canberra: Australian Institute of Aboriginal Studies.
- 1975b. Swallowing and Regurgitation in Australian Myth and Rite. In *Australian Aboriginal Mythology*. Ed. L.R. Hiatt, 143–62. Canberra: Australian Institute of Aboriginal Studies.
- 1984. Your Mother-in-law Is Poison. *Man*, 19: 183–98.
Hiatt, L.R., ed. 1978. *Australian Aboriginal Concepts*. Canberra: Australian Institute of Aboriginal Studies.
Hobson, A. 1988. *The Dreaming Brain*. New York: Basic Books.
Howitt, A.W. 1904. *The Native Tribes of South-East Australia*. London: Macmillan and Co.
Ingold, Tim. 1996. Hunting and Gathering as Ways of Perceiving the Environment. In *Redefining Nature: Ecology, Culture and Domestication*. Ed. Roy Ellen and Katsuyoshi Fukui, 117–55. Oxford: Berg.
- 2000. *The Perception of the Environment: Essays in Livelihood, Dwelling and Skill*. London: Routledge.
Iteanu, André. 1990. The Concept of the Person and the Ritual System: An Orokaiva View. *Man*, 25: 35–53.
Jedrej, M., and R. Shaw, eds. 1992. *Dreaming, Religion and Society in Africa*. Leiden: E.J. Brill.
Kaberry, Phyllis. 1938. Totemism in East and South Kimberley, North-West Australia. *Oceania*, 8 (3): 265–88.
- 1939. *Aboriginal Women, Sacred and Profane*. London: Routledge and Kegan Paul.
Keen, Ian. 1994. *Knowledge and Secrecy in an Aboriginal Religion*. Oxford: Clarendon.
Keesing, Roger. 1974. Theories of Culture. *Annual Review of Anthropology*, 73–98.
- 1982. *Kwaio Religion: The Living and the Dead in a Solomon Island Society*. New York: Columbia University Press.
Kendon, Adam. 1988. *Sign Languages of Aboriginal Australia: Culture, Semiotic and Communicative Perspectives*. Cambridge: Cambridge University Press.
Kilani, Mondher. 1983. *Les cultes du Cargo: Mythe et rationalité en Anthropologie*. Paris: Le Forum Anthropologique.
Kilborne, B. 1981. Moroccan Dream Interpretation and Culturally Constituted Defense Mechanism. *Ethos*, 9 (4): 294–313.
Kimber, R.G. 1995. Politics of the Secret in Contemporary Western Desert Art. In *Politics of the Secret*. Ed. Christopher Anderson, 123–42. Sydney: University of Sydney Press.

Kolig, Erich. 1979. Djuluru: Ein synkretistichen Kult Nordwest-Australien. *Baessler-Archiv,* neue folge, 27: 419–48.

– 1980. Noah's Ark Revisited: On the Myth-Land Connection in Traditional Aboriginal Thought. *Oceania,* 51 (2): 118–32.

– 1981. *The Silent Revolution: The Effects of Modernization on Australian Aboriginal Religion.* Philadelphia: Institute for the Study of Human Issues.

– 1989. *Dreamtime Politics: Religion, World View and Utopian Thought in Australian Aboriginal Society.* Berlin: Dietrich Reimer Verlag.

Kuper, Adam, ed. 1992. *Conceptualizing Society.* London: Routledge.

Lakoff, George, and Mark Johnson. 1980. *Metaphors We Live By.* Chicago: University of Chicago Press.

Latour, Bruno. 1993. *We Have Never Been Modern.* New York: Harvester Wheatsheaf.

Leach, Edmund. 1966. Virgin Birth. *Proceedings of the Royal Anthropological Institute of Great Britain and Ireland,* 39–49.

Lee, Richard, and I. DeVore, eds. 1966. *Man, the Hunter.* Chicago: Aldine.

Le Goff, Jacques. 1985. *L'imaginaire médiéval.* Paris: Gallimard.

Le Goff, J., J. Gauvin, L. Marin, et al., 1986. *Histoire et imaginaire.* Paris: Poiesis.

Lévi-Strauss, Claude. 1947. *Les structures élémentaires de la parenté.* Paris: Mouton.

– 1962. *La pensée sauvage.* Paris: Plon.

– 1985 [1950]. Introduction à l'œuvre de Marcel Mauss. In *Sociologie et anthropologie.* Marcel Mauss. Paris: Quadrige/Presses Universitaires de France.

– 1985. *La potière jalouse.* Paris: Plon.

Levy-Bruhl, L. 1960 [1922]. *La mentalité primitive.* Paris: Presses Universitaires de France.

Liberman, Kenneth. 1985. *Understanding Interaction in Central Australia: An Ethnomethodological Study of Australian Aboriginal People.* Boston: Routledge and Kegan Paul.

Lincoln, J.S. 1970 [1935]. *The Dream in Primitive Cultures.* New York: Johnson Reprint Corporation.

Long, Jeremy. 1989. Leaving the Desert: Actors and Sufferers in the Aboriginal Exodus from the Western Desert. *Aboriginal History,* 13 (1): 9–43.

Lotman, Yuri. 1990. *Universe of the Mind: A Semiotic Theory of Culture.* Bloomington: Indiana University Press.

Maddock, Kenneth. 1972. *The Australian Aborigines: A Portrait of Their Society.* London: Penguin Press.

– 1976. Communication and Change in Mythology. In *Tribes and Boundaries.* Ed. Nicolas Peterson, 162–79. Canberra: Australian National University Press.

Marriott, McKim. 1976. Hindu Transactions: Diversity without Dualism. In *Transaction and Meaning*, 109–42. Ed. Bruce Kapferer. Philadelphia: Institute for the Study of Human Issues Publications (Association of Social Antropologists of the Commonwealth Essays in Anthropology 1).

Mauss, Marcel. 1985 [1950]. *Sociologie et anthropologie*. Paris: Quadrige/Presses Universitaires de France.

Meggitt, M.J. 1962a. *Desert People*. Sydney: Angus and Robertson.

– 1962b. Dream Interpretation among the Mae Enga of New Guinea. *South Western Journal of Anthropology*, 18: 216–20.

– 1966a. *Gadjari among the Walbiri Aborigines*. Oceania Monograph, Sydney: University of Sydney Press.

– 1966b. Marriage Classes and Demography in Central Australia. In *Man, the Hunter*. Ed. Richard Lee and I. DeVore, 176–84. Chicago: Aldine.

Merlan, Francesca. 1981. Land, Language and Social Identity in Aboriginal Australia. *Mankind*, 13 (2): 133–48.

– 1986. Australian Aboriginal Conception Beliefs Revisited. *Man*, 21 (3): 474–93.

– 1988. Gender in Aboriginal Social Life: A Review. In *Social Anthropology and Australian Aboriginal Studies*. Ed. Ronald Berndt and Robert Tonkinson, 15–76. Canberra: Australian Aboriginal Studies.

– 1992. Male-Female Separation and Forms of Society in Aboriginal Australia. *Cultural Anthropology*, 169–93.

– 1998. *Caging the Rainbow: Places, Politics and Aborigines in a North Australian Town*. Honolulu: University of Hawaii Press.

Merrill, W. 1987. The Raramuri Stereotype of Dreams. In *Dreaming: Anthropological and Psychological Interpretations*. Ed. Barbara Tedlock, 194–219. Cambridge: Cambridge University Press.

Micha, F.J. 1970. Trade and Change in Australian Aboriginal Cultures: Australian Aboriginal Trade as an Expression of Close Culture Contact and as a Mediator of Culture Change. In *Diprotodon to Detribalization: Studies of Change among Australian Aborigines*. Ed. A.R. Pilling and R.A. Waterman, 285–313. East Lansing: Michigan State University Press.

Morphy, Howard. 1984. *Journey to the Crocodile's Nest*. Canberra: Australian Institute of Aboriginal Studies.

– 1991. *Ancestral Connections: Art and an Aboriginal System of Knowledge*. Chicago: University of Chicago Press.

– 1995. Landscape and the Reproduction of the Ancestral Past. In *The Anthropology of Landscape: Perspectives on Place and Space*. Ed. E. Hirsch and M. O'Hanlon, 184–209. Oxford: Clarendon Press.

– 1997. Empiricism to Metaphysics: In Defence of the Concept of the Dreamtime. In *Prehistory to Politics: John Mulvaney, the Humanities and the Public Intellectual.* Ed. T. Bonyhady and T. Griffiths, 163–89. Melbourne: Melbourne University Press.

Morton, John. 1985. *Sustaining Desire: A Structuralist Interpretation of Myth and Male Cult in Central Australia* (2 vols). PhD diss., Australian National University, Canberra.

Mountford, C.P., and Robert Tonkinson. 1969. Carved and Engraved Human Figures from North Western Australia. *Anthropological Forum*, 2 (3): 371–90.

Moyle, Richard. 1979. *Songs of the Pintupi.* Canberra: Australian Institute of Aboriginal Studies.

Mulgan, Richard. 1998. Citizenship and Legitimacy in Post-colonial Australia. In *Citizenship and Indigenous Australians: Changing Conceptions and Possibilities.* Ed. Nicolas Peterson and Will Sanders, 179–95. Cambridge: Cambridge University Press.

Munn, Nancy. 1970. The Transformation of Subjects into Objects in Walbiri and Pitjantjara Myth. In *Australian Aboriginal Anthropology.* Ed. Ronald Berndt, 141–63. Nedlands: University of Western Australia Press.

– 1973. The Spatial Presentation of Cosmic Order in Walbiri Iconography. In *Primitive Art and Society.* Ed. J.A.W. Forge, 193–220. London: Oxford University Press.

– 1986a [1973]. *Walbiri Iconography.* Chicago: Chicago University Press.

– 1986b. *The Fame of Gawa.* Cambridge: Cambridge University Press.

Myers, Fred. 1979. Emotions and the Self: A Theory of Personhood and Political Order among Pintupi Aborigines. *Ethos*, 7: 343–70.

– 1982. Always Ask: Resource Use and Land Ownership among Pintupi Aborigines of the Australian Western Desert. In *Resource Managers: North American and Australian Hunter-Gatherers.* Ed. N.M. Williams and E.S. Hunn, 173–96. Boulder: Westview Press.

– 1986a. *Pintupi Country, Pintupi Self: Sentiment, Place and Politics among Western Desert Aborigines.* Washington, DC: Smithsonian Institution Press.

– 1986b. The Politics of Representations: Anthropological Discourse and Australian Aborigines. *American Ethnologist*, 13 (1): 138–53.

– 1988a. Locating Ethnographic Practice: Romance, Reality and Politics in the Outback. *American Ethnologist*, 15 (4): 609–24.

– 1988b. The Logic and Meaning of Anger among Pintupi Aborigines. *Man*, 23: 589–610.

– 1989. Truth, Beauty and Pintupi Painting. *Visual Anthropology*, 2: 163–95.

– 1992. Representing Culture: The Production of Discourse(s) for Aboriginal Acrylic Paintings. In *Rereading Cultural Anthropology.* Ed. George Marcus, 319–55. Durham, NC: Duke University Press.

– n.d. What Is the Business of the 'Balgo Business'? A Contemporary Aboriginal Religious Movement. Manuscript.

– 2002. *Painting Culture: The Making of an Aboriginal High Art*. Durham, NC:
Duke University Press.

Myers, Fred, and Betty Clark. 1983. *A Claim to Areas of Traditional Land by the
Warlpiri, Kukatja and Ngarti*. Alice Springs: Central Land Council.

Nathan, P., and D.L. Japanangka. 1983. *Settle Down Country*. Malmsbury, Victoria: Kibble Books.

Obeysekere, Gananath. 1981. *Medusa's Hair: An Essay on Personal Symbols and
Religious Experience*. Chicago: University of Chicago Press.

– 1992. *The Apotheosis of Captain Cook: European Myth-Making in the Pacific*.
Princeton: Princeton University Press.

O'Flaherty, Wendy. 1984. *Dreams, Illusions and Other Realities*. Chicago: University of Chicago Press.

O'Nell, C.W. 1976. *Dreams, Culture, and the Individual*. San Francisco: Chandler
and Sharp Publishers.

Ortner, Sherry. 1984. Theory in Anthropology since the Sixties. *Comparative
Studies in Society and History*, 26 (1): 126–66.

– 1995. Resistance and the Problem of Ethnographic Refusal. *Comparative Studies in Society and History*, 37 (1): 173–93.

Overing, J. 1985. Introduction. In *Reason and Morality*. Ed. J. Overing, 1–29. London: Tavistock Publications.

Parman, Suzan. 1991. *Dream and Culture: An Anthropological Study of the Western
Intellectual Tradition*. New York: Praeger.

Payne, Helen. 1989. Rites for Sites or Sites for Rites? The Dynamics of Women's
Cultural Life in the Musgraves. In *Women, Rites and Sites*. Ed. P. Brock. Sydney: Allen and Unwin.

Peile, Anthony. 1985. Le concept du vent, du souffle et de l'âme chez les
Aborigènes dans le désert de l'Australie. *Bulletin ethnomédical*, 33: 75–83.

– 1997. *Body and Soul: An Aboriginal View*. Carlisle, WA: Hesperian Press.

Pentony, B. 1938. *The Dream in Australian Culture*. Master's thesis, University of
Western Australia, Perth.

– 1961. Dreams and Dream Beliefs in North Western Australia. *Oceania*, 32:
144–9.

Perrin, Michel. 1992. *Les praticiens du rêve: Un exemple de chamanisme*. Paris:
Presses Universitaires de France.

Peterson, Nicolas. 1970. Buluwandi: A Central Australian Ceremony for
the Resolution of Conflict. In *Australian Aboriginal Anthropology*. Ed.
Ronald Berndt, 200–15. Nedlands: University of Western Australia
Press.

- 1972. Totemism Yesterday: Sentiment and Local Organization among the Australian Aborigines. *Man*, 7: 12–32.
- 1975. Hunter-Gatherer Territoriality: The Perspective from Australia. *American Anthropologist*, 77: 53–68.
- 1986. *Australian Territorial Organization*. Oceania Monograph. Sydney: University of Sydney Press.
- 1998. Introduction. In *Citizenship and Indigenous Australians: Changing Conceptions and Possibilities*. Ed. Nicolas Peterson and Will Sanders, 1–32. Cambridge: Cambridge University Press.
- 1999. Hunter-Gatherers in First World Nation States: Bringing Anthropology Home. Eighth International Conference on Hunting and Gathering Societies: Foraging and Post-Foraging Societies. *Bulletin of the National Museum of Ethnology* (Osaka, Japan), 23 (4): 847–61.
- 2000. An Expanding Aboriginal Domain: Mobility and the Initiation Journey. *Oceania*, 70 (3) 205–18.
Peterson, Nicolas, ed. 1976. *Tribes and Boundaries*. Canberra: Australian National University Press.
Petri, H., and G. Petri-Odermann. 1970. Stability and Change: Present-day Historic Aspects among Australian Aborigines. In *Australian Aboriginal Anthropology*. Ed. Ronald Berndt, 248–76. Nedlands: University of Western Australia Press.
Poirier, Sylvie. 1992a. Cosmologie, personne et expression artistique dans le désert occidental australien. *Anthropologie et Sociétés*, 16 (1): 41–58.
- 1992b. Nomadic Rituals: Networks of Ritual Exchange among Women of the Australian Western Desert. *Man*, 27 (4): 757–76.
- 1994. Présentation: Rêver la culture. *Anthropologie et Sociétés*, 18 (2): 5–11.
- 1999. Une anthropologie du rêve est-elle possible? *Anthropologie et Sociétés*, 23 (3): 175–81.
- 2000. Contemporanéités autochtones, territoires et (post)colonialisme: Réflexions sur des exemples canadiens et australiens. *Anthropologie et Sociétés*, 24 (1): 137–53.
- 2001. Les politiques du savoir rituel: Réflexions sur les relations de genre chez les Kukatja (Désert occidental australien). In *Sexe relatif ou sexe absolu? De la distinction de sexe dans les sociétés*. Ed. Catherine Alès and Cécile Barraud, 111–34. Paris: Editions de la Maison des sciences de l'homme.
- 2004. Ontology, Ancestral Order, and Agencies among the Kukatja (Australian Western Desert). In *Figured Worlds: Ontological Obstacles in Intercultural Relations*. Ed. J. Clammer, S. Poirier, and E. Schwimmer. Toronto: University of Toronto Press.

Poirier, Sylvie, and Alain Sachel. 1992. Le mouvement des outstations australiennes. *Anthropologie et Sociétés*, 16 (3): 119–26.

Povinelli, Elizabeth. 1993a. *Labor's Lot: The Power, History and Culture of Aboriginal Action*. Chicago: University of Chicago Press.

– 1993b. 'Might be something': The Language of Indeterminacy in Australian Aboriginal Land Use. *Man*, 28: 679–704.

– 1995. Do Rocks Listen? The Cultural Politics of Apprehending Australian Aboriginal Labor. *American Anthropologist*, 97 (3): 505–18.

– 1998. The State of Shame: Australian Multiculturalism and the Crisis of Indigenous Citizenship. *Critical Inquiry*, 24: 575–610.

Radcliffe-Brown, A.R. 1930. The Social Organization of Australian Tribes. *Oceania*, 1: 34–63, 322–41, 426–56.

Reay, Marie. 1970. A Decision as Narrative. In *Australian Aboriginal Anthropology*. Ed. Ronald Berndt, 164–73. Nedlands: University of Western Australia Press.

Reid, Janice. 1983. *Sorcerers and Healing Spirits: Continuity and Change in an Aboriginal Medical System*. Canberra: Australian National University Press.

Ricoeur, Paul. 1963. Structure et herméneutique. *Esprit*, 322: 596–628.

– 1965. *De l'interprétation: Essai sur Freud*. Paris: Editions du Seuil.

– 1986. *Du texte à l'action: Essais d'herméneutique II*. Paris: Editions du Seuil.

Rodman, Margaret. 1992. Empowering Place: Multilocality and Multivocality. *American Anthropologist*, 94 (3): 640–56.

Róheim Géza. 1945. *The Eternal Ones of the Dreams*. New York: International Universities Press.

– 1988. *Children of the Desert II: Myths and Dreams of the Aborigines of Central Australia*. Ed. John Morton and Werner Muensterberger. Oceania Ethnographies 2. Sydney: University of Sydney Press.

Rosaldo, Renato. 1980. *Ilongot Headhunting 1883–1974: A Study in Society and History*. Stanford, CA: Stanford University Press.

– 1986. Ilongot Hunting as Story and Experience. In *The Anthropology of Experience*. Ed. Victor Turner and Edward Bruner, 97–138. Urbana: University of Illinois Press.

Rose, Deborah. 1992. *Dingo Makes Us Human: Life and Land in an Australian Aboriginal Culture*. Cambridge: Cambridge University Press.

– 1994. Whose Confidentiality? Whose Intellectual Property? In *Claims to Knowledge, Claims to Country*. Ed. Mary Edmunds, 1–11. Canberra: Australian Institute of Aboriginal and Torres Strait Islander Studies, Native Title Research Unit.

– 2000. To Dance with Time: A Victoria River Aboriginal Study. *The Australian Journal of Anthropology*, 11 (3): 287–96.

Roseman, Marina. 1991. *Healing Sounds from the Malaysian Rainforest: Temiar Music and Medecine*. Berkeley: University of California Press.

Rumsey, Alan. 1994. The Dreaming, Human Agency and Inscriptive Practice. *Oceania*, 65: 116–30.

Ryder, B.O. 1935. La vie sauvage dans le nord-ouest de l'Australie. *La Géographie*, 63: 219–29.

Sahlins, Marshall. 1981. *Historical Metaphors and Mythical Realities: Structure in the Early History of the Sandwich Islands Kingdom*. Ann Arbor: University of Michigan Press.

– 1985. *Islands of History*. Chicago: University of Chicago Press.

– 1993. Goodbye to Tristes Tropes: Ethnography in the Context of Modern World History. *Journal of Modern History*, 65: 1–25.

– 1995. *How 'Natives' Think: About Captain Cook, for Example*. Chicago: University of Chicago Press.

Sansom, Basil. 1980. *The Camp at Wallaby Cross*. Canberra: Australian Institute of Aboriginal Studies.

– 1988. A Grammar of Exchange. In *Being Black: Aboriginal Cultures in 'Settled' Australia*. Ed. Ian Keen, 159–77. Canberra: Aboriginal Studies Press.

Schneider, D.M., and L. Sharp. 1969. *The Dream Life of a Primitive People: The Dreams of the Yir Yoront of Australia*. Anthropological Studies, 1. Washington, DC: American Anthropological Association.

Schwimmer, Erik. 1986. Le discours politique d'une communauté papoue. *Anthropologie et Sociétés*, 10 (3): 137–58.

Spencer, B., and F.J. Gillen. 1899. *The Native Tribes of Central Australia*. London: Macmillan.

– 1927. *The Arunta*. London: Macmillan.

Stanner, W.E.H. 1961. A Reply to Goody: The Classification of Double Descent Systems. *Current Anthropology*, 2 (1): 20–1.

– 1965. Aboriginal Territorial Organization: Estate, Range, Domain and Regime. *Oceania*, 36 (1): 1–26.

– 1966. *On Aboriginal Religion*. Oceania Monograph 11. Sydney: University of Sydney Press.

– 1979. *White Man Got No Dreaming: Essays 1938–1973*. Canberra: Australian National University Press.

States, B.O. 1988. *The Rhetoric of Dreams*. Ithaca: Cornell University Press.

Stephen, Michele. 1979. Dreams of Change: The Innovative Role of Altered State of Consciousness in Traditional Melanesian Religion. *Oceania*, 50 (1): 3–22.

– 1982. Dreaming Is Another Power! The Social Significance of Dreams among the Mekeo of Papoua New-Guinea. *Oceania*, 53 (2): 106–22.

Strathern, Marilyn. 1980. No Nature, No Culture: The Hagen Case. In *Nature, Culture and Gender*. Ed. C.P. MacCormack and M. Strathern, 174–222. Cambridge: Cambridge University Press.

– 1988. *The Gender of the Gift: Problems with Women and Problems with Society in Melanesia*. Berkeley: University of California Press.

– 1992. *Reproducing the Future: Anthropology, Kinship and the New Reproductive Technologies*. New York: Routledge.

Strehlow, T.G.H. 1968 [1947]. *Aranda Traditions*. Melbourne: Melbourne University Press.

– 1970. Geography and the Totemic Landscape in Central Australia. In *Australian Aboriginal Anthropology*. Ed. Ronald Berndt, 92–140. Nedlands: University of Western Australia Press.

– 1971. *Songs of Central Australia*. Sydney: Angus and Robertson.

– 1978. *Central Australian Religion: Personal Monototemism in a Polytotemic Community*. Adelaide: Flinders University Press.

Sutton, Peter. 1988. The Morphology of Feeling. In *Dreamings: The Art of Aboriginal Australia*. Ed. Peter Sutton, 59–88. New York: George Braziller Publishers.

– 1999. The System as It Was Straining to Become: Fluidity, Stability, and Aboriginal Country Groups. In *Connections in Native Title: Genealogies, Kinship and Groups*. Ed. J.D. Finlayson, B. Rigsby, and H.J. Bek, 13–57. Canberra: Center for Aboriginal Economic Policy Research, Research Monograph 13.

Sutton, Peter, ed. 1988. *Dreamings: The Art of Aboriginal Australia*. New York: George Braziller Publishers.

Swain, Tony. 1993. *A Place for Strangers: Towards a History of Australian Aboriginal Being*. Cambridge: Cambridge University Press.

Tamisari, Franca. 1998. Body, Vision and Movement: In the Footprints of the Ancestors. *Oceania*, 68 (4): 249–70.

Tedlock, Barbara. 1981. Quiché Maya Dream Interpretation. *Ethos*, 9 (4): 313–31.

– 1987a. Dreaming and Dream Research. In *Dreaming: Anthropological and Psychological Interpretations*. Ed. Barbara Tedlock, 1–30. Cambridge: Cambridge University Press.

– 1987b. Zuni and Quiché Dream Sharing and Interpreting. In *Dreaming: Anthropological and Psychological Interpretations*. Ed. Barbara Tedlock, 105–31. Cambridge: Cambridge University Press.

– 1992. The Role of Dreams and Visionary Narratives in Mayan Cultural Survival. *Ethos*, 20 (4): 453–76.

Tedlock, Barbara, ed. 1987. *Dreaming: Anthropological and Psychological Interpretations*. Cambridge: Cambridge University Press.

Tedlock, Dennis. 1983. *The Spoken Word and the Work of Interpretation*. Philadelphia: University of Pennsylvania Press.

Tonkinson, Robert. 1970. Aboriginal Dream-Spirit Beliefs in a Contact Situation: Jigalong, Western Australia. In *Australian Aboriginal Anthropology*. Ed. Ronald Berndt, 277–91. Nedlands: University of Western Australia Press.

– 1974. *The Jigalong Mob: Aboriginal Victors of the Desert Crusade*. Menlo Park, CA: Cummings.

– 1978. Semen versus Spirit-Child in a Western Desert Culture. In *Australian Aboriginal Concepts*. Ed. L.R. Hiatt, 81–92. Canberra: Australian Institute of Aboriginal Studies.

– 1991 [1978]. *The Mardu Aborigines: Living the Dream in Australia's Desert*. New York: Holt, Rinehart and Winston.

Tonkinson, Robert, and Myrna Tonkinson. 2001. 'Knowing' and 'Being' in Place in the Western Desert. In *Histories of Old Ages: Essays in Honor of Rhys Jones*. Ed. Atholl Anderson, Ian Lilley, and Sue O'Connor, 133–9. Canberra: Pandanus Books.

Trigger, David. 1992. *Whitefella Comin': Aboriginal Responses to Colonialism in Northern Australia*. Cambridge: Cambridge University Press.

Turner, David. 1987 [1985]. *Life before Genesis: A Conclusion*. New York: Peter Lang.

Turner, Terence. 1991. Representing, Resisting, Rethinking: Historical Transformation of Kayapo Culture and Anthropological Consciousness. In *Colonial Situations: Essays on the Contextualisation of Ethnographic Knowledge*. Ed. G. Stocking, 285–313. Madison: University of Wisconsin Press.

– 1995. Social Body and Embodied Subject: Bodiliness, Subjectivity, and Sociality among the Kayapo. *Cultural Anthropology*, 10 (2): 143–70.

Tylor, E.B. 1958. *Religion in Primitive Culture*. New York: Harper and Brothers.

Valiquette, Hilaire, ed. 1993. *A Basic Kukatja to English Dictionary*. Wirrimanu: Luurnpa Catholic School.

Van Gennep, A. 1905. *Mythes et légendes d'Australie*. Paris: E. Guilmoto.

Viveiros de Castro, Eduardo. 1999. Comments on Bird-David, "Animism" Revisited. *Current Anthropology*, 40, Supplement: S79–80.

Wagner, Roy. 1991. The Fractal Person. In *Big Men and Great Men: Personifications of Power in Melanesia*. Ed. Maurice Godelier and Marilyn Strathern. Cambridge: Cambridge University Press.

Wallace, A.F.C. 1956. Revitalization Movements. *American Anthropologist*, 58: 264–81.

– 1958. Dreams and the Wishes of the Soul. *American Anthropologist*, 60: 234–48.

Warner, W.L. 1958 [1937]. *A Black Civilization: A Social Study of an Australian Tribe*. Chicago: Harper and Brothers.

Watson, Christine. 1996. *Kuruwarri, the Generative Force. Balgo Women's Contemporary Paintings and Their Relationship to Traditional Media.* MA thesis. Canberra: Australian National University.

– 1997. Re-embodying Sand Drawing and Re-evaluating the Status of the Camp: The Practice and Iconography of Women's Public Sand Drawing in Balgo, W.A. *The Australian Journal of Anthropology,* 8 (1): 104–24.

– 1999. Touching the Land: Towards an Aesthetic of Balgo Contemporary Painting. In *Art from the Land: Dialogues with the Kluge-Ruhe Collection of Australian Aboriginal Art.* Ed. Howard Morphy and M. Smith Boles. Richmond: University of Virginia.

Williams, Nancy. 1982. A Boundary Is to Cross: Observations on Yonlgu Boundaries and Permission. In *Resource Managers: North American and Australian Hunter-Gatherers.* Ed. Nancy Williams and E. Hunn, 131–54. Boulder: Westview Press.

Young, E., and K. Doohan. 1989. *Mobility for Survival: A Process Analysis of Aboriginal Population Movement in Central Australia.* Darwin: North Australia Research Unit.

Index

Aboriginal and Torres Strait Islanders Commission (ATSIC), 37
Aboriginal Arts Board, 40
Aboriginal Land Rights (Act 1976) (Northern Territory), 28, 201
agency, 61, 67, 199, 245, 246, 250, 262n3
Akerman, Kim, 30, 215, 217, 218, 271n17
Alice Springs, 16, 31, 108, 132, 150, 151, 171, 234, 264n2, 272n29
Alroe, M.J., 260n7
ancestors, 40, 43, 46, 52, 55, 57, 60–4, 67–9, 80, 82–6, 89, 91, 92, 99, 100, 102, 103, 111, 113, 118, 119, 122, 123, 129, 139, 141, 151, 152, 156, 164, 165, 180, 193–5, 199, 200, 203, 231, 232, 240, 242, 244–6, 248, 250, 255, 260n11, 261n3, 266n14, 267n9
ancestral, ancestrality (*see also* law, *Tjukurrpa*), 52–64, 66–8, 70, 72, 74, 75, 77, 79–91, 94–8, 100, 102–6, 109, 112, 114, 117–19, 121, 122, 128, 130–6, 141, 144, 146, 148, 152, 154, 155, 158, 164, 165, 168, 172, 176, 179, 182, 184–6, 188, 190–4, 196–201, 204, 206, 207, 209, 210,
217, 218, 220, 224, 231, 232, 238, 240–55, 262n10, 262–3n12; ancestral beings, 41, 46, 60–2, 67, 75, 84, 85, 89, 90, 98, 100, 103, 109, 112, 114, 118, 129, 130, 131, 141, 146, 176, 179, 186, 191, 194, 201, 221, 224, 231; ancestral lands, 27, 40, 41, 42, 44, 87, 250; ancestral order, 90, 121, 192, 194, 198, 200, 232, 238, 243, 244, 254; ancestral power, 55, 67, 68, 75, 79, 148, 190, 192; ancestral realm, 46, 193, 241, 262–3n12
Anderson, C., 44
Arnhem Land, 41, 42, 261n3, 266n9
Ashley-Montagu, M.F., 266n8
Augé, M., 262n4
Australian Government Publishing Service (AGPS), 42

Bakhtin, M.M., 197
Balgo (Wirrimanu), 15, 18, 19, 20, 22–35, 37, 39–46, 53, 56, 60, 65, 66, 70, 71, 73–7, 79, 80, 81, 84–8, 93–7, 99, 100, 104, 107, 108, 109, 110, 112, 115–17, 122, 124, 127, 132, 134–40, 145–8, 150, 151, 155, 157, 162, 165, 168, 171, 175–8, 183, 187, 190, 193,

302   Index

Spencer, B., 53, 264n26, 266n8,
271n18
spirit-child (*see also* conception, *kuru-warri*), 60, 61, 67, 68, 117, 133, 139,
142, 153, 184, 188, 192, 195
spirits (evil) (*see also wanya*), 174, 187,
188
Stanley, O., 46
Stanner, W.E.H., 4, 13, 14, 52–4, 57,
58, 98, 265nn7, 9, 268nn12, 13,
269n22
Stansmore Range (Mungkayi), 4, 17,
19, 21, 43, 46, 71, 75, 76, 79–81, 87,
88, 96, 102, 103, 105–8, 113, 158,
165, 202, 224, 261n17
State Department of Education, 33,
37, 40
Stephen, M., 258n10
story, 33, 37, 40, 66, 70, 73, 74, 76,
77–80, 82, 84, 85, 88, 89, 91, 99, 101,
102, 115, 123, 124, 131, 134, 136,
137, 155, 157–61, 166, 169, 174, 178,
180, 181, 186–96, 204, 266n5, 270n5;
'good story,' 158, 159, 161, 174, 180,
181, 187, 195, 246, 266n5; telling,
12, 185, 189, 190; 'true story,' 82,
185, 187
Strathern, M., 258n13, 259nn19, 20,
265n12
Strehlow, T.G.H., 261n1, 265n1,
266n8
Sturt Creek, 16, 28, 202
subjectivity, 13, 61, 246
subsection, 58, 71, 73–5, 77–9, 109,
110–12, 114–18, 130, 141, 193, 202–4, 206, 208, 213, 223, 224, 227, 229,
265n10, 270n11; system, 58, 109–12,
118, 265n10
Sutton, P., 257n4
Swain, T., 215, 218, 221, 271n11

Tamisari, F., 261n3, 266n9
tarruku, 66, 75, 76–9, 181, 204, 214,
226
Tedlock, B., 257n7, 258n10
temporality, 57, 58
territoriality, 12
territories (*see also* country, local
groups, *ngurra*), 18, 21, 43, 71, 75,
84–6, 96, 103, 108, 119
Three Ks, 141, 148, 150, 151, 250
time (Aboriginal approach to),
58–60
Tingarri, 75–81, 107, 205, 206, 208,
209–12, 218, 220, 263nn20, 21,
271n23
Tjarada, 24, 221, 222–5, 227–30, 237,
271n20, 272n27
Tjaru, 4, 27, 28, 38, 74, 75, 93, 97
Tjawa Tjawa (Point Moody), 44,
79
Tjukurrpa (the Dreaming) (*see also*
ancestrality, cosmological order,
itineraries, law), 5, 30, 52–60, 62–8,
70, 71, 73, 79–83, 85–90, 92–105,
107, 108, 110, 113, 118, 119, 121–5,
127–9, 130–40, 145, 148, 152, 154,
155, 156, 162–4, 166, 167, 172, 174,
175, 177, 182, 184, 186, 189, 190–3,
195, 200–2, 204, 207–11, 213, 215,
220, 223–5, 227, 230–6, 238, 240,
242–4, 248, 262n8, 263nn14, 17, 18,
265n1, 267n9
Tjulurru, 22, 137, 148, 149, 150, 181,
215, 216–21, 224, 226, 238, 268n10,
271n9
Tonkinson, R., 18, 92, 93, 99, 104, 107,
128, 133, 135, 245, 246, 258n11,
260nn9, 10, 261nn16, 18, 263n15,
265nn7, 8, 266nn8, 11, 267n5,
268n15

ANTHROPOLOGICAL HORIZONS

Editor: Michael Lambek, University of Toronto

Published to date: